Flash® CS4
ALL-IN-ONE
FOR
DUMMIES®

Cheat Sheet

Getting to Know the Flash CS4 Interf.

D1199645

Filename — Display bar — Menu bar — Stage — ...tor — Tools panel

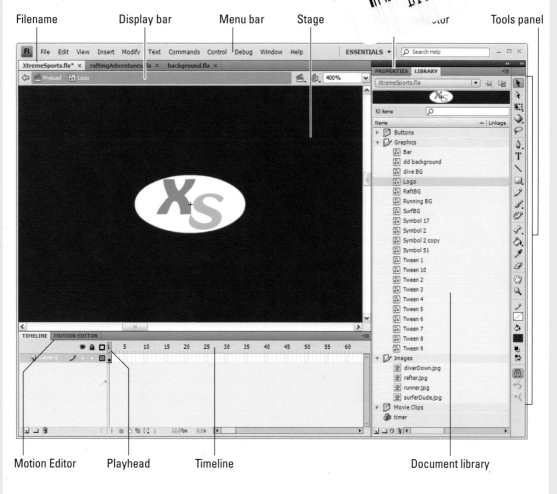

Motion Editor — Playhead — Timeline — Document library

Flash® CS4
ALL-IN-ONE
FOR
DUMMIES

Cheat
Sheet

Keyboard Shortcuts for Selecting Tools

Tool	Icon	Shortcut	Tool	Icon	Shortcut
Selection		V	Pencil		Y
Subselection		A	Brush		B
3D Rotation		W	Spray Brush		B
3D Translation		G	Deco		U
Lasso		L	Bone		X
Pen		P	Bind		Z
Text		T	Paint Bucket		K
Line		N	Ink Bottle		S
Rectangle		R	Eyedropper		I
Rectange Primitive		R	Eraser		E
Oval		O	Hand		H
Oval Primitive		O	Zoom		Z

For Dummies: Bestselling Book Series for Beginners

Flash® CS4

ALL-IN-ONE

FOR

DUMMIES®

Flash® CS4

ALL-IN-ONE

FOR

DUMMIES®

by Doug Sahlin and Bill Sanders

Wiley Publishing, Inc.

Flash® CS4 All-in-One For Dummies®

Published by
Wiley Publishing, Inc.
111 River Street
Hoboken, NJ 07030-5774
www.wiley.com

For general information on our other products and services, please contact our Customer Care Department within the U.S. at 800-762-2974, outside the U.S. at 317-572-3993, or fax 317-572-4002.

For technical support, please visit www.wiley.com/techsupport.

Wiley also publishes its books in a variety of electronic formats. Some content that appears in print may not be available in electronic books.

Library of Congress Control Number: 2008939711

ISBN: 978-0-470-38539-5

Manufactured in the United States of America

10 9 8 7 6 5 4 3 2 1

WILEY

About the Authors

Doug Sahlin: Doug Sahlin is an author, a photographer, and a Web designer living in Lakeland, Florida. He is the author of more than 20 books on Web design, image editing, and digital photography. Recent titles include *How To Do Everything: Adobe Acrobat 9.0* and *Digital Photography Workbook For Dummies* (Wiley). Many of his books have been bestsellers at Amazon.com. Doug uses Flash to create Web content and multimedia presentations for his clients.

Bill Sanders: Bill Sanders is faculty in the University of Hartford's Multimedia Web Design and Development program and owner of Sandlight Productions. He also works as a developer, software architect, and consultant for Adobe Flash Media Server and Flash. His latest project is Sandlight Green, a series of applications to replace carbon-burning commutes with interactive software for Internet-based management. He has published 49 books on computer-related topics including several on Flash and ActionScript.

Dedication

Doug Sahlin: Dedicated to the memory of my loving mother, Inez. Miss you, kiddo!

Bill Sanders: Dedicated to my folks, William and Eleanor Sanders.

Authors' Acknowledgments

Doug Sahlin: Thanks to Steve Hayes, for making this project possible. Kudos to my coauthor, Bill Sanders, for his knowledge of ActionScript and for being a great guy to work with. A tip of the hat to project editor extraordinaire Kim Darosett, for keeping my inbox full and making this a better book. Thanks to Rebecca Whitney, for understanding my sense of humor, being a kindred spirit, and manicuring the text in this book to perfection. Kudos to the entire Wiley publishing team — you guys and gals are the greatest! Special thanks to Margot Hutchison, for being legally blonde and the best agent an author could hope for. As always, thanks to my friends, mentors, and fellow authors for your support and inspiration. Special thanks to my family, especially you, Karen and Ted. A tip of the hat too to Niki, the furball who shares my space, who is also known as Queen of the Universe.

Bill Sanders: Thanks to Doug Sahlin for being a perfect coauthor, knowledgeable, and amiable. The folks at Adobe were most helpful in providing assistance with queries about Flash as were fellow designers and developers who share the Flash adventure. Steve Hayes and Kim Darosett deftly steered the project and myself through the unique style of this series. Likewise, I want to thank Kathy Simpson, Becky Whitney, and James Russell who contributed to the copy and developmental editing. I imagined them having a tag team to replace each other as they fell exhausted from my manuscript, and after being given a stiff shot of brandy, gamely returning to do battle with the tome. Danilo Celic did the technical editing made sure that all the code worked as promised, and I'm glad he did! Margot Hutchinson did her usual marvelous job of bringing author and publisher together. My wife Delia was as supportive as always. My dogs WillDe and Ruby liked the fact that I was available for a pat on the head and so encouraged further writing.

Publisher's Acknowledgments

We're proud of this book; please send us your comments through our online registration form located at www.dummies.com/register/.

Some of the people who helped bring this book to market include the following:

Acquisitions, Editorial, and Media Development

Project Editor: Kim Darosett

Executive Editor: Steven Hayes

Copy Editors: James Russell, Kathy Simpson, Rebecca Whitney

Technical Editor: Danilo Celic

Editorial Manager: Leah Cameron

Media Development Project Manager: Laura Moss-Hollister

Media Development Assistant Project Manager: Jenny Swisher

Media Development Assistant Producers: Angela Denny, Josh Frank, Kit Malone, Shawn Patrick

Editorial Assistant: Amanda Foxworth

Sr. Editorial Assistant: Cherie Case

Cartoons: Rich Tennant (www.the5thwave.com)

Composition Services

Project Coordinator: Katherine Key

Layout and Graphics: Reuben Davis, Stephanie Jumper, Christin Swinford, Ronald Terry

Proofreaders: Laura Albert, Linda Seifert

Indexer: Slivoskey Indexing Services

Contributions:

Corbis Digital Stock: pgs. 33, 47, 77, 91, 241, 445

Nic Miller/Digital Vision/Getty Images: pg. 207

PhotoDisc, Inc.: pgs. 123, 141, 179, 385

PhotoDisc/Getty Images: pg. 233

Publishing and Editorial for Technology Dummies

Richard Swadley, Vice President and Executive Group Publisher

Andy Cummings, Vice President and Publisher

Mary Bednarek, Executive Acquisitions Director

Mary C. Corder, Editorial Director

Publishing for Consumer Dummies

Diane Graves Steele, Vice President and Publisher

Composition Services

Gerry Fahey, Vice President of Production Services

Debbie Stailey, Director of Composition Services

Contents at a Glance

Table of Contents

Introduction

Welcome to *Flash CS4 All-in-One For Dummies*. Our goal when writing this book was to share our enthusiasm for Flash and, at the same time, demystify the application. You can do so many things with Flash that it becomes mind boggling. The minibooks in this reference are designed to take the boggle out of your mind and show you how to use Flash to create Web banners, animations, and other delights. We also delve into the topics of ActionScript and Flash video.

If you're reading this introduction in a bookstore and deciding whether this Flash book is the one for you, we want to give you a few facts. The authors of this book are card-carrying geeks who love working in Flash. We're also professional authors, which means that we value our readers. We don't overload you with technical terms. Each section was written as though we were looking over a friend's shoulder while they were working with Flash and then showing them how to work smarter and not harder. We've also injected enough humor to keep you awake while learning Flash, and (we hope) to make you chuckle out loud at least once per chapter.

About This Book

This book isn't meant to be read from front to back. It's more like a reference: Each chapter is divided into sections, each of which has self-contained information about something you can do in Flash CS4.

You don't have to memorize anything in this book. The information here is what you need to know to get by and see how Flash works. When you need specific information, let your fingers do the walking to the table of contents or the index, and then open the book to that page and read. We recommend that you use those little sticky flags to mark pages that interest you. Feel free to highlight text and scribble in the borders (it's your book). We request that you keep this book on your desk and out of harm's way — for some reason, poodles love to chew *For Dummies* books.

Wherever we mention a new term or are possessed by the need to get geeky with our technical descriptions, we let you know so that you can decide whether to read them or ignore them. You can thank us now, or you can thank us later.

Conventions Used in This Book

We realize that doing something the same way over and over again can be boring (such as always having to put on your socks before your shoes), but sometimes consistency is a good thing. For one thing, it makes stuff easier to understand. In this book, those consistent elements are *conventions*. In fact, we use italics to identify and define new terms.

Our book is cross-platform. In fact, your friendly authors are cross-platform: Doug uses Flash on a PC; Bill, on a Mac. Whenever we show a keyboard shortcut, we list the keyboard sequence for both platforms.

Whenever you have to type something to complete a task, we put the stuff you need to enter in a **bold** type so that it's easy to see.

When we type URLs (Web addresses) within a paragraph, they look like this: www.pixelicious.info.

What You Don't Have to Read

We've added little tidbits of interest in many parts of this book. You'll see sidebars with information relating to the topics being discussed and icons that list technical information relating to tasks we're showing you how to do. Treat these little tidbits like snacks: You can devour them when you see them, ignore them, or read them when you get a chance.

Foolish Assumptions

This is the spot where we help you determine whether you've got the stuff that's needed to do what we show you how to do in this book. First, if you thought that this book was about flashing, you're in the wrong section of the bookstore. Second, we assume that you have a computer capable of running Flash CS4. Third, we assume that you have Flash CS4 installed on your computer, or will have it installed soon. If you're blushing because we've assumed incorrectly, quietly put this book back on the shelf and slowly walk away, carefully avoiding any closed-circuit TV monitors in the store.

How This Book Is Organized

We've divided this book into minibooks, which are organized by topic. The minibooks point out the most important aspects of Flash CS4. If you're looking for information on a specific Flash topic, such as motion tweens or ActionScript, skim the table of contents or check the headings in it, or check out ye olde index.

By design, this book enables you to find as much (or as little) information as you need at any particular moment. If you need to know something superfast for your meeting with a new client who wants an all-singing, all-dancing Flash site, for example, just skim the index until you find the topic, and then read that section. By design, *Flash CS4 All-in-One For Dummies* is your desktop companion for all things Flash. When you're working on a project and you're stumped, pick up this book and quickly find the information you need.

Book I: Introducing Flash

When you launch Flash and first see all that stuff on your monitor, you might let loose with an expletive that we can't print in this book because our editors would delete it. But we agree: Flash has a lot of features. If you're not familiar with Flash, you'll find Book I rather comforting because our sole purpose when writing it was to show you what you can do with Flash and familiarize you with the application. If you're a Flash veteran, you may be tempted to skip this minibook, but we advise you to skim through it so that you can see some of the cool new Flash features.

Book II: Creating Graphics

Flash has a Tools panel filled with neat-looking icons. In Book II, we show you how to use these icons to create objects for your Flash movies. In addition to showing you the Flash drawing tools, we show you how to create text. And because it seems that nothing in today's world is black and white, we show you how to add color to your Flash projects. And while we're on the subject of projects, in Book II we show you how to streamline your projects by creating symbols for the items you use repeatedly and how to organize your work with layers. If your project involves digital images, fear not: We devote one chapter of this minibook to that topic.

Book III: Animating Graphics

Animation is a moving subject, which is why we devote an entire minibook to it. If you've seen Flash animations, you know that they can be complex. Fortunately, Flash CS4 makes it easier than ever to create an interesting animation. In Book III, we show you how to create motion tween and shape tween animations. We also show you how to animate text.

Book IV: Adding ActionScript 3.0 Magic

ActionScript 3.0 is used to show you how to control every aspect of your Flash CS4 creation. Although powerful, ActionScript 3.0 is perfectly manageable, and you will quickly find out how to create the effects and functionality that you always wanted but didn't know how to produce. We show you how to use the latest ActionScript classes in ActionScript files and how to make simple Timeline entries using the Actions panel.

Book V: Working with Flash Audio

Flash is alive, with the sound of music. Well, not by default, but if you want to add music to your Flash projects, Book V is the place to go. We show you how to import sound into your Flash projects, synch it with the Timeline, edit the sound, optimize it for your project, and much more. We also show you how to create buttons that make noises when you click them.

Book VI: Working with Flash Video

One of the best new benefits of Flash CS4 is the ease with which you can incorporate video into your Flash project. You can create a video using anything from a humble Webcam to a state-of-the-art digital video camera to either stream live or create recorded video to be played at the user's leisure. We show you how to use the FLVPlayback component to set up a video in a few steps and to create your own video player using ActionScript 3.0. On top of all of this, Flash CS4 allows you to use the crystal-clear H.264 format for high-quality playback.

Book VII: Getting Interactive

In Book VII, we start by showing you how to create buttons and then use ActionScript to make them do interesting things when users click them. You also find out how to use the components for making menus, text displays with scrollbars, interactive buttons that change dynamically when the user presses them, and a host of other powerful components to add a highly professional touch to your Flash masterpiece. In addition, Book VII shows you how to use the newest version of AIR to create desktop versions of the same Flash applications that are launched on the Web.

Book VIII: Finalizing a Flash Project

Creating a Flash document is a lot of fun. But at some point, you have to publish the document so that you can share it with the world, or at least with a few close friends. In Book VIII, we show you how to test and preview your Flash creations. We also show you how to debug the ActionScript code in your Flash projects. The last chapter of this minibook shows you how to publish your creation for the Web and other destinations.

Companion Web site

Graphic files, text files, AIR files, source code (FLA) files, ActionScript (.as) files, and other necessary files for the featured projects in the book are available for downloading at the book's companion Web site: www.dummies.com/go/flashallinone. Everything has been tested (and retested) so that if you make a typo in one of the project applications, you still have what you need.

Icons Used in This Book

To make your experience with this book easier, we use various icons in the margins to indicate particular points of interest. If fact, you can use these icons to skim through a chapter and find sections that interest you.

Whenever we give you a hint or a tip that makes an aspect of Flash CS4 easier to understand, we mark it with this little Tip doohickey — it's our way of sharing the tidbits of wisdom we've learned by being charter members of the School of Hard Knocks — so that you don't have to.

This icon is a friendly reminder or a marker for information that you want to make sure to keep in mind when performing a task.

Ouch! Warnings give you important directions to keep you from doing something that throws a giant roadblock in your path or that, even worse, causes Flash to crash and obliterates your hard work. We know what *not* to do, and this handy little icon can prevent you from having to struggle through the same pitfalls we once encountered.

Sometimes we feel obligated to share some geek stuff with you that's interesting but not essential to your knowledge of Flash. We mark that information with our supergeeky hero so that you know that it's just background information.

This icon identifies files available for downloading from the book's companion Web site (`www.dummies.com/go/flashallinone`).

Where to Go from Here

Now you're ready to use this book. Look over the table of contents and find something that catches your attention or a topic that you think can help you solve a problem. Launch Flash and then read about the topics that interest you. We find it best to just jump in and perform a task, so if you follow along while you read, you'll get the knack of Flash rather quickly.

Book I
Introducing Flash

The 5th Wave   By Rich Tennant

"What you want to do, is balance the image of the pick-up truck sittin' behind your home page, with a busted washing machine in the foreground."

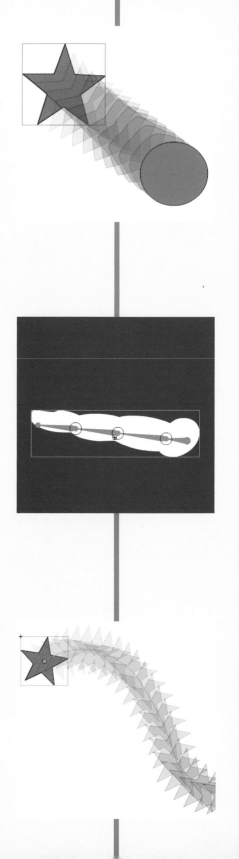

*F*lash CS4 is new. And, it's different. You can do the same tasks with Flash CS4 that you could do with Flash CS3 — and then some. If you want to find out about all the things you can do with Flash, and get a preview of the features we show you in this book, you've parked your bifocals on the right minibook.

In Book I, we show you what's new and different in Flash, and we show you some of the works of art you can expect to create if you finish reading this book in its entirety. So, if you want to see what Flash and this book are all about, flip the page.

Chapter 1: Exploring Flash

In This Chapter

✔ Discovering what's new in Flash CS4

✔ Examining the Flash workspace

✔ Exploring the Flash tools

✔ Customizing Flash

*J*ust when you thought you had Flash all figured out and believed that it was safe to continue merrily with your old Flash CS3 habits, along comes Flash CS4. The fact that you hold this book in your hands means that you own Flash CS4 and want to know more about the application. Flash CS4 is an extremely sophisticated piece of software. And — yikes! — it has come a long way since Adobe purchased Macromedia in December 2005. It seems like only yesterday that Flash 4 (and its medieval ActionScript and shape tweening) were considered the best thing since sliced bread.

Using a program like Flash has a tendency to organize you. Organized authors that we are, we figured the best place to start a book is by getting to know the lay of the land, so to speak. This process is kind of like a car manual: You don't start out by showing the driver how to change a tire — you start with a diagram that shows the nut behind the wheel where to park and then show him how to start his fuel-efficient hybrid car that takes dainty sips of gas when it's not running on electricity. First, we tell you what's new and exciting in Flash CS4, and then we familiarize you with the new workspace. And, because we know that no two people work alike (that's why they created preferences), we show you how to customize Flash to suit your working preference.

Finding Out What's New in Flash CS4

It's always something with new software, and for that matter, with life. Just when you think that you know something like the back of your hand, technology raises its pointy little head and turns your beloved application into an 800-pound gorilla that must be tamed.

As authors, we're glad that technology keeps changing, because it gives us something to write about. When we find a new application, the software maker sends us a prerelease version of the software because it's not ready for prime time yet. The first thing we do is "lift the hood" and poke around until we find the new features. After that, our next job is to figure out just what the heck the feature is and why it was added. The following sections highlight some of the flashy stuff we found in Flash CS4.

Discovering the new features

Working with a new version of an application is like peeling an onion: The outside looks familiar, but then you start revealing its layers. And, without documentation, using a program's new features can bring you to tears. Don't worry: We already peeled Flash CS4. The following list shows you the new features we found:

- **Inverse kinematics:** If you feel the need to add an animation of a dancing chicken to a Web site, you can do it with Flash CS4, thanks to the Inverse Kinematics animation tool. You can use it to create animations such as people walking across the screen or working with machinery. You use the Flash drawing tools to create, in essence, the parts of the dancing chicken, dancing dude, or dancing fool. Then you create an inverse kinematics chain, which creates your character's bones. We show you how to get bad to the bone with inverse kinematics in Book III, Chapter 2.

- **Kuler:** Adobe Kuler is an online resource for creating color palettes for Web pages and illustrations, for example. Flash CS4 comes with a Kuler panel that you use to view color palettes created by other designers and to create your own color palettes. We show you how to be cooler with Kuler in Book II, Chapter 2.

- **Scrubby sliders:** A *scrubby slider* is an interactive way of entering a value. When you see a value in blue with a line underneath it, pause the cursor over the value. The cursor becomes a hand with a pointing forefinger sprouting a dual-headed arrow. Click and drag to interactively change the value. Hold down the Shift key while dragging to change the value in large increments, or hold down the Ctrl key (Windows) or the Command key (Macintosh) while dragging to change the value in small increments. Use scrubby sliders to enter precise, minty-fresh, ecologically safe values. (No pixels were harmed or destroyed in the creation of this paragraph.)

✓ **Motion tweening:** If you've used Flash for a while, you've no doubt created a *motion tween animation*. As its name implies, you move an object from Point A to Point B, and Flash calculates the frames between the start and end of the animation. The designers of Flash CS4 have now made motion tweening child's play, and you have more control than ever. For example, if you need to create an animation of a ball jumping through many hoops (which is similar to getting a bill through Congress), we show you everything you need to know about motion tweening but were afraid to ask in Book III, Chapter 2.

✓ **Motion Editor:** If you're a veteran Flash animator, you may be familiar with the term *easing*, which determines how the animation starts and ends. You can ease into the animation slowly, and ease out quickly, like a car accelerating, or vice versa. In Flash CS4, the new Motion Editor tool enables you to edit any facet of your animation, not just the beginning and end. In the Motion Editor, you use straight lines, curved lines, graphs, and grids, for example. In other words, the Motion Editor is a virtual treasure trove for animators who want to precisely control every facet of an animation. And yes, Virginia, the Motion Editor has scrubby sliders.

Introducing the new tools

When you have new features, you have new tools. (It's a law, you know.) Many new Flash tools were created for use with the new features listed in the previous section. Some of the other new tools have absolutely nothing to do with new features, but are welcome additions to the Tools panel. The following list discusses the new tools and what you can do with them:

✓ **3D Rotation:** Gives you the power to take an object for a spin. Create a motion tween animation, add this tool, and spin gently (or not), and you end up with a cool animation when the object appears to flutter through space in three dimensions. Can you envision an animation of falling leaves? This tool can do it.

✓ **3D Translation:** Has three axes — X, Y, and Z — that you use to move an object left and right, up and down, forward and backward. We know what you're thinking: Flash is 2D. And you're right. But in a motion tween animation, this tool makes it possible for you to simulate a 3D experience. Don't preview animations made with this tool in front of your pet because it may make the critter dizzy.

✓ **Deco:** Used with the default graphic to populate a Flash project with vines and flowers. Or, you can use symbols from the document library to put your own spin on the graphic created by the tool. You can also animate the graphic created by the tool.

- **Bone:** Helps define the structure of your object when you delve into the world of inverse kinematic animations. In essence, you use this tool to give the object a skeleton. When you add bones to an object, Flash creates a new layer named Armature. You can use as many bones as you need in order to animate an object, and you can create additional branches to create sophisticated animation. Yep, Flash is still 2D, but this tool takes your animations to the next level.

- **Bind:** Used in conjunction with the Bone tool, but, contrary to its name, not to bind things. If an animation isn't performing the way you want, you use the Bind tool to tell Flash which points should be connected to which bone.

- **Spray Brush:** Extra! Extra! Read all about it: Creates graffiti in Flash designer. You use this interesting addition to the Flash toolbox to spray color that looks like it was applied with an airbrush. Or, you can load the brush with a symbol from the document library and have some fun. You can use this virtual spray gun to add decoration to any Flash project with no toxic fumes or messy clean-up from clogged spray heads.

Flash CS4 and you

Like the proverbial well, Flash CS4 is deep. How deep you go is entirely up to you. This book gives you a full-course serving of Flash, from soup to nuts. And, the fact that this book is thicker than most phone books means that Flash CS4 has lots of features. As card-carrying geeks and fastidious authors, it's our job to show as much as we possibly can about Flash CS4 in this book. That's why we give you eight minibooks to get the job done. It's a smorgasbord with a heaping helping of everything Flash has to offer. The good news is that if you need just a little snack, you can cut right to the chase and read a minibook, or a chapter of a minibook.

There's so much you can do with Flash that the mind boggles. If you just dip your toe in the shallow end of the pool, you can create some awesome animations for Web pages. If you've ever seen Web site banners that move and thereby move the visitor, you've seen only the tip of the iceberg. Figure 1-1 shows a Web site (phoenixfl.com) with an all-singing, all-dancing banner.

The Flash intros that were all the rage a few years ago have gone the way of the dodo. Would *you* want to see the same thing every time you visit a certain Web site? Flashy intros fail to thrill after a couple of visits.

Figure 1-1: If you use your imagination, you can see all the dancing text at the top of this page — or just visit the site.

Here's a taste of the interactivity that Flash CS4 provides:

- **ActionScript:** You can also use Flash to build full-fledged interactive Web sites with all kinds of bells and whistles or flashy games. Interactive Flash designs and games rely heavily on ActionScript. ActionScript 3.0 has been around since Flash CS3. You can still create interactive designs using ActionScript 2.0, but that version of ActionScript will eventually be relegated to history. In this book, we show you how to use ActionScript 3.0. Although this version can seem a little daunting if you want to create an interactive Web site, we do our best to demystify it in Book IV. Figure 1-2 shows an interactive, online Flash portfolio for an aspiring model (dasdesigns.net/demo).

Figure 1-2: Interactive Flash Web sites are a thing of beauty and a joy forever.

- **Flash video:** Flash video is a wonderful thing. Flash CS4 supports high-definition video. And yes, you can put high-definition video on the Web for visitors to see and enjoy. If you or a client records video using a standard camcorder, you still see great results when converting it to Flash video. The file format for Flash Video is FLV.

- **Adobe Media Encoder:** Flash CS4 also ships with the Adobe Media Encoder, which makes it possible for you encode video while you sleep. All you do is load the encoder with your videos, choose a setting for each video, click a button, and let the media encoder do its thing while you solve the world's problems or tackle a less lofty goal. The media encoder has a wide variety of presets, or you can modify a preset to suit a particular video or Web site. We show you how to master the video encoder and much more in Book VI. Figure 1-3 shows a Web site with some Flashy video (`www.antonioswinterhaven.com/video.htm`).

Those are just a few of the tasks you can do with Flash. As you become more familiar with the application, you may venture into creating games that can be played online or on devices. When you're armed with a creative mind, Flash CS4, and a little help from your friendly authors, the possibilities to create compelling content with Flash are virtually endless.

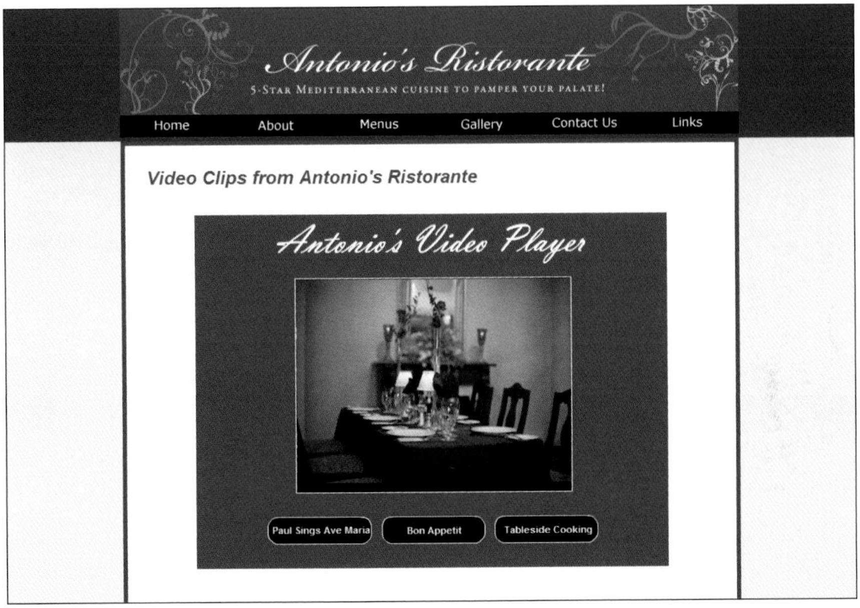

Figure 1-3: Flash video is squeaky clean, and it streams.

Exploring the Flash Workspace

The Flash CS4 interface has all the familiar parts you've come to know and love in Flash CS3 — and a couple of new ones. Adobe's first iteration of Flash was CS3, and the interface looked decidedly Adobe. The Flash CS4 interface is even more Adobe-like — if that's possible. Adobe interfaces are similar to German sports cars, where form follows function. The new interface has been well thought out. In the following sections, we show you the nuts and bolts of the interface and the manner in which it's constructed. But, hey — if you don't like the way it's constructed, we also show you how to deconstruct it and set it up to your liking. Figure 1-4 shows the new interface in all its glory.

Now that you know what the new interface looks like, roll up for a magical mystery tour of it. The lists in the following sections demonstrate the closest we could come to an actual survey of the new workspace:

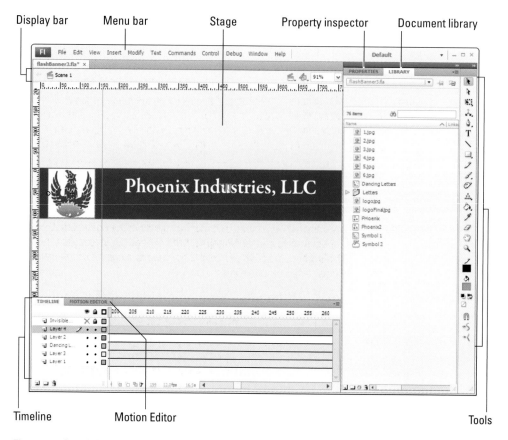

Figure 1-4: I can't find anything in this new interface. Please pass the GPS.

Getting to know the menu bar

When you create a new document in Flash, or open an existing one, the menu bar changes to display all menu groups. It's almost the same as the one you came to know and love in Flash CS3, and it's at the top of the interface, which is why we decided to start there. The menu bar is divided into the groups described in Table 1-1.

Table 1-1	The Menu Bar
Menu	*What You Can Do with It*
File	Create new documents, open existing documents, and close and save documents. You also find commands for publishing and printing documents.
Edit	Cut, copy, paste, duplicate, and find objects; work with the Timeline; and edit symbols, for example. Because Flash has many Timeline commands, they're conveniently grouped on a submenu.
View	Zoom in and out, change the level of magnification, enable rulers, show the grid, enable snapping to other objects and the grid, plus much more. The Go To submenu is especially useful because it lists symbols in the document. Click a symbol name to go to that symbol.
Insert	Insert symbols, create motion or shape tweens that you use to animate objects in your project, and create scenes. You can use the Timeline submenu to create layers, layer folders, frames, keyframes, and blank keyframes.
Modify	Modify the document, and modify objects in the document. Use submenus to modify bitmaps (photorealistic digital images), symbols, shapes, and the Timeline. You also find commands to transform, arrange, and align objects.
Text	If you're going to have text in your document, you can use this menu group to specify fonts, sizes, and styles, for example. You can even find a command to check your spelling.
Commands	Although the name of this menu group may seem redundant, you use the group to manage commands you create, find more commands from Adobe, and run commands, for example.
Control	Navigate the Timeline; play, rewind, and test a movie; test a scene, and much more.
Debug	Ensure that everything in your Flash production runs without a hitch. When you debug a movie, you can stop it at critical points to see what's happening and to make sure that any ActionScript is executing as expected.
Window	Display Tools panels or libraries or switch to another workspace, for example.
Help	Use this menu when you need to get by with a little help from Flash — but not before you check the index in this book.

Examining the display bar

This part of the interface changes to let you know where you're at in the Flash universe. When you are working on the main Timeline, the current scene is displayed. When you edit a symbol, the symbol name is displayed with a Back button you click to exit Symbol Editing mode.

Additionally, the display bar contains these standard elements:

- **Edit Scene icon:** Click this icon to display all scenes in your production. Click a scene name to edit it.

- **Edit Symbol icon:** Click this icon to display a list of the symbols in your document. Click a symbol name to edit it.

- **Magnification drop-down menu:** Change the magnification or fit the project on the stage, for example. Figure 1-5 shows a symbol being edited and the choices from the Magnification drop-down menu.

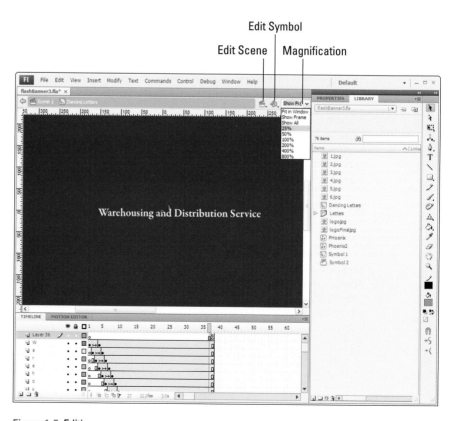

Figure 1-5: Editing a scene.

Taking the stage

Published Flash projects are known as *movies,* so it's only fitting that the spot where you do your animation wizardry is the Stage.

Exploring the panels

The default workspace has two panel docks: one on the right side of the interface, and one on the bottom. The right panel dock is home to the document library and the Property inspector. The lower panel dock is home to the Timeline and Motion Editor. But nothing is cast in stone, of course. If you don't like this setup, you can customize it, a task we show you in a later section.

Property inspector

The Property inspector tells you everything you want to know about a selected object. You also use it to modify the parameters of tools used to create shapes, to change the properties of an object on the Stage, name (in Symbol Editing mode) movie clips that will be accessed by ActionScript, and much more.

The Property inspector has a chameleon nature. It changes on the fly when you select an object or tool. Figure 1-6 shows the Property inspector as a floating window, displaying the parameters for a document.

Document library

The document library displays all objects used in a Flash project and helps you stay organized. You can also check out items from the document library for use in your current Flash project. For that matter, you can open a library from a different document and use items from it in your current project. Figure 1-7 shows a document library as a floating window.

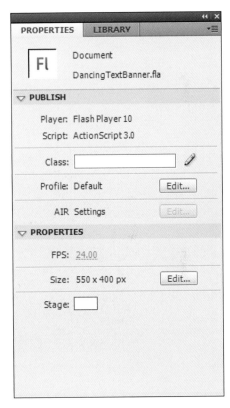

Figure 1-6: Properties that aren't on the real estate market.

Figure 1-7: A library you don't need a card for.

Timeline

The Timeline is sort of a roadmap: It shows you the frames, keyframes, layers, and layer folders that were created for your Flash project. We show you how to master the Timeline (which is shown as a floating window in Figure 1-8) in Book III, Chapter 1.

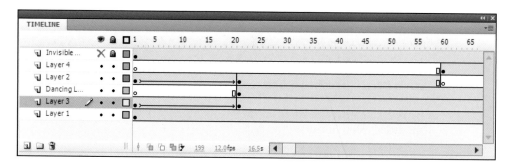

Figure 1-8: Timelines stand still for no man.

Motion Editor

The Motion Editor is a new addition to Flash. You can use it to precisely control the speed at which an animation starts and finishes. You can control other parameters by using the Motion Editor, such as object opacity during the animation. You can also add keyframes and manually adjust any parameter from within the Motion Editor. It's shown as a floating window in Figure 1-9.

MOTION EDITOR					
Property	Value	Ease		Keyframe	Graph
				1	5 1
▽ Basic motion		☑ No Ease ▾	🔁		
X	164.9 px	☑ No Ease ▾	◀ ⌃ ▷		165.0
Y	126 px	☑ No Ease ▾	◀ ⌃ ▷		125.0
Rotation Z	0 °	☑ No Ease ▾	◀ ⌃ ▷		0.0
▽ Transformation		☑ No Ease ▾	🔁		
Skew X	0 °	☑ No Ease ▾	◀ ⌃ ▷		0.0
Skew Y	0 °	☑ No Ease ▾	◀ ⌃ ▷		0.0
Scale X	100 %	☑ No Ease ▾	◀ ⌃ ▷		100.0

☰ 20   ▭ 201   ▥ 9   ◀   ▶

Figure 1-9: The Motion Editor controls animations without inducing motion sickness.

Other panels

Flash has panels — lots of panels. If you read the preceding sections, you already know what to use the panels for that are displayed in the workspace by default. Other panels remain incognito — wherever that is — until you select them from the Window menu. You can have as many panels as you want floating in the workspace. You can also access panels by using keyboard shortcuts.

Figure 1-10 shows the Align panel. The little X icon at the top is used

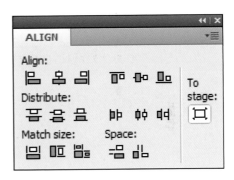

Figure 1-10: You can float panels in the workspace.

to close the panel, and the left-pointing double arrows collapse the panel to an icon. Keeping a frequently used panel in the workspace is an efficient way to work. We give you the straight scoop on individual panels when they're needed to perform a task.

Getting chummy with the Tools panel

On the right side of the default workspace, dangerously close to the document library and a few scant pixels away from the Property inspector, is the lean, mean Tools panel. It's lean because it's one tool wide and quite tall, and it's mean because it packs a lot of wallop. The Tools panel gives you the power to create and move objects and do much more.

Figure 1-11 shows the Tools panel floating in a separate window. The panel has so many tools that some of them share space on the Tools panel. Whenever you see a triangle in the lower-right corner of a tool, click it to have access to the other tools that share the space, as shown in Figure 1-11. The last tool used is always displayed when multiple tools occupy the same space.

Table 1-2 gives you the lowdown on the tools at your disposal.

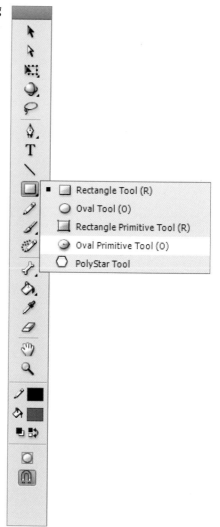

Figure 1-11: A Flashy Tools panel, if there ever was one.

Table 1-2	The Tools Panel
Tool	*What You Can Do with It*
Selection	Select and move objects.
Subselection	Select points on a path.
Free Transform	Transform an object. You can resize an object proportionately, change its width or height, and skew or rotate the object.
Gradient Transform	Transform the position of a gradient that fills an object. This tool resides on a fly-out menu with the Free Transform tool.
3D Translation	Change the X, Y, and Z positions of an object in a motion tween animation. Flash isn't 3D, but the tool can make an object appear as though it's traveling in three dimensions.
3D Rotation	Rotate a tool along its X, Y, or Z axis in a motion tween animation. It works well for mimicking objects fluttering in space.
Lasso	This tool is used to select objects, or round up if you will; hence the name Lasso.
Pen	Create paths. This tool has several buddies on the fly-out menu that are used to add, delete, and convert anchor points on the path.
Text	Add text to a document. Flashes uses three flavors of text: Static, Input, and Dynamic. Input and Dynamic text are used in conjunction with ActionScript to accept text (Input text), or display text (Dynamic text). Static text is used when you want to display text, and can also be used to display hyperlinks in a Flash project.
Line	Create a straight line from Point A to Point B.
Rectangle	Create rectangles and rounded rectangles.
Oval	Create objects of the elliptical variety, known as ovals. You can also use this tool to create objects that look like pies with wedges and a piece missing.
Rectangle Primitive	Create rectangles and rounded rectangles. The beauty of using a primitive shape is that you can edit all its attributes at any time by using the Property inspector.
Oval Primitive	Create ovals that can be edited in the Property inspector any time after they're created.
Polystar	Create multisided polygons and stars.

(continued)

Table 1-2 *(continued)*

Tool	What You Can Do with It
Pencil	In the Property inspector, specify the color and width of the stroke and many other attributes. (This tool is the virtual equivalent of a 2H Eberhard Faber pencil.) Flash smoothes shapes that you create with the Pencil tool. You determine how much smoothing by choosing a modifier from the bottom of the Tools panel.
Brush	Add splashes of color to a Flash project, or, if you're really talented, to actual artwork. You determine how the brush stroke looks by choosing options in the Property inspector and choosing modifiers from the bottom of the Tools panel.
Spray Brush	Add graffiti-like splashes of color to a document. You can change the color that sprays out of the nozzle, or spray a symbol from the document library out of the nozzle.
Deco	Draw a shape that looks like a flowering vine. You specify the colors in the Property inspector, and you can also choose a symbol from the document library for the leaf and the vine.
Bone	Create an inverse kinematics (IK) animation. You use this tool to add bones to the object you're animating. The bones comprise the inverse kinematics chain: You tug on a bone and the bones that are higher in the chain move.
Bind	Fine-tune an IK animation that's not performing up to snuff (that's bound up, if you will). You use this tool to bind points from an object with a bone.
Paint Bucket	Fill a shape with color or a gradient.
Ink Bottle	Change the outline (the *stroke,* in Flash-speak) of an object.
Eye Dropper	Sample a fill color.
Eraser	Erase parts of objects. You can specify how the tool works by choosing a modifier from the bottom of the Tools panel.
Hand	Pan from one part of the document to another.
Zoom	Change the level of magnification. You specify whether the tool zooms in or out by choosing a modifier from the bottom of the Tools panel.
Stroke Color	Show the selected color for strokes (outlines) created with the drawing tools.
Fill Color	Show the selected fill for shapes. A fill can be a solid color or a gradient.
Default Colors	Revert the stroke and fill to the default colors, which are black and white, respectively, just like in a newspaper.
Swap Colors	Swap the current stroke and fill colors.
No Color	Change the current color to no color.

Customizing the Workspace

If you're one of those right-brained people using Flash, which was obviously designed by left-brained people, you'll be happy to know that you can customize the workspace to suit the way you work and, for that matter, think. You can customize the layout of the workspace, the Tools panel, and much more. If you're interested in changing the way the Flash workspace is set up, the following sections are just for you.

Customizing the Tools panel

The default Tools panel shows you every tool that the Flash designers have known, and that's quite a few tools. You'll be happy to know that if you don't use every tool on the Tools panel, you can customize the panel by removing tools and rearranging the locations of the others. To customize the Tools panel, follow these steps:

1. **Choose Edit⇨Customize Tools Panel.**

   The Customize Tools Panel dialog box appears (see Figure 1-12).

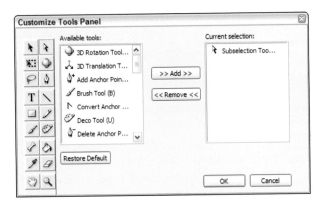

Figure 1-12: Create your own, special Tools panel.

2. **Select the tool you want to modify from the facsimile of the Tools panel on the left side of the dialog box.**

   The name of the tool appears in the Current Selection pane. If other tools are available from a fly-out menu, they're listed as well.

3. **Do one of the following:**

   • *Make a tool available as a choice on a fly-out menu:* Select the tool from the Available Tools pane and then click Add. You can add as many tools as you want to a fly-out menu.

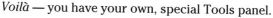

- *Remove a tool from the Tools panel*: Select the tool in the Current Selection pane and then click Remove. This action leaves a blank space on the Tools panel, which you fill by choosing a tool from the Available Tools pane and then clicking Add.

4. **Continue arranging the Tools panel to suit your needs and then click OK.**

   Voilà — you have your own, special Tools panel.

You can always revert to the default Flash workspace by choosing Window⟶Workspaces⟶Default.

Rearranging the workspace

The easiest way to change the Flash workspace is to change where items are located. And, you don't need an interior designer to show up with a bunch of color swatches and talk about applying feng shui (whoever he is!) to your space. Here are some ways to customize your workspace:

- ✔ **Undock a panel.** Click the panel's title and drag it into the workspace.

- ✔ **Dock a floating panel.** Click the panel's title bar and drag it to the one of the interface sides. When you see an opaque vertical bar, release the mouse. The panel docks to a side of the workspace. When you see an opaque, horizontal black bar, release the mouse to dock the panel at the top or bottom of the workspace.

- ✔ **Dock one floating panel with another.** Drag one panel's title bar toward the other panel. When an opaque blue overlay appears over the other panel, release the mouse button to dock the panels together. If you see an opaque blue line appear over the panel to which you're docking, the panel you're moving docks on top of the other panel.

- ✔ **Change the size of a panel.** Move the cursor toward a corner of the screen. When the panel becomes a line with a double-headed arrow, click and drag to resize the panel.

Saving a custom workspace

When you rearrange the workspace to suit your preferences, Flash remembers the setting when you close the application. The next time you launch Flash, all the panels and Tools panels are right where you left them. However, if another Flash designer shares your computer, she may want to arrange the workspace differently. After she uses the computer, you're stuck with her custom workspace, and a Battle of the Designers ensues. This unfortunate situation doesn't have to happen. You can save a custom workspace by following these steps:

1. **Rearrange the workspace to suit your needs.**

2. **Customize the Tools panel.**

   If you don't know how to customize the Tools panel, we show you how in the section "Customizing the Tools panel," earlier in this chapter.

3. **Choose Window⇨Workspace⇨ New Workspace.**

   The New Workspace dialog box appears (see Figure 1-13), in which you can save a custom workspace for posterity.

Figure 1-13: Saving a custom workspace.

4. **Enter a name for the workspace.**

5. **Click OK.**

   The new workspace is saved and is added to the Workspace submenu.

To change from the current workspace to a saved workspace, choose Window⇨Workspace, and then click to select a workspace. Figure 1-14 shows a custom workspace that Doug created, which looks a lot like the Flash CS3 workspace. If you don't like the new workspace, you can create a reasonable facsimile of the old one.

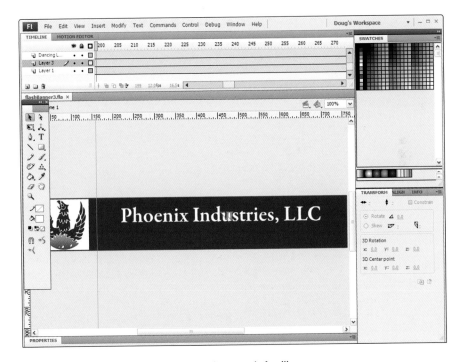

Figure 1-14: A custom workspace that looks vaguely familiar.

Managing workspaces

Flash designers and developers can change their minds whenever they want. If you've experimented with different workspace designs and find that you have too many lurking about on the Workspaces submenu, you can alleviate the clutter by managing your workspaces as outlined in these steps:

1. **Choose Window⇨Workspaces⇨ Manage Workspaces.**

   The Manage Workspaces dialog box appears (see Figure 1-15). You can manage your custom workspaces at any time.

2. **Select the workspace you want to modify.**

   From here, you can either rename or delete the workspace.

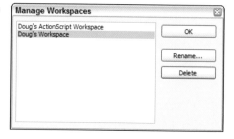

Figure 1-15: Managing custom workspaces.

To rename the workspace, follow these steps:

1. **Click Rename to rename the selected workspace title.**

   The Rename Workspace dialog box appears.

2. **Enter a new name for the workspace and click OK.**

   The workspace is renamed.

3. **Click OK again to close the Manage Workspaces dialog box.**

To delete the workspace, follow these steps:

1. **Click Delete.**

   Flash displays a message box telling you that the deletion cannot be undone.

2. **Click Yes to delete the workspace, or No to save the selected workspace.**

   If you click Yes, the workspace vanishes into the great cyberspace ether.

3. **Click OK to apply your changes.**

   Your changes are saved, and the Manage Workspaces dialog box closes.

Changing keyboard shortcuts

Keyboard shortcuts are tremendous timesavers. (Doug uses them all the time.) Adobe has a default set of keyboard shortcuts for Flash CS4, which may or may not be ideally suited to your working preferences. For example, if you remember a set of keyboard shortcuts from another application that has commands similar to Flash and the Flash keyboard shortcuts are different, you can modify the default set to match the shortcuts you memorized. To change keyboard shortcuts, follow these steps:

1. Choose Edit⇨Keyboard Shortcuts.

The Keyboard Shortcuts dialog box appears (see Figure 1-16).

Figure 1-16: Use this dialog box to make keyboard shortcuts work the way you want.

2. Click the Duplicate Set button.

The Duplicate dialog box appears. You cannot modify the default set, but you can modify a duplicate set.

To match the keyboard shortcuts of popular applications, choose a set from the Current Set drop-down menu. You can choose to match the keyboard shortcut set of applications such as Flash 5, Photoshop 6, or Illustrator 10, for example.

3. **Enter a name for the duplicate shortcut set.**

   You can give it any name you want. However, if you're creating multiple keyboard shortcut sets, it makes sense to give the keyboard shortcut a name that reflects the task for which you use the shortcut set; for example, My ActionScript Shortcuts.

4. **Choose an option from the Commands drop-down list.**

   The list includes all command groups, such as Actions Panel Commands, Debug Movie Commands, and Drawing Menu Commands.

5. **Click the plus sign (+) icon next to a command group.**

   The command group expands to display all commands.

6. **Select the menu command for which you want to assign a keyboard shortcut, or change an existing keyboard shortcut.**

   If the command has a keyboard shortcut, it's displayed in the Shortcuts pane. If the command doesn't have a keyboard shortcut, the pane is empty.

7. **To create a keyboard shortcut for a command the doesn't have one, click the plus sign to the right of the Shortcuts title.**

   The word <empty> appears in the Shortcuts pane and the Press Key pane.

8. **Press the key sequence you want to use as a shortcut for the command.**

   You can use keys such as Backspace or Delete or the arrow keys without a modifier. If you use a letter or number for a shortcut, you must use it in conjunction with the Ctrl key; for example, Ctrl+T. If you press a keyboard shortcut used by another command, a warning message appears underneath the Press Key pane.

9. **Press Change to apply the keyboard sequence to the command.**

   If you choose a keyboard sequence assigned to another command, the Reassign dialog box appears. Click Reassign to reassign the keyboard shortcut sequence or press Cancel. When you reassign a keyboard shortcut, it's no longer associated with the other command (to avoid any potential conflicts).

10. **Continue modifying and adding keyboard shortcuts to suit your working preferences.**

11. **Click OK to apply the changes to your new keyboard shortcut set and then close the Keyboard Shortcuts dialog box.**

    The new keyboard shortcuts remain in effect until you invoke the Keyboard Shortcuts command again and choose a different keyboard shortcut set from the Current Set drop-down menu.

Setting Flash preferences

Flash is a popular application that's used by a wide variety of people. Some of them are card-carrying geeks, like your friendly authors, and others are mild-mannered designers. Yes, even some soccer moms use the application to create cool animations for their kids' soccer teams.

Of course everyone is different and works differently, so you'll be glad to know that, in addition to modifying the Tools panel, workspace, and keyboard shortcuts, you can change other Flash elements to suit your own working preferences. For example, if you've worked behind a computer so long that the text in the Actions panel looks positively miniscule, you can change the font type and size by modifying ActionScript preferences.

If we showed you the steps involved to modify every single Flash preference, our editors would pull their hair out because we would exceed our allocated page count. Besides, many of the options are self explanatory. The following steps give you a jumping-off point:

1. **Choose Edit⇨Preferences.**

   The Preferences dialog box appears (see Figure 1-17).

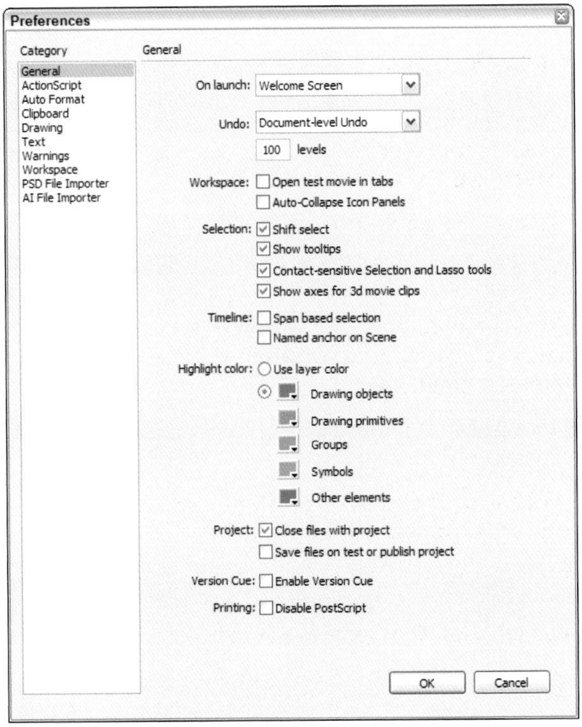

Figure 1-17: You can change Flash preferences to suit the way you work.

2. **Choose the category you want to modify from the Category pane.**

   The title changes and the dialog box is updated to show the options you can modify.

3. **Modify the options however you want.**

   Most options are self explanatory. For example, if you use Adobe Illustrator to create artwork for your Flash projects, the options in the AI File Importer category should be familiar to you. If you don't use Adobe Illustrator to create artwork for your Flash projects, you have no business mucking about in that category.

4. **Continue modifying categories and options as needed.**

5. **Click OK to apply the changes and close the Preferences dialog box.**

Chapter 2: Introducing Graphics, Symbols, and Animations

*F*lash is an extremely versatile application. You can create interactive Flash projects with audio and video and other bells and whistles. But Flash's humble beginnings were all about graphics and animations. Combine great-looking graphics with interactivity, and the sky's the limit.

If you're a first-time user of Flash CS4, you might feel like a kid in a candy store — you literally want to experiment with every tool. But, like anything else that's new, before you dive into the deep end of the pool, you have to dip your toe in the shallow end. In this chapter, we show you what you can accomplish with the Flash tools, and we introduce you to the backbone of any lean, mean Flash production: symbols, which are reusable graphics. But we're getting ahead of ourselves. In this chapter, you get an introduction to the type of things you can create with the drawing tools, plus an introduction to symbols and the document library.

Working with Flash Graphics

Great-looking graphics separate a ho-hum Flash production from something that grabs viewers by the scruff of the neck and makes them want to view the entire project, whether it's a game, an interactive Web site, or a great-looking Flash banner on a Web site. If you're artistically inclined, you can use the Flash drawing tools to create compelling graphics. In the following sections, we introduce you to some of the things you can accomplish using the drawing tools and the Text tool, and we show you how to get colorful with the Swatches panel.

Creating graphics with drawing tools

Flash has a plethora (one of Doug's favorite words) of drawing tools. You can draw lines, rectangles, ovals, polygons, and stars. You use several tools to create a finished drawing. For example, to create a facsimile of a storefront, you can use the rectangle tool to create the basic shape and windows and then use the Oval tool to create some objects in the store window, the sun, and perhaps a sign or two. If you have a street in your project, you can use the Polystar tool to create a stop sign. Figure 2-1 shows a logo that was created with the Primitive Oval tool and the Text tool.

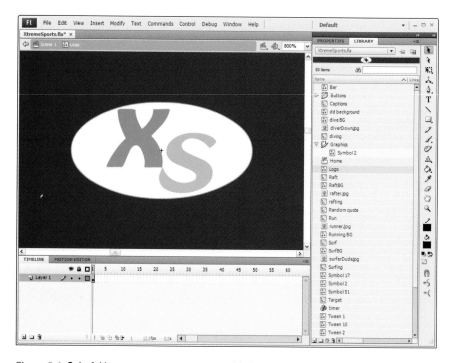

Figure 2-1: Colorful logos are a snap to create with the drawing tools.

The Pencil and Brush tools

If you know how to get the most out of a pencil or a paint brush, you'll be happy to know that Flash has the digital equivalent of these tools in its Tools panel. When you create graphics with the Pencil tool, you can modify the tool so that each stroke you draw is a separate object, or you can use the old paradigm of the Flash drawing tool, where each stroke of the same color develops a magnetic attraction to those you draw over. The Brush tool also works in a similar manner. If you're drawing with these tools using a mouse, Flash automatically smoothes the shape after you draw it.

Use a pressure-sensitive tablet and stylus to gain precise control over your work. Flash still smoothes the lines and brush strokes you draw, but the resulting artwork looks more professional.

The Pen tool

Another drawing tool in the Flash Tools panel enables you to create shapes and paths with point-by-point accuracy. If you work with illustration programs, you're familiar with what the Pen tool can do. If you don't work with illustration programs and you're brand-new to Flash, you create paths with the Pen tool. The path is composed of points, which come in two flavors:

- Straight
- Curve

You use the Pen tool to create an *open* path (a series of connected points resulting in a curved line or several connected straight line segments), or a *closed* path (an outline or solid shape filled with color).

The control you have with the Pen tool enables you to create sophisticated shapes and artwork. You can edit the paths by moving the points or by changing straight points to curve points and vice versa. You can also edit curve points by changing the tangent handles. If you're new to the wonderful world of paths and Bezier curves, we give you a full-course serving in Book II, Chapter 1.

If you own Adobe Illustrator, you can use the program to create vector artwork for your Flash projects. Illustrator has a robust toolset for creating sophisticated vector illustrations. You can import Illustrator artwork into Flash and preserve layers, and you can import an Adobe Illustrator EPS file or Adobe PDF file by saving it in the AI format and then importing the file into Flash. You can also import the file to the stage or into the document library.

Introducing the Text tool

If you have (or your client has) something to say and you're going to say it in Flash, you have to use the Text tool. Text in Flash comes in three flavors:

- **Static:** Displays text in a document. When you create the text, you can specify the font type, size, and color, for example. You can even embed fonts that may not be on your viewer's computers.
- **Input:** Captures user input.
- **Dynamic:** Creates a text field that can be dynamically changed during the course of a Flash movie. You use ActionScript to determine the text that's displayed in the field. You can also convert text into a vector

object that can be manipulated on a point-by-point basis. Figure 2-2 shows a published Flash movie in which the Text tool was used to create informational text, text for the navigation menu, and text for the banner.

Figure 2-2: Using the Text tool for fun and profit.

Getting colorful

A Flash production without color would be, well black and white. And a day without sunshine is night. But seriously, if you're going to attract visitors to a Flash Web site or create Flash projects for a living, you have to use color. We don't tell you which colors to use, but we do show you how to specify which colors are used for object strokes, fills, and backgrounds, for example. Figure 2-3 shows the Color panel, which has been used to mix the radial gradient that you see as the background for the Flash project.

You can use solid colors or gradients as fills:

- **Solid color:** The Solid Color option fills an object with one color. (We know that seems blatantly obvious, but we have to cover all the bases. You never know when an alien might find our Internet and download this book in electronic format.)

- **Gradient:** A blend of two or more colors. You can create one of these types of gradients:

- *Linear:* Blends colors from Point A to Point B in a straight line
- *Radial:* Blends colors from the center out in a concentric pattern
- *Bitmap:* Uses a photograph as the fill

Use the default colors and gradients from the Swatches panel, or mix your own by using the Color panel. After you master working with colors, you can create cool items, such as facsimiles of tie-dyed T-shirts and much more.

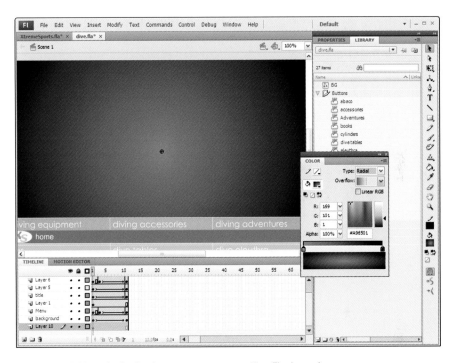

Figure 2-3: Add a splash of color to create a compelling Flash movie.

Finding Out about Symbols and Instances

Symbols and instances are the lifeblood of any Flash project. When you use instances of symbols rather than create a new symbol every time you need one, it's like feeding your Flash project one of those diets used by the rich and incredibly vain (diets with fancy names that are copyrighted and therefore can't be used in our book). That's right: Symbols decrease the file size of a published Flash project.

You can create a symbol from scratch or convert an object to a symbol. Symbols are stored in the document library. When you use a symbol in a Flash project, you're creating an *instance* of a symbol. And then disaster strikes. Suppose that the client (the guy with the fat wallet) calls you up and tells you that he wants to change the color of the soup can symbol, which is used a gazillion times in the project, from green to red. When this happens, you must be stern and tell the client that completing this task will take a long time. Then when you hang up the phone, you simply edit the symbol and change the color from green to red, and each instance of the symbol is instantly updated.

Understanding graphic symbols

Graphic symbols are static symbols that you create by using drawing tools or by importing vector artwork from an application such as Adobe Illustrator. When you create complex graphic symbols that are composed of many objects, you use layers to segregate the objects, which makes it easy to edit complex symbols.

You can also use an image as the basis for a symbol. This capability is useful when you need to display the image several times in a Flash project or animate the symbol. That's right: You can animate graphic symbols, and they're static. The later section on animation makes this perfectly clear.

Buttons, buttons, and more buttons

Buttons are everywhere. You see them on jackets and shirts and on Web sites. It's the clickable type we're referring to, although you can create a graphic symbol that looks like a shirt button. A *button* in Flash is a symbol with four states:

- ✔ Up
- ✔ Down
- ✔ Over
- ✔ Hit

The graphic in each state defines what the viewer sees when the button is first visible, when the cursor is paused over the button, and when the button is clicked. The Hit state defines the size of the active area of the button. You can create multiple layers when creating a button. You can also use sounds in a button. For example, if the button is used for a shopping cart checkout, you can have a "ka-ching" sound play when the button is clicked. Figure 2-4 shows a button being created.

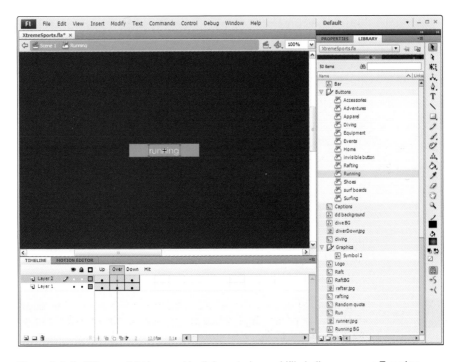

Figure 2-4: As Wimpy might have said, click me today and I'll gladly pay you on Tuesday.

Changing movie clip properties

Movie clips serve several purposes: You can use them as self-contained animations, as targets for external content that will be loaded into a project, or as containers for ActionScript. You create a movie clip when you want to create multiple instances of an animation in a Flash project. Why work harder when you can work smarter instead?

Movie clips can also be addressed by ActionScript. You can use ActionScript to change various properties of a movie clip. For example, if you want the movie clip to change dimensions, give the Movie Clip instance a name, and then change its .xscale and .yscale properties. Figure 2-5 shows a movie clip on the Stage that's being addressed by ActionScript. Notice that the instance name in the Property inspector is also present in the Actions panel. We show you how to control movie clips in Book IV, Chapter 1.

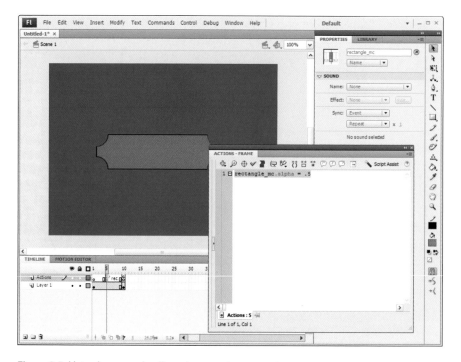

Figure 2-5: Listen here, movie clip — become transparent.

Checking out symbols from the library

When you create a symbol, it's added to the document library. Each symbol type can be identified by a unique icon. When you select a symbol, you see a preview at the top of the library. If the symbol is a movie clip, you can play it before adding it to your production.

Tools in the library make it possible for you to segregate objects into folders. This capability is useful when you have a huge Flash show with lots of graphics, movie clips, and buttons. You can create a folder for each symbol type, as shown in Figure 2-6. When you finish perusing a folder, you can collapse it to get a better look at the other items in the document library. You can also modify objects from another document library to suit the current document.

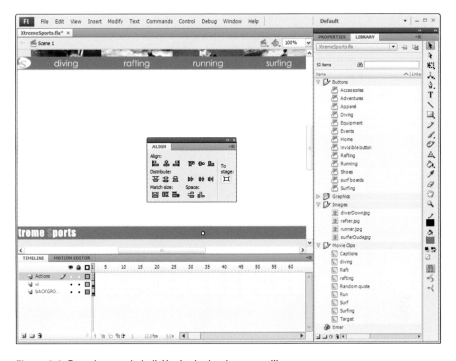

Figure 2-6: Be quiet, numbskull. You're in the document library.

Introducing Flash Animation

Flash began life as the animation program FutureSplash. Macromedia bought the application and developed it, and then Adobe bought Macromedia and developed Flash into the application you use today. In every iteration of Flash, animation has always been a strong Flash feature. And it's gotten even better with Flash CS4. In the following sections, we introduce you to Flash animation, and we cover the topic in more detail in Book III.

Frame-by-frame animation (the old school)

If you've watched cartoons, you've seen frame-by-frame animations at work. Artists draw the characters in different poses and motions. The whole thing is assembled as a video, and you see seamless motion. Flash gives you easier ways to create animation. However, frame-by-frame animation can sometimes still be used to good effect without causing you to break much of a sweat. You have to create lots of frames, however. Creating an image slideshow and typewriter text are two uses we can think of for frame-by-frame animation. Figure 2-7 shows the timeline for a frame-by-frame animation.

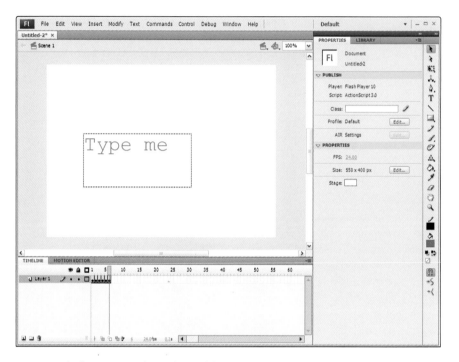

Figure 2-7: Let's see — one frame for each letter and then. . . .

Motion tweening will move ya

Suppose that your client wants, on the home page of his Web site, a Flash animation that moves an object from Point A to Point B to Point C. If you are new to Flash and just finished reading the preceding section, on frame-by-frame animation, you're probably thinking, "Yikes. That will take three forevers." Calm down, Flash Grasshopper. Breathe deeply and chant the mantra: Motion tween. When you need to create a complex animation, you create the symbol you want to animate (or not) and then choose Motion Tweening, and Flash creates the in-between frames. Get it? In between! Motion Tween.

After Flash creates the initial frames, you can add frames and keyframes to create the animation you want. And, if that's still not enough, you can tweak the animation 57 ways to Tuesday in the Motion Editor. Figure 2-8 shows a motion tween animation. We enabled onion skins so that you can see each frame of the animation. If we add ActionScript, we can have a "Twinkle, twinkle, little star" motion tween animation.

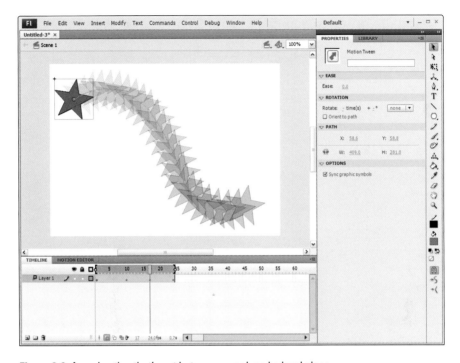

Figure 2-8: An animation that's not between a rock and a hard place.

Shape tweening will morph ya

Did you ever wish that you could change one thing into another — such as turn your former significant other into a piece of coal? Flash can't help you with your significant other, but it can morph one shape into another by using shape tweening. All you have to do is create two keyframes on which there are two separate shapes, apply shape tweening, and watch the fun begin. There's a bit more to it than that, so we show you how to morph the shape of your choice into another shape in Book III, Chapter 2.

Figure 2-9 shows a Shape Tween animation in which a star is morphing into an oval while moving. Onion skins are enabled so that you can see the in-between frames. If the thought of onion skins brings you to tears, you probably haven't tweaked a Shape Tween animation, a task we show you how to do in Book III, Chapter 4.

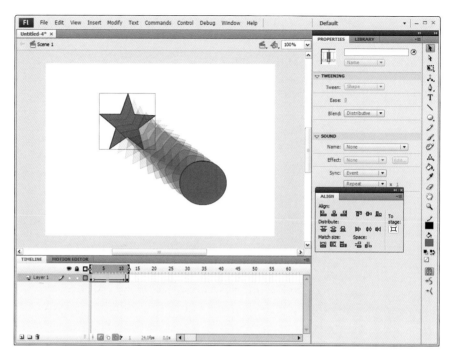

Figure 2-9: Morphing magic with shape tweening.

Inverse kinematics is bad to the bone

Character animation is loads of fun. (Doug did a lot of character animation in 3D programs.) Now you can create 2D character animations in Flash. If you want a character to strut her stuff into your Flash project, you can do so by creating an Inverse Kinematics animation. After you create your character using Flash drawing tools, you use the Bone tool to give the character form. And, if your character is a dog, for example, you use the Bone tool to give the dog a skeleton (see Figure 2-10).

If the animation doesn't play properly, you use the Bind tool to unbind the parts that were bound and determined to not make your animation run smoothly. We show you how to bone and bind in Book III, Chapter 2.

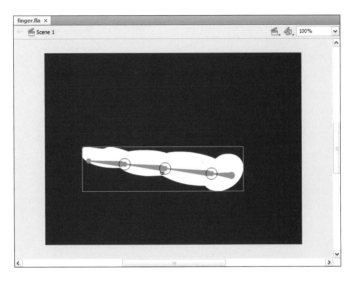

Figure 2-10: Knick, knack, paddy whack, bone the dog a skeleton.

Chapter 3: The Engine Beneath Flash: ActionScript 3

ActionScript 3 is the programming language that can be used with Flash CS4. If you're new to Flash, you will find ActionScript to be a powerful and extensive language. However, you will also find that just a little goes a long way. Experienced Flash hands will see how to use ActionScript and shift from many of the old practices to new techniques for getting the most out of ActionScript 3's new features.

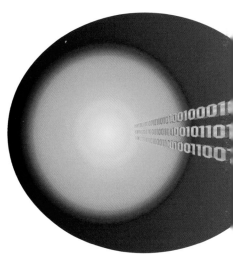

Book IV, which is dedicated to ActionScript 3, guides you through several uses of ActionScript and its levels of sophistication. In this chapter, we provide you with an introduction to ActionScript and tell you how to start using it. Also, if you have used ActionScript in Flash CS3, you will be delighted to find that the CS4 version has changed little from the CS3 version, which means that you don't have to figure out how to use the language all over again (as has often been the case in past revisions).

Understanding What ActionScript 3 Can Do for You

We like to treat ActionScript as the engine beneath your Flash creation. Think of it as you would after building a beautiful automobile chassis and body: You need an engine and a steering mechanism to make the device go and to guide it through the many different possibilities you plan for your project.

Suppose that you build an eye-catching animation with a beautiful design and that viewers see your Flash page on the Web. The first time a viewer sees your page, she's impressed and shows it to her friends. After a few views of the page with your animation on it, however, the viewer becomes bored. It's similar to telling a joke: The first time you tell it, it's funny. However, with every retelling, the joke loses its flavor and you need to dip into your repertoire to pull out another one. Unless you want to go through life repeatedly telling the same joke (or repeatedly showing the same Flash movie), you need ActionScript in order to make practical and interesting Web sites with Flash CS4.

Controlling the Timeline

In many ways, the Flash Timeline is like a runaway train: After the playhead starts moving through the different frames and your animation begins, the viewer can do nothing other than watch whatever you created. In even the earliest versions of Flash, the software engineers realized that Flash viewers needed some way to start and stop the playhead on the Timeline. Thus, the first ActionScript version consisted of a simple set of commands to control the Timeline. (It was ActionScript in diapers!)

To let viewers control the playhead, early versions of Flash had Button symbols that could be programmed with ActionScript. The Button symbols were bandwidth friendly because, as symbols, they could be reused as different instances. You could create a single Button symbol and then make 100 instances, and only a single symbol's code was hauled over the Internet. (Buttons are *still* bandwidth friendly, as are movie clips.)

When ActionScript was updated, the plan of putting it into buttons and movie clips got progressively worse. The more movie clips and buttons in a Flash application, the more little pieces of disconnected ActionScript that need to be dealt with. Trying to track down hundreds of buttons and movie clips that had snippets of code on each one was similar to playing Where's Waldo? in a house of mirrors. Even the addition of Movie Explorer was of little help because, after you located the code in Movie Explorer, you had to try to find the object's frame in what might be a very long Timeline with lots of layers.

With ActionScript 3, Flash's key language is no longer at the proverbial children's table of Internet programming languages. ActionScript is all grown up now, and although many users miss the old ways, it's similar to missing a bad habit, such as smoking. So use the new ActionScript to see how to move along the Timeline without adding code directly to the button. (See Book IV, Chapter 1 for a more detailed example.)

Working with the Timeline

In a nutshell, working with the Timeline, you must

- **Make a button.** You can do it on the Stage or by using ActionScript.

- **Attach a listener to the button.** The listener tells the button what to listen for — usually a click on the button.

- **Write a function that alters movement on the Timeline.** Actions include moving to a frame and stopping, moving to a frame and restarting stopped movement, or starting play from the Timeline's current position.

Of course, the best way to show this process is to create an example.

Creating Timeline Functions with ActionScript

In this section, you create two buttons: a winning choice and a losing choice. (If only life were that simple! Sigh.)

Creating two buttons

To create the buttons, follow these steps:

1. **Open a new Flash file (ActionScript 3), and save it as `Fate.fla`.**

2. **Add two layers by clicking the New Layer icon below the Timeline, naming the top layer** Actions, **the second layer** Frames, **and the bottom layer** Buttons, **as shown in Figure 3-1.**

3. **In the Actions layer, click Frame 3, and press F5 to insert keyframes out to Frame 3.**

4. **In the Frames layer, click Frames 2 and 3, and press F6 to add keyframes.**

5. **In the Buttons layer, click Frame 3, and press F5 to add three frames.**

6. **Click the lock icon in both the Actions and Frames layers.**

   This step locks the layers to help prevent you from making mistakes.

7. **Click the first frame of the Buttons layer.**

8. **Using the Oval tool, draw a circle to be used as a button; select the oval and press F8 to open the Convert to Symbol dialog box.**

9. **Type** Btn **for the name, select Button as the type, select the Export for ActionScript check box, and click OK.**

   (If you don't see the check box, click the Advanced button.)

   Now you should have a button on the Stage.

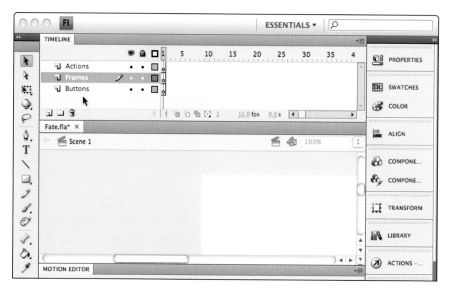

Figure 3-1: Setting up layers in an application.

10. **Select the button, and while holding down the Ctrl key (the Option key on the Mac), drag the button to create a duplicate.**

11. **Position one button above the other.**

Formatting the buttons

Now you're ready to apply some properties to the buttons. Follow these steps:

1. **Select the top button by clicking on it.**

2. **Choose Window⇨Properties (Ctrl+F3, ⌘+F3 on the Mac) from the menu bar to open the Property inspector. In the Instance name box, type** Win, **as shown in Figure 3-2.**

3. **Select the bottom button.**

4. **In the Instance name box of the Property inspector, type** Lose.

5. **Next to the top button, type** Win; **next to the bottom button, type** Lose.

6. **Lock the Buttons layer by clicking the column beneath the lock icon.**

    A lock icon appears in the layer.

7. **Unlock the Frames layer by clicking the lock icon.**

8. **Click the first frame, and select the Text tool.**

9. **Select a 36-point font, and type** Choose your fate **(see Figure 3-3).**

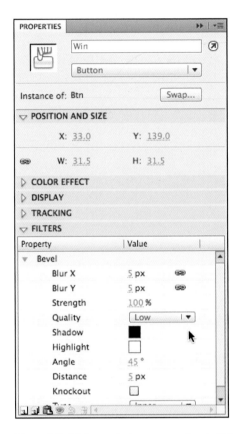

Figure 3-2: Adding an instance name to a button.

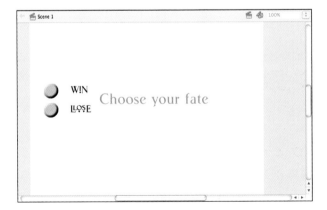

Figure 3-3: Added static text labels.

10. **Select Static Text in the pop-up menu in the Property inspector, if it isn't already selected.**

11. **Click the second frame, and then using the Text tool, type** You won! You can program in ActionScript 3.0.

12. **Click the third frame with the Selection Tool, and then with the Text Tool, type** You lost your fear of programming in ActionScript 3.0!.

13. **Lock the layer.**

Adding the ActionScript

The last part of the process is adding the code. Follow these steps:

1. **Click the Actions layer, and choose Window⇨Action.**

   The Actions panel opens.

2. **Click inside the Actions panel and add the following script:**

   ```
   stop();
   Win.addEventListener(MouseEvent.CLICK,goWin);
   Lose.addEventListener(MouseEvent.CLICK,goFearless);

   function goWin(e:MouseEvent):void
   {
           gotoAndStop(2);
   }

   function goFearless(e:MouseEvent):void
   {
           gotoAndStop(3);
   }
   ```

3. **Save the .fla file.**

The ActionScript's actions

The following points show exactly what the ActionScript did to the flow on the Timeline:

1. The playhead was stopped with the stop() statement.

2. The event listener was added to both the Win and Lose instances of the buttons. Each one listens for a button CLICK.

3. The Win button's function is goWin(); the Lose button's function is goFearless(). Each function moves the playhead to the appropriate keyframe.

As you can see, the example used the simple sequence of `Make` (you made the button), `Listen` (the button listened for the `CLICK`), and `Action` (the ActionScript functions moved the playhead where specified.)

Test the movie by choosing Control⇨Test Movie. The message you see depends on which button you click. Figure 3-4 shows what happens when you click the Lose button.

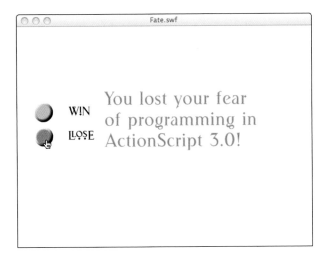

Figure 3-4: Clicking the Lose button leads to this output.

Bringing in New Objects

One persistent challenge in developing Web sites — whether it's in HTML or Flash or any other Internet language — is sending an object over the Internet. The *size* of the object you're sending determines the experience of the person on the receiving end.

Big objects take more time to transport than small ones do. Suppose that you're making a Flash site for a travel agency. The agency wants a Flash animation on every page along with a photograph to accompany the animation. The site will have a total of ten pages. Your client tells you that under *no circumstances* can any page be larger than 50KB. However, because you know Flash, you want to place each page in a keyframe with each one taking up no more than 50KB. By using buttons to control the Timeline, you can then have viewers quickly change content, including the animation and graphic.

If you place all ten elements in the Flash document at the same time, it has a load cost of 500KB. That takes a while to load, and impatient users may not wait — the deadly Back button in a browser always beckons whenever a page loads slowly.

On the other hand, you can display ten pages by using ActionScript to load a movie clip whenever it's needed. At only 50KB, the clip should load quickly, and users may not even be able to notice. Also, after the materials are in the *cache* (temporary memory), they load even more quickly the second time around. The other pages simply wait on the server until requested. Because the pages aren't loaded, users don't have to wait for pages they haven't asked to see.

Figure 3-5 illustrates the difference between the two approaches.

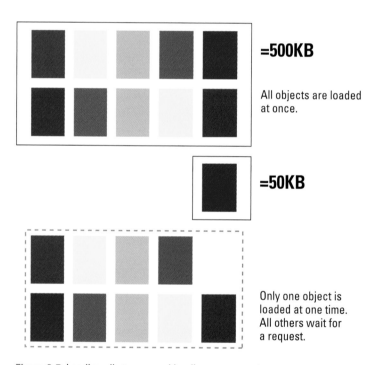

Figure 3-5: Loading all at once and loading on request.

Both techniques require ActionScript, and because it makes more sense in the context of real-world Web use to load pages only when requested, that technique is the one you want to use. (See Book IV for examples.)

You reuse the same code repeatedly. Just dust off the old code and reuse it whenever you need it. There's no sense in reinventing the wheel every time you use ActionScript.

Providing information just in time

The concept of organizing your Flash application so that ActionScript loads materials only when requested is related to another important consideration — getting what you want when you want it. Some materials may be requested, but the information need not be in front of viewers until a specified time. For example, a recipe doesn't require its baking instructions until all the ingredients have been prepared and mixed. Other types of information may arrive in real time, such as a Web service that tracks thunderstorms. By breaking down tasks into smaller parts and keeping them on the server until needed, you avoid cluttering your screen or overworking your computer's processor. You get what you need *just in time*.

Organizing tasks

When you're developing Flash Web sites, you can depend on two events taking place:

1. Your site will change.
2. Your site will grow.

By breaking down a Flash site into smaller parts and using ActionScript to control those parts, you make your life easier. Suppose that a client runs a grocery store and wants to run weekly specials, and that you have to change the site weekly. If that client then decides to expand her services to include a soup-and-salad bar, you have to add another component. Figure 3-6 compares two ways to approach that problem.

By taking a more granular approach to your application, you create far more flexibility for growth and change. The "parts" are really just little Flash programs in .swf format. These smaller Flash files (in .swf format) make it easy to find out about Flash and to build sophisticated applications.

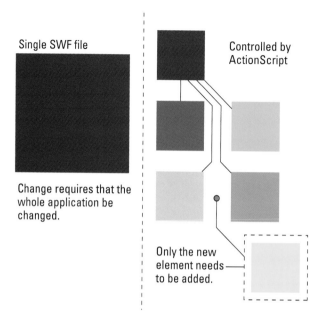

Single SWF file

Change requires that the whole application be changed.

Controlled by ActionScript

Only the new element needs to be added.

Figure 3-6: Organizing for change and growth.

Looking at the Many Levels of ActionScript

Working with ActionScript 3 in Flash CS4 provides you with a wide range of options. Flash CS4 can use earlier versions of ActionScript (ActionScript 1 and ActionScript 2), but we don't cover these earlier versions. ActionScript 3 was introduced in Flash CS3, so it's not even brand-new. If we were to spend time discussing earlier ActionScript versions, we would just be going backward, and many of the functions in those earlier versions have been deprecated.

The Timeline code

If you use ActionScript on the Timeline, you're best served by keeping it in a single frame on a single layer. It can be tempting to add code in keyframes wherever you think you need to, but you can bet that doing so will lead to problems. As you can see in Figure 3-1, the top layer is the Actions layer, and you can see in the first frame the little a, indicating that the frame has ActionScript.

When you place your script on the Timeline, use the Actions panel. It helps you write ActionScript and provides aid in the form of code hints and available options. Figure 3-7 shows the Actions panel and all its parts.

Insert Target Path ┐ Debug Options ┌ Apply Block Comment

Add   Auto   Collapse Remove
Item   Format Section Comment

Toolbox   Help

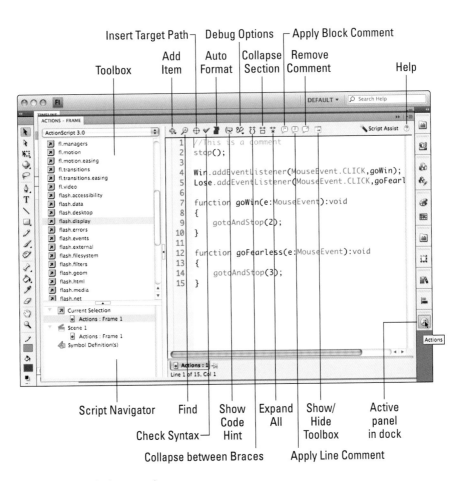

Script Navigator   Find   Show   Expand   Show/   Active
                              Code   All   Hide   panel
                              Hint   Toolbox   in dock

Check Syntax ┘

Collapse between Braces   Apply Line Comment

Figure 3-7: The Actions panel.

For the most part, you just use your keyboard to write in ActionScript. However, the following list briefly describes each part of the panel:

- **Toolbox:** A library of ActionScript language that's organized into classes. At the end is an index with all the terms arranged alphabetically.

- **Script Navigator:** Helps you find where you placed your code. Put it all in one place, and the Script Navigator shows the current selection and scene with ActionScript. (If you put your code all over the place on the Timeline, the Script Navigator can't save you! You still have to select each element with ActionScript to show it in the Script Navigator.)

✔ **Add Item:** Allows you to click an ActionScript statement to enter it into the program (an alternative to typing).

✔ **Find:** Lets you search for terms in the program.

✔ **Insert Target Path:** Helps to define the absolute or relative path to an object, such as a movie clip.

✔ **Check Syntax:** Checks for syntax errors and reports them.

✔ **Auto Format:** Formats code and makes your code more readable. It automatically adds semicolons where needed and checks for syntax errors.

Rather than use Check Syntax, we favor using Auto Format. If no errors are found, your code is formatted; if it's not, all syntax errors are reported.

✔ **Show Code Hint:** Helps you figure out how to use ActionScript far better than the Script Assist feature does. (We keep this feature turned on all the time.) For example, if you place a period (.) next to an object, all the properties and methods associated with that object's class appear.

✔ **Debug Options:** Adds little red dots to the left of the line number. In longer programs, these little red dots make it easier to find a problem you're working on.

✔ **Collapse between Braces, Collapse Selection, Expand All:** Three tools used to hide or show code that can be useful in longer programs.

✔ **Apply Block Comment, Apply Line Comment, Remove Comment:** Assist in creating and removing *comments,* which are notes that a programmer inserts into the code.

✔ **Show/Hide Toolbox:** A toggle button that displays and hides the Toolbox on the left side of the Actions panel.

✔ **Script Assist:** The original ActionScript entry mode. Some people see it as the greatest thing since solar power, and others see it as an awkward programming tool. It shows the options available and helps display the structure of statements. (Code hints are, in our opinion, a better alternative.)

✔ **Help (?):** An essential tool that helps you use ActionScript. Rather than a typical Help resource, this one instead opens the ActionScript 3.0 Reference, including examples, in your browser. You can select a term, and the Help (?) button immediately displays the term in the ActionScript 3.0 Reference.

Keep in mind that the Actions panel is used *only* for programs developed by placing the code in the Timeline. However, there's a better way to develop ActionScript wholly independently of the Timeline that we introduce in the next section.

ActionScript files and classes

Writing code on the Timeline leaves a lot to be desired. For programmers, it's an unnatural place for programs. For designers, while offering certain advantages, has long-range consequences for applications that are likely to fail at some point. Also, scripts linked to the Timeline hinder changing code and reusing the same code in another project.

To write scripts that are independent of the Timeline, you use ActionScript files along with the familiar Flash file. The Flash (.fla) file's primary use is to hold the symbols in its library and hold the name of the class to be loaded and run.

From Timeline to ActionScript file

Preparing to program using an ActionScript file begins with the Flash file. You simply open a new Flash file and put the name of the ActionScript file in the Class window, found in the Property inspector, as shown in Figure 3-8.

If you have any movie clips or buttons in the Flash file, you can address the movie clips and buttons by using ActionScript statements. Suppose that you build some buttons that you want to use. All you have to do is to leave them in the library and let ActionScript put them where you want them on the Stage. Figure 3-9 shows code that's similar to the code shown in Step 2 of the section "Adding the ActionScript," earlier in this chapter.

Figure 3-8: Placing the class name in the Property inspector.

```
Fate.as ×   Fate.fla ×   FateFree.fla ×
                                                              Target:  FateFree.fla
 1   package
 2   {
 3       import flash.display.Sprite;
 4       import flash.events.MouseEvent;
 5       public class Fate extends Sprite
 6       {
 7           private var Win:Btn;
 8           private var Lose:Btn;
 9           public function Fate()
10           {
11               Win=new Btn();
12               Win.x=33,Win.y=139;
13               addChild(Win);
14               Lose=new Btn();
15               Lose.x=33,Lose.y=183;
16               addChild(Lose);
17
18               Win.addEventListener(MouseEvent.CLICK,goWin);
19               Lose.addEventListener(MouseEvent.CLICK,goFearless);
20           }
21           function goWin(e:MouseEvent):void
22           {
23               trace("You won! \nYou can program \nin ActionScript 3.0\n");
24           }
25           function goFearless(e:MouseEvent):void
26           {
27               trace("You lost your fear\nof programming in\nActionScript 3.0!\n");
28           }
```
Line 24 of 30, Col 4

Figure 3-9: All ActionScript is in the ActionScript file.

Notice that the buttons named Win and Lose in the code shown in Figure 3-9 make a reference to the same buttons that you saw in the example using the Actions panel (see the section "Creating Timeline Functions with ActionScript," earlier in this chapter). The only difference is that rather than provide instance names for them, each one is named in the code.

Don't expect to understand much of the ActionScript coding at first. Just look at the statements and how they're used. Even though ActionScript is a little more difficult to use initially, it has a consistent logic that makes it much easier in the long run. Book IV has more examples and explanations to ease you through the process.

When you test an application that was created with ActionScript files rather than on the Timeline, the results can be either similar or identical. In this case, you can see the differences by comparing Figure 3-10, which uses the `trace()` statement to send the text messages to the Output panel, and Figure 3-4, which places messages on the Stage.

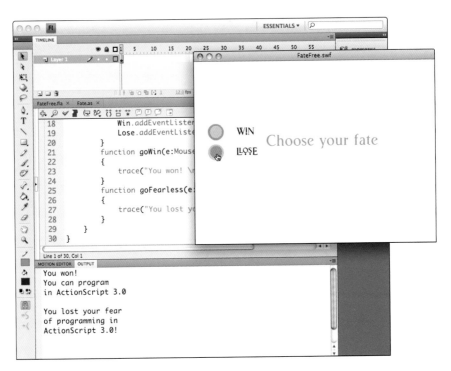

Figure 3-10: The ActionScript structure is similar to the one used on the Timeline.

Taking it in a little at a time

When you start using ActionScript and Flash, slow and steady works best. Because ActionScript is so powerful, it must have a large set of ActionScript statements. Figure out how to use the basics and then extend your knowledge (and power!) a little at a time. Book IV is dedicated to showing you how to use ActionScript, and it gets you going.

Chapter 4: Creating Your First Flash Project

In This Chapter

✓ **Planning your project**

✓ **Creating your first Flash document**

✓ **Creating your first animation**

Every project has a beginning and an end, which is the point where you breathe a sigh of relief and then sit back and bask in the glow of accomplishment of a job well done. But the beginning isn't where you think it might be. If you begin a project without planning, it's like trying to go somewhere you've never been without using a road map. If you don't know where you're going, *any* road will take you there. So, the first step when you're creating a Flash project, whether it's for fun or for hire, is to plan.

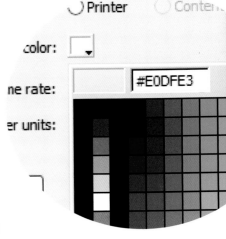

The amount of planning you do is directly proportionate to the scale of your project, and whether you're creating the project for a client. If you're planning the project for a client, the 90/10 rule takes effect: The first 90 percent of any phase of a project takes 90 percent of the allotted time. The final 10 percent of any phase of a project is equal in duration to the first 90 percent of the project. When the planning phase is over, you can roll up your sleeves and launch Flash.

In this chapter, we discuss some things you should consider when planning your project, and we show you how to create your first Flash document and animation. Let's delve into the wonderful world of Flash.

Planning Your Project

The loftiest goal in the world isn't anything more than a dream until you write it down on paper along with a list of action steps you have to take to accomplish the goal. Creating a project in Flash is similar: We like to start with a clean sheet of paper and start *noodling* — a technical term for daydreaming on paper with a purpose in mind. During the initial planning stage, you come to grips with the scope of your project and determine what you need in order to — as Larry the Cable Guy would say — get 'er done.

Mapping out the project

When Doug starts a new project, he uses the *mind-mapping* technique: He starts with a blank piece of unlined paper and draws circles to define the various parts of the project. This strategy is especially useful if you're creating a large project that has a lot of content. For example, if you're creating a Flash Web site, you have the home page and the other sections of the site (see Figure 4-1). Mapping out a site in this manner helps you envision the entire project. You also have associated items, such as the interface, background music, and images. After you have all the items listed, you draw lines to show how the various objects are connected.

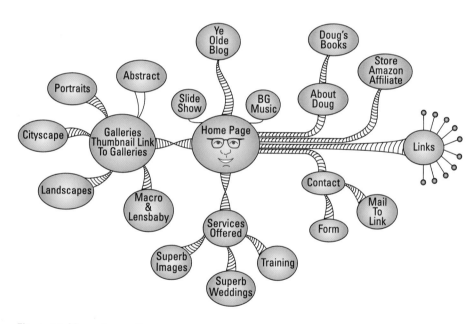

Figure 4-1: Map out your site.

If you're creating a complex animation or game, you can use *storyboarding*, a filmmaking technique. In a nutshell, you create a facsimile of each major scene in the animation. Your storyboard doesn't have to be a work of art; it's just a visual reference to keep you on track. Your storyboard can consist of several rectangles that are the approximate aspect ratio of your Flash project. Create one rectangle for each keyframe or scene in your project and draw stick figures. If you're working out a storyboard in a restaurant with your client, you may end up using napkins to sort out your storyboard. Just make sure that the napkins don't get wet after you create the storyboard. Whether you create your storyboard on a legal pad, computer screen, or napkin, the result is your vision of the final project.

Different people work in different ways, so mind mapping and storyboarding may not work for you. But we urge you to do some kind of planning when you tackle a complex Flash project, even if you just make some notes on a legal pad. When you put it in writing, what you see in your mind's eye may not be as cut and dried as you first thought.

Determining the scope of your project

After you do your initial planning, you have a good idea of what you need to get the job done. At this stage, you have an idea of the approximate amount of time it will take to finish your project. This information is useful if a client is chomping at the bit to post your Flash masterpiece on the Web.

If you're dealing with a client and the project is grand in nature, create some milestones and discuss them with the client. The milestones help keep you focused, especially if you're juggling more than one project.

Your initial planning also gives you an idea of whether you have the necessary knowledge to create your grand vision. If the project involves a lot of ActionScript and you don't know how to use the actions necessary to pull off the project, you may have to

- Find some assistance.
- "Dummy down" (big grin) the project.
- Thumb through the index of the reference book you hold in your hands and find the information you need to get the job done. We packed a lot of gems of wisdom — and blood, sweat, and tears — into this handy reference.

Planning a project may seem like a huge expenditure of time, and we agree that planning isn't as much fun as working in Flash. However, if you spend a little extra time up front, it can save you a huge amount of time when you're working on a project. Another benefit of planning ahead of time is that you don't reach the end of a project (or what you *thought* was the end of it) and realize that it has a fatal flaw or that you forgot to do one little thing at the start of the project. When you're dealing with hundreds of frames or hundreds of lines of ActionScript code, trying to find a flaw is like trying to find the proverbial needle in the haystack.

Making a list and checking it twice

Creating a checklist is a handy way to manage a project. Your list shows you everything you need to create for the project. The objects you need to create in Flash are assumed, but listing them helps you recognize areas where you can save time and bandwidth by creating symbols, which help keep the resulting project rather svelte in regard to file size. Even with today's fast Internet connections, file size is still a factor. When you're listing the objects you need to create in Flash, begin with symbols, which are reusable. For example, you can create a rounded rectangle graphic symbol that can be used as a background for text. The same symbol can double as the basis for a button. Creating reusable symbols means less work for you. Then add to the list the other items you need to create, such as the user interface, movie clips, and animations.

The last part of the list consists of the objects you need from your client, such as photos, text, and logos. Here are some tips for gathering those items:

- **Images:** Make sure that you tell your client the size and resolution you require for the project images. Better yet, ask the client to send you the original digital file on disc, as long as it meets or exceeds your minimum requirements.

- **Video and audio files:** If your client supplies video and audio files, make sure that they're in the proper format. If the client is supplying video, ask for the original video captured by the camcorder. If she gives you video that has already been compressed, she won't like the results. Compressing a compressed file isn't just redundant — it doesn't produce good results, either. Plop the original file into the Adobe Media Encoder and do something exciting while the application renders a squeaky-clean FLV file for your project.

Covering your assets

After you create your list, you know what you need in order to create the project. We recommend rounding up all necessary items ahead of time. It's extremely counterproductive to realize, right in the middle of a project, that you're missing a vital element. We also recommend that you store all project assets in the same folder. Eventually, they'll end up in the document library, but being organized ahead of time is helpful. When your creative juices are flowing like the mighty Niagara Falls, it's not a good idea to slow down and try to remember where you stored an asset. Nothing stifles creativity quicker.

Creating Your First Flash Document

After you know where you're going and all your assets are safely nestled away in a folder, it's time to get down and get funky with Flash. When you create a Flash document, you have choices: You can start with a template or create your own document from scratch. If you use a template, it has all the information you need to start your project. However, if you create a document from scratch, you specify the document type, width, height, background color, and frame rate.

In the following sections, we show you how to create a simple Flash animation. If you're new to Flash, this information is extremely helpful. If you're an old hand at Flash, it's still helpful because animation is done slightly differently in Flash CS4.

Ye olde Welcome screen

When you launch Flash for the first time, you see the Welcome screen (see Figure 4-2). From there, you can do several things: Create a new document, click links to view online tutorials, find out about new features, or check out online resources, for example.

Figure 4-2: Welcome back, my friends, to the show that never ends.

You can find the same Welcome-screen resources on the Help menu, including the Flash Exchange. (No, unfortunately, you cannot exchange an old version of Flash for a new one.) What you can do in the Flash Exchange is find extensions for Flash. *Extensions* are similar to plug-ins in an image editing application: They enable you to create some cool elements, such as Flash slide shows, without breaking a sweat. We leave it up to you to decide whether you want to display the Welcome screen each time you launch Flash, or disable it by selecting the Don't Show Again check box (which is what Doug will do as soon as he finishes writing this sentence.) From now on, we use menu commands to create new documents.

Creating a document from a template

A template is a wonderful thing. It's all set up for a specific application, waiting for you to add your own splash of creativity to turn the published project into something special. Flash templates are in several categories: You can choose a template to create a Flash advertising banner, create a Flash project for a mobile device, create a photo slide show, or create a Flash project.

To create a document from a template, follow these steps:

1. **Choose File⇨New.**

   The New Document dialog box appears.

2. **Click the Templates tab.**

   The dialog box refreshes and displays the template categories (see Figure 4-3).

Figure 4-3: Creating a Flash document from a template is easy.

3. **Choose a category from the left pane.**

   Flash displays all templates associated with the category.

4. **Select a template.**

   A description of the typical use of the template appears in the lower-right corner of the dialog box.

5. **Click OK to close the dialog box.**

   Your shiny, new document is front and center on the Stage.

Creating a document from scratch

Flash has a default template for each document type. You can modify the document to suit your specific project after you create the document. The document type determines what the published document will be used for. To create a new document, follow these steps:

1. **Choose File⇨New.**

   The New Document dialog box appears (see Figure 4-4).

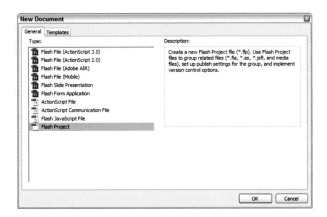

Figure 4-4: Which type of document do you want to create today?

2. **Review the available document types.**

   The document type determines the ultimate use of the published file. Your choices are described in this list:

   - *Flash File (ActionScript 3.0):* Creates a new Flash FLA file in the Document window using the default dimensions. The resulting document is published as a Flash ActionScript 3.0 SWF file that plays in the Adobe Flash Player.

   - *Flash File (ActionScript 2.0):* Creates a new Flash FLA file in the Document window using the default dimensions. The resulting document is published as a Flash ActionScript 2.0 SWF file that plays in the Adobe Flash Player.

   - *Flash File (Adobe AIR):* Creates a new Flash FLA file in the Document window using the default dimensions. The Publish settings are for Adobe AIR, which enables you to publish a desktop application that's played on the Adobe AIR runtime. The published file is cross-platform.

Adobe AIR makes it possible for you to create an application in Flash. The published file can be installed and executed on any computer that has the free Adobe AIR extension for the Flash Player (`http://get.adobe.com/air`).

- *Flash File (Mobile):* After you choose this option, the Adobe Device Central CS4 application appears. Choose a device, a player version, an ActionScript version, and a content type, which creates a new document tailored to the device you select.

- *Flash Slide Presentation:* Choose this option to create a Flash slide-show presentation that's published as a Flash SWF file.

- *Flash Project:* Choose this option to create a Flash Project, which is essentially a folder in which you store project content. This option is handy when you have many SWF and ActionScript files for a project.

3. **Choose ActionScript 3.0 and then click OK.**

   Flash creates a document with publish settings that are tailor-made for an ActionScript 3.0 document.

Setting the document size, background color, and frame rate

When you create an ActionScript 2.0 or 3.0 document, the default size is 550 x 400 pixels, the frame rate is 24 fps (frames per second), and the default Stage color is white, which isn't terribly useful if you're creating an animation of a polar bear in a snowstorm. You can change any of these options to suit your project by following these steps:

1. **After creating a new document, choose Window➪Properties.**

   The Property inspector opens (see Figure 4-5). If you're using the default workspace, you can open the Property inspector by clicking its tab in the Panel Dock on the right side of the workspace. In Figure 4-5, notice the options to change the Publish settings.

2. **Click the Edit button in the Properties area.**

   The Document Properties dialog box opens (see Figure 4-6).

3. **Enter some dimensions in the (width) and (height) fields.**

4. **Choose a Match option:**

   - *Default:* The default option matches the document to the default dimensions of the ones you specify.

   - *Printer:* If you choose Printer, the document size changes to match the dimensions of the paper now in the default printer, minus the printer margin size.

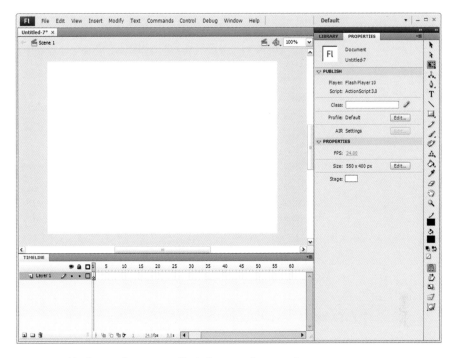

Figure 4-5: It's time to change your Flash document's properties.

- *Contents:* If you have objects on the Stage when you modify document properties, the Contents radio button becomes available. Choosing this option leaves an equal margin around the content on all sides.

5. **Click the Background color swatch.**

   The Swatches panel opens (see Figure 4-7).

6. **Click to select a swatch.**

   The Background color swatch changes to the selected color.

7. **Enter a value in the Frame Rate field.**

Figure 4-6: Every document has properties. It's a Flash law.

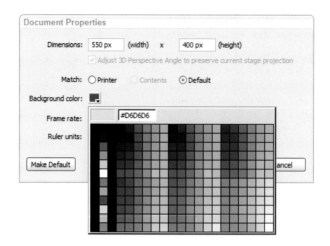

Figure 4-7: Is there a sky-blue pink in this panel?

The default frame rate of 24 frames per second (fps) is ideal for many projects, including those with external streaming video that loads into the published file. However, if you're creating a project for people who will be accessing the Internet with a slow connection, you can specify a frame rate as low as 12 fps and still produce good results with motion tweening and shape tweening animations.

8. **Choose a unit of measure from the Ruler Units drop-down menu.**

   This option changes the unit of measure for the document. The default option is pixels. Your choices include inches, inches (decimal), points, centimeters, millimeters, and pixels. The change is reflected in every dialog box that changes the size or location of an object.

   If you create lots of documents with the same dimensions, background color, and frame rate, you should create a new document, change the document properties as outlined in this section, and then click the Make Default button in the Document Properties dialog box before clicking OK.

9. **Click OK.**

   The dialog box closes, and your changes are applied to the document.

Creating your first animation

After you create a document, it's time to make something happen. In this section, we show you how to create a basic animation using motion tweening. To create your first animation, follow these steps:

1. **Create a new document, as outlined earlier in this chapter.**

   If you rushed to this section to find out how to create your first animation and you don't know how to create a new document, take a deep breath and flip back a few pages to the section about creating a document from scratch.

2. **In the Tools panel, select the Oval Primitive tool.**

   If you haven't used the tools yet, click the triangle to the lower-right of the Rectangle tool and select the Oval Primitive tool from the fly-out menu (see Figure 4-8).

3. **Click and drag on the Stage to create the oval.**

   Create a relatively small oval on the left side of the Stage.

4. **Right-click (Windows) or Control+click (Macintosh), and choose Create Motion Tween from the context menu.**

   Flash displays a dialog box telling you the shape because it cannot be tweened. You have the option to have Flash automatically convert it.

5. **Click OK.**

   Flash converts the object to a symbol and adds several frames to the Timeline. The last frame is selected (see Figure 4-9).

6. **Select the Selection tool.**

   It's the solid, left-pointing arrow at the top of the Tools panel.

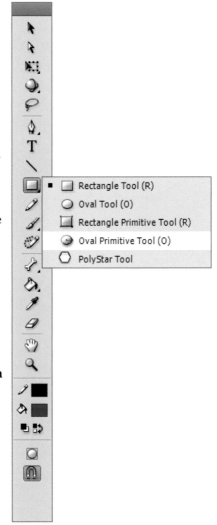

Figure 4-8: Allow us to introduce the Oval Primitive tool.

7. **Drag the oval to the right side of the Stage and down.**

   Flash creates a solid green line with a point for each frame. A keyframe is also added to the end of the Timeline (see Figure 4-10).

8. **Move the Selection tool close to the green line.**

   When you see a curve icon appear below the tool, click and drag to arc the line (see Figure 4-11).

9. **Release the mouse button when the arc looks like the one shown in Figure 4-11.**

   Flash curves the line, which in Flash-speak is known as the path.

10. **Choose Control⇨Test Movie.**

    Flash opens another window and your animation plays again and again and again. After you tire of looking at your handiwork, click the red X to close the dialog box.

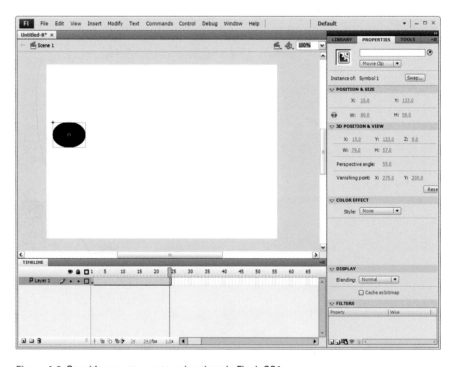

Figure 4-9: Gee, it's easy to create animations in Flash CS4.

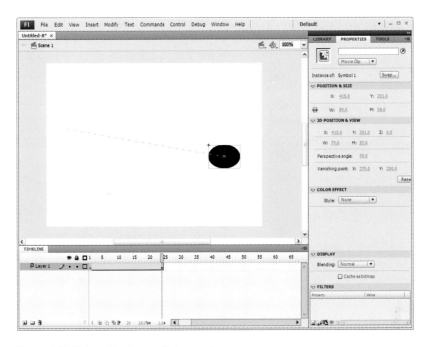

Figure 4-10: Holy motion tween, Batwoman!

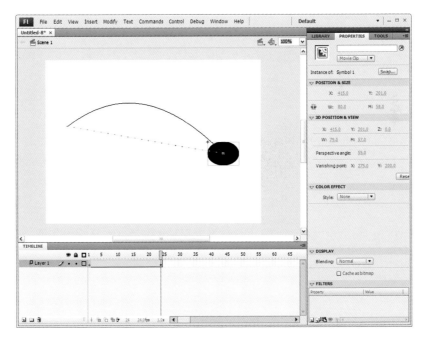

Figure 4-11: Bend me, shape me, any way you want to.

11. **If you want to save your first animation for posterity, choose File⇨ Save and follow the prompts to save the document in its native FLA format.**

When you combine animation with ActionScript and the other delightful features we discuss in this book, you create compelling Flash projects that will amaze your friends and family members and, if you're learning to use Flash for a living, your clients.

Chapter 5: Pushing the Panic Button — Help!

lash is a multifaceted software application. You can use it to create animations, multimedia presentations, interactive applications, and much more. You might say that Flash is *vast:* If it had only 50 percent of its current features, it would be half-vast. But even a half-vast program can present stumbling blocks. Your first line of defense is this book. Suppose that you're working in a client's office, though. Faced with an insurmountable problem, you don't want to whip out a *For Dummies* desk reference, so you can always resort to using the Help information supplied with the Flash application. It doesn't have any traces of the authors' charm and wit, but it provides help, and fast.

In this chapter, we show you how to summon Flash Help. We also show you how to use the other goodies lurking on the Flash Help menu. And, if you're a communal kind of Flash designer or developer, we show you the way to the Adobe online forums. Something for everyone, a Forum tonight.

Getting By with a Little Help from Flash

Flash can stump you when you least expect it. You may be working away, merrily drawing vectors and shapes and symbols and adding interactive snippets of ActionScript when Murphy (the guy who wrote the law) rains on your parade. Fear not, trepid Flash groupie, when Murphy strikes with a vengeance, an umbrella and some sunshine are just a few mouse clicks away.

Using Flash Help

The Flash Help menu, like the program, is bi-i-ig. With a bit of work, though, you can cut to the chase and find the information you're seeking. To summon Flash Help, follow these steps:

1. **Choose Help⇨Flash Help.**

    Alternatively, you can press F1 to get help. The menu command or keyboard shortcut displays an HTML page with Flash CS4 Help loaded and awaiting your command (see Figure 5-1).

Figure 5-1: Help me, Flash.

If you like to have information at your fingertips, click the PDF link in the upper-right corner of the Flash Help pages. A PDF file called Using Adobe Flash CS4 Professional loads in your browser. On the Acrobat toolbar, click the Save button to save a copy of the document on your computer.

If you're online when you summon Flash Help, pages from an Adobe Web site load in your default Web browser. If you're offline when you summon Flash Help, you see HTML pages that were added to your hard drive when you installed Flash.

2. **Choose an option from one of the menus.**

    The menu consists of several topics that contain information about every conceivable nook and cranny in Flash, minus the sage wisdom and humor of your friendly authors, Bill and Doug. If you want to cut to the chase, choose a book that appears to be the logical choice for the topic about which you need help. For example, to find information on ActionScript 3.0 components, choose the book with that title.

3. **Click the plus sign (+) icon to the left of a topic to see a list of information related to that topic.**

If you're searching for information on a topic like ActionScript, you'll find more topics with more plus signs. Click the applicable plus sign to reveal more topics. When you see the title that contains the information you're looking for, click it, and the related information appears on the right side of the Help window. You may have to click another plus sign to find what you're seeking. When you select a topic of interest, you see a list of items related to the topic.

4. **Click an item of interest.**

   The Flash help menu gives you detailed information about the item the piques your curiosity — the topic that had you stumped just a few seconds ago (see Figure 5-2).

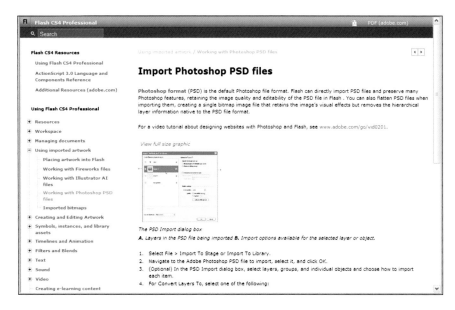

Figure 5-2: Finally, the information I'm looking for!

You can also find information by entering a word or phrase in the Search text box and then pressing Enter or Return. This returns a page of results from Adobe Community Help. The topics are listed in order of relevance. You can refine your search by choosing a topic from the list below your search query.

Getting ActionScript help

ActionScript is a whole different kettle of fish. When you're knee-deep in code and trying to create an interactive jigsaw puzzle before it rains any-more and Murphy's Law takes over, you need to get help. But you don't want help for everything — just information about what a specific action does and how to properly format the code.

To get ActionScript help, open the Actions panel and then follow these steps:

1. **From the left side of the Actions panel, select the action that has you stumped.**

   Don't double-click the action, or else you add it to your script.

2. **Right-click (Windows) or ⌘+click (Mac) and choose View Help.**

   Help information for the object appears in a different window, in HyperText Markup Language (HTML). In other words, it's an HTML document from Adobe's Web site. Figure 5-3 shows ActionScript help for the Date object, which is used for telling the time (and not for wowing unmarried Flash designers of the opposite sex).

Figure 5-3: Getting ActionScript help is easy.

Updating Flash

The people who designed Flash are like Santa's elves: They're continually working to make the product the best possible application it can be. To that end, they periodically make application updates available. If you use Flash on a computer that's always connected to the Internet, available updates

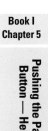

are installed automatically weekly or monthly whenever you start your computer. You see a warning message to this effect that shows the updates to be
installed. If you have additional Adobe applications on your machine, available updates for those applications are also displayed.

You can also update Flash manually by following these steps:

1. **Launch Flash and then choose Help⇨Updates.**

   The Adobe Updater appears, displaying the message shown in Figure 5-4.

Figure 5-4: And now, the latest and greatest Flash updates will
appear.

After the Adobe Updater scans for Flash updates, the dialog box
refreshes and shows you whether updates are available for Flash — and
other Adobe applications installed on your computer (see Figure 5-5).

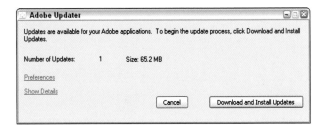

Figure 5-5: Update now!

2. **Choose one of the following options:**

   • *Preferences:* Click this link to open the Adobe Updater Preferences
     dialog box (see Figure 5-6). From within this dialog box, you can
     determine whether your computer automatically checks for updates,
     how often the Updater scans for updates to your Adobe applica-
     tions, whether the updates are downloaded automatically or you're
     prompted when updates are available, and which applications are
     automatically updated.

Figure 5-6: Setting Updater preferences.

To disable automatic updates, deselect the *Automatically Check for Adobe Updates* check box. After disabling automatic updates, you can manually scan for updates by choosing Help⇨Updates.

- *Show Details:* Click this link to open a dialog box that shows the available updates for each Adobe application installed on your computer. When you choose this option, a check box appears next to each update (see Figure 5-7). Deselect an update's check box if you don't want to install it.

- *Download and Install Updates:* Click this button to install the updates — or selected updates, if you choose not to install all available updates — to your computer. If you choose this option, a dialog box appears, showing you which update is being downloaded. A bar shows you the progress of the update. Below the progress bar, the Updater displays the time remaining to complete the update.

  After the download is complete, the Installation Progress dialog box appears, showing you which update is being installed. You have the option to cancel the install or minimize the Installation Process dialog box to the system tray (Windows). The dialog box notifies you if an installation fails and tells you what you need to do to apply the update to the application in question. When the update is complete, a message to that effect appears and the dialog box disappears.

Extending Flash

Lots of geeks out there love to write extensions for Flash. The majority of the extensions are pretty cool and do just as they're advertised to do — give you the capability to do something different from within the Flash application. You extend Flash by taking a short and tumble journey from Flash to the Flash Exchange. Here you find all kinds of extensions: some for video and some for ActionScript, for example.

The *Flash Exchange* is a popular place where lots of designers and developers upload extensions for Flash and other Adobe applications. Some of the extensions are free, and others aren't. But if an extension makes it possible for you to do something with Flash that you couldn't do before, it must have some value.

Finding Flash extensions

If you want to explore which Flash extensions are available, follow these steps:

1. **Launch Flash and choose Help⇨Flash Exchange.**

   Your default Web browser opens to the Adobe Exchange.

2. **In the Exchanges by Product section, click Flash.**

   The page refreshes to show the Flash Exchange (see Figure 5-7). The Flash Exchange is divided into four tabs: Staff Picks, Most Recent, Most Popular, and Highest Rated.

3. **Click to select a tab.**

   The page refreshes and shows the extensions filtered to all license types.

4. **Choose an option from the License Type drop-down menu, and then click Filter.**

   For example, one of the license options is Freeware. If you're on a budget and looking to extend Flash, this is the place to start.

5. **Click the Download button to the right of any extension to download it. The applications that cost money have a Buy button next to them. Click the button to purchase and download the extension.**

   Alternatively, you can click the extension title to display a page that has more information about the extension. If, after reading the description, you decide that the extension is for you, click Download or Buy. If you download an extension, you're prompted for your Adobe ID and password. If you don't have an Adobe account, you can set one up at this page. (It's free — what are you waiting for?) After signing in, the download begins.

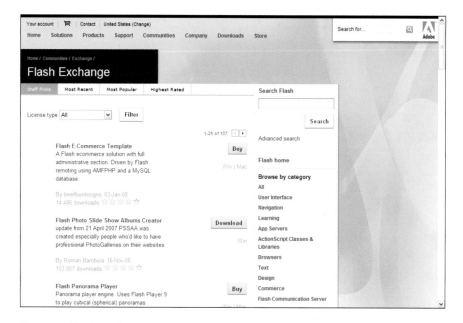

Figure 5-7: The Flash Exchange is chock-full of extensions for Flash.

Installing Flash extensions

After you download some Flash extensions, you install them. After you install them, you can use them to extend Flash in ways that may boggle your mind. To install an extension, follow these steps:

1. **From within Flash, choose Help⇨Manage Extensions.**

   Alternatively, you can double-click an extension. Either method launches the Adobe Extension Manager CS4. When you launch the Extension Manager for the first time and have extensions installed in the previous version of it, you have the option to migrate them to the current version.

2. **Click Yes to migrate extensions from the previous version of the Extension Manager into the current one.**

If you're pressed for time, click Later. If you don't want the old extensions, click Never. If you click Yes, the Extension Manager migrates the extensions. Click OK to complete the migration, and then restart the Adobe Extension Manager CS4.

3. **Click Install.**

   The Select Extension to Install dialog box appears.

4. **Navigate to the extension you want to install.**

   We generally download extensions to the computer desktop. They're easy to find there, and you can delete them after the Extension Manager installs them.

5. **Select the extension you want to install, and then click Open.**

   The Extension Manager displays the extension disclaimer. In essence, the disclaimer says that a third party created the extension and that Adobe doesn't warrant or support it. (It says a lot more, but we're not from Philadelphia, nor are we lawyers.) We suggest that you read the disclaimer thoroughly before accepting it.

6. **Click Accept to install the extension.**

   The extension is installed, and a message to that effect is displayed, which also notes that you must restart Flash CS4 for the extension to be recognized.

7. **Click OK.**

   The message box closes.

8. **Close Adobe Extension Manager CS4 and then restart Flash.**

   After installing an extension and restarting Flash, you can use the extension. Whether it appears as a tool or a menu command is predetermined by its designer. Refer to the Adobe Extension Manager CS4 for information.

Managing Flash extensions

After you download and install extensions for any Adobe application, you use Adobe Extension Manager CS4 to manage your extensions. You can disable an extension, remove an extension, or visit the Flash Exchange from within Adobe Extension Manager CS4. To manage your extensions, follow these steps:

1. **Launch Flash and choose Help➪Manage Extensions.**

   The Adobe Extension Manager CS4 appears.

2. **Select from the Products column the application whose extensions you want to manage.**

The check box in the Enabled column is selected for any extension that's enabled (see Figure 5-8).

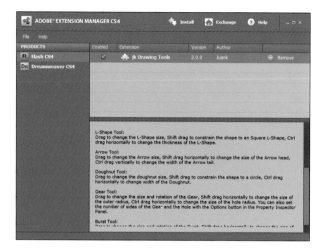

Figure 5-8: Manage your extensions with ease by using Adobe Extension Manager CS4.

3. **Click a selected check box next to an extension to disable it.**

   A bar appears, showing the progress, and then a message appears, telling you that the extension was successfully disabled.

4. **Click Remove to remove the extension.**

   A message appears, telling you that you're about to remove an extension.

5. **Click OK to remove the extension.**

From within Adobe Extension Manager CS4, click Exchange to visit the Adobe Exchange.

Flash Online Resources

Adobe believes that its customers should be informed and have access to a plethora of online resources. And, you don't have to do a Google search to find these resources. You can access a wealth of information by choosing one of these options from the Help menu:

✔ **Flash Support Center:** Opens the Flash Support Center, where you can search the Flash Knowledge Base by entering a few key words in the Search For text field. You also see a Search Tips link and an Advanced Search link.

✔ **Adobe Online Forums:** Opens the Flash Support Forums Web page, which is divided into several categories. Click a category that interests you to read the posts. You can add your two cents to a thread or use the forums as a resource for ideas or to search for information about a design problem that has been bothering you.

✔ **Adobe Training:** Leads you to the Flash Resources section of the Design Center tutorial, where you find tutorials, articles, and reference materials as well as links to blogs and other resources.

Book II
Creating Graphics

The 5th Wave — By Rich Tennant

"I'm not sure—I like the mutual funds with rotating dollar signs, although the dancing stocks and bonds look good too."

*F*lash! The very name of this application leads you to believe that you can create compelling projects. That's right — we're talking flashy here. To create flashy projects to present on the Web, you need to create good-looking graphics. Flash has all the tools you need to create rectangles, ovals, stars, and other shapes. You can add artistic splashes of color to the shapes you create with the Flash drawing tools. You can also kick up your projects a notch or two by importing photorealistic images. And, when you need to get the word out, you can use the Text tool.

Creating graphics can be time consuming, though. You'll be happy to know that you can create a symbol, which is in essence a reusable graphic. You can also organize your work with layers. We show you how to do all of the above and more in Book II.

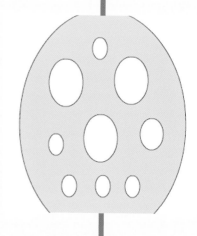

Scarg

Chapter 1: Creating Flashy Graphics

In This Chapter

✓ **Understanding vectors and bitmaps**

✓ **Creating shapes with the Drawing tools**

✓ **Modifying shapes**

A thing of beauty is a joy forever. If you want your Flash design to be a thing of beauty, you need to have eye-catching graphics. Can you imagine an interface with just text? You don't see one of those in modern designs. If you've been around for a few years, like your friendly authors have, you may remember when the Internet was text-only. When you opened a Web page, it looked like a giant outline from a word processing application. That was back when computers had black-and-white monitors and not much processing power. Even the most basic modern computer can handle pretty much anything the Web or Flash can throw at it.

So, unless you want your Flash project to look like something from the Jurassic period of the Internet, you need to become friendly with the tools that are used to add shapes to a design. In this chapter, we show you how to come to grips with the tools you use to create shapes and the drawing tools.

A Tale of Two Graphic Types

Flash graphics have a split personality. The shapes you draw with the shape and drawing tools can be scaled almost infinitely, with the exception of graphics that are filled with complex gradients. (Color is covered in the next chapter, so we stick with shapes here.) The shapes you create with the Flash drawing and shape tools are known as *vector graphics*. (Give me a vector, Victor.) When you import photorealistic images into Flash, you're importing *raster graphics*, mon. Raster graphics come in many flavors, but have one thing in common: If you try to greatly increase the size of a raster graphic, the result doesn't look good. If it all seems about as clear as a gallon of molasses, read the following sections to discover the difference between the two.

Understanding vector graphics

When you create a graphic using a Flash drawing or shape tool, the resulting graphic is composed of points and line segments. In essence, it's pure math. When you increase the size of a vector graphic, mathematical formulas preserve the placement of the points, whether the point is a straight or curve point or the relative length of the line segment between the points, for example. Figure 1-1 shows a shape created with the Polystar tool. The shape has been selected with the Subselect tool to show you the points that make up the shape.

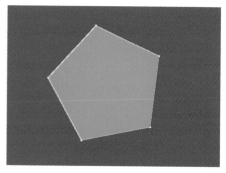

Figure 1-1: Vector images are all about the math.

Understanding bitmap (raster) graphics

A photograph taken with a digital camera or scanned into a computer is known as a bitmap, which you shouldn't confuse with the Windows .bmp format — also called bitmap. A *bitmap* is a pixel-based image (see Figure 1-2). A *pixel* is a square of color. If you zoom in on a bitmap — we're geeks, so we prefer the term *raster* — you can see the individual pixels, as shown in Figure 1-3.

Figure 1-2: It's a bitmap image, mon.

Bitmaps are resolution dependent. For example, an 8x10-inch image, with a resolution of 300 ppi (pixels per inch) has a document size of 2400 (8 inches x 300 ppi) x 3000 (10 inches x 300 ppi) pixels. A resolution of 300 pixels per inch is perfect for printing, but is more than you need for your Flash projects. A resolution of 96 or 72 ppi is perfect for viewing images on a computer monitor, which is where most Flash projects are viewed.

We don't launch into a long dissertation on sizing images. Just keep the size of your Flash project in mind when you're optimizing images for a Flash project. If you use the default document size of 550 x 400 pixels, resize your images so that they don't exceed either dimensions with a resolution of 96 pixels per inch. You can also shrink them to the size you want in Flash, but if you try to increase them, you don't produce good results because you're asking Flash to increase the size of each pixel. For more information on working with bitmaps, check out Chapter 6 of this minibook.

Figure 1-3: Pixels are a bitmap's lowest common denominator.

Creating Shapes

You can get a lot of mileage out of shapes. You can use your garden-variety rectangle as a background for text, the framework for a building, part of an interface, and much more. You can create five basic shapes: lines, ovals, polygons, rectangles, and stars. These five basic shapes are the framework for your Flash artwork. Rectangles and ovals have special status in Flash: primitive rectangles and ovals, and basic rectangles and ovals. You can modify primitive rectangles and ovals at any time. This isn't the case with basic ovals and rectangles, but basic ovals and rectangles have other tricks up their vector sleeves. In the following sections, we show you how to get the most bang for your buck by using the shape tools.

Using the Primitive Oval and Rectangle tools

The Primitive Oval and Primitive Rectangle tools are anything but primitive. In fact, they're downright sophisticated. However, referring to a tool as sophisticated might seem a little snobbish, so the Flash guys and gals settled on the moniker Primitive. Using these tools, you can create a rectangle with rounded or chamfered corners or an oval that looks like a slice of pie or a doughnut.

Creating a Primitive Oval shape

A primitive oval can be perfectly round or elliptical in nature. You can create lots of interesting shapes with the Primitive Oval tool. To check out this powerful tool, follow these steps:

1. **Select the Primitive Oval tool.**

   The Primitive Oval tool hangs out with his other shape pals on the ninth slot of the Tools panel. The last used tool is always at the top of the heap.

2. **Click on the Stage to define the starting point for your shape, and then drag to create the shape.**

   As you drag the tool, an oval outline appears, designating the current size of the oval. Hold down the Shift key to constrain the oval to a circle.

3. **Release the mouse button when the oval is the shape you want.**

   This step gives you a garden-variety oval. But you can do so much more with this tool after the shape is created. If you're using the Shift modifier to constrain the tool to a circle, make sure to release the mouse button before you release the Shift key.

4. **Choose Window⇨Properties.**

   The Property inspector appears.

   By default, the drawing tools snap to grid points as you create objects with them. To disable snapping to the grid, click the magnet icon in the Tool Options section of the Tools panel.

5. **In the Oval Options section, drag the Start Angle slider to the right.**

   An alternative method is entering a value in the Start Angle text field, but we find that using the slider is more intuitive and more rewarding. As you drag the slider, watch the shape change into something like a pie with a couple of slices gone.

6. **In the Oval Options section, drag the End Angle slider to the right.**

   The missing slice starts getting smaller.

   Experiment with the Start Angle and End Angle sliders to see the variety of shapes you can create with these options.

7. **Click the Reset button.**

   The garden variety ho-hum oval returns.

8. **Drag the Inner Radius slider to the right.**

   Holy doughnut hole, Batman!

9. **Drag the Start Angle and End Angle sliders to see the different variety of shapes you can create with the tool.**

   Figure 1-4 shows a shape created with the tool. Notice the parameters in the Oval Options section.

10. **Click the Close Path check box to deselect the default option.**

    If you changed any of the Oval Options, you see a path with the current Stroke color.

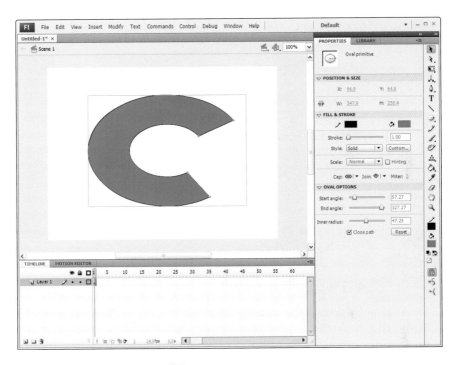

Figure 1-4: This is a primitive oval? Hmm.

Creating a Primitive Rectangle shape

You can create some unique shapes with the Primitive Rectangle tool. If you like rectangles or squares with corners that aren't square, this tool is the one for you. Follow these steps to try it out:

1. **Select the Primitive Rectangle tool.**

   The Primitive Rectangle tool hangs out with his other shape pals on the ninth slot of the Tools panel. The last used tool is always at the top of the heap.

2. **Click on the Stage to define the starting point for your rectangle, and then drag to create the shape.**

   As you drag the tool, a rectangular outline appears, designating the current size of the rectangle. Hold down the Shift key to constrain the tool to a square.

3. **Release the mouse button when the rectangle is the shape you want.**

   This step creates a rectangle with square corners, and that may or may not be cool. If you use the Shift modifier to constrain the tool to a square, make sure to release the mouse button before you release the Shift key.

4. **Choose Window⇨Properties.**

   The Property inspector appears.

5. **In the Rectangle Options section, drag the slider to the right.**

   The Rectangle now sports round corners.

6. **In the Rectangle Options section, drag the slider to the left.**

   As you drag the slider, the corners are squared off. Drag the slider until negative values appear and the corners are chamfered (see Figure 1-5).

   You can create rounded or chamfered corners while creating the shape. Press the down-arrow key while creating the shape for rounded corners or the up-arrow key for chamfered corners.

7. **Click the Reset button.**

   You have a rectangle with sharp, pointy corners again.

8. **Click the Lock icon.**

   You can now create a rectangle with a different radius or chamfer on each corner. When you choose this option, the slider is no longer functional.

9. **Enter a value in a corner text field.**

   Enter a negative value to chamfer the corner, or a positive value to round the corner.

10. **Continue experimenting with different values to see the variety of shapes you can create with this tool.**

You can set the parameters for the Primitive Oval and Rectangle tools before you draw the shape by selecting a tool, opening the Property inspector, and then entering values or dragging sliders in the Oval or Rectangle Options section. The options remain in effect for every shape you draw with the tool until you change the values.

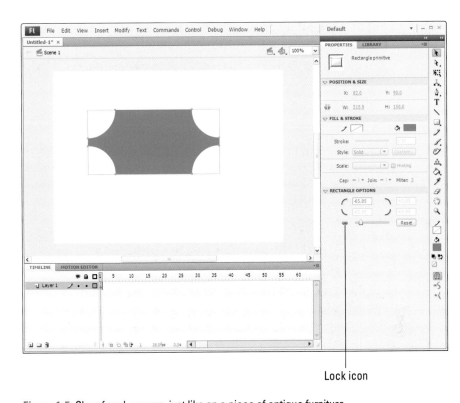

Lock icon

Figure 1-5: Chamfered corners, just like on a piece of antique furniture.

Modifying Primitive Ovals and Rectangles

As you create shapes for your Flash project, you may decide that a shape you created with the primitive tool needs a little tweaking or touching up. You can easily modify a shape by following these steps:

 1. **Select the shape with the Selection tool.**

2. **Chose Window➪Properties.**

    The Property inspector opens.

3. **Modify the values in the Oval Options (shape created with the Primitive Oval tool) or Rectangle Options (shape created with the Rectangle Primitive tool) for the shape.**

    From the Property inspector, you can also modify the size and position of the shape, a topic we cover in the "Modifying Objects with the Property Inspector" section, later in this chapter.

Creating shapes with the Oval and Rectangle tools

When you create ovals and rectangles with these tools, you can create the same type of shapes as the tool's primitive counterparts, but you can't edit the options after the fact. But these tools have two different drawing modes: Standard Drawing mode and Object mode. We explain the difference in the following sections.

The Oval tool

The Oval tool creates shapes that look identical to what you can create with the Oval Primitive tool (discussed earlier in this chapter), with two exceptions:

✔ You have to set your parameters in the Property inspector before you create the shape.

✔ You can't edit the parameters in the Property inspector after you create the shape.

Follow these steps to create a shape with the Oval tool:

1. **Select the Oval tool.**

   The Oval tool bunks with his other shape pals on the ninth slot of the Tools panel. The last used tool is displayed at the top of the heap.

2. **Choose Window⇨Properties.**

   The Property inspector appears, looking like that famed TV detective in a rumpled raincoat. ("Err, just one more thing, Oval tool.")

3. **In the Oval Options section, drag the Start Angle slider to the right.**

   An alternative method is entering a value in the Start Angle text field, but we find that using the slider is more intuitive and more rewarding. Larger values create a shape that looks like a pie with a couple of pieces missing. Larger values create a shape that looks like a piece of pie.

4. **In the Oval Options section, drag the End Angle slider to the right.**

   The type of shape that results depends on the start angle value. If you have a high start angle value, the wedge gets larger. If you have a small start angle value, you end up with a smaller wedge missing from the circle.

5. **Drag the Inner Radius slider to the right.**

   This step is similar to punching a hole in a doughnut. You modify this option in conjunction with the start and end angle values to produce a shape that looks like the letter *C,* or a curve.

6. **Click the Stage to define the starting point for your shape, and then drag to create the shape.**

   As you drag the tool, an oval outline appears, designating the current size of the oval. Hold down the Shift key to constrain the oval to a circle.

7. **Release the mouse button when the oval is the shape you want.**

   This step results in a nice shape that can't be edited. The parameters you specify in the Property inspector are used with other shapes you create with the tool until you specify different options.

The Rectangle tool

You use the Rectangle tool to create rectangles with pointy, round, or chamfered corners. You can modify the rectangle corners as you create the shape, or by modifying parameters in the Property inspector. To create a ho-hum, or not so ho-hum, rectangle, follow these steps:

 1. **Select the Rectangle tool.**

   This rascal sublets space on the ninth slot of the Tools panel.

2. **Click to define the starting point for your rectangle and then drag diagonally.**

   As you drag the tool on the Stage, a rectangular outline shows the current size of the shape. Hold the Shift key to create a square. Press the down-arrow key to create rounded corners or the up-arrow key to create chamfered corners. Release the arrow key when the corners are the way you want them.

   You can modify the corner radius by opening the Property inspector after you select the tool and before you create the shape. This action is counterintuitive, however, because you can't see the result. And you cannot modify the options after you create the shape. The only bonus for setting rectangle options in the Property inspector is when you want a different radius on each corner. To achieve this effect, click the Lock icon and then manually enter values in the text fields.

3. **Release the mouse button when the rectangle is the size and shape you want.**

   The Property inspector plays the ultrasmart detective and records the radius values for the shape you just created. These values are applied to future shapes you create with the tool until you either click the Reset button in the Property inspector and manually enter values or create a new rectangle and define the shape of the corners by using the arrow keys.

Mastering the Polystar tool

You have a Flash project with a boring, jet black midnight sky in need of a star or 50. Or, perhaps you have a project that needs a multisided shape. When either occasion occurs, you need look no further than the Tools panel. Check out the Polystar tool — Poly is short for *polygon,* which is a multi-sided shape, and *star* represents twinkle, twinkle, big or little. You use this multifaceted tool to create multisided shapes. Talk about your ultimate mul-titasker. (Yikes — our copy editor will probably tell us that using *multi* that many times is redundant.)

To master the Polystar tool, follow these steps:

1. **Select the Polystar tool.**

   The tool is a tad introverted and may be hidden on the fly-out menu, on the ninth slot of the Tools panel.

2. **In the Tool Settings section of the Property inspector (Window⇨Property Inspector), click the Options button.**

   The Tool Settings dialog box appears (see Figure 1-6).

3. **Choose an option from the Style menu.**

   You have a choice: Polygon or Star.

4. **Enter a value for the number of sides.**

   We advise that you don't get too carried away here. If you create a shape with a lot of sides, it's hard to edit, and it increases the file size of the published movie.

5. **Enter a value between 0 and 1 in the Star Point Size field.**

   This value determines the depth of the star, when you choose that option. If you specify a value closer to 0, the star has longer points. This option has no effect on polygons.

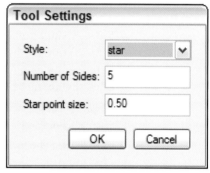

Figure 1-6: Okay, Polystar — this is a set-up.

Creating unique shapes with the Oval Rectangle and Polystar tools

When you create shapes with the Oval and Rectangle tools with no stroke, the shapes have an affinity for each other. You can create unique shapes in one of two ways. Here's the first one:

1. **Select the Oval, Rectangle, or Polystar tool.**

   Don't select one of the Primitive tools. They're independent critters who like to maintain their own identity.

2. **Select a fill color and no stroke.**

   We know: We haven't covered selecting stroke and fill colors yet. But, hey: Which came first — the chicken or the egg? We show you how to specify strokes and fills in Chapter 2 of this minibook.

3. **Create a shape on the Stage.**

4. **Create another shape with the Oval, Rectangle, or Polystar tool with the same fill color and no stroke.**

   When you create the second shape, make sure that it overlaps the first.

5. **Release the mouse button after you create the second shape.**

6. **Select the Selection tool and click the shape to select it.**

7. **Drag the shape to a different spot on the Stage.**

   Notice that the two shapes are joined at the hip (see Figure 1-7). You can stack multiple shapes to create some truly unique shapes. You can also use the Brush tool to add to a shape when painting a brush stroke that's the same color over an existing shape.

Book II
Chapter 1

Figure 1-7: I declare, Lance, the sum is better than the parts.

If you prefer more control when combining basic shapes to create unique shapes, create the second shape, but don't overlap it with the first one. Select the shape with the Selection tool and then overlap it with the first shape. You can now freely move the second shape until you have it exactly where you want it. It doesn't join with the first shape until you click a blank area of the Stage with the Selection tool.

When you overlap shapes that aren't the same color, one shape cuts away from the other. This oil-and-vinegar relationship makes it possible for you to create some truly unique shapes. Follow these steps to get an idea of how this second method works:

1. **Select the Oval tool.**

2. **Open the Property inspector (choose Window⇨Properties) and select a fill color but no stroke.**

   We know we haven't covered color yet. Here's your baptism by fire. In the Fill & Stroke section of the Property inspector, click the Stroke swatch (it's next to the pencil icon) and click the No Stroke icon (the white rectangular icon with a red diagonal slash in the Swatches panel, as shown in Figure 1-8). Then click the fill color swatch (it's next to the paint bucket icon), and click one of the color swatches in the Swatches panel.

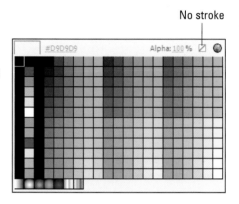

   Figure 1-8: To stroke or not to stroke. . . .

3. **Draw an oval on the Stage.**

4. **With the Oval tool still selected, click the fill color swatch in the Property inspector and choose a different color.**

   It doesn't matter which color you choose. You delete the shape when you're done.

5. **Create a smaller oval that doesn't overlap the first shape you created.**

6. **Select the shape with the Selection tool.**

   The Selection tool is the head honcho at the top of the Tools panel.

7. **Drag the second shape over the first shape until it's in the position you want.**

8. **Click anywhere outside the shape.**

   This step deselects the shape.

9. **Click the smaller oval and drag it outside the first shape.**

   A hole appears in the first shape. You can continue using the different-colored oval to cut out of the first oval. Just drop it into position, deselect it, and then move it someplace else. With a bit of work, you could create a piece of Swiss cheese for your favorite digital mouse (see Figure 1-9). Oh, you noticed the outlines around the cheese and the holes. These were created with the Ink Bottle tool, which we show you in Chapter 2 of this minibook.

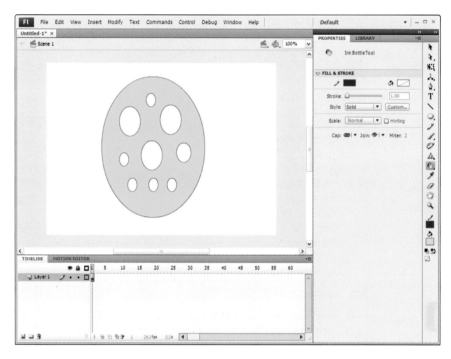

Figure 1-9: Look! It's Flash Swiss cheese! Where's my digital Swiss Army knife?

Creating lines — the straight and narrow

If you have a Flash project that needs to toe the line, so to speak, summon the Line tool. You use the tool to create straight lines. When you feel the need to draw a straight line, follow these steps:

1. **Select the Line tool.**

   This tool is prominently displayed on the eighth slot of the Tools panel.

2. **Click on the Stage to define the starting point, and then drag to create the line.**

   As you drag the tool, a crosshair signifies the current position of the tool.

3. **Release the mouse button when the line is the length you want.**

   We were going to include an illustration, but realized that you already know what a straight line looks like.

Hold the Shift key while dragging the line tool diagonally to constrain the line to a 45-degree angle. Hold the Shift key while dragging from left to right (or from right to left, if you're so inclined) to create a horizontal line, or while dragging from top to bottom (or from bottom to top) to create a vertical line.

Using the basic shape tools in Object Drawing mode

You have seen the basic shape tools in their default mode. In this section, we show you how to use the basic shape tools in Object Drawing mode. When you use this mode, you create a unique object that cannot be merged with other objects. You can, however, edit the basic shape after you create it. To create a shape in Object Drawing mode, follow these steps:

1. **Select the Line, Oval, Rectangle, or Polystar tool.**

   The Line tool appears in the eighth slot of the Tools panels, and the other tools appear on the fly-out menu in the ninth slot of the Tools panel (see Figure 1-10).

Figure 1-10: Choosing a shape tool.

    2. **Click the Drawing Object icon at the bottom of the Tools panel.**

3. **Create a shape.**

   After you create the shape, a border appears around the shape, which signifies that it's an object (see Figure 1-11).

Modifying basic shapes

The basic shapes you create with the Line, Oval, Rectangle, or Polystar tool can be modified to create unique shapes. As discussed previously, you can overlap shapes of the same color to create a new shape, or use a different-colored shape to take a chunk out of another shape. You can also mold a shape like putty with the Selection tool, or use the Line tool like a scalpel to carve up a shape as long as you don't click the Object Drawing icon in the Tool Options section. To modify a basic shape:

 1. **Select the Selection tool.**

2. **Use the tool to select, move, or modify the shape as follows:**

   • Click the shape to select it. If the shape has a stroke, double-click the fill to select both the stroke and the fill. After selecting a shape, drag it to a position on the Stage.

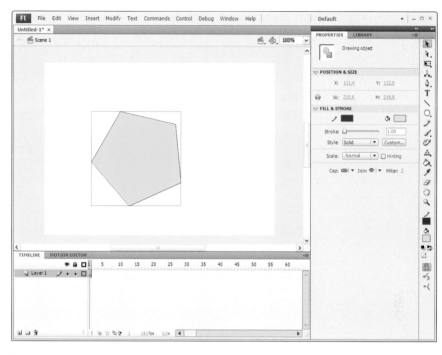

Figure 1-11: Creating an object with a shape tool.

- To select several shapes, click and drag the Selection tool around the shapes you want to select.

- Move the Selection tool toward a shape that hasn't been selected. When a curve icon appears beneath the tool icon, click and drag to change the shape (see Figure 1-12).

The Line tool can also be used to cut a basic shape into two or more pieces. To cut a shape down to size, follow these steps:

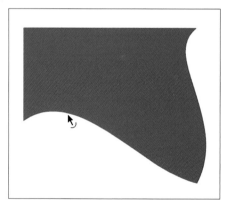

Figure 1-12: Bend me, shape me, any way you want to.

1. **Select the Line tool.**

   It's the diagonal line icon right below the T (Text tool) on the Tools panel.

2. **Create a line that intersects and is wider than or taller than the shape you want to cut.**

3. **Select the Selection tool.**

4. **Select one part of the shape and drag it away from the other.**

   What was once joined is now parted (see Figure 1-13). If the shape has a stroke, make sure that you double-click it to select both the shape and the stroke.

5. **You can now select the line, which is now in three segments, and delete it by pressing the Delete key.**

   Thank you, line. You have served us well.

You can also use a line to slice and dice another line. Move one line over another, and then select a piece with the Selection tool and move it to another position.

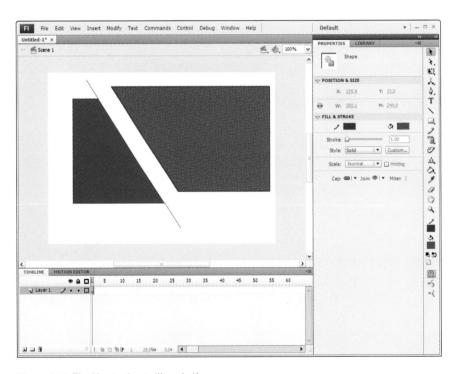

Figure 1-13: The Line tool cuts like a knife.

Using the Drawing Tools

If you're the artistic type who likes to doodle with a pen or brush (Doug's drawing tool of choice when he was a kid was an Etch-A-Sketch), you'll enjoy working with the drawing tools. If you like creating freeform shapes, become familiar with the Pencil and Brush tools. If you like point-by-point accuracy when creating shapes, the Pen tool has your initials carved on it.

Drawing with the Pencil tool

The Pencil tool should be colored yellow to resemble the good old Eberhard Faber pencil that also made a good impromptu drum stick that could be used to good effect when trying to drive a substitute teacher absolutely bonkers. But it's a boring gray, just like the other tools. Don't let that fool you, though. This single tool is the equivalent of every pencil you've ever used and then some. To create lines with the Pencil tool, follow these steps:

1. **Select the Pencil tool.**

   It's the tenth tool in the Tools panel.

2. **Choose Window⇨Properties.**

   The Property inspector appears, displaying the parameters you can modify for the tool (see Figure 1-14).

3. **Select a stroke color.**

   Click the color swatch next to the pencil icon and choose a color from the Swatches panel. For more information on working with the Swatches panel, see Chapter 2 of this minibook.

4. **Drag the Stroke slider to specify the width of lines you draw with the tool.**

   Alternatively, you can enter a value from 1 to 200 in the text field to the right of the slider.

5. **Choose an option from the Style drop-down menu.**

   You can draw a hairline or a solid, dashed, dotted, ragged, stippled, or hatched line.

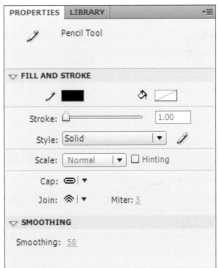

Figure 1-14: Even a pencil stroke has properties.

TIP

To create with the Pencil tool a line that doesn't interact with other shapes, click the Object Drawing icon in the Options section of the Tools panel.

To create a custom style, click the Edit Stroke Style icon (it looks like a pencil) in the Property inspector to open the Stroke Style dialog box. Follow the prompts to create your custom line. The parameters you can modify depend on the style you start with.

6. **Choose a scale option.**

These options determine how the stroke is scaled in Flash Player. Your options are described in this list:

- *Normal:* Scales the thickness of the stroke.

- *Horizontal:* Doesn't scale the thickness if the object is resized horizontally.

- *Vertical:* Doesn't scale the thickness if the object is resized vertically.

- *None:* Doesn't scale the stroke.

7. **Select the Hinting check box to enable stroke hinting.**

This option positions anchor points on pixels, which prevents blurry lines.

8. **Choose one of the following options from the Cap drop-down menu:**

- *None:* Makes the cap flush with the end of the line.

- *Round:* Adds to the end of the line a round cap that's half the width of the stroke.

- *Square:* Adds to the end of the line a square cap that's half the width of the stroke.

9. **Choose one of the following options from the Join drop-down menu:**

- *Miter:* Creates a 45-degree miter joint where path ends join.

- *Round:* Creates a rounded corner where path ends join.

- *Square:* Creates a square corner where ends join.

10. **If you choose Miter for the Join option, specify a Miter value.**

This option is a scrubby slider. Drag the slider to specify the Miter value, which prevents the join from being beveled. For example, if you specify a value of 2 for a three-point stroke width, when the length of the join is more than six points, the join is squared off.

11. **Specify a smoothing option.**

This option appears in the Modifier section of the Tools panel. Your choices are described in this list:

- *Straight:* Straightens lines. Use it when you want to draw objects, such as triangles and rectangles.

- *Smooth:* Smoothes lines. This option is useful when you use a mouse with the Pencil tool.

• *Ink:* Applies no smoothing to lines. Use this option when you're creating freeform artwork with the Pencil tool.

12. Specify a smoothing value.

This option determines the degree to which Flash smoothes a line. The default value is 50. Specify a higher value for a smoother line. Note that this is a scrubby slider. Hover the cursor over the current value until you see a pointing finger icon with two arrows, and then click and drag to change the value.

13. Drag the tool on the Stage to create the line.

The default drawing mode creates a basic shape, which acts like a line drawn with the Line tool. If you draw it over other shapes, the line you create bisects the other shape.

Alternatively, you can click the Object Drawing button (shown in the margin) to draw a line that becomes an object and doesn't interact with other shapes.

Painting with the Brush tool

If you like dabbling with a paint brush and watercolor, oil, or acrylic paint, check out the Brush tool. It gives you the power to add artistic or calligraphic splashes of color to your Flash projects. If you're truly talented and use a digital tablet and stylus, you'll love the artistic strokes you can create with this tool. To grace your Flash projects with eye-catching strokes from the Brush tool, follow these steps:

1. Select the Brush tool.

We love truth in advertising. This tool's icon, which occupies the eleventh slot on the Tools panel, looks just like an artist's paint brush.

2. Select a fill color.

We know: We haven't covered color yet. That happens in the next chapter. The quick and easy way is to click the fill color swatch (it's next to the paint bucket icon in the Property inspector or the Tools panel), and choose a color from the Swatches panel.

3. Choose a painting mode.

By default, the tool creates strokes just like a normal brush. When you paint over something, it disappears. You can change the way the tool creates strokes by choosing a different painting mode in the Options section of the Tools panel (see Figure 1-15).

You have these options:

• *Paint Normal:* Paint over lines and fills on the same layer.

• *Paint Fills:* Paint within closed paths (outlines) and blank areas of the Stage without affecting lines.

- *Paint Behind:* Paint color on blank areas of the Stage on the active layer, without affecting lines and fills. In other words, you're painting behind the lines and fills you already created.

- *Paint Selection:* Paint within selected objects.

- *Paint Inside:* Paint within a closed path (shape outline) without affecting other lines. You can also paint on blank areas of the Stage without affecting other fills and lines on the same layer. After choosing this mode, click inside the object with the fill you want to change.

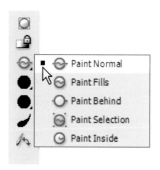

Figure 1-15: Choosing a different painting mode.

4. **Choose a brush tip size.**

   You choose this option from the Options section of the Tools panel (see Figure 1-16).

5. **Choose a brush tip shape.**

   You choose this option from the Options section of the Tools panel (see Figure 1-17).

 6. **If you use a Wacom tablet and stylus, click the Use Pressure icon.**

   This option changes the size of the brush tip depending on the amount of pressure you apply against the stylus.

 7. **If you use a Wacom tablet and stylus, click the Use Tilt icon.**

   This option changes the angle of calligraphic brush tips when you tilt the stylus.

8. **Create something nice to look at.**

   You can dabble with the tool until you're good enough to create something nice to look at.

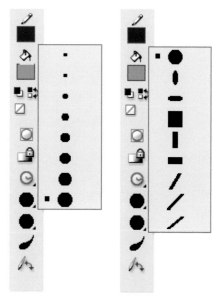

Figure 1-16: Do I need a teeny-weeny brush or a big 'un?

Figure 1-17: I'm in a calligraphic state of mind.

Using the Spray Brush tool

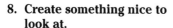

If you have the urge to spray graffiti in parts of a Flash project, check out the Spray Brush tool. It's multifunctional. In this section, we show you how to use this tool to spray color.

1. **Select the Spray Brush tool.**

   This tool is introverted by nature and shares space with the Brush tool on the eleventh slot of the Tools panel.

2. **Choose Window⇨Properties.**

   The Property inspector opens, displaying the properties you can modify for the Brush Spray tool (see Figure 1-18). Don't fret about the Symbol section yet. We show you how to spray symbols in Book II, Chapter 4.

3. **In the Brush section, specify the width and height.**

   These options determine how large a burst of color one click of the tool produces. The default sprays a burst of color 92 x 92 pixels. These values are changed by using scrubby sliders. Position the cursor over the current value, and when the icon becomes a pointing finger with two arrows, drag left to decrease the size or right to increase the size.

4. **In the Brush section, specify the brush angle.**

   This option determines the angle at which the spray disperses from the tool. The default option sprays horizontally. Vary the angle to achieve different effects.

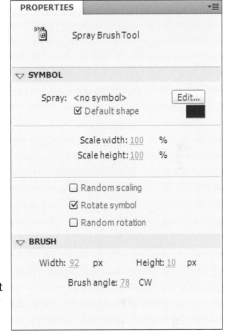

Figure 1-18: And the mother skunk said to her children, "Let us spray."

5. **Spray with the tool.**

   We know you want to. That's right: Experimentation is the key to success with any new tool. We had lots of fun using the tool to spray graffiti on a blank Flash document.

Creating paths with the Pen tool

If you like precision, you'll like the Pen tool. When you create a shape with the Pen tool (known as a *path* in vector-speak), you create points. It's like that connect-the-dots artwork you find in restaurants that keep your kids endlessly amused while you decide whether to order a salad or indulge and have a decadent appetizer, like deep-fried mozzarella. When you create a path with the Pen tool, you can create straight points or curve points. To create a basic path with the Pen tool, follow these steps:

1. **Select the Pen tool.**

2. **Choose Window⇨Properties.**

   This step opens the Property inspector and displays the properties you can modify for the Pen tool. The options are identical to those for the Pencil tool (refer to Figure 1-14). Please refer to our words of wisdom in the "Drawing with the Pencil tool" section, earlier in this chapter, for concise instructions on how to set these properties.

   To create a shape with the Pen tool that doesn't interact with other shapes, click the Object Drawing icon in the Modifier section of the Tools panel.

3. **Click to define your first point.**

   The first anchor point appears as a hollow dot.

4. **Click to define the second point.**

   A line segment appears between the two points. Shift+click to constrain the line segment to a 45-degree angle. Shift+drag to create a curve point. When you create a curve point, tangent handles appear and the outer tangent handle is active. If you continue to drag the tangent handle, the radius of the curve increases. You can also change the angle of the tangent handle as you create the curve point.

5. **To finish creating the path, do one of the following:**

   - *To create an open path:* Select a different tool.

   - *To close the path:* Click the first anchor point (the hollow dot). Figure 1-19 shows a closed path and an open path.

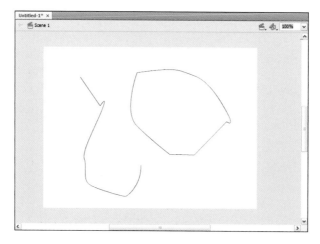

Figure 1-19: A tale of two paths.

The Eraser tool — the quicker picker-upper

Digital erasers are the greatest thing since the invention of computer image-editing applications. You get to eradicate your mistakes, and you don't have to deal with a bunch of pink or white eraser crumbs. You might think that you know how to use an eraser, but the Flash Eraser tool has some special modes you should know about. To use the Eraser tool, follow these steps:

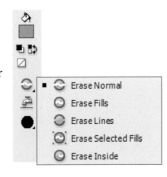

 1. **Select the Eraser tool.**

This tool looks like the pink erasers your friendly authors used in grade school.

Figure 1-20: Erasers are a digital artist's best friend.

2. **Select an eraser mode.**

You choose Eraser mode in the Options section of the Tools panel (see Figure 1-20).

Your options are described in this list:

- *Erase Normal:* Erase lines and fills on the same layer.

- *Erase Fills:* Erase fills within closed paths (outlines) and blank areas of the Stage without affecting lines.

- *Erase Lines:* Erase color on blank areas of the Stage on the active layer, without affecting lines and fills. In other words, you erase behind lines and fills that you already created.

- *Erase Selected Fills:* Erase fills within selected objects.

- *Erase Inside:* Erase within a closed path (shape outline) without affecting other lines. After choosing this mode, click inside the object whose fill you want to erase either partially or totally.

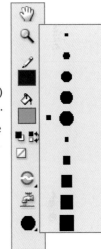

Figure 1-21: Do square erasers erase square pixels and round erasers remove dots?

3. **Choose an eraser tip size and shape.**

You choose this option from the Tool Modifiers section of the Tools panel, shown in Figure 1-21. The sizes are identical to those of the Brush tool.

Wait — there's more. If you need to erase line segments, or fills within shapes, select the Eraser tool, select the Faucet modifier from the Tools panel Options section, and then click the fill you want to remove. Like magic, the tool and selected option suck it up, just like one of those superfantastic paper towels. To remove a line segment, select it with the Selection tool, and then select the Eraser tool and enable the Faucet modifier. Click the selected line segment and it is, to quote the raven, "Nevermore."

Modifying Objects

After you create an object, you have the option to modify it. You can modify objects using menu commands or tools or both. Modifying objects isn't rocket science, or brain surgery, but you have to choose the right menu command or tool for the job. After all, you don't drive home a finishing nail with a sledgehammer. In the following sections, we show you how to use the drawing tools to modify the shapes you create.

Selecting objects

After you populate a Flash project with a bunch of objects, you need to grab the critters by the scruff of their pixels so that you can modify them. After you select one or more objects, you can use menu commands or tools to modify them.

 You select objects with the Selection tool. We know that's a case of the blatantly obvious, but you can use the tool in different ways. To master the Selection tool, create a Flash document and then create a couple of objects with the drawing tools. Select the Selection tool and do the following:

- **To select a stroke segment of an object created in Basic Drawing mode:** Click the segment.

- **To select the stroke of an object created in Basic Drawing mode:** Double-click any stroke segment.

- **To select the stroke and fill of an object created in Basic Drawing mode:** Double-click the object's fill.

- **To edit an object created in Object Drawing mode:** Double-click the shape to display the object in another window. You can then use the Selection tool to select individual stroke segments or modify the object on a point-by-point basis, as outlined in the following section.

- **To select several objects:** Click and drag the tool around the objects you want to select. As you drag the tool, Flash displays a bounding box that shows the current selection area. Release the mouse button when the bounding box surrounds the objects.

✔ **To add objects to the selection:** Select an object and then Shift+click. To add an object created in basic Shape Drawing mode, Shift+double-click the object's fill to add it to the selection.

✔ **To round up objects:** Select the Lasso tool (it's on the fly-out menu in the fourth slot of the Tools panel), and drag it around the objects you want to round up.

Modifying shapes point by point

When you create a shape with one of the shape tools or drawing tools, you create a Vector object that's composed of points and line segments (see Figure 1-22). You can modify these shapes on a point-by-point basis. In this section, we show you how to move points, add points, convert points, and perform other, similar tasks.

Book II
Chapter 1

Creating Flashy Graphics

When you select an object with the Subselection tool, which is like the Selection tool on steroids, you can modify the shape on a point-by-point basis. To quickly get to the point with the Subselection tool, follow these steps:

1. **Select the Subselection tool.**

2. **Click the perimeter of the shape you want to modify.**

   The points that make up the shape are displayed as hollow dots.

3. **Click a point to select it.**

   The dot is filled, which signifies that the point is selected.

4. **Drag the point to a new location.**

   The shape changes.

5. **Click a curve point.**

   The point and the tangent handles for the connecting line segments are displayed.

6. **Drag a tangent handle to modify the line segment.**

   As you drag the handle, Flash displays a preview of what the resulting line segment will look like. If you select a point with two tangent handles (the intersection of two curve line segments), the handles move in lock-step. Press the Alt key (Windows) or Option key (Macintosh) and then one tangent handle to modify it and not the adjoining tangent handle. If you select a point that is the intersection of a straight and curve line segment, you have only one tangent handle to modify (see Figure 1-22).

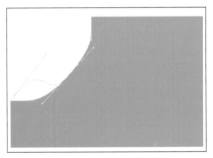

Figure 1-22: A tangent handle that twists a curved line segment into submission.

Modifying objects with the Pen tool and friends

What you create with the Pen tool, you can modify with the Pen tool. In fact, you can modify any Vector shape with the Pen tool or one of his pals that hang out on the same fly-out menu. You can modify a Vector shape by adding anchor points and convert straight anchor points to curve anchor points and vice versa.

 To modify an object's anchor points, select the object with the Subselection tool and do one of the following:

 ✐ Select the Add Anchor Point tool, and click a line segment to add an anchor point. This action adds a straight point to the line segment. Click and drag the point to convert it to a curve point.

 ✐ Select the Delete Point tool, and click a point to remove it.

 ✐ Select the Convert Anchor Point tool and click a curve point to convert it to a straight point.

✐ Select the Convert Anchor Point tool, and then click and drag a straight point to convert it to a curve point and modify the tangent handles at the same time.

 You can also use the Pen tool to modify the anchor points of an object you select with the Subselection tool. As you move the tool toward a line segment, you see a plus sign (+) to the lower right of the tool icon, indicating that you can click the line segment to add a point. If you move the tool toward an anchor point and see a minus sign appear to the lower right of the tool icon, you can click the point to delete it. If you move the tool toward an anchor point and see an angled inverted lowercase v to the lower left of the icon, you can convert the anchor point to its polar opposite by clicking it. Make sure that you click the point you intend to modify; if you don't, you start creating a new path.

Modifying objects with the Property inspector

You use the Property inspector to set the properties for a drawing tool before you use it. After you create the shape, you can also use the Property inspector to modify it. The properties you can modify depend on the type of object you created. To modify a basic shape:

1. **Select the shape with the Selection tool.**

2. **Choose Window↷Properties.**

   The Property inspector appears, displaying the properties you can modify for the selected object. Figure 1-23 shows the properties for a shape created with the Oval tool. You can modify all basic properties for the shape, such as fill color, stroke color, stroke width, and style.

You can also modify the following factors for any object you select:

- *X:* The position of the object registration point from the left side of the document.

- *Y:* The position of the object registration point from the top of the document.

- *W:* The width of the object.

- *H:* The height of the object.

You use scrubby sliders to change these values. Position the cursor over a value. When it changes to a pointing finger with two arrows, drag left to decrease the value, and drag right to increase it.

The unit of measure for values in the Property inspector is the same unit of measure you specify for the document.

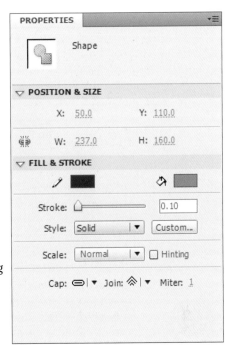

Figure 1-23: Modifying a basic shape.

Using the Free Transform tool

Another way to transform an object is by using the Free Transform tool. The tool isn't free, of course. You or your boss paid for Flash, the application in which you find the tool. But you do use the tool to freely transform an object into something that suits your Flash project. To freely transform an object, follow these steps:

1. **Select the Free Transform tool and then click the object you want to transform.**

   If the object was created using Basic Drawing mode, double-click the center of the object to select the stroke and fill. After selecting the object with the tool, eight handles appear around the object, as shown in Figure 1-24.

2. **To freely change the dimensions of the object, do one of the following:**

   - *To change the height:* Click the middle handle on the top or bottom of the object, and then drag up or down.

   - *To change the width:* Click the middle handle on the right or left side of the object, and then drag right or left.

   - *To resize the object:* Click a corner handle and then drag diagonally.

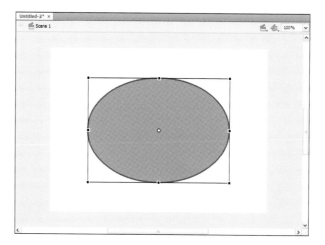

Figure 1-24: The buck doesn't stop here with the Free Transform tool.

Hold the Shift key while dragging a corner handle to resize the object proportionately. Remember to release the mouse button before releasing the Shift key, or else the object may not resize proportionately.

3. **To move the object, place the cursor in the center of the object. When it becomes a left-pointing arrow, with a four-sided arrow at the lower left, click and drag the object to the position you want.**

If the Free Tranform tool isn't enough for you, choose Modify⇨ Transform⇨Envelope. This command creates an envelope with eight handles. Each handle is a Bezier point with two tangent handles. You can click and drag the Bezier point to distort the object, and then further distort the object by dragging the tangent handles. Such fun!

4. **To rotate the object, move the cursor toward one of the corner handles. When it becomes a curved line with a downward-pointing arrow, click and drag left or right to rotate the object.**

5. **To skew the object, move the cursor to a line between the handles. When the cursor becomes two lines with arrows pointing in opposite directions, click and drag to skew the object.**

6. **To transform an object using only one of the corner handles, press Ctrl (Windows) or ⌘ (Macintosh) and move the cursor toward the handle you want. When the cursor becomes a hollow arrow, click and drag to transform the object from only that handle (see Figure 1-25).**

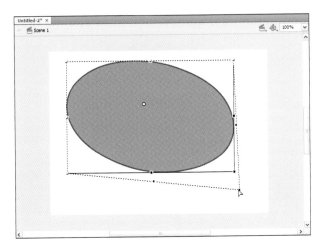

Figure 1-25: Ouch! You got me by the short handle.

The Transform panel — a geek's best friend

Some Flash designers are card-carrying, pocket-protector-wearing, duct-taped-glass-wearing folks who think that math rules. If you find yourself in that category, the Transform panel is your best friend. To transform an object using the Transform panel, follow these steps:

1. **Select the object you want to transform.**

2. **Choose Window⇨Transform.**

   The Transform panel appears (see Figure 1-26).

3. **To change the dimensions of the object, do one of the following:**

   - Drag the scrubby slider that's located to the right of the horizontal, dual-headed arrow to the left to decrease the width or to the right to increase the width.

   - Drag the scrubby slider that's to the right of the vertical dual-headed arrow to the right to increase the height or to the left to decrease the height.

   - Click the Constrain slider and then change the width or height. Flash changes to other dimensions to resize the object proportionately.

4. **To rotate the object, click the Rotate radio button (the default selection), and drag the scrubby slider to the right to rotate the object clockwise or to the left to rotate the object counterclockwise.**

5. **To skew the object, click the Skew radio button and drag the first scrubby slider to skew the object horizontally, and the second scrubby slider to skew the object vertically.**

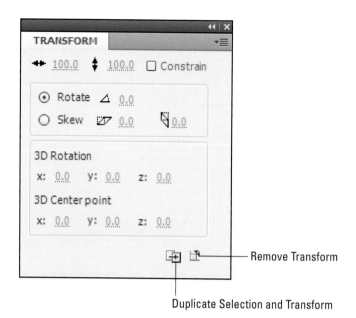

Remove Transform

Duplicate Selection and Transform

Figure 1-26: It's time to transform an object.

The 3D Rotation section is used for animation, a topic we cover in Book III.

6. **To remove all transformations applied to the object, click the Remove Transform icon in the lower-right corner of the panel.**

7. **To duplicate the object and transformation, click the Duplicate the Selection and Transform icon in the lower-right corner of the dialog box.**

   This option is quite useful. For example, to create spokes for a wheel, use the Line tool to create a vertical line. Then open the Transform panel and rotate the line 15 degrees. After applying the first transformation, click the Duplicate and Transform icon 11 times to spin your spokes.

The Info panel — read all about it

Sometimes you need precise information. When this need occurs, you can find out the size of an object and its position from one handy little panel. You can also use the panel to change the object's dimensions and position and to specify the coordinates of the cursor and the RGB values under the cursor. (Talk about your multitasker!) To find out almost everything you ever wanted to know about an object, follow these steps:

1. **Select the object.**

2. **Choose Window⇨Info.**

The Info panel appears, displaying information about the dimensions and position of the selected object (see Figure 1-27).

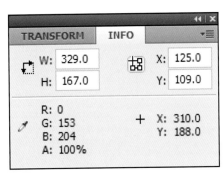

3. **To change the size of the object, enter different values in the W and H fields.**

   The Info dialog box doesn't change the size proportionately. Use at your own risk.

4. **To change the position of the selected object, enter different values in the X and Y fields.**

Figure 1-27: Extra! Extra! Read all about it.

The X value controls the horizontal position of the object, and the Y value controls the vertical position of the object.

5. **Hover the cursor over an object to display its color values.**

   The Info panel displays color information using the RGB color model, and also displays the alpha (transparency) value of the object.

6. **Move the cursor to different positions on the Stage.**

   As you move the cursor, its current position (X and Y coordinates) are displayed in the lower-right corner of the panel.

The Align panel — when precision counts

Freeform can be fun. But sometimes you have to align objects with precision. At other times, you have to distribute a selection of objects equally (you know, get your ducks in a row?), match their size, or space them equally. When one of these tasks confronts you, there's no need to whip out a calculator — or abacus or slide rule, if either one is your preferred calculation tool. All you need to do is summon the Align panel and let it take care of the grunt work for you. You can perform the following tasks with the Align panel:

✔ **To align an object to Stage:** Select the object, open the Transform panel (choose Window➪Align), shown in Figure 1-28, click the To Stage icon, and then click to select vertical and horizontal alignment icons. The Transform panel is the one to use when your objects are out of alignment.

✔ **To align objects relative to each other:** Select the objects you want to align, open the Transform panel, deselect the To Stage option, and select the horizontal or vertical alignment icons you want.

✔ **To evenly distribute selected objects relative to each other:** Open the Transform panel, deselect the To Stage option, and then select the vertical or horizontal distribution buttons you want.

✔ **To evenly distribute selected objects relative to Stage:** Open the Transform panel, click the To Stage icon, and then select the vertical or horizontal distribution buttons you want.

✔ **To match the size of selected objects:** Open the Transform panel, deselect the To Stage option, and then click an icon to match the width or height, or both. If you select the To Stage option and choose one of the Match Size options, Flash matches the selected objects to the width, height, or both dimensions of the Stage.

✔ **To space three or more selected objects relative to their current positions:** Open the Transform panel, deselect the To Stage option, and then click the space-vertically icon or space-horizontally icon (or both).

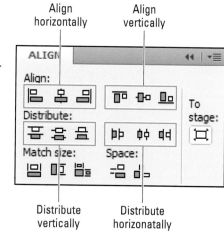

Figure 1-28: The panel to call when your objects are out of alignment.

✔ **To space two or more selected objects relative to the Stage:** Open the Transform panel, select the To Stage option, and then click the space-vertically icon or the space-horizontally icon (or both).

When you use the Align panel to match sizes or alignment of objects, Flash uses the last selected object as the reference.

Creating groups

When you create a complex object that's composed of many shapes, it's time to round them all up into a group. When you create a group, it behaves like an individual object on the Stage, which is a good thing when your group is a complex character. You can edit individual objects in the group, and you can disband the group at any time, which can be useful if you're creating a Flash project that documents the history of a rock-and-roll band that changed members more often than most people change underwear. Here are some ways to work with groups:

✔ **To create a group:** Select the objects you want to group and then choose Modify⇨Group.

✔ **To edit individual objects in the group:** Double-click the group. This action opens the group in a new window. You can now select individual objects in the group and edit them using one of the many methods described in this chapter. After you edit a group, click the Back or Scene button.

✔ **To ungroup a group:** Select it and then choose Modify⇨Ungroup.

Chapter 2: A Splash of Color, S'il Vous Plaît

In This Chapter

- ✓ Choosing the stroke color
- ✓ Choosing the fill color
- ✓ Using the Swatches panel
- ✓ Working with the Color panel
- ✓ Creating gradients

A Flash document without color would be black and white — or, in other words: boring. Fortunately, Flash gives you all the tools you need to create stunning full-color or, if you're so inclined, Web-safe color documents. Whether you're creating ho-hum rectangles, rotund circles, or curvy paths, you can get wild and crazy, like Van Gogh or Dalí, or take a slightly more sedate route by just adding a splash of Web-safe color. If you like rainbows of color, you'll love our section on creating gradients.

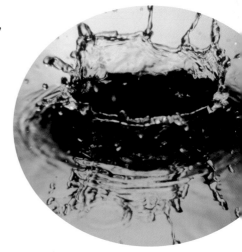

Color is what this chapter is all about. So put on your rose-colored sunglasses and mix up a frothy glass of pink lemonade while we show you everything you need to know to create a colorful Flash document.

Getting to Know Color: The Skinny on RGB, HSB, and Hexadecimal

When you mix up a color for your Flash project, you mix a combination of red, green, and blue; in other words, the *RGB color model*. In Flash, you can specify the color by entering values for red, blue, and green or for hue, saturation, and brightness. In another method, you enter the hexadecimal value for a color. Here's the lowdown on these methods for expressing color values:

✔ **RGB:** When you use the RGB color model to mix a color, you work with 256 hues of each color. When you do the math, you see that you can choose from 16,777,216 colors. Even the trendiest interior designer would go slightly bonkers from working with that many colors. But the possibility exists. When you specify colors using RGB values, lower numbers mean darker hues. Pure black is 0,0,0, and pure white is 255,255,255. Pure red is 255,0,0; pure green is 0,255,0, and pure blue is 0,0,255.

✔ **HSB:** When you specify colors using H,S,B values, you enter values for the hue, saturation, and brightness. The Hue value is from 0 to 360 degrees, and pure black is 0 or 360. Yellow is 120 degrees, green is 180 degrees, and blue is 240 degrees. The Saturation value is from 0 to 100 percent; 0 is totally unsaturated, and 100 is fully saturated. The Brightness value is also a percentage, with darker colors falling on the lower end of the spectrum and brighter colors falling at the high end of the spectrum.

✔ **Hexadecimal values:** When you specify colors using hexadecimal values, you use a combination of numbers from 0 to 9 and letters from A to F (six digits total). Pure black is #000000, and pure white is #FFFFFF. The first two digits represent the Red value; the next two digits, the Green value; and the last two digits, the Blue value. The possible combinations give you 256 hues of each color. Yep, you guessed it: Hexadecimal is just a different way of expressing RGB values.

There's no right or wrong way of expressing color values. If you're a photographer or you're familiar with Photoshop, you probably prefer the RGB method of expressing color. If you were born to be wild on HTML, you may prefer hexadecimal. (We're not sure about HSB, but we think that it may have originated in France after a night of Brie and Bordeaux.) Now that you know everything — or perhaps more than you wanted to know — about color, it's time to work it into your Flash workflow.

Stroked and Filled, but Not Punched

When you create a shape with one of the shape tools, you have the option of creating an outline for the shape — which, in Flash-speak, is known as the *stroke* — and filling the shape with color or a gradient. The color inside the outline is the *fill*.

A shape can have a stroke but no fill, or a fill but no stroke. If you like to cover all the bases, you can create a shape that has no stroke and no fill, but unless you're creating a Flash version of a polar bear in a snowstorm, we advise against this strategy. In the following the sections, we show you how to define the stroke and fill colors.

Defining the stroke color

When you create a shape such as a circle or rectangle, you can add a stroke to the shape, which in essence is a border. When you use the Pencil, Pen, or Line tool, a stroke is all you've got. And, if you use the Pen tool to create a sword — that's another kettle of fish. To define the stroke color, follow these steps:

1. **Click the color swatch below the Stroke icon.**

   It looks like a pencil, near the bottom of the Tools panel.

   The Swatches panel opens, as shown in Figure 2-1. The selected color is shown in the upper-left corner of the panel. Notice the number next to the color. That's the hexadecimal — Gesundheit! — value for the color. You also see an Alpha value, which determines the opacity of the color.

Book II
Chapter 2

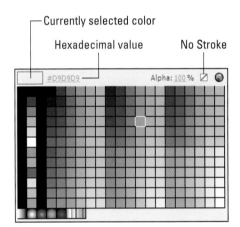

Figure 2-1: Defining the stroke color.

2. **To create a shape with no stroke, click the No Stroke icon.**

3. **To specify the stroke color, do one of the following:**

   - Click a swatch. After you click a swatch, the panel closes, and the Stroke color swatch changes to reflect your choice.

   - Double-click the current hexadecimal value and enter a value.

   - Click the color wheel in the upper-right corner to open the system color picker. From within the color picker, click a color swatch or enter values in the Red, Green, and Blue fields or the Hue, Sat, and Lum fields.

After clicking the current stroke color swatch, move the cursor to the Stage and click an object whose color you want to match perfectly. This technique is an ideal way to match a color from an image or a logo.

4. **Accept the default Alpha value or drag the scrubby slider to specify a different value.**

   Alternatively, you can double-click the current value and enter one you want. When you specify a value less than 100 percent, the color of underlying objects or the background is visible, which changes the hue of the stroke. When you specify a low value, more of the underlying color influences the color of the stroke.

You can also specify the stroke for objects you create with a tool in the Property inspector. Select the tool, and in the Property inspector, click the Stroke icon and follow these steps again.

Defining the fill color

Whether you create a cool shape by mixing and matching regular shapes or create a shape using one of the drawing tools, your next step is to flesh out your creation by filling it with color. To define the fill color, follow these steps:

1. **Click the color swatch below the Fill icon, which looks like a paint bucket, near the bottom of the Tools panel.**

   The Swatches panel opens (refer to Figure 2-1). The selected color is shown in the upper-left corner of the panel. The number next to the color is the Hexadecimal value for the color. You also see an Alpha value, which determines the transparency of the color. (We discuss hexadecimal values in the section "Getting to Know Color: The Skinny on RGB, HSB, and Hexadecimal," at the beginning of this chapter.)

2. **To create a shape with no fill, click the No Color icon (which is the white square with the diagonal red slash).**

3. **To specify the fill color, do one of the following:**

   - Click a swatch. After you click a swatch, the panel closes, and the Stroke color swatch changes to reflect your choice.

   - Double-click the current hexadecimal value and enter a value.

   - Click the color wheel in the upper-right corner to open the system color picker. From within the color picker, select a color swatch or enter values in the Red, Green, and Blue fields or the Hue, Sat, and Lum fields.

After clicking the current fill color swatch, move the cursor to the Stage and click an object whose color you want to match perfectly. This technique is an ideal way to match a color from an image or a logo.

4. **Accept the default Alpha value, or drag the scrubby slider to specify a different value.**

    Alternatively, you can double-click the current value and enter one of your own. When you specify a value less than 100 percent, the color of underlying objects or the background is visible, which changes the hue of the stroke. When you specify a low value, more of the underlying color influences the color of the stroke.

Finding Your Way around the Swatches Panel

The Swatches panel is what you see when you specify a stroke or fill color. There are, however, other ways to access this color collection of cubes that may have inspired Rubik. If you're the adventurous type, you'll be glad to know that you have full control over the colors in the panel. You can delete colors, add colors, and export colors, for example. We show you how to use the Swatches panel in the following sections.

Understanding Web-safe colors

In a perfect world, you could use any color and it would look the same in all Web browsers and all operating systems. But don't forget the infamous browser wars and whether 'tis nobler to Mac or PC — facts that leave the poor Flash designer in a color-choosing quandary. Most modern monitors and video cards can display any color you can throw at them. However, if you're creating a Flash project that will be viewed on a device that doesn't support 16- or 24-bit color, choose your colors from the default Flash color palette, which consists of 216 colors that are unsafe at any speed — er, we mean safe in any browser viewed on any platform.

Getting to know the Swatches panel

The Swatches panel has color swatches (216, to be exact) and gradient swatches. You use the Swatches panel to select colors for the fill and stroke of objects created with the drawing tools. You also use the Swatches panel to manage and export color sets, for example. Follow these steps for a quick tour of the Swatches panel:

1. **Choose Window⇨Swatches.**

    The Swatches panel (see Figure 2-2) appears. If you're into keyboard shortcuts like we are, press Ctrl+F9 (Windows) or ⌘+F9 (Mac) to open the panel.

2. **To add a color to the panel from an object in the workspace,** move the cursor over the object whose color you want to sample and then click. Move the cursor inside the Swatches panel (the icon becomes a paint bucket) and then click to add the sampled color to the panel.

3. **Click the icon to the far right of Swatches.**

   The Swatches panel Options menu (see Figure 2-3) opens.

4. **Choose one of the following options from the menu:**

   • *Duplicate Swatch:* Duplicates the selected swatch.

   • *Delete Swatch:* Deletes the selected swatch.

   • *Add Colors:* Opens the Import Color Swatch dialog box, which enables you to add a Flash color set (using the .CLR extension) or a color table (using the .ACT extension). You also have the option to import colors from an existing image in the GIF format. When you choose the latter option, Flash recognizes the colors in the image and creates a swatch for each color.

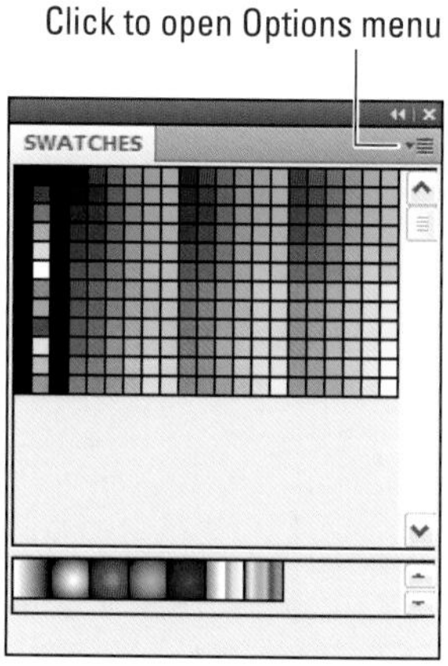

Click to open Options menu

Figure 2-2: The Swatches panel has lovely cubes of color.

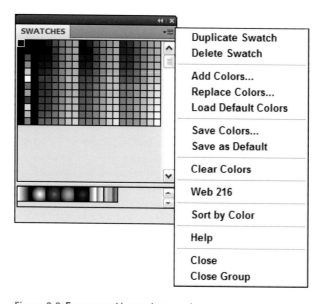

Figure 2-3: Every panel has to have options.

If you're creating a Flash project for a client and you need to match the colors from the client's logo, import the logo into your favorite image-editing application and save it as a GIF file. Use the Add Colors command from the Swatches panel Options menu and then select the image to add the colors to the existing color set.

- *Replace Colors:* Opens the Image Color Swatch dialog box. Select a Flash color set or a color table. The colors from the imported color set or table replace the existing colors. Another option is to select an image in the GIF format. Flash recognizes the colors in the image and uses them to replace the existing colors.

- *Load Default Colors:* Loads the default color set.

- *Save Colors:* Opens the Export Color Swatch dialog box, in which you can save the colors that are currently in the Swatches panel as a Flash color set with the .CLR extension or a color set with the .ACT extension.

If you're going to use an exported color set in another Adobe application, such as Fireworks or Photoshop, save the exported colors as a color set with the .ACT extension.

- *Save as Default:* Saves the current colors as the default color set for creating new documents.

- *Clear Colors:* Removes all color swatches except for the default black and white colors. This choice is excellent if you're creating a color set from scratch using the Color panel or by adding colors from an existing color set or .GIF image.

- *Web 216:* Loads the Web Safe palette with 216 colors.

- *Sort by Color:* Arranges the swatches according to hue.

Creating a custom color set

If you're creating Flash projects for clients and use the same colors regularly, you may find it beneficial to create a custom color set. You can easily do so from within the Swatches panel by following these steps:

1. **Choose Window⇨Swatches.**

   The Swatches panel appears.

2. **Delete the colors you don't want saved with the custom color set.**

   To delete a color, select the swatch you want to delete and then choose Delete Swatch from the Swatches panel Options menu.

3. **Add colors to the color set.**

   You can add colors by choosing Add Colors from the Swatches panel Options menu and then importing a color set or having Flash create the color swatches from an existing GIF image.

4. **To sample a color from an object on the Stage, select the eyedropper tool, click the color you want to sample, move the cursor into the Swatches panel, and then click to add the sampled color to the color set.**

5. **Add and delete additional colors as needed.**

6. **After customizing the color set, choose Save Colors from the Swatches panel Options menu.**

   The Export Color Swatch dialog box appears, as shown in Figure 2-4.

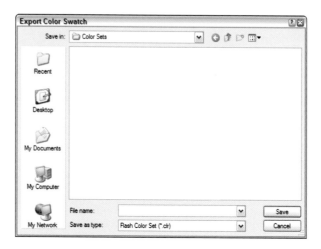

Figure 2-4: Exporting a custom color set.

7. **Navigate to the folder in which you want to save the color set.**

   Store the file in a folder you can easily find. You may want to create a new folder named Color Sets in either your client's folder or your Documents folder.

8. **Enter a name for the color set.**

   Choose a name that reflects the purpose for which the color set is used. If it's for a client, use the initials of the client's company as the filename.

9. **Choose an option from the Save as Type drop-down menu.**

   Your choices are Flash Color Set (.CLR), or Color Set (.ACT). If you're only using the color set in Flash, save it as a Flash color set. For maximum compatibility with other Adobe image-editing applications that use color sets, choose Color Set.

10. **Click Save.**

    Flash saves the color set for future use.

Mixing a Color

Yellow, blue, what'll you do?

Maybe you should mix a color.

Black, white, is all right

Living color may be what you need.

The Swatches panel is a useful starting point when you need to choose a color for a Flash project. But sometimes the color you need isn't in the Swatches panel. Mixing a color, though, isn't just about mixing up a solid color like the paint department down at your local hardware store does. You can mix *gradients,* which are blends of two or more colors. When you need a hipper-than-hip-funkier-than-funky color or a gradient that contains a plethora of colors, look no further than on the Color panel. In the following sections, we show you how to mix a color and gradient.

Getting up close and personal with the Color panel

A swatch is a cool tool when you need to get down, get funky, and grab a color quickly. But if you're creating a Flash project on a rainy day while you're dreaming away, you can create any color — even sky-blue pink — in the Color panel. The Color panel also makes it possible for you to mix *gradients* — blends of two or more colors — that come in different flavors. We show you everything you need to know about mixing colors and gradients with the Color panel in the following sections.

Mixing a swatch of color

When you need a color for a stroke or fill that's not present on the Swatches panel, you can easily mix what you need by using the Color panel. You can mix a color by dipping the cursor into the color well or by entering the values of the color, if you know them. To mix a color by using the Color panel, follow these steps:

1. **Choose Window⇨Color.**

   The Color panel appears, as shown in Figure 2-5. The panel gives you the option of mixing a color for strokes or fills created by using the drawing tools. You can also revert to the default stroke and fill colors (black and white), specify no color, or swap the existing stroke and fill colors.

2. **Click the Stroke or Fill color icon.**

   This step determines whether the mixed color appears in the Stroke or Fill color swatch in the Tools panel.

3. **Choose an option from the Type drop-down menu.**

   Your options are None, Solid, Linear, Radial, or Bitmap. The Linear and Radial options are for gradients, which are covered in the "Creating a gradient" section, later in this chapter. (Creating a bitmap fill is covered in Chapter 6 of this minibook.)

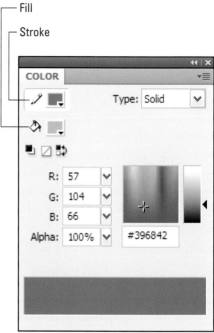

Fill

Stroke

Figure 2-5: Mix a color without getting paint on your hands.

4. **If you know the color values, enter them.**

   If you know the RGB, HSB, or hexadecimal values, you can enter them in the appropriate fields. If the color model you want isn't displayed, you can choose it from the Color panel Options menu (see Figure 2-6), which is accessed by clicking the icon in the upper-right corner of the panel.

5. **To mix a color from scratch, drag inside the color well until the swatch is the hue you want, and then drag the Brightness slider.**

   As you change the color and brightness, the Current Color Swatch is updated in real time.

Color well

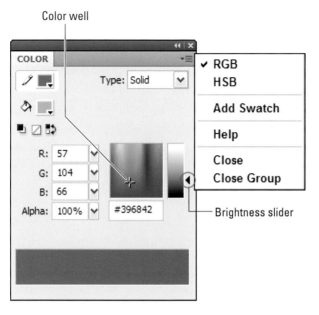

Figure 2-6: Options are a good thing.

6. **Drag the Alpha slider to change the opacity of the color.**

   Alternatively, you can enter a value from 0 to 100. When you specify a value less than 100 percent, the color becomes partially transparent, and you can see the underlying colors.

7. **Choose Add Swatch from the Color panel Options menu to add the color to the Swatches panel.**

   After mixing a color for the stroke or fill, you can keep the panel open to mix the other color. If you're creating a custom color set from scratch, you can continue mixing colors and choose Add Swatch from the Color panel Options menu to finish creating the custom color set.

Creating a gradient

The Flash Swatches panel has a couple of default gradients you can use. But if you or your client think that the project needs custom color gradients, you can mix your own in the Color panel. You can create a *linear gradient,* which mixes the colors from left to right, or a *radial gradient,* which mixes the colors concentrically. Figure 2-7 shows both a linear and radial gradient.

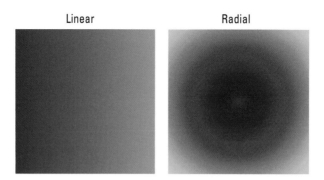

Linear   Radial

Figure 2-7: Gradients come in two flavors — linear and radial.

To create a gradient, follow these steps:

1. **Choose Window⇨Colors.**

   The Color panel appears.

2. **Click the Fill icon.**

   You wouldn't specify a gradient for a stroke, would you?

3. **Select a gradient type from the Type drop-down menu.**

   Your choices are Linear and Radial. The default gradient colors are black and white (see Figure 2-8). (Black-and-white gradients are only one stop removed from monotone, from which the word *monotonous* is derived.)

4. **Choose an option from the Overflow drop-down menu.**

   This option determines how colors are applied when they extend beyond the gradient. You have three overflow options:

   - *Extend:* The default option applies the colors past the end of the gradient.

   - *Reflect:* The colors of the gradient are repeated in a pattern from beginning to end and then reversed, which fills a shape with a mirror-like reflection.

   Figure 2-8: Black-and-white gradients — boring.

   - *Extend:* Repeats the gradient colors from beginning to end until the shape is filled.

5. **Select the Linear RGB check box to create a gradient that's SVG (Scalable Vector Graphics) compliant.**

   You can scale the vector object to which the gradient fill is applied, and the fill scales properly with no degradation.

6. **Select the first color stop and specify a color for it.**

   The default gradients have two stops. You add a stop wherever you want to introduce a new color. You can specify a color for a stop in several ways: You can double-click the stop to open the Swatches panel, drag the cursor in the color well, and then drag the brightness slider, enter the RGB, HSB, or hexadecimal values for the color you want, or drag the individual color sliders.

7. **Specify the Alpha value for the first color stop.**

   To specify the Alpha value, enter a value in the text field or drag the slider.

8. **Select the second color stop and specify its color and Alpha value.**

   We know what you're thinking: Are two stops all we get? If that question weighs heavily on your mind, please read Step 9.

9. **Move the cursor toward the color bar and click when it becomes a left-pointing arrow with a plus sign (+).**

   Another color stop is added. You can add as many color stops as you need.

10. **To remove an unneeded color stop, select it and drag it off the color bar.**

    The secretary disavows any record of its existence.

11. **Specify the color and Alpha value for any color stops you add.**

    Figure 2-9 shows a radial gradient with more colors than a psychedelic ice cream concoction you'd find in a Haight-Ashbury ice cream store.

If you want to save a gradient for future use, choose Add Swatch from the Color panel Options menu.

When you create a radial gradient, the leftmost stop is the color in the center of the gradient.

Figure 2-9: Two scoops of Strawberry Alarm Clock, please.

Using the Transform Gradient tool

After you apply a gradient to a shape, you can change the way the gradient is mapped to the shape by using the Transform Gradient tool. You can use it to scale the gradient, rotate the gradient, and change the width of the gradient. To modify a gradient with the Transform Gradient tool, follow these steps:

1. **Select the Transform Gradient tool.**

   The Transform Gradient tool shares the third slot on the Tools panel. If the tool isn't visible, click the Free Transform tool and select the Transform Gradient tool from the fly-out menu.

2. **Click the shape whose gradient you want to transform.**

   If you click an object with a linear gradient, two handles appear around the object, and one hollow dot appears in the center (see Figure 2-10). If you click an object with a radial gradient, three handles appear around the object, and one hollow dot appears in the center (see Figure 2-11).

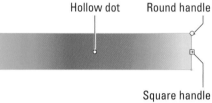

Figure 2-10: Transforming a linear gradient.

3. **If you're transforming a linear gradient, these are your options:**

   - *Rotate the gradient:* Position the cursor over the round handle, and when it becomes a circle with four curved arrows, drag clockwise or counterclockwise to rotate the gradient relative to the shape.

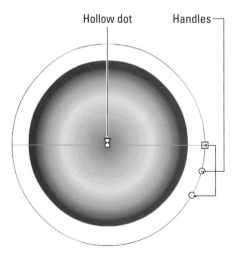

Figure 2-11: Transforming a radial gradient.

- *Change the width:* Position the cursor over the square handle, and when it becomes a dual-headed arrow, drag left or right to decrease or increase the width of the gradient.

- *Change the center:* Position the cursor over the hollow dot, and when it becomes a cross with four arrows, drag to change the center of the gradient relative to the object.

4. **If you're transforming a radial gradient, here are your options:**

- *Change the width:* Position the cursor over the uppermost handle, and when it becomes a dual-headed arrow, drag left or right to decrease or increase the width of the gradient.

- *Change the scale:* Position the cursor over the uppermost circular icon, and when it becomes a hollow circle with a diagonal arrow, drag in or out to increase or decrease the scale of the gradient.

- *Rotate the gradient:* Position the cursor over the lower circle, and when it becomes a hollow circle with four curved arrows, drag clockwise or counterclockwise to rotate the gradient relative to the shape.

- *Change the center:* Position the cursor over the hollow dot, and when it becomes a cross with four arrows, drag to change the center of the gradient relative to the object.

Changing Colors

Editing colors on Flash objects is a piece of cake. You can change the stroke or fill of an object at any time. You change the stroke by using the Ink Bottle tool and change the fill by using the Paint Bucket tool.

Using the Ink Bottle tool

You use the Ink Bottle tool to change an object's stroke. You can change an object's stroke at any time by following these steps:

1. **Select the Ink Bottle tool.**

2. **In the Property inspector, click the Stroke color swatch and select a color from the Swatches panel.**

3. **In the Property inspector, specify the stroke width and style.**

4. **Click the object whose stroke you want to change.**

   The object's stroke changes to reflect the stroke parameters you specify in the Property inspector. If the object has no stroke, a stroke is applied to it.

Using the Paint Bucket tool

When you need to ch-ch-ch-change the fill of an object, you use the Paint Bucket tool. The ability to quickly change the fill of any object comes in handy when you have a client who can't seem to make up her mind, and a blinding flash of artistic insight tells you that every pink object in your Flash project should be mellow yellow. To change the fill of an object with the Paint Bucket tool, follow these steps:

1. **Select the Paint Bucket tool.**

2. **In the Property inspector, click the Fill color swatch and select a color from the Swatches panel.**

3. **Click the object whose fill you want to change.**

Using the Kuler Extension

If you want to have a colorful Flash design (and who doesn't?), consider using the Kuler extensions. We're not sure how this term is pronounced or how Adobe came up with the name, but we're pronouncing it "cooler." So whenever you want a cooler Flash design, call up the Kuler extension and mix up some masterful color:

1. **Choose Window⇨Kuler.**

   The Kuler panel appears (see Figure 2-12). Notice the colorful round area — the color wheel.

2. **Select an option from the Rule menu.**

   Your choices are described in this list:

   - *Analogous:* Creates a color palette using colors that are adjacent to the base color on the color wheel. This color scheme is also referred to as harmonious.

   - *Monochromatic:* Creates a color palette using different values the base color.

   - *Triad:* Creates a color palette using colors that are 120 degrees from the base color on the color wheel.

   - *Complementary:* Creates a color palette using colors that are opposite each other on the color wheel.

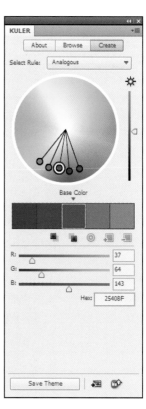

Figure 2-12: Kuler rhymes (we think) with cooler.

- *Compound:* Creates a color palette using a combination of the rules.

- *Shades:* Creates a color palette using colors that are shades of the base color. If your client is a blues guitarist, this option is an excellent choice. Choose blue as the base color and you'll have several shades of blue for your Flash creation.

- *Custom:* Creates a palette based on your input.

3. **Select a base color.**

   You can select a base color by dragging the R, G, and B sliders. Alternatively, you can enter the R, G, B, or hexadecimal values of a color.

4. **Modify the color scheme.**

   The beauty of Kuler comes into play in this step. You can drag any of the dots to modify the color scheme. You can also double-click any color to make it the active color and then modify the R, G, B, or hexadecimal values. You can also control the brightness of the active color by dragging the brightness slider. This action creates a darker or lighter shade of the color.

   To create a color scheme based on the current stroke color, click the Add Current Stroke Color as Base Color icon. To create a color scheme based on the current fill color, click the Add Current Fill Color as Base Color icon.

5. **Click a color swatch and the click the Remove This Color from the Theme icon.**

   The color is removed from the palette. After you remove a color from the palette, the Add a New Color to the Theme icon becomes available. After clicking the icon, you can mix a new color by entering R, G, B, or hexadecimal values. The other colors are changed based on the color rule you specify in Step 2. You can remove any color from the palette except the base color.

   You can also modify the color palette by clicking the Affect the Other Colors in the Theme Based On Harmony icon.

6. **Click the Stroke color swatch and then click a color from the Kuler color palette you created.**

   The stroke color is updated to reflect your choice.

7. **Click the Fill color swatch and then click a color from the Kuler color palette you created.**

   The fill color is updated to reflect your choice.

8. **Click Save Theme.**

   The Save Theme dialog box appears.

9. **Enter a name for the theme and click OK.**

The color palette is saved to the Kuler panel. To use the saved theme, click Browse and then choose Saved from the drop-down menu.

10. Click Add This Theme to Swatches.

The color palette is added to the Swatches panel.

11. Click Upload to Kuler.com.

Choose this option if you want to share your creation with other Kuler fans. When you choose this option, you're prompted for your username and password.

If you're not feeling terribly creative or you just want to see what other Kuler users are doing, click Browse. The Kuler panel refreshes to show color palettes created by other Kuler users. You can sort the palettes by choosing an option from the drop-down menu. For example, you can choose the highest-rated or most popular palettes. You can fine-tune your search by limiting the time period in which the palettes were uploaded to Kuler. The default is All Time, but you can limit the number of palettes by choosing Last 7 Days or Last 30 Days. After navigating the themes, you can add a selected theme to the Swatches panel or edit the theme as outlined in this section.

Chapter 3: Getting the Word Out with Text

In This Chapter

- ✓ **Mastering the Text tool**
- ✓ **Stylizing text**
- ✓ **Creating text**
- ✓ **Editing text**
- ✓ **Finding and replacing items**

*W*riters love words. So do readers. If you create Flash projects with information from writers that will be read by site visitors, it's your job to add the words to the Flash project. You do so with the Text tool. We know that sounds like a case of the blatantly obvious, but the Text tool isn't as easy to use as some would think. In fact, each of the three text types has different properties: garden-variety static text when you need to get the word out; dynamic text when you're creating a project with text that changes frequently or otherwise need to be addressed with ActionScript; and input text when you want site users to enter information such as their names or credit card numbers. (In fact, you can even animate text, but that's a subject for another chapter.) In this chapter, we show you how to master the Text tool.

Using the Text Tool

The Text tool is similar to one of those pens with three colors of ink and a PDA stylus all wrapped in one neat container. With the Flash text tool, you can create static text, dynamic text, or input text. In the following sections, we show you how to use the Text tool to create each text type.

Creating static text

Static text may sound somewhat boring, but you can get a charge out of it. You can use any font on your system when creating static text. You can stylize the text, have a multiline text field, and do much more. To create static text, follow these steps:

1. **Select the Text tool.**

2. **In the Property inspector (choose Window⇨Properties), choose Static Text from the uppermost drop-down menu (see Figure 3-1).**

3. **Click and drag the area where you want the text to appear.**

   When you create static text boxes, you can only set the width of the text box. The default option is to display a single line of text.

4. **Set the text parameters in the Property inspector.**

   The parameters for static, dynamic, and input text are almost identical. We cover them in the later section "Formatting Text."

5. **Select an option from the Orientation section of the Property inspector.**

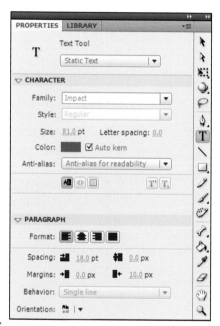

Figure 3-1: Creating static text.

   The default option is horizontal. You can also create vertical text that goes from left to right or from right to left.

   You can change the orientation of the text after creating it and then choosing an option in the Orientation section of the Property inspector.

6. **Type some text.**

   As you enter text, it automatically wraps to the next line.

7. **Modify the width of the text box in the Property inspector.**

   You cannot modify the height of a static text field.

8. **When you finish creating text, click outside the text box or select another tool.**

As long as the cursor is inside the text field, the Text tool is still active, primed, and ready.

Adding a hyperlink to text

When you create static text, you can apply a hyperlink to a selection of text. After you create the hyperlink, you specify whether it opens in the same window or a different window. To create a hyperlink, follow these steps:

1. **Create a block of static text.**

If you don't know how to create a block of static text, read the "Creating Static Text" section, earlier in this chapter.

2. **Using the Text tool, select the text to which you want to apply the hyperlink.**

3. **In the Options section of the Property inspector (choose Window⇨Properties) enter the URL for the Web page that will open when the link is clicked.**

4. **Choose an option from the Target drop-down menu (see Figure 3-2). Your choices are shown in this list:**

- *_blank* opens the page in a new window.

- *_parent* opens the page in the parent of the current frame.

- *_self* opens the page in the current frame in the current window.

- *_top* opens the page in the top-level frame in the current window.

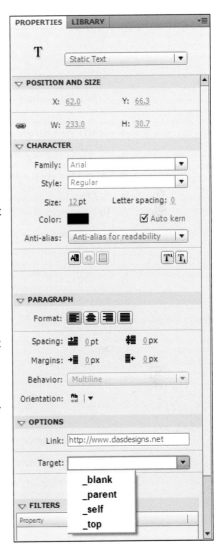

Figure 3-2: Aim to load the URL in the target.

Creating input text

You create an input text field when you want the Flash application to accept input from the user. Input text fields can be formatted to accept a single line of text or multiple lines of text. You can also specify whether the text wraps to a new line when it exceeds the width of the field. And you can and limit the maximum number of characters that users can input into the field. To create an input text field, follow these steps:

1. **Select the Text tool.**

2. **In the Property inspector, choose Input Text from the Text drop-down menu.**

3. **Enter an instance name for the text box.**

   You use the instance name when you address the text box with ActionScript.

4. **Click and drag the area where you want the text to appear.**

   When you create input text boxes, you can set the dimensions as you drag the tool on the Stage.

5. **Set the text parameters in the Property inspector.**

   The parameters for static, dynamic, and input text are almost identical. We cover those in the later section "Formatting Text."

Creating dynamic text

Dynamic text boxes display text that's updated dynamically at runtime or by the use of ActionScript. Dynamic text boxes can also be used to display text that's loaded from an external file. To create a dynamic text box, follow these steps:

1. **Select the Text tool.**

2. **In the Property inspector, choose Dynamic Text from the Text drop-down menu.**

3. **Enter an instance name for the text box.**

   You use the instance name when you address the text box with ActionScript.

4. **Click and drag the area where you want the text to appear.**

   When you create dynamic text boxes, you can set the dimensions as you drag the tool on the Stage.

5. **Set the text parameters in the Property inspector.**

    The parameters for formatting static, dynamic, and input text are almost identical. We cover those in the later section "Formatting Text."

To make an input or dynamic text box that's scrollable, create the text field and then choose Text⇨Scrollable. After you issue this command, a black dot appears in the lower-left corner of the text box. You can fill it to overflowing. When the file is published, a user can click inside the text box and drag the mouse to scroll the text.

If you have a lot to say, create your text in a word processing application, press Ctrl+A (Windows) or ⌘+A (Mac) to select the text and then press Ctrl+C (Windows) or ⌘+C (Mac) to paste the text to the Clipboard. In Flash, place the cursor inside the text field and then press Ctrl+V (Windows) or ⌘+V (Mac). Note that some of the formatting you apply in a word processing application may not be preserved when you paste it into Flash.

Formatting Text

Text without formatting is boring. When you create static, input, or dynamic text, you can specify all the usual suspects, such as font, size, style, and color. You can also determine whether viewers of your Flash masterpiece (why would you create anything less?) can select text. In the upcoming sections, we show you how to set character parameters, format paragraph text, and resize text fields.

Specifying text character parameters

Formatting text in Flash is almost like formatting text in your favorite word processing application. The options are almost identical for static, dynamic, and input text, which is why we're conserving paper and showing you how to specify character styles in one section. When a parameter is unique to a specific type of text, we tell you which type of text for which the parameter is used. To specify character parameters, follow these steps:

1. **Create a text field.**

    Vive la difference. Specify whether the text is input, dynamic, or static in the Property inspector. The Character section of the Property inspector updates to show you the available options. Figure 3-3 shows the Property inspector after creating a dynamic text box.

2. **In the Property inspector, select a font type from the Family drop-down menu.**

   You have lots of choices; one for each font you installed on your computer.

3. **Select a style from the Style drop-down menu.**

   This is Word Processing 101 — you can choose from Regular, *Italic*, **Bold**, or ***Bold-Italic***.

4. **Drag the scrubby slider to specify the text size.**

   Alternatively, click the current size to reveal a text field, and then enter a value.

5. **Drag the scrubby slider to specify text spacing.**

   Alternatively, click the current value to reveal a text field and then enter a value. Positive values space the letters farther apart, and negative values scrunch the text closer together.

6. **Accept the default text color or click the color swatch.**

   Clicking the color swatch reveals the Swatches panel. Select a color. If you want the text to be semitransparent, specify an alpha value less than 100. For more information on color, refer to Chapter 2 of this minibook.

7. **Accept the default Auto Kern option, or click the check box to deselect it.**

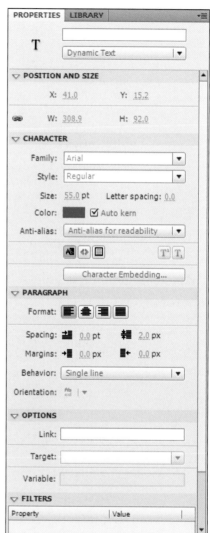

Figure 3-3: Dynamic, isn't it?

Auto Kern uses the font family information to determine the spacing between characters. If you disable this option, all characters are spaced equally, which may cause certain character pairings to look a bit odd.

8. **Choose an option from the Anti-Alias drop-down menu. Your choices are**

   - *Use Device Fonts:* Anti-aliases text according to the fonts installed on a user's computer. If you choose this option, make sure that you use one of the Flash device fonts when creating the text: _sans, _serif, or _typewriter.

   - *Bitmap Text (No Anti-Alias):* Disables anti-aliasing and renders crisp text, which results in a larger file size because font outlines are embedded with the resulting SWF file. The text renders well at the original size but doesn't scale well.

   - *Anti-Alias for Animation:* Alignment and kerning information are disregarded, which results in a smoother animation. This option results in a larger file size because font outlines are embedded. When using this option, in order for the text to be legible, make sure that the font size is 10 or larger.

   - *Anti-Alias for Readability:* The Flash text engine renders the font to ensure high quality and legibility. The file size increases because the font outlines are embedded. When you use this option, the file must be published for Flash Player 8 or later.

   - *Custom Anti-Alias:* The Custom Anti-Aliasing dialog box opens, which enables you to modify the font by specifying the thickness of the font anti-alias transition and the sharpness of the transition between the font and the background. This option increases the file size. To specify custom anti-aliasing, you must publish the file for Flash Player 8 or later.

9. **(Optional) Click the Selectable icon.**

   This option enables users to select the text.

10. **(Optional) Click the Render Text as HTML icon.**

    This option enables you to use HTML formatting on an external text file that's loaded into the field. For example, to make text boldface, you use the <b> and </b> tags. Any text between the tags conforms to the tag attribute.

11. **To create an outline around the text field, click the Show Border around Text icon.**

12. **To add superscripting or sub-scripting to selected text, click the applicable icon.**

You can apply character settings to an entire block of text or apply settings to a selected set of characters or, in non-geek-speak, a word or selection of words.

13. **To embed font characters with the published file, click the Character Embedding button.**

This step opens the Character Embedding dialog box (see Figure 3-4). Select a character set from the list. You can select multiple character sets by pressing Ctrl and then clicking the sets you want to embed. You can have Flash determine which characters need to be embedded based on what you already entered in the field by clicking the Auto Fill button. After selecting a character set, click OK to close the dialog box.

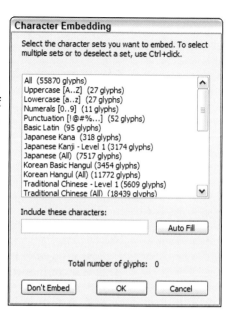

Figure 3-4: Yikes! We're gonna be embedded.

Working with paragraph text

If you're creating a simple banner or one line of input or dynamic text, you're finished after you specify the character settings. However, if you have multiple lines of text, you can format the text just like you would format a paragraph in your favorite word processing application. To apply paragraph settings to a text field, follow these steps:

1. **Create a text field.**

   Select Static, Input, or Dynamic from the Type drop-down menu. If you select Static, you can't apply paragraph settings to the field until you create several lines or paragraphs of text. Figure 3-5 shows the Paragraph section in the Property inspector when formatting a dynamic text box.

2. **Choose an option from the Format section.**

   Your choices are align left, align center, align right, or justify.

3. **Drag the Indent Spacing scrubby slider to set an indent for the first sentence in each paragraph.**

   Alternatively, you can click the current value and enter a value.

4. **Drag the Line Spacing scrubby slider to set the spacing between lines.**

   Alternatively, you can click the current value and enter a value.

5. **Drag the Left Margin scrubby slider to set the left margin.**

   Alternatively, you can click the urrent value and enter a value.

6. **Drag the Right Margin scrubby slider to set the right margin.**

   Alternatively, you can click the current value and enter a value.

7. **Choose an option from the Behavior drop-down menu.**

   The option you choose determines how the text flows. Your choices are Single Line, Multiline, Multiline No Wrap, and (if you're creating input text) Password.

8. **If you're creating input text, in the Options section drag the Max Chars scrubby slider to the value you want.**

   Use this optional step if you want to limit the number of characters that the characters using the published file can enter into the text box. Alternatively, you can click the current value and enter a value.

Figure 3-5: Formatting paragraph text.

Creating Text

A Flash project without text is just graphics. If you already read the previous sections, you know that you have a great deal of flexibility when you need to add text to a Flash project. However, sometimes even the best-laid plans go to waste and you end up with a document with gobs of text. In this section, we point out some issues you need to consider when creating text for your documents — and some solutions.

Font considerations

Some designers get carried away when using fonts. They mix and match font types and mix boldface and italicized fonts, for example. This creates a confusing message to viewers because it looks like the designer cashed in on a font sale at Font's Fifth Avenue and finally found a design in which to use them. In addition to presenting a confusing message, it bloats the file size. So, whenever possible, think "less is more" when choosing fonts. In the following sections, we offer more sage advice for choosing fonts.

Choosing fonts for static text fields

When you specify a font for a static text field, Flash embeds the font outline in the resulting SWF file to ensure that the text looks identical when played in the Flash Player on other users' computers. However, if you have a large amount of text in a Flash project that uses different font families and styling, you run the risk of creating a large file that takes a while to load. When you plan a project that contains a lot of text, make sure to stick with one font family. If file size is a real issue, consider using device fonts because they aren't embedded in a Flash SWF file. When you use a device font, the Flash Player uses the closest match from the user's computer to render the text. As a bonus, device fonts result in more legible text when you specify a font size of 10 points or smaller. To convert a text field to device fonts, follow these steps:

1. **Select the Text tool.**

2. **Double-click the text field you want to convert to device fonts.**

   All the text is selected.

3. **In the Character section of the Property inspector, choose one of the following choices from the Family drop-down menu:**

   - *_sans:* Resembles Arial or Helvetica

   - *_serif:* Resembles Times Roman

   - *_typewriter:* Resembles Courier

Some font outlines cannot be embedded in a Flash SWF file. To ensure that you choose fonts that can be embedded, choose View⇨Preview⇨Anti-Alias Text. If any text you create with a font family has jagged edges, don't use that family in your project.

Choosing fonts for input and dynamic text fields

When you create input or dynamic text fields and specify a font family, Flash records the name with the published SWF file. When the file is played, Flash Player renders the text using the same font or a similar one from the user's computer. To ensure that the file renders correctly, you can embed font outlines with the file, but that increases file size. You can also specify a device font as outlined in the previous section.

Converting text to graphics

Sometimes you pick a cool font that you want to use for a banner or for an animation. You can embed a font with the file, which increases the file size. If you already have lots of other text, embedding your way-cool text bloats the file size. So, if the text is just another pretty face, you can convert each letter to a graphic. Here's how:

1. **Create some text.**

   If you're in an experimental state of mind, try something big and bold using the Impact font family.

2. **Select the text with the Text tool.**

3. **Choose Modify⇨Break Apart.**

   Flash breaks the text into individual pieces; one piece per letter.

4. **Choose Modify⇨Break Apart.**

   No, we're not being redundant. The first time you break the text apart, it's still text and can be edited as text. The second time you apply the command, each letter is converted into a shape. You can now convert each shape to a symbol or, if you want to have some fun, select a letter with the Subselection tool. Now you can select and manipulate each point. You can also modify each shape with the Selection tool. For more information on folding, spindling, mutilating, and performing other edits on shapes, refer to Book II, Chapter 1. Figure 3-6 shows a letter that has been modified after it was converted to a shape.

Figure 3-6: Shaken but not stirred.

Editing Text Fields

When you have a document with lots of text, you almost always end up making some kind of change. The client may change his mind, or you may decide that a text field is a little too large. You may also find that your spelling isn't perfect. Nothing is worse than a Flash project with typos. Unfortunately, text is infinitely editable in the native FLA document, except when you convert it to a shape. Then it becomes infinitely malleable. In the upcoming sections, we show you some of the most common edits you need to perform.

Resizing a text field

The great thing about text fields is that you can resize them at any time. You can resize text fields in two ways, and neither distorts the text within the field. To resize a text field, do one of the following:

- Select the text field with the Selection tool, and then drag one of the handles.

- In the Property inspector, use a scrubby slider to change the width or height of the text field. Click the icon that locks the width and height values (it looks like a broken link) if you want to resize the field proportionately.

Editing text

To err is human, and to change one's mind is also human. The fact that Flash designers and developers work for humans means that at some point you have to edit text on one of your projects. Before you can edit text, you have to select it. Here are your options for selecting text:

- Drag the text tool over the character, word, or sentence you want to edit.

- Double-click a word with the Text tool to select it.

- Select the Text tool, click to designate the beginning of a selection you want to edit, and then Shift+click to designate the end of the selection.

- Select the Text tool, click inside a text field, and then Press Ctrl+A (Windows) or ⌘+A (Mac) to select all text within a field.

Spell-checking text fields

Don't you just hate it when you have tons of text to type, your fingers go numb, your finger slips from F to V, and without knowing it you make a couple of *bad* typos. If you miss the mistake when you proofread, — you do proofread your stuff before you post it to the Web, don't you?— after you upload the published file to your client's Web site, you're up the proverbial creek without a paddle, not to mention the copious amounts of egg you'll have to wipe off your face. Typos are bad, but typos posted to the Web can be fatal to your career as a Flash designer. Fortunately, there's a backup for your proofreading. It's known as spell check.

Setting up the Flash spell check

Before you can run a spell check, you have to tell Flash the items you want spell-checked, what to ignore, or which dictionary to use. You can also add words to a personal dictionary (like your last name if it's not common) that might otherwise be listed as suspects for correction. To set up the Flash spell check feature, follow these steps:

1. **Choose Text⇨Spelling Setup.**

   The Spelling Setup dialog box appears (see Figure 3-7).

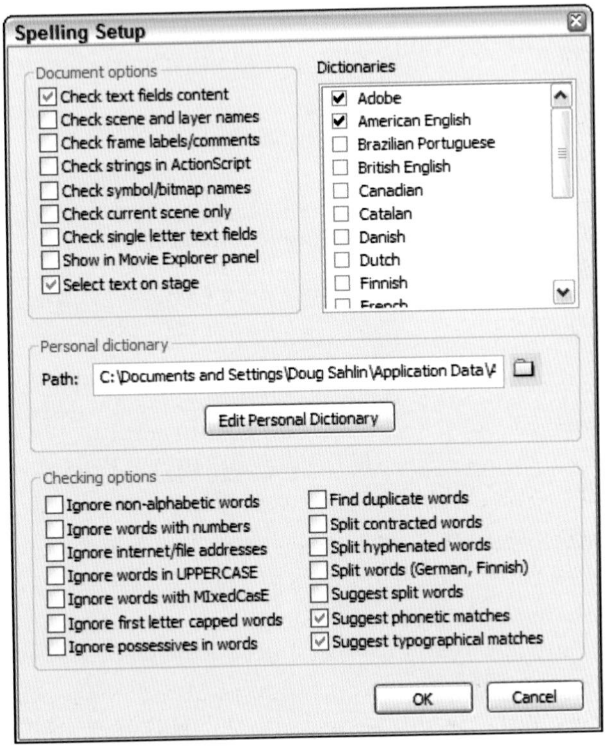

Figure 3-7: Setting up the Flash spell check.

2. **Select the options you want Flash to include when you invoke the Check Spelling command.**

   You see two groups of options: Document and Checking. To prevent you from nodding off, we refrain from listing every option, because they're self explanatory. Note that you have options to spell-check scene and layer names, which is something we use so that our editors don't send screen shots back because of misspelled words.

3. **Choose a dictionary.**

   You can include multiple dictionaries, if you want. You can also switch dictionaries, which is a handy option if you're creating a Flash document in a different language.

4. **Click Edit Personal Dictionary.**

   The Edit Personal Dictionary dialog box appears (see Figure 3-8).

5. **Enter words that Flash may list as suspects for correction.**

Figure 3-8: Flash lets you set up your own, personal dictionary. How great is that?

   Press Enter or Return after entering a word. Add words like your last name, the name of your client's business, or any unusual technical terms that may not appear in the dictionaries Flash is using as resources when checking spelling.

6. **Click OK to close the Edit Personal Dictionary dialog box, and then click OK to close the Spelling Setup dialog box.**

   You're now ready to let Flash check your documents for spelling errors.

Running the Flash spell checker

After spending hours sprinkling a Flash document full of graphics, animations, and text fields, it's time to test your handiwork. We cover testing the entire document in Book VIII, Chapter 1. Now we show you how to check the document for spelling errors:

1. **Choose Text⇨Check Spelling.**

   The Check Spelling dialog box appears and Flash highlights the first word that it suspects is spelled incorrectly. If suggested corrections are available, Flash lists them in the Suggestions pane (see Figure 3-9).

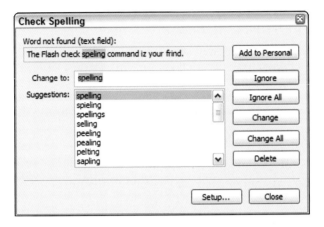

Figure 3-9: Oops. Somebody spelled something wrong!

2. **When Flash highlights a suspect, click one of the following buttons:**

   - *Add to Personal:* Adds the highlighted word to your personal dictionary.

   - *Ignore:* Ignores this instance of the suspect word, and Flash continues to check the document for spelling errors.

   - *Ignore All:* Ignores all instances of the suspect word.

   - *Change:* Changes this instance of the suspect to a suggested replacement that you select in the Suggestion pane. When you select a suggestion, it appears in the Change To field. Alternatively, you can enter a word in the Change To field.

   - *Change All:* Changes all instances of the suspect to a suggested replacement that you select in the Suggestion pane. When you select a suggestion, it appears in the Change To field. Alternatively, you can enter a word in the Change To field.

   - *Delete:* Deletes the suspect word from the object that Flash is spell-checking.

   - *Setup:* Opens the Spelling Setup dialog box, which is a handy option if you notice that Flash isn't handling the spell checking the way you want it to.

   - *Close:* Exits the spelling check before Flash finishes checking the document.

3. **After Flash finishes checking the document, a dialog box appears, telling you that the spelling check has been completed. Click OK to close the dialog box.**

Using the Find and Replace Command

When your client changes her mind and needs you to change some text, it can be a time-intensive task if you're working on a large project. Fortunately, you can find and replace text in a document. For that matter, you can find and replace almost anything in a Flash document. To use the Find and Replace command, follow these steps:

1. **Choose Edit➪Find and Replace.**

   The Find and Replace dialog box appears (see Figure 3-10).

2. **Select an option from the Search In drop-down menu.**

   You can search in the entire document or the current scene.

3. **Choose an option from the For drop-down menu.**

   You can search for the following:

   - *Text:* Search for a word or block of text. You can also enter text that replaces the text for which you're searching. You also have the usual suspects for options, such as searching for the whole word or for matching case.

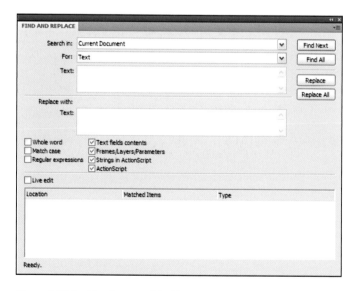

Figure 3-10: Looking for something?

- *Font:* Search for instances of text using a specific font. You can narrow your search by specifying a style and a size. You can replace all instances of the font with a different font.

- *Color:* Search for all instances of a specific color. You choose the color to search for by clicking a swatch, which opens the Swatches panel. Click to choose the color or enter its hexadecimal value. You choose the replacement color in the same manner. You can replace the color in fills or strokes or text or any combination thereof.

- *Symbol:* Search for all instances of a symbol and replace them with another symbol, if you want. Drop-down menus list each symbol you created for the document. Think of this option as the Swap Symbol command on steroids.

- *Sound:* Search for a sound file in the document and replace it with another, if you want. Drop-down menus list each sound you imported into the document.

- *Video:* Search for a video file in the document and replace it with another, if you want. Drop-down menus list each video you imported into the document.

- *Bitmap:* Search for an image file in the document and replace it with another, if you want. Drop-down menus list each image you imported into the document.

4. **After selecting an object, click one of the following:**

- *Find Next:* Finds the next instance of the object for which you're searching.

- *Find All:* Finds all instances of the object for which you're searching.

- *Replace:* Replaces the current instance of the object with the replacement object.

- *Replace All:* Replaces all instances of the object for which you're searching with the replacement object.

**Book II
Chapter 3**

**Getting the Word
Out with Text**

Chapter 4: Creating Graphic Symbols for Fun and Profit

*W*hen you need to create a Flash project with lots of graphics that are similar, you don't have to reinvent the wheel. When you create a graphic symbol, it appears in the document library. You can use the symbol whenever and wherever you need, even in another document. You can even duplicate an existing symbol and use it as the basis for a new symbol. (Talk about recycling resources! We wonder whether using a symbol repeatedly reduces Flash's carbon footprint on the planet and can be considered "going green.") If the judicious use of symbols requires less time behind the computer, which enables a Flash designer to turn off her computer sooner, thereby conserving energy, we guess that symbols *can* be considered going green. In the spirit of conserving resources, we'll cut to the chase and show you how to use symbols in your own Flash project.

Understanding Symbols and Instances

When you create a graphic symbol in a Flash document, it's a stand-alone object, kind of like a stand-up comic. It can entertain, but if you need more than one graphic, you have to create another. When you create a symbol, it's like creating a DVD of a stand-up comic. You can play it in other places, and it looks and sounds just like the original. When you create a symbol, it resides in the document library. You can create an instance of the symbol at any time by dragging it from the document library to the Stage. When the Flash Player sees an instance of a symbol in a Flash movie, the player uses the information from the document library to reconstruct the symbol, which means a smaller file size — and less work for you.

Creating Symbols

Symbols are the lifeblood of any Flash document. As we mention elsewhere, you can create a symbol and then use instances of it as needed. In the following sections, we explain the different symbol types and show you how to create a symbol from scratch or convert an object to a symbol. A symbol can be edited at any time. When you edit a symbol, all instances are affected. The carte blanche use of graphics increases file size. However, when you use instances of symbols in lieu of creating new graphics, you greatly reduce the file size.

Understanding symbol types

You can create three types of symbols in Flash: Movie Clip, Button, and Graphic. When you examine the symbol names, you may think that the movie clip is the only symbol that can be animated. You can animate a graphic and have an animated button too. Each symbol type has a unique icon in the document library. The following list explains the differences between the symbol types:

 ✔ **Movie Clip:** Can have multiple frames and be an animation. A Movie Clip symbol can also be a single object on a single frame. When you create an instance of a movie clip and give it a unique name, you can address the symbol instance with ActionScript and get it to do some cool stuff, such as change dimensions and move, for example. When you create an animation inside a movie clip, the parent Timeline doesn't need to have the same number of frames as the movie clip. An animation in a movie clip loops endlessly unless you address its Timeline with ActionScript.

 ✔ **Button:** An interactive critter that responds to mouse clicks. You can use ActionScript to determine what happens when a button is clicked. A Button symbol has four frames, which enables you to display different graphics when the user hovers the mouse over the button and clicks it. You can use a short animation in a button frame to create a unique button.

 ✔ **Graphic:** Can contain multiple graphics and be an animation. However, an instance of a Graphic symbol cannot be addressed with ActionScript. A Graphic symbol is locked to the main Timeline. If you create a graphical symbol with multiple frames, the main Timeline must have enough frames from the point where you add it to the Timeline to play the entire animation.

Converting an object to a symbol

If you create a graphic on the Stage and decide that you need to use it repeatedly, you can convert the object into a symbol. Then you can choose the type of symbol that the object becomes and do much more. To convert an object to a symbol, follow these steps:

1. **Select the object you want to convert to a symbol.**

2. **Choose Modify⇨Convert to Symbol.**

   The Convert to Symbol dialog box appears (see Figure 4-1).

Figure 4-1: Converting an object to a symbol.

3. **Enter a name for the symbol.**

   Use a logical name with no spaces or special characters. Even though the document library provides methods for organizing a project, we add prefixes to our symbols that further identify their use. For example, our graphic symbols might be GCar01; our movie clip, McCar01; and our button, Btn01.

4. **Choose the symbol type from the Type drop-down menu.**

   Your choices are Movie Clip, Button, or Graphic. If you fast-forwarded to this part of the chapter, and don't know about symbol types, rewind to the section "Understanding symbol types."

5. **Choose the registration point.**

   We prefer to use the upper-left registration point, which makes it easy to align objects relative to the edge of the Stage, which is x=0, y=0.

6. **Click Advanced.**

   This step expands the dialog box to show the advanced options for converting an object to a symbol (see Figure 4-2). The options differ for a button and movie clip. If you're converting an object to a graphical symbol, you have no advanced options.

7. **If you're converting a graphic into a movie clip that will have instances to scale, click the Enable Guides for 9-slice Scaling option.**

   When you choose this option, you have more control when you scale instances of a symbol. A movie clip with 9-slice scaling has a visual overlay with nine sections. When you scale the instance, each section is sized individually, without scaling the corners. This option maintains the visual integrity of movie clip instances when scaled.

Book II
Chapter 4

Creating Graphic
Symbols for Fun and
Profit

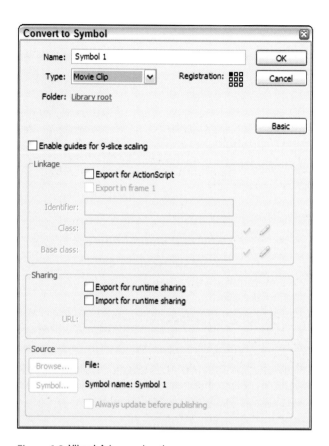

Figure 4-2: Yikes! Advanced options.

8. **If applicable, select the Export for ActionScript check box.**

   This step reveals the Identifier, Class, and Base Class fields. It also gives you the option to export the symbol in the first frame, which means that it's accessible to ActionScript during the course of your Flash project. For more information on the ActionScript identifiers, classes, and base classes, see Book IV.

9. **If applicable, select the Export for Runtime Sharing check box.**

   This step allows you to treat the symbol as a class and to instantiate instances of it from ActionScript. For more information on importing and exporting for runtime sharing, see Book IV.

10. Click OK.

The object is converted to a symbol and added to the document library.

Creating a new symbol

If you plan out your project ahead of time (you did plan out your project, didn't you?), you know exactly how many symbols you need for your project. Whenever possible, we like to take care of the grunt work before creating instances of symbols on the Stage, adding frames to the Timeline, writing ActionScript code, and performing other delightful tasks. To create a new symbol, follow these steps:

1. **Choose Insert⇨New Symbol.**

   If you like keyboard shortcuts, press Ctrl+F8 (Windows) or ⌘+F8 (Mac). Both methods open the Create New Symbol dialog box (see Figure 4-3).

Figure 4-3: It's time to get symbolic and create a new symbol.

2. **Enter a name for the symbol.**

   Use a logical name with no spaces or special characters. Even though the document library provides methods for organizing a project, we add prefixes to our symbols that further identify their use. For example, our graphical symbols might be GCar01; our movie clips, McCar01; and our buttons, Btn01.

3. **Choose a symbol type from the Type drop-down menu.**

   Your choices are Button, Graphic, or Movie Clip. If you don't know a graphic from a movie clip, check out the section "Understanding Symbol Types," at the beginning of this chapter.

4. **Accept the default folder (the Library root) or click the default folder name to open the Move To dialog box (see Figure 4-4).**

Figure 4-4: Moving the new symbol to a different folder.

We're strong believers in being organized. If your project has lots of Button, Movie Clip, and Graphic symbols, we recommend storing them in separate folders. Notice in Figure 4-4 that we already created a folder for each symbol type. Step 5 assumes that you think our advice is sage, Rosemary, and segregates your symbols in separate folders.

5. **Select the folder in which to store the symbol, or create a new folder.**

   To create a new folder, enter the name in the New Folder text field. Alternatively, click the Existing Folder radio button, and then select a folder. If you like the idea of creating your folders ahead of time, like we did, check out the section "Creating library folders," later in this chapter.

6. **Click Advanced.**

   The dialog box expands to show the Advanced options for creating a symbol (see Figure 4-5). The options differ for a button and movie clip. If you're converting an object to a graphical symbol, you have no advanced options.

7. **If you're converting a graphic into a movie clip that will have instances to scale, click the Enable Guides for 9-Slice Scaling option.**

   When you choose this option, you have more control when you scale instances of a symbol. A movie clip with 9-slice scaling has a visual overlay with nine sections. When you scale the instance, each section is sized individually, without scaling the corners. This option maintains the visual integrity of movie clip instances when scaled.

8. **If applicable, select the Export for ActionScript check box.**

   This step reveals the Identifier, Class, and Base Class fields. It also gives you the option to export the symbol in the first frame, which means that it's accessible to ActionScript during the course of your Flash project. For more information on the ActionScript identifiers, classes, and base classes, see Book IV.

9. **If applicable, select the Export for Runtime Sharing check box.**

   This step lets you treat the symbol as a class and instantiate instances of it from ActionScript. For more information on importing and exporting for runtime sharing, see Book IV.

10. **Click OK.**

    If you've never used Flash, don't freak out — you haven't crashed the program. A new window opens when you create a symbol from scratch.

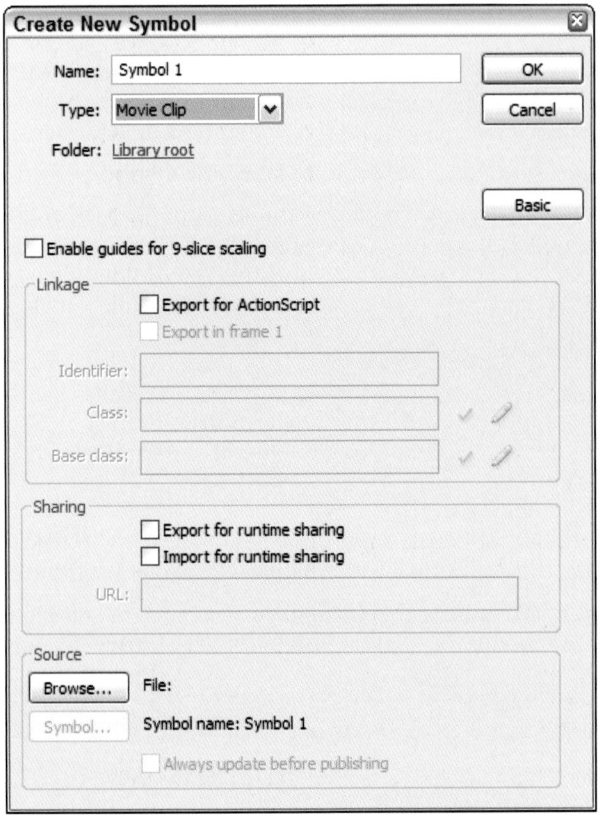

Figure 4-5: Advanced symbols go to the head of the class.

11. **Use the Flash tools to create the symbol.**

    You can also use images you imported into the document library as part of your symbol. You can also use multiple layers when creating a symbol. Figure 4-6 shows a button symbol being constructed.

12. **When you finish creating the symbol, click the Back button or the current scene button.**

    The symbol is added to the document library.

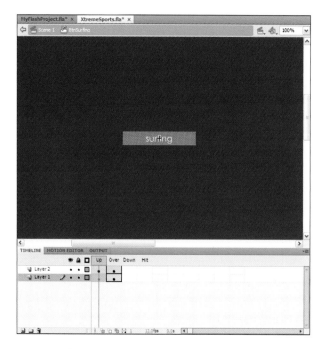

Figure 4-6: Build me a button, my lovely.

Spraying symbols

The Spray Brush tool lets you spray graffiti-like strokes of color wherever you want, as outlined in Chapter 1 of this minibook. But you can also load the Spray Brush tool with a symbol. This sprays instances of the symbol, which reduces the document file size. For example, if you need a sky full of stars, use the Polystar tool to create a star and then use the Spray Brush tool to sprinkle the sky full of stars. To spray symbols, follow these steps:

1. **Select the Spray Brush tool.**

2. **In the Symbol section of the Property inspector, click the Edit button.**

   The Swap Symbol dialog box appears (see Figure 4-7).

3. **Select the symbol you want to load in the Spray Brush tool and click OK.**

   The tool is primed and ready for you to set the rest of the parameters in the Property inspector.

4. **Set parameters in the Symbol section of the Property inspector (see Figure 4-8).**

   You can scale the size of the symbol by changing the Width and Height values. We advise you to change both parameters to the same value; otherwise, the tool sprays a distorted variation of your lovely (or not so lovely, depending on your artistic capabilities) symbol. You can add some variety to the sprayed symbol by choosing one or more of the following options: Random Scaling, Rotate Symbol, and Random Rotation.

5. **Change the parameters in the Brush section.**

   You can change the brush width and height as well as the angle of rotation.

6. **Click on the Stage where you want to spray the symbol.**

   Figure 4-9 shows a starry, starry night, courtesy of the Spray Brush tool and a symbol created with the Polystar tool.

Figure 4-7: Swapping symbols to load the Spray Brush tool.

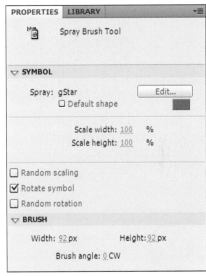

Figure 4-8: The Spray Brush tool will soon be locked and loaded.

Figure 4-9: Are the stars out tonight?

Editing Symbols

Symbols are a wonderful thing, especially when you get a document library filled with them. Then when your client comes up with a "brainstorm" when you're 90 percent done with the project, you wince and then smile as you remember that you did most of your work with symbols. When you edit a symbol, all instances of the symbol are updated. What could be simpler?

Editing symbols in place

When you need to edit a symbol and it's imperative that you know what effect your edits will have on the rest of your project, you can edit a symbol in place. In reality, you're editing a symbol instance, but the changes are applied to every symbol instance in the document. To edit a symbol in place, follow these steps:

1. **Select the Selection tool.**

2. **Right-click (Windows) or Control+click (Mac). Select the symbol you want to edit.**

   A context menu appears.

3. **Choose Edit in Place.**

   The rest of the objects on the current frame are dimmed. The symbol name is listed to the right of the scene (see Figure 4-10).

   You can also edit a symbol in place by double-clicking any instance of it on the Stage.

Figure 4-10: You can edit a symbol in place.

4. **Perform any edits you want.**

   You can use any tool to change the symbol. In addition, you can add objects to the symbol.

5. **Click the Back button or the current scene button.**

   Alternatively, you can choose Edit⇨Edit Document. Your edits are applied to the symbol and all instances thereof.

Using symbol-editing mode

When you edit a document in symbol-editing mode, you edit it separately from the main Timeline. This action is similar to creating a new symbol. To edit a symbol in symbol-editing mode, follow these steps:

1. **Do one of the following to invoke symbol-editing mode:**

   • Double-click the symbol's icon in the document library.

   • Right-click (Windows) or Control+click (Mac) a symbol instance on the Stage and choose Edit from the context menu.

   • Select an instance of the symbol on the Stage and choose Edit⇨Edit Symbols.

   • Select the symbol in the document library and choose Edit from the context menu, or choose Edit from the Library panel Options menu.

2. **Apply any edits you want to the symbol.**

   You can add graphics to the symbol or nest graphics or other symbols within the symbol, for example.

3. **To leave symbol-editing mode, click the Back button or current scene button.**

   Alternatively, you can choose Edit⇨Edit Document. Your edits are applied to the symbol and all instances thereof.

Editing symbols in another window

Another option for editing a symbol is to edit it in another window. When you edit the symbol in another window, you have access to the symbol and the main Timeline. To edit a symbol in another window, follow these steps:

1. **Select an instance of the symbol on the Stage, right-click (Windows) or Control+click (Mac) and then choose Edit in New Window.**

2. **Perform any edits you want on the symbol.**

3. **Click the Close button to return to the main Timeline and apply your edits to all instances of the symbol.**

Swapping symbols

When a client changes his mind when a project is almost complete, you can use *another* method to thwart the fork he puts in your road. Suppose that your client represents an insurance company whose symbol is a duck and you created an animation designed to "quack up" the viewer. Then your client switches insurance companies, and now the mascot is an English bulldog. Don't fret — just create a new symbol with a dancing bulldog (with or without stiff upper lip) and swap the symbol. To swap a symbol, follow these steps:

1. **Select the symbol instance on the Stage.**

   To open the Swap Symbol dialog box (see Figure 4-11), do one of the following:

   - Right-click (Windows) or Control+click (Mac) and choose Swap Symbol from the context menu.

   - In the Property Inspector, click Swap.

2. **Select a symbol and click OK.**

   Presto-chango. The symbol is swapped.

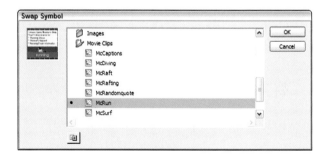

Figure 4-11: Swapping one from Column A with one from Column B.

Modifying symbol instance properties

You edit a symbol to modify every instance of it in a Flash project. However, you can also modify the properties of a symbol instance. You can change the dimensions of a symbol instance, tint it, and change its brightness or Alpha (transparency) value. To modify the properties of a symbol instance, follow these steps:

1. **Select the symbol instance on the Stage.**

2. **Choose Window⇨Properties.**

   The Property inspector opens.

3. **Change the position and size of the symbol instance by entering values in the applicable fields in the Position and Size section of the Property inspector.**

4. **To change the appearance of the symbol instance, choose an option from the Style drop-down menu in the Color Effect section. Your options are described in this list:**

   - *Brightness:* Displays a slider that enables you to change the brightness of a symbol. Drag the slider to the right to make the symbol instance brighter, or to the left to make it darker.

   - *Tint:* Displays four sliders (see Figure 4-12). Drag the sliders until the object becomes the color you want, and then drag the Tint slider to specify the amount of tint to be applied to the object. The Red, Green, and Blue sliders enable you to precisely "dial in" the color by using the RGB color model. (See Chapter 2 of this minibook.)

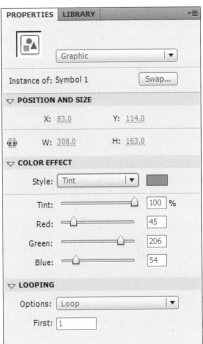

Figure 4-12: Tinting a symbol instance.

- *Advanced:* Displays eight values (see Figure 4-13). You can use the values on the left to reduce the transparency or color in the symbol instance by a specific percentage from –100 to 100, and use the values on the right to modify the red, green, and blue values of the symbol instance from –255 to 255.

- *Alpha:* Displays a slider you can use to change the transparency of the object. Values less than 100 percent render the symbol instance partially opaque.

5. **Use the Free Transform tool to skew, scale, rotate, or move the symbol instance.**

   As its name implies, you use this tool to freely transform the object. For more information about the Free Transform tool, see Chapter 1 of this minibook.

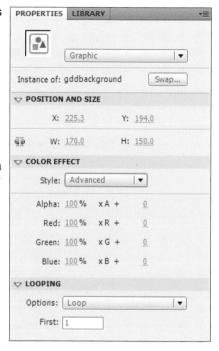

Figure 4-13: And now, the Advanced Color Effect.

Using the Document Library

When you create a symbol or import an image clip or a video or sound clip, it ends up in the document library. If you create complex Flash projects, you can end up with a lot of items in your document library. The document library takes up a relatively small spot in the Flash workspace; therefore, a document library with lots of items ends up looking cluttered. But you can whip the document library of any Flash project into shape — without resorting to a professional organizer — by reading the following sections.

Creating library folders

When you create a new Flash document, you start with an empty document library, which you can quickly fill to the brim by creating symbols and importing media, for example. When you create a symbol, you can create a folder at the same time. When you import external media, it's placed in the root folder of the document library. You can quickly alleviate clutter by creating a separate folder for each type of object that you plan to use in your Flash project. To create a folder in your document library, follow these steps:

1. **Choose Window⇨Library.**

   The document library appears (see Figure 4-14) without that musty old book smell. (This document library isn't an example of the way we work. We create folders for each type of object in our Flash projects.)

2. **Click the New Folder icon at the bottom of the document library.**

   A folder icon appears at the bottom of the document library, with the default name Untitled Folder 1. The folder name is highlighted, which indicates that you can rename it. We strongly advise you to never accept default names.

3. **Enter a new name for the folder.**

   The logical choice is a name that indicates what you're storing in the folder. For example, Movie Clips is a logical name for a folder that you stuff full of movie clips.

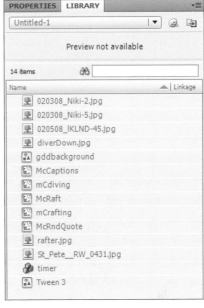

Figure 4-14: A document library in need of some TLC.

4. **Select the items you want to store in the folder, and then drop them on top of the folder.**

   The selected items are no longer visible, but the arrow to the left of the folder indicates that the folder can be expanded to reveal the contents within.

5. **Continue creating new folders as needed and populate them with the applicable objects.**

   We create a folder for each object type that we intend to use in a project. Working in this manner keeps us organized from the get-go. Figure 4-15 shows our squeaky-clean document library with a folder for everything, and everything in its folder. One folder has been expanded to reveal its contents.

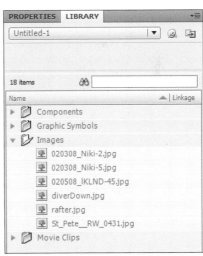

Figure 4-15: A neat and tidy document library.

Duplicating symbols

When you need to create a new symbol, there's no need to reinvent the wheel. For example, if you're creating a navigation bar with buttons that use identical graphics with the exception of the button name, you can save a lot of time by duplicating a symbol, and then editing it. To duplicate a symbol, follow these steps:

1. **Open the document library and then select the symbol you want to duplicate.**

2. **Right-click (Windows) or Control+click (Mac) and choose Duplicate from the context menu.**

   The Duplicate Symbol dialog box appears, as shown in Figure 4-16.

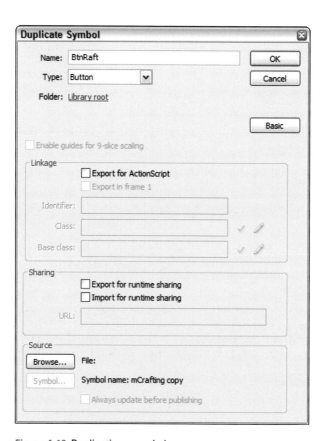

Figure 4-16: Duplicating a symbol.

3. **Enter a name for the duplicate symbol.**

   Give the symbol a meaningful name.

   If you're exporting the duplicate symbol for ActionScript, click the Advanced button. The options are the same as the Create New Symbol dialog box, which we cover in the section "Creating a new symbol," earlier in this chapter.

Understanding that default names are not your friends

As we mention earlier in this chapter, in the section "Creating a new symbol," you should never, never, never (we apologize for being redundant, but this advice is important) use the default name that Flash assigns for a symbol. The default names don't make a lot of sense, especially if you're using ActionScript. The same rule applies for folders you create in the document library or the media you import into the document library. If you're using someone else's assets (in case you don't have your own assets covered) that have less-than-desirable names, you can easily rename them in the document library. Follow these steps:

1. **Open the document library and double-click the item you want to rename.**

   The current name of the item is highlighted, indicating that you can enter a new name.

2. **Enter a new name for the item and then click Enter or Return.**

   The object has a new moniker.

Keeping the document library neat and tidy: The Felix Unger factor

Sometimes you err on the side of caution and create more items than you need for a project. If you publish a Flash project with more items in the Library than you need, you increase its file size. Therefore, it's in your best interest to keep the document library fastidiously clean. Follow these steps:

1. **Choose Window⇨Library.**

   The document library appears.

2. Click a symbol to preview it.

The preview appears at the top of the Library panel. If the symbol is a movie clip, a Play button appears next to it (see Figure 4-17).

3. Press Delete to remove a selected symbol from the document library.

Alternatively, you can click the Delete button. It looks like a trash can at the bottom of the Library panel. Either method deletes the symbol from the document library and removes all instances of it from the document. Flash doesn't warn you before you delete a symbol. Make sure that you don't need the symbol before deleting it.

4. To see all unused symbols in the document, choose Select Unused Items from the Library panel Options menu.

All unused items are highlighted. You can now delete them by clicking the Delete button at the bottom of the Library panel.

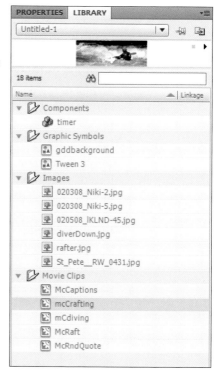

Figure 4-17: This library's a mess. Call in the cleaning crew.

 The document library has other tricks up its sleeve. Click the Library panel Options icon to reveal the Library panel Options menu, from which you can create new symbols; rename, delete, or duplicate selected symbols; move a selected symbol to another folder; edit, play, or update a symbol; or display symbol properties, for example.

Importing symbols from another Flash document

If you've already spent a lot of time creating symbols for a Flash project and you create a new Flash project that can use the same or similar symbols, you have no need to re-create them. Simply grab the symbols from the other Flash project and drag them into the current document library. Here's how to do it:

1. **Choose Window➪Library.**

   The document library appears (see Figure 4-18).

2. **Click the New Library Panel icon.**

   A copy of the document library appears on the Stage.

3. **In the new library panel, click the Pin Current Library icon.**

   This step keeps the duplicate library open, even when you open another document.

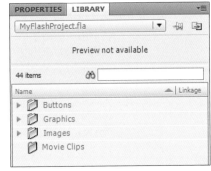

Figure 4-18: You can pin a document library.

4. **Open the document that contains the symbols you want to use in the current document.**

   The document opens and is designated by another tab. The document library from your other project is on the Stage.

5. **Select a symbol from the library of the document you just opened, and drag the symbol into the document library from your other project.**

   When you drag the symbol into the other document library, a plus sign appears, indicating that the symbol will be added to the pinned document library (see Figure 4-19).

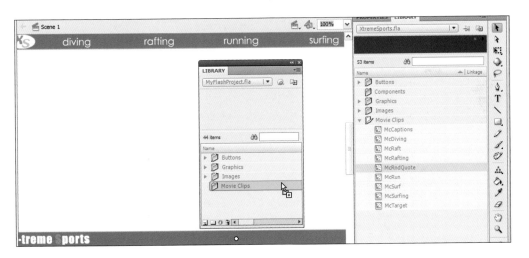

Figure 4-19: Robbing from Peter to pay Paul.

6. **Release the mouse button.**

   The symbol is added to the document library.

7. **Continue dragging symbols between libraries.**

   Work smarter, not harder. It's a creed we authors live by.

Chapter 5: Organizing Your Work

In This Chapter

- ✔ **Understanding layers**
- ✔ **Adding layers to a document**
- ✔ **Using layer folders**
- ✔ **Viewing rulers and grids**

*B*eing organized is a good thing, especially when you're dealing with a document full of symbols, movie clips, and buttons, not to mention ActionScript. When you have this much going on in a document, trying to stuff it all on one layer is like storing your clothes in a dresser with no drawers. (You can't find nothing, honey.) In the last chapter — you did read it, didn't you? — we showed you how to organize your symbols in the document library. In this chapter, we get down to brass tacks and show you how to organize the stuff on Stage.

Organizing a Project with Layers

When you create a new document, you have one layer with which to work. No, the Flash guys and gals weren't being stingy when they designed the program; they just wanted to give you options. The option to create a layer whenever you need to gives you a tremendous amount of flexibility. You can think of layers as a place to put your Flash stuff. But if you have lots of Flash stuff on lots of Flash layers, you have a hard time finding your stuff. When that happens, you create a layer folder that neatly collapses to a single icon. Figure 5-1 shows a Flash document with a lot of stuff neatly segregated on layers, and neatly packed away in layer folders. (This paragraph was inspired by the late George Carlin, who taught us everything we needed to know about stuff.)

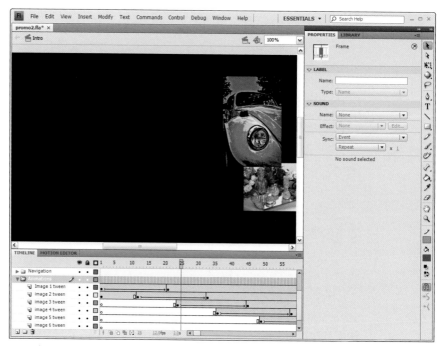

Figure 5-1: Layers and layer folders are places to put your Flash stuff.

It's useful to think of layers as clear sheets of plastic. The objects on an upper layer eclipse the objects directly below them on underlying layers. When you work with objects on one layer, it doesn't affect the objects on the underlying layers. When you have a lot of objects on many layers, getting a good grasp on what you're doing is difficult, especially when you're trying to edit objects on the bottommost of five layers. When that happens, you can temporarily hide a layer. And, when the magic moment arrives and you have everything on a layer just the way you want it, you can lock it. Don't worry about having to locate a key — you unlock a layer by clicking an icon. In upcoming sections, we show you how to organize your work with layers.

Creating a new layer

You know when you need to create a layer — when the Stage looks like a dressing room for a troupe of ballet dancers with shoes scattered everywhere, topped with tutus and boas. You get the picture. Layers don't make a crowded Stage look less cluttered, but they make it easier for you to find objects and edit them. To create a new layer, follow these steps:

1. **Select the layer below the spot where you want the new layer to appear.**

   When you have only one layer, it's a no-brainer. But when you have multiple layers, the new layer you create is directly above the selected layer.

2. **To create the layer, do one of the following:**

   - Right-click (Windows) or Control+click (Macintosh) and choose Insert Layer from the context menu.

   - Click the New Layer icon at the bottom of the Timeline panel.

3. **Accept the default layer name, or double-click it and enter a new layer name.**

   Unless you're dealing with a two- or three-layer document, we strongly advise you to give your layers meaningful names.

Creating layer folders

When a Flash project has a heaping helping of layers, you have somewhat of a logistical nightmare: You use the scrollbar incessantly to move from one layer to the next. Fortunately, the Flash designers added a layer folder to the application. A *layer folder* can be filled with layers and then collapsed to a single icon on the Timeline. How convenient. Of course, you have to expand the layer folder again to edit the Timelines. But that's a small price to pay for the convenience of not having to slog through layer after layer after layer. To create a layer folder, follow these steps:

1. **Open the Timeline panel.**

   You can open the Timeline panel by clicking its title or choosing Window➪Timeline.

2. **Select the layer below the spot where you want the layer folder to appear.**

   If you have an extremely busy Timeline, the obvious place to create the layer folder is just above the last object in the stack that you want to add to the layer folder.

3. **Click the Layer Folder icon.**

   A layer folder is born.

4. **Double-click the default folder name.**

   The text is highlighted, indicating that you can enter a new title name.

   We strongly advise you to give everything in the project a unique name.

5. **Enter a new name for the folder.**

   Create a name that reflects the folder contents.

6. **Drag and drop some layers into the folder.**

   Make sure that you stack the layers in the same order that they previously appeared on the Timeline.

7. **Collapse the layer folder.**

   Click the downward-pointing arrow to the left of the folder's name to collapse the folder. Click it again to expand the folder. Figure 5-2 shows a Timeline that has been organized with named layers and layer folders.

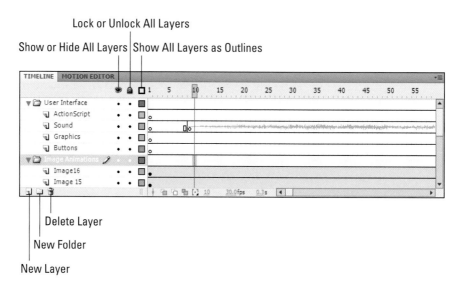

Figure 5-2: A group of layers whipped into shape by a fastidious Flash designer.

Editing layers

After you organize your work with layers and layer folders, you can edit them as needed. In this section, we show you everything you need to know about editing objects on layers and editing layers.

Hiding one or more layers is beneficial when you have a lot of objects on the Stage stacked in different layers. When you have this much going on, it can be hard to select an individual object on a layer. To select, reveal, or hide a layer:

✔ **To select a layer for editing:** Click the layer name. This action makes the layer the active layer (as indicated by the pencil icon), which enables you to edit objects on only that layer.

✔ **To hide a single layer:** Click the dot to the right of the layer's name and below the eyeball icon.

✔ **To hide all layers except the selected layer:** Right-click (Windows) or Control+click (Macintosh) and choose Hide Others from the context menu.

✔ **To hide all layers:** Click the eyeball icon.

✔ **To reveal hidden layers:** Right-click (Windows) or Control+click (Macintosh) and choose Show All from the context menus.

Locking one or more layers is beneficial when things are just the way you want them. When you lock a layer, it prevents you from inadvertently selecting an object that's in pixel-perfect position. To lock or unlock layers:

Book II
Chapter 5

Organizing Your Work

✔ **To lock a single layer:** Click the dot to the right of the layer's name and below the lock icon.

✔ **To lock all layers except the selected layer:** Right-click (Windows) or Control+click (Macintosh) and choose Lock Others from the context menu.

✔ **To lock all layers:** Click the lock icon.

✔ **To unlock a locked layer:** Click the lock icon to the right of the layer's name.

Displaying layer objects as outlines is another way to alleviate clutter and make it easier to see what's going on in a busy project. To display objects on layers as outlines, do one of the following:

✔ **To display objects on a single layer as outlines:** Click the Show Objects as Outlines icon to the right of the layer's name.

✔ **To display all layers as outlines:** Click the Show Layers as Outlines icon in the upper-left corner of the Timeline panel.

Editing layer properties

Everything in Flash has properties, even layers. You can edit layer properties to change the manner in which the layer is displayed on the Timeline, the layer type, or the layer name, for example. To edit layer properties, follow these steps:

1. **Select the layer whose properties you want to edit.**

2. **Right-click (Windows) or Control+click (Macintosh) and choose Properties from the context menu.**

   The Layer Properties dialog box appears (see Figure 5-3).

3. **Accept the current name for the layer or enter a new name.**

If you suddenly decide to get organized and the current name is the default name, we strongly suggest that you give the layer a meaningful name.

4. **Select the Show check box to toggle visibility of the layer.**

   If the layer is visible, the check box is selected.

5. **Select the Lock check box to lock or unlock the layer.**

   If the layer is unlocked, the check box isn't selected.

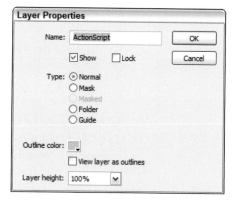

Figure 5-3: Layers have properties that make no sense to Realtors.

6. **Accept the current layer type or click a different radio button.**

   Unless you're a Flash veteran, the choices other than Normal and Folder may seem strange to you. Don't worry; we describe each layer type as needed in later chapters. Just remember how to change them and you're good to go.

7. **Accept the default layer outline color or click the swatch, which opens the Swatches panel and enables you to select a different color for the layer outline.**

   This color is the one that's used to designate objects when you choose to display the layer contents as outlines.

8. **Select the View Layer as Outlines check box to specify whether the layer objects are displayed as outlines.**

   When the check box is selected, layer objects are displayed as outlines.

9. **Choose an option from the Layer Height drop-down list.**

   The default layer height is 100 percent. You can increase the height to 200 or 300 percent. Increasing the layer height makes it easier to work with keyframes and frame spans.

10. **Click OK to apply the new properties to the layer.**

Being Precise with Rulers and Guides and the Grid

Flash has a powerful trio of features that are quite useful when you're creating a document. Using rulers and guides and the grid enables you to precisely place objects. In fact, you can choose options to have objects snap to the grid or guides when you move them. If you're a precise kind of person, read the following sections, where we show you how to be precise when working on a Flash project.

Using rulers

Rulers are displayed on the top and left sides of the Stage. The unit of measure for rulers is the same unit of measure as the document. When you move an object, lines appear on the applicable ruler to designate the width and height plus the x and y position of the object. To display rulers and modify the unit of measure, follow these steps:

✔ **To display or hide rulers,** choose View➪Rulers.

✔ **To change the rulers' unit of measure,** choose Modify➪Document and choose an option from the Ruler Units drop-down menu.

Creating guides

Guides are a wonderful thing unless you have a mouthy global positioning system (GPS) in your vehicle. When you work in Flash, you can create as many guides as you need to align the objects in your project. Guides are useful when you're creating a navigation menu and you want to align buttons with pinpoint accuracy. To create guides, follow these steps:

1. **Position the cursor over a ruler, and then click and drag a guide onto the Stage.**

   The current position of the guide is indicated by a line that's parallel to the ruler from which the guide is created. You also see the current position marked off on the opposite ruler.

2. **Release the mouse button when the guide is in the position you want.**

   The new guide is designated by a line that is the default guide color.

After adding one or more guides to a Flash document, you can do the following:

✔ **Move a guide:** Click it with the Selection tool and drag it to another position.

✔ **Make objects snap to guides:** Choose View➪Snapping➪Snap to Guides.

✔ **Lock guides in their current positions:** Choose View➪Guides➪Lock Guides.

✔ **Toggle visibility of guides:** Choose View➪Guides➪Show Guides.

✔ **Edit guides:** Choose View➪Guides➪Edit Guides. This command opens the Guides dialog box, which enables you to change the color of guides and determine whether guides are shown, whether objects can snap to them, and whether guides are locked. You can also choose a snap accuracy from a drop-down menu. Your snap accuracy choices are

   • *Must Be Close*

   • *Normal*

   • *Can Be Distant*

You can also remove all guides from the document by clicking Clear All.

✔ **Remove all guides from the document:** Choose View⇨Guides⇨Clear Guides.

Using the grid

Flash has a grid that's hidden by default. When you choose to view the grid, it looks like somebody put a piece of transparent graph paper over the Stage. We don't think the default grid is particularly useful because the grid spacing is so small (10x10 pixels is the default size of each grid square). However, with a little work, the grid can be extremely useful. To use the grid, follow these steps:

1. **Choose View⇨Grid⇨Show Grid.**

   The grid is displayed. However, the default size and color may not suit your project.

2. **To edit the grid, choose View⇨Grid⇨Edit Grid.**

   The Grid dialog box appears (see Figure 5-4).

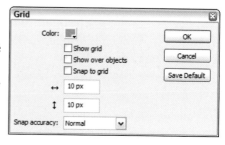

3. **Accept the default grid color, or click the swatch to specify a different color from the Swatches panel.**

   This step is useful when you're working on a document that's almost the same color as the grid. When this is the case, select a color that contrasts well with the background.

Figure 5-4: Edit the grid to suit your document and preferences.

4. **Click the Show Grid check box to toggle grid visibility.**

5. **Select the Show Over Objects check box to display the grid on top of the objects.**

   We're not crazy about this option especially with the default grid size, but try it — you might like it.

6. **Select the Snap to Grid check box.**

   When this option is selected, objects develop a magnetic attraction to grid intersections.

7. **Accept the default grid measurements or enter different values.**

   You can change the width independently of the height and vice versa. If you're creating a document with a lot of objects that have similar dimensions, you may want to change the dimensions of the grid to a common dimension for your most-often-used object. (You know — similar to navigation menu buttons.)

8. **Choose an option from the Snap Accuracy drop-down menu.**

   This option determines how close an object must be to the grid before it can be snapped to a grid intersection. Your snap accuracy choices are

   • *Must Be Close*

   • *Normal*

   • *Can Be Distant*

9. **Click OK.**

   The changes are applied to the grid. Figure 5-5 shows a grid that has been modified to suit a specific document.

If you use the grid frequently on similar documents, modify the grid as outlined in this section and then click Save Default. You have to close Flash and then relaunch the application for the new default settings to take effect.

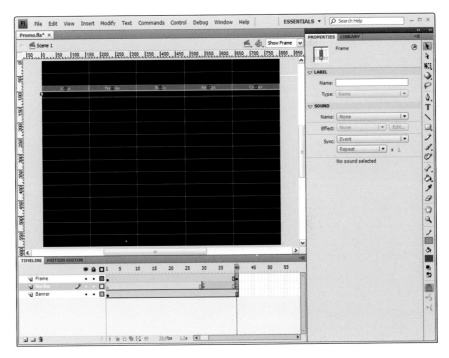

Figure 5-5: Flash grids are better than gridlock.

Chapter 6: Working with Images (Or, Bumpin' with Bitmaps)

In This Chapter

✔ Understanding compatible file formats

✔ Getting images ready for Flash

✔ Working with image sequences

✔ Tracing bitmaps

✔ Editing images

✔ Creating a bitmap fill

✔ Swapping images

Images can make or break a Flash project. The size and quality of your images determine the file size and quality of the resulting Flash movie. If you or your client starts out with crisp images, you get good results. On the other hand, if your client presents you with a bunch of images that have already been severely compressed, you have no way to create a decent-looking Flash movie. In this chapter, we're letting Doug take the lead. He has published books on digital photography and knows Photoshop and Fireworks inside and out. In this chapter, Doug shows you how to create Flash movies with great-looking images.

Knowing Your File Formats

Flash supports the popular image file formats. Unfortunately, if you don't deal with images regularly, choosing the right image format for a Flash project can be daunting. The following list describes some characteristics about the image file formats supported by Flash.

✔ **PNG File:** The PNG (PNG) file format is the native Fireworks file format. In Fireworks, the format supports layers and slices and all the other goodies you need in order to create image documents for the Web. Other applications can also export PNG files. The PNG format supports 8-, 16-, 24-, and 32-bit depth. If you're using this file format in a Flash document, the best bet is a 24-bit (true color) PNG file. You can, however, use an 8-bit PNG file if you're working with an image, such as a logo, that has large areas of solid color.

✔ **Photoshop:** The Photoshop image format (PSD) supports layers, multiple color models, adjustment layers, and much more. When you import a Photoshop image, you have the option to import each layer. Certain Photoshop layers aren't supported by Flash and cannot be imported.

✔ **Bitmap:** The Bitmap image format (BMP) can be exported from many image editing applications. The term *bitmap* is often confused with the generic reference to all photorealistic images as bitmaps. One drawback to bitmap images is that the file size is quite large as a result of an image-editing application applying no compression when saving images to this file format. Some image editing applications use Zip lossless compression when saving in this file format, which results in a smaller file size.

✔ **GIF Image:** The GIF image format (GIF) is widely used for Web page images. This format is best suited to images with large areas of solid color. It also works well for images that have lots of text. As a rule, you're better off creating your text in Flash because you can edit Flash text at any time. The only time you should consider using a GIF file in a Flash project is when you're working with a logo, which generally has large areas of solid color.

✔ **JPEG Image:** The widely used JPEG image format (JPG) uses full (24-bit) color. The JPEG format is known as a *lossy* format because data is lost when images are compressed. The amount of data that's lost depends on the amount of compression you apply to the image when saving it. In Photoshop and many other image editing applications, you have the option of setting the quality of the image on export. In Photoshop, image quality ranges from 0 (high compression, poor image quality, and small file size) to 12 (little or no compression, high image quality, and large file size). Some image editing applications use a range from 0 to 100; the latter yields the best image quality and the largest file size.

✔ **Macintosh PCT Image:** The Macintosh PCT Image format (PCT) was originally a Macintosh-only image format. Many image editing applications, including image editing programs in the Windows operating system, can export in the PCT format. The image format is full (24-bit) color.

✔ **MacPaint Image:** The MacPaint Image format (PNTG) is a Macintosh format. Images using this file format are similar to images created with the Windows Paint program and are not compressed.

✔ **TGA Image:** The TGA Image file format (TGA) can be created by most popular image editing programs. The resulting file doesn't support layers and isn't compressed.

✔ **TIFF Image:** The TIFF image format (TIF, TIFF) is widely used. TIFF images support layers, and the file format can be saved from most popular image editing applications. The format supports layers and can be compressed on export. Flash, however, cannot import TIFF files compressed using the Zip or JPEG compression options.

Preparing Images for Flash

If you read the previous section, you know that you can import most popular file formats into Flash. However, just because you can import an image into Flash doesn't mean that it's the right image for the job. Image editing applications refer to image size in document dimensions, which is a combination of the image size in pixels and the resolution of the image in pixels per inch. For example, an 8-x-10-inch image with a resolution of 300 pixels per inch (ppi) has dimensions of 2400 x 3000 pixels with a whopping file size of 20.6MB. The same image at 72 pixels per inch has dimensions of 720 x 576 pixels and a relatively svelte file size of 1.19MB. Using the right commands in a good image-editing application enables you to get an even smaller file size on the order of about 50K or smaller. For monitor viewing, a resolution of 72 pixels per inch is sufficient. If you've ever saved a properly optimized image from a Web site (shame on you!) and printed it, you noticed that the image is blocky. That's because the image doesn't have a resolution that's high enough for printing.

To give you an example of the impact that image size and resolution can have on a Flash project, consider the following. The 8-x-10-inch image noted in the previous section was exported from Photoshop with no compression using the TIFF format and then imported into Flash. The image size was huge — much larger than needed for the document. The image was cut down to size using the Transform command. However, the original image was in the document library; the same bloated 20.6MB file that was imported to Flash. Flash applies image compression when exporting a file. The document was published using the default compression settings, resulting in a file size of 410K; it's relatively small compared to the size of the original image, but imagine what the file size would be if you added other elements, such as graphic objects, text, or animation.

The same image was exported from Photoshop in the JPEG format with a Quality setting of 10 after being resampled to dimensions of 400 x 320 pixels with a resolution of 72 ppi. The image that was imported into Flash was the proper size. The file when published was 58K, considerably smaller than the first published file. In Photoshop, the original image was resampled to the same dimensions and resolution as the previous example, and exported with a Quality setting of 7. The visual difference between the two images was negligible. The image with a quality setting of 7 was imported into Flash. The published file size was 28K — a considerable savings.

As you can see from the previous example, preparing images ahead of time is beneficial when you start to work with the images in Flash. Here are some recommendations you should consider when optimizing images for a Flash project:

✔ Resample the image to pixel dimensions that aren't wider than or taller than your Flash document.

✔ Change the image resolution to 72 ppi.

✔ If you're creating lots of Flash movies with images, consider investing in an application such as Fireworks, which gives you the capability of comparing, side by side, the original image (2-Up, if you're being technical) and the image with compression applied (see Figure 6-1).

✔ If you're working in an application like Photoshop and using the Adobe RGB color profile or working with images from a digital camera that uses the Adobe RGB color profile, convert the color profile to sRGB IEC61966-2.1. If you don't, the image doesn't display properly.

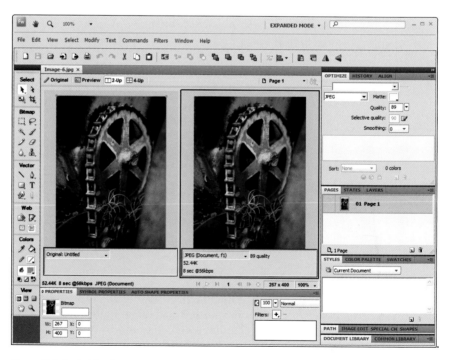

Figure 6-1: Optimizing images in Fireworks CS4.

✔ Export the image using the JPEG format with Medium quality. However, if you export at a higher quality, you can optimize the image in Flash.

✔ If you're creating images for a Flash file show, give the images sequential names, such as img_01, img_02, and so on. You see why in the next section.

Importing Image Sequences

Creating Flash slide shows is fairly easy: Stack some images on the Timeline, add a few frames to determine how long each image is displayed, add a little ActionScript on the back end to loop the show, and you have something you can plug into an HTML page or use as part of a Flash project. The trick is to rename the images before you import them into Flash. Here's how:

1. **Rename the images that will be in your image sequence.**

   Give the images sequential names, such as img_01, img_02, and so on.

2. **In Flash, choose File➪Import➪Import to Stage.**

   The Import dialog box appears.

3. **Select the first image of your image sequence and click Open.**

   Logic may tell you to select them all. Don't. It creates more work if you do. If you select the first image, you see the dialog box shown in Figure 6-2.

Figure 6-2: Yes, you can easily import an image sequence.

4. **Click Yes.**

   Flash imports each image in the sequence and creates a keyframe for each one on the Timeline (see Figure 6-3). Notice that the image you can see isn't aligned properly. If you're a Flash veteran, you may know how to correct it. If you don't, or if you've never worked with frames, this is your indoctrination by fire.

5. **Click the Edit Multiple Frames icon.**

   Three frames are selected.

Figure 6-3: Imported and stacked on the Stage.

6. **Drag the first handle to the first keyframe.**

   Now all the frames created from importing the image sequence are selected for editing (see Figure 6-4).

7. **Select the Selection tool, and then drag to marquee-select all images.**

   The easiest way to select all images is to click and drag outside the perimeter of the Stage.

8. **Choose Window⇨Align.**

   The Align panel appears.

9. **Align the select images to the vertical and horizontal center of the Stage.**

   For more information on using the Align panel, see Book II, Chapter 1.

Now that you have all your ducks in a row — er, we mean *images aligned* — you can start adding frames between each keyframe, which determines how long each image is displayed. Detailed information on working with the Timeline is in Book III, Chapter 1.

Figure 6-4: Selected, not rejected.

Importing a Photoshop Document with Layers

If you've created a document in Photoshop with objects on different layers, you can preserve the layers when importing the document into Flash. After the document is in Flash, you can move the objects on the layers to suit your project. Imagine the power! You could create a collage in Photoshop with each image on a different layer. Import the document into Flash and apply a motion tween (see Book III, Chapter 2) to each image, and you have an animated collage. To import a Photoshop document with layers, follow these steps:

1. **Choose File⇨Import to Stage.**

   The Import dialog box appears.

2. **Select the Photoshop document (with the PSD extension) you want to import and then click Open.**

   The Import [Name of Document] to Stage dialog box appears, as shown in Figure 6-5. All layers supported in Flash are selected for import by default.

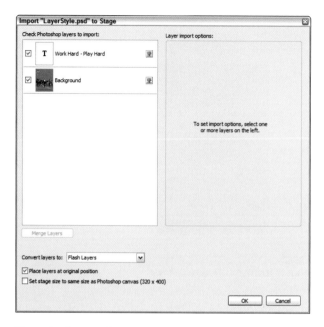

Figure 6-5: Import a Photoshop document to the Stage.

3. **To deselect a layer, select its check box.**

4. **Choose an option from the Convert Layers To drop-down menu.**

   Your choices are Flash Layers and Keyframes.

5. **Accept the default option, Place Layers at Original Position.**

   This option places the layers in the same position as they were in Photoshop. If you deselect this option, the layers are centered to the Stage.

6. **(Optional) Choose Set Stage Size to Same Size as Photoshop Canvas.**

   This option resizes the stage to the same size as the image.

7. **Click OK to import the document.**

Tracing Bitmaps

If you have an image you want to convert to vector objects, you can easily do so with the Trace Bitmap command. When you convert an image to vectors, it's no longer linked with the bitmap in the document library. To trace a bitmap, follow these steps:

1. **Select the image you want to trace.**

   Figure 6-6 shows a photo of a flower that will be traced.

Figure 6-6: You're going to trace a bitmap!

2. Choose Modify⇨Bitmap⇨Trace Bitmap.

The Trace Bitmap dialog box appears (see Figure 6-7).

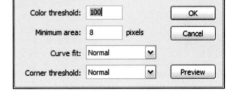

3. Accept the default Color Threshold value or enter a different value.

Figure 6-7: Tracing a bitmap.

Increase the value to decrease the number of colors in the traced bitmap, or decrease the value to increase the number of colors in the traced bitmap. If you choose a lower value, the traced bitmap looks more like the original image, but the file size is larger.

4. Accept the default Minimum Area value or enter a different value.

This value determines the number of surrounding pixels to consider when Flash determines which colors are assigned to which pixels. Smaller values prevent banding if your image has lots of colors.

5. Choose an option from the Curve Fit drop-down menu.

The Pixels option creates a traced bitmap that looks close to the original. These options work differently depending on the number of curves in your image and the complexity of the image. Our best advice is to experiment. If you don't like the result, undo the Trace Bitmap command and try different settings until you find something you like.

6. Choose an option from the Corner Threshold drop-down menu.

The Many Corners option creates a traced bitmap that looks more like the original bitmap. Again, we advise you to experiment.

7. **Click OK.**

Flash traces the bitmap. Alternatively, you can click the Preview button to get a sneak peek at what the traced bitmap looks like with the current settings. If you don't like what you see, change the settings and click Preview again. Figure 6-8 shows the traced bitmap that results from the following settings:

- Color Threshold = 30
- Minimum Area = 4
- Curve Fit = Pixels
- Corner Threshold = Many Corners

Figure 6-8: The traced bitmap.

8. **After you trace a bitmap, all the pixels are still selected. At this stage, we advise you to choose Modify⇨Group.**

If you don't, you run the risk of inadvertently selecting several pixels and moving them. When you create a group, it acts as one object.

Editing Images

After you import images into Flash, you can edit them. No, we're not talking about transforming them; we're talking about editing the actual image and changing its image properties. In the following sections, we show you how to edit images in an external image editor and how to change image properties.

Editing images in an external editor

After you import an image into Flash, you can edit the image in an external editor. What happens is that you make a round trip from Flash to the external editor (Fireworks CS4 by default) and back again. When you finish the round trip, the image is updated to reflect your edits. To edit an image in an external editor, follow these steps:

1. **In the document library, select the image you want to edit.**

2. **Right-click (Windows) or Control+click (Macintosh) and choose Edit with Fireworks from the context menu.**

   After you choose this command, Fireworks launches and the Find Source dialog box appears. This action gives you the option of choosing a Fireworks source file in the application's native PNG format or using the file you imported into Flash.

3. **Choose the source file option.**

   After choosing a source file option, the file opens in Fireworks. The Flash symbol and the message "Editing from Flash" appear above the image, which is a handy reference in case you become flummoxed and forget the application in which you're working.

4. **Use the Fireworks image editing tools to perform the edits you want.**

   Unfortunately, a tutorial on editing images in Fireworks is beyond the scope of this book.

5. **After editing the image, click Done.**

   The image is updated to reflect your edits in Fireworks.

If you don't own Fireworks, choose Edit With from the context menu and from the Select External Editor dialog box, locate the EXE file for your image-editing application.

If you edit an image in an external editor without taking a round trip from Flash, your edits aren't reflected in the image you imported into Flash. You can easily rectify this situation by selecting the image and then choosing Update from the context menu.

Editing image properties

You can affect the file size of a published document and the quality of the images by editing image properties. You can modify the compression method and the amount of compression applied to an image. To edit image properties, follow these steps:

1. **In the document library, select the image whose properties you want to update.**

2. **Right-click (Windows) or Control+click (Macintosh) and choose Properties from the context menu.**

   The Bitmap Properties dialog box appears (see Figure 6-9). From within this dialog box, you can modify the compression settings and test the next settings before committing to them. If the dialog box opens in Advanced mode, don't worry — be happy. Advanced mode is used when ActionScript is involved. ActionScript is covered in Book IV.

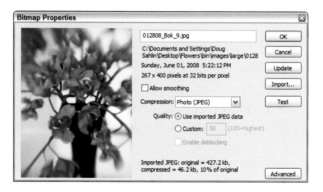

Figure 6-9: Editing image properties.

3. **Accept the default label (the image filename) or enter a different label.**

   Changing the label makes it easier to indentify what's in the image when you see the label in the document library. This is useful when you work with images from a digital camera with filenames such as img2641.jpg. If you change the label, the link to the original file is still intact.

4. **(Optional) Select the Allow Smoothing check box.**

   This option anti-aliases the edges of the bitmap. In our experience, you don't need this option if you're working with a sharp digital image. Smoothing makes the image look a little fuzzy around the edges.

5. **Select an option from the Compression drop-down menu.**

   Choose Photo (JPEG) for photorealistic images or choose Lossless (PNG/GIF) if the image contains large areas of solid color.

6. **Accept the default image quality, which is based on the original image, or click Custom.**

   If you choose Custom, a text box appears.

7. **If you choose Custom, enter a value.**

   The highest quality is 100, which matches the quality of the original image. Lower values result in smaller file sizes at the expense of image quality.

8. **Click Test.**

   This step tests your custom settings. The image in the dialog box is updated to reflect the current quality setting. If you're not happy with the results, enter a different value and test the settings again. When you change compression settings, text at the bottom of the dialog box notes the current compression setting, the original file size, and the com-pressed file size.

   If you decide to accept a low quality setting, you may notice that the image looks blocky. Click Enable Deblocking to smooth the blocky pixels.

9. **Click OK.**

   The new properties are applied to the image.

Creating a Bitmap Fill

If you read Chapter 2 of this minibook, you might recall that we show you how to specify a fill for an object. In case you didn't read the chapter (sniff — it's some of our best work), you have your solid fills and you have your gradient fills. Guess what? If you have images in your document library, you can create a bitmap fill. That's right: You can fill an object with an image by following these steps:

1. **Select the object you want to fill with a bitmap.**

2. **Choose Window⇨Color.**

   The Color panel appears.

3. **Choose Bitmap from the Type drop-down menu.**

   The dialog box refreshes, and the first bitmap in the document library replaces the previous fill. Thumbnails of all images in the document library appear at the bottom of the panel (see Figure 6-10).

4. **Move the cursor over the thumbnails in the bottom of the Color panel.**

   The cursor becomes an eyedropper.

Figure 6-10: Fill me with a bitmap.

5. **Click a bitmap.**

The object is filled with the bitmap.

If you don't see a bitmap worthy of filling your object, click Import to open the Import to Library dialog box. Select an image and click Open to import it to the library. The imported image appears at the bottom of the Color panel and can be selected to fill the object.

6. **After selecting a bitmap, close the Color panel.**

If the bitmap doesn't fill the image the way you want, use the Transform Gradient tool to resize the bitmap fill relative to the object, rotate it, or skew it, for example. For more information on the Transform Gradient tool, see Chapter 2 of this minibook. Figure 6-11 shows a rectangle that has been filled with a bitmap. The fill was transformed by using the Transform Gradient tool.

Figure 6-11: Oh, my — filled with a bitmap.

Click the Fill icon in the Tools panel to open the Swatches panel. At the bottom of the panel, next to the gradients, you see thumbnails of bitmaps you imported to the Stage or to the document library. Click the thumbnail and it becomes the current fill.

Swapping Bitmaps — It's Legal in All 50 States

After you import a bunch of bitmaps into the document library and start using them, you may find that a different image is needed. And then there's the scenario in which you have almost finished the project and your client suddenly decides that the picture that was sent to you looks horrible and wants a recent glamour shot used instead. When either event occurs, you can swap a bitmap quicker than this paragraph was typed. Here's how:

1. **With the Selection tool, select the bitmap you want to swap.**

2. **Right-click (Windows) or Control+click (Macintosh) and choose Swap Bitmap from the context menu.**

   Alternatively, you can choose Modify⇔Bitmap⇔Swap Bitmap. Either method opens the Swap Bitmap dialog box (see Figure 6-12). The Swap bitmap dialog box shows the selected bitmap and a list of all bitmaps in the document library.

3. **Click a filename.**

   Figure 6-12: Shhh — we're swapping a bitmap.

   The dialog box is updated to show the replacement bitmap. Unfortunately, the dialog box doesn't show thumbnails of the other bitmaps in the document library. If you didn't pick the right file, you can select a different one.

4. **Click OK to swap the bitmap.**

**Book II
Chapter 6**

Working with
Images (Or, Bumpin'
with Bitmaps)

Book III
Animating Graphics

The 5th Wave   By Rich Tennant

@RICHTENNANT

"I can't explain it, but everytime I animate someone swinging a golf club, a little divot of code comes up missing on the home page."

*F*lash has always provided the tools to create compelling animations. However, in previous versions of Flash, you had to jump through a couple of hoops before you could create even the simplest animation. Flash CS4 makes it easier than ever to animate graphics. You can make a shape go from Point A to Point B and back again, or you can morph one shape into another without having to do a bunch of work on the Timeline.

In Book III, we show you how to harness the power of Flash to create your own animations. We also show you how to master the Timeline, simulate 3D animation, and create character animations with the new Inverse Kinematics feature. So if you have the notion to get a move on, take this minibook for a spin.

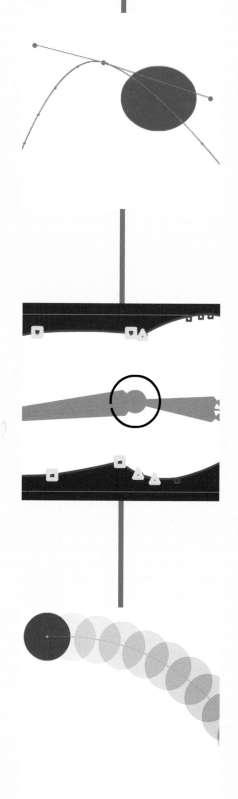

Chapter 1: Working with the Flash Timeline

In This Chapter

⮡ **Understanding the Timeline**

⮡ **Creating frames and keyframes**

⮡ **Editing frames**

*W*hen you create a Flash document, the default settings give a Timeline with one keyframe, which is great if you're creating something static. But Flash is all about motion and animation, so 1-frame Timelines just don't cut the mustard. The Timeline determines what happens during the course of your Flash movie. Keyframes on Timelines are places where things change, because if something didn't change, it wouldn't be Flash. When you create animations, you use the Timeline to designate where action starts and stops. In this chapter, we present a timely treatise on keyframes, frames, and Timelines. And the Timeline signifies that it's time to stop the intro and start writing.

Getting to Know the Timeline

Someone told us that it's all happening on the Timeline. We do believe it. We do believe it's true. In Flash, the Timeline is used to arrange content over time. You can put forks in the road, known as *keyframes,* where things happen. The document frame rate determines how the action on each frame occurs. The default document frame rate of 12 frames per second (fps) means that you need 12 frames for each second of action and that each frame is $\frac{1}{12}$ of a second. And, we computed all that without the aid of a calculator or an abacus.

Each layer has its own Timeline. Each layer's Timeline runs independently of other Timelines. Flash gives you the tools to create a sophisticated animation. When you work with the Timeline, you can navigate from frame to frame (also known as *scrubbing* the Timeline) by dragging the playhead across the Timeline. Figure 1-1 shows the Timeline of a Flash project.

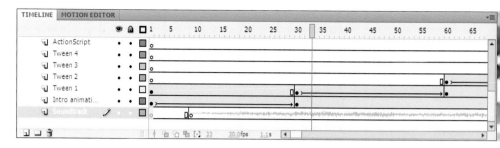

Figure 1-1: The Flash Timeline is a happening place.

Frames and Keyframes and Blank Keyframes

Flash has three kinds of frames: frames (no, we aren't being redundant), keyframes, and blank keyframes. A Flash Timeline is composed of frames, keyframes, blank keyframes, and frame spans. Figure 1-2 shows the anatomy of a Timeline.

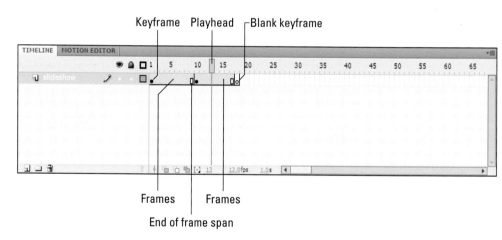

Figure 1-2: A Timeline waits for no man.

This list describes the elements on the Flash Timeline:

✐ **Frame:** A placeholder; a place where content stays the same — at least at this stage of the game. In Chapter 2 of this minibook, when we show you how to create motion tween animations, you'll see that frames become in-between frames, where Flash takes the reins and determines what happens. Frames are designated by blank spaces on the Timeline.

✐ **Keyframe:** Designates where something changes in your animation. You create a keyframe when you need a fork in the road. The keyframe can contain a different graphic, or the graphic from the previous keyframe in a different position. A keyframe is identified by a solid dot on the Timeline.

✐ **Blank keyframe:** Signifies that a change is going to happen, but the frame is empty. You can create blank keyframes at the beginning of a project to set up the timing. You can then populate the blank keyframe by selecting it and dragging an item from the document library to the Stage.

✐ **Frame span:** Consists of a keyframe and the following frames exclusive of the next keyframe. The end of a frame span is indicated by an unfilled rectangle.

Now that you know who all the players are, we suggest that you rock on to the next section, where we show you how to create frame, keyframes, and blank keyframes.

Creating Frames, Keyframes, and Blank Keyframes

After you map out your Flash project, you know where you need to add frames, blank keyframes, or frames to your Timeline. In this section, we show you how to add these gems to your Timeline.

If you do a lot of work with frame spans, you may prefer the option of clicking a frame in the sequence to select the entire sequence. To enable this selection option, choose Edit⇨Preferences to open the Preferences dialog box. In the Timeline section of the General tab, choose Span Based Selection. Click OK to close the dialog box and immediately enable the feature.

Adding a frame

To add a frame to the Timeline, follow these steps:

1. **Click the spot on the Timeline where you want to add the frame.**

   If you click in a frame span, the frame is added at that place in the frame span. If you click an unused frame beyond the last frame in the Timeline, Flash adds frames up to that point.

If you enabled span-based selection in the Preferences dialog box, Ctrl+click (Windows) or ⌘+click (Mac) to select a single frame.

2. **To add the frame, do one of the following:**

   - Choose Insert⇨Timeline⇨Frame.
   - Press F5.

Adding multiple frames

To add multiple frames to the Timeline, follow these steps:

1. **Click the spot where you want to add multiple frames to the Timeline.**

   Congratulations. You successfully selected a frame.

   If you enabled span-based selection in the Preferences dialog box, Ctrl+click (Windows) or ⌘+click (Mac) to select a single frame.

2. **Drag right or left to increase the selection to the number of frames you want to add.**

   Alternatively, you can Shift+click the final frame you want to select.

   If you enabled span-based selection in the Preferences dialog box, hold down the Ctrl key (Windows) or ⌘ key (Mac) while dragging. Alternatively, you can press Ctrl+Shift (Windows) or ⌘+click (Mac) to select the final frame you want to select.

3. **Choose Insert⇨Timeline⇨Frame.**

   Alternatively, you can press F5. Either method adds the same number of frames to the Timeline you selected.

Adding a keyframe

To add a keyframe to the Timeline, follow these steps:

1. **Click the spot on the Timeline where you want to add the keyframe.**

   If you click in a frame span, the keyframe is added at that place in the frame span. If you click an unused frame beyond the last frame in the Timeline, Flash adds a keyframe at the point and adds frames to fill the gap.

2. **To add the frame, do one of the following:**

   - Choose Insert⇨Timeline⇨Keyframe.
   - Press F6.

Adding multiple keyframes

If you're creating a project such as a frame-by-frame animation, you need to add multiple keyframes to the Timeline. To add multiple keyframes to the Timeline, follow these steps:

1. **Click the spot where you want to add multiple keyframes to the Timeline.**

   One frame of the Timeline is selected.

   If you enabled span-based selection in the Preferences dialog box, Ctrl+click (Windows) or ⌘+click (Mac) to select a single frame.

2. **Drag right or left to increase the selection to the number of keyframes you want to add.**

   Alternatively, you can Shift+click the final frame you want to select.

   If you enabled span-based selection in the Preferences dialog box, hold down the Ctrl key (Windows) or ⌘ key (Mac) while dragging. Alternatively, you can press Ctrl+Shift (Windows) or ⌘+click (Mac) to select the final frame you want to select.

3. **Choose Insert⇨Timeline⇨Keyframe.**

   Alternatively, you can press F6. Either method adds the same number of keyframes to the Timeline as the number of frames you selected.

Adding a blank keyframe

Did you ever have to make up your mind? Well, sometimes you know that something is going to happen, and you know where it's going to happen, but you don't know *what* is going to happen. If that's what's troubling you, just walk right in and sit right down because we show you how to add a blank keyframe to the Timeline. To add a blank keyframe to the Timeline, follow these steps:

1. **Click the spot on the Timeline where you want to add the blank key-frame.**

   If you click in a frame span, the blank keyframe is added at that location in the frame span. If you click an unused frame beyond the last frame in the Timeline, Flash adds a blank keyframe at that point and add frames to fill the gap.

   If you enabled span-based selection in the Preferences dialog box, Ctrl+click (Windows) or ⌘+click (Mac) to select a single frame.

**Book III
Chapter 1**

**Working with the
Flash Timeline**

2. **To add the blank keyframe, do one of the following:**

- Choose Insert➪Timeline➪Blank Keyframe.
- Press F7.

Editing Frames

Sometimes, you hit it right the first time, and your Flash project plays just the way you want it to. And sometimes things happen too fast or too slow. You may also find the need to cut frames or copy frames to another layer, for example. Like the heading says, in this section we show you how to edit frames.

Selecting a frame

You can select one of your frames by doing one of the following:

- ✔ Click a frame to select it.

  If you enabled span-based selection in the Preferences dialog box, Ctrl+click (Windows) or ⌘+click (Mac) to select a single frame.

- ✔ Click one frame and then drag to select a range of frames.

- ✔ Click one frame and then Shift+click another frame to select contiguous frames.

- ✔ Double-click inside a frame span to select the entire frame span.

  If you enabled span-based selection in the Preferences dialog box, click any frame in-between keyframes to select a frame span.

- ✔ To select the entire Timeline, select a frame and then choose Edit➪Timeline➪Select All Frames. Alternatively, you can press Ctrl+Alt+A (Windows) or ⌘+Option+A (Mac).

Copying a frame

Another change you may need to make is to copy and paste a frame of a frame span. To copy and paste, do one of the following:

- ✔ Alt+click (Windows) or Option+click (Mac) a keyframe and drag it to the location to which you want to paste it.

- ✔ Select a frame or frame span, choose Edit➪Timeline➪Copy Frames, click inside a frame span, and then choose Edit➪Timeline➪Paste Frames to replace the frame span.

Alternatively, click a blank frame at the end of the Timeline, and then choose Edit⇨Timeline⇨Paste Frames to add the copied frames to the end of the Timeline. You can also paste frames to another layer.

Managing a Timeline

There are many other ways to manage a Timeline. You can remove frames and copy and paste frames, for example. The following list describes the different options you have for managing a Timeline filled with frames and keyframes and frame spans and — whew!

✔ If you enabled the span-based selection option, you can change the duration of a frame span by moving the cursor over the last frame in the frame span. When the cursor becomes a line with two arrows, click and drag to the right to extend the frame span, or drag to the left to shorten it.

✔ To delete a frame or frame sequence, select the frame or frame sequence, and then choose Edit⇨Timeline⇨Remove Frames. After invoking the command, Flash moves the upstream keyframes and frame spans to fill in the gap.

✔ To move a keyframe or frame sequence, select it and drag it to a location you want. After you move the selection, Flash extends the appropriate selection to fill the gap.

✔ To clear a keyframe, select it and then choose Edit⇨Timeline⇨Clear Frames.

✔ To convert a keyframe to a frame, choose Edit⇨Timeline⇨Convert to Keyframes. Flash fills the converted frame with the contents of the previous keyframe.

We wouldn't be doing our job if we didn't introduce you to the power of the context menu. Right-click (Windows) or Ctrl+click (Mac) a keyframe to reveal the context menu shown in Figure 1-3. Every conceivable command you can use is just a mouse click away.

Figure 1-3: The Timeline context menu.

Chapter 2: Creating a Flash Animation

In This Chapter

✓ **Creating a frame-by-frame animation**

✓ **Creating a motion tween animation**

✓ **Creating a shape tween animation**

✓ **Animating with tools**

✓ **Creating an IK animation**

Animation has always been a staple of Flash projects. Motion tweening and shape tweening have been part of Flash since we can remember, and that was just before the Watergate scandal. (Kidding.) Tween animations are slightly younger than dirt, and creating a tween animation has changed considerably in Flash CS4. You no longer have to create a symbol and then beginning and ending keyframes before applying a motion tween. That's too much work.

Instead, you create a shape and tell Flash that you want it to be a motion tween animation, and Flash adds enough frames for a 1-second animation. You move the object to the last frame, and Flash fills in the in-between frames to create your animation. Tween, in between. Logical, isn't it? In this chapter, we show you how to create animations with motion and shape tweening. Careful with the motion tween, Eugene!

Creating an Animated Background

The new Art Deco tool makes child's play out of creating a background that draws itself. Yes, that's right — the background is animated. It makes an interesting background for certain projects. You can use the Art Deco tool to replace the default symbols with any symbol you've added to the document library. To create an animated background with the Art Deco tool, follow these steps:

1. **Select the Art Deco tool and then select the frame where you want the animation to start.**

   If you're creating a background, select the first frame.

2. **In the Drawing Effect section of the Property inspector, accept the default symbols or click Edit to choose a symbol from the document library.**

   Our experiments indicate that you'll be happy if you accept the default leaf shape and choose a flower shape from a symbol in the document library. For example, you can create a star Graphic symbol with the Polystar tool and use vines of stars for the background. (That might work for a rock star's Web site.)

3. **In the Advanced Options section, change the branch angle, pattern scale, and segment length to suit your project.**

   For more information on setting up the Art Deco tool, see Book II, Chapter 4.

4. **Select the Animate Pattern check box.**

   This option creates keyframes as you drag the tool across the Stage.

5. **Specify the Frame Set option.**

   This step determines how many frames it takes for each step of the animation to occur. If you accept the default option, Flash creates lots of keyframes and your published file has more baggage than your ex-girlfriend or -boyfriend does, which means that it's a large file. If you choose a value of about 30, the file size is manageable.

6. **Click on the Stage.**

   Sit back and relax while the tool fills the Stage with vines and leaves and creates a keyframe for each step (see Figure 2-1).

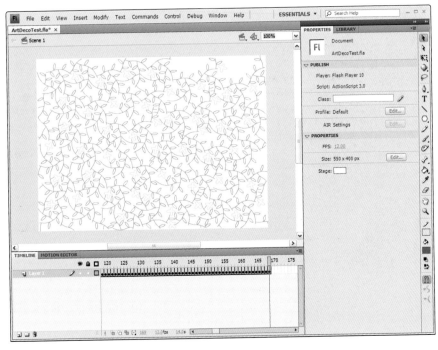

Figure 2-1: Creating an animated background with the Art Deco tool.

Creating a Frame-by-Frame Animation

A frame-by-frame animation is similar to the way cartoonists work. A cartoonist creates a separate drawing for each frame of the cartoon, and when the frames are compiled, they play back smoothly. You might have created flip books when you were young, in which you draw stick figures at the top of the pages on a small pad, change the character ever so slightly on each page of the pad, and then quickly thumb through the pages to make the stick figure move. This process is similar to a frame-by-frame animation, and you know that it involves a lot of work.

In a nutshell, what you do is create an object on a keyframe. Then you create additional keyframes and change the object ever so slightly in each keyframe. When the keyframes are played back, you see relatively smooth motion. We don't show you the steps for creating a frame-by-frame animation in this chapter because it's not used often with graphics. It's useful when you're animating text, though, so we show you how to create a frame-by-frame animation in Chapter 3 of this minibook.

Making a Motion Tween Animation

Motion tween animations have been around forever in Flash. In Flash CS4, you can create a motion tween animation more easily (*much* more easily) than you could do it in previous versions of Flash. When you create a motion tween animation in Flash, you use keyframes, which is where the changes in motion take place. Flash interpolates the motion on the in-between frames. When you play the animation, you see smooth motion. To create a motion tween, follow these steps:

1. **Create a new document and create an object, and then position the object where you want it on the Stage.**

   For the purpose of this exercise, create an oval; any color you like. When you create your own animations, you can place the object anywhere you want. For the purpose of this exercise, place the object in the lower-left corner of the Stage.

2. **Double-click the object with the Selection tool to select it.**

   You have to double-click an object to select both the stroke and the fill.

3. **Choose Insert⇨Motion Tween.**

   Alternatively, you can right-click (Windows) or Ctrl+click (Mac) and choose Motion Tween from the context menu. Either method displays a dialog box warning you that the symbol cannot be tweened but notifying you that Flash will gladly convert it to a symbol for you.

   The dialog box doesn't appear if you select a Graphic or Movie Clip symbol from the document library.

4. **Click OK.**

   Flash adds 23 frames to the animation and positions the playhead on the twenty-fourth frame of the animation, to give you a 1-second animation.

5. **Move the object to a different position on the Stage.**

   For the purpose of this exercise, move the object to the upper-right corner of the Stage. After you move the object, Flash creates a keyframe in the twenty-fourth frame and a line with dots from the starting point of the animation to the ending point of the animation (see Figure 2-2).

6. **Drag the playhead to preview the animation.**

   You see smooth motion from Point A to Point B.

7. **Click the sixth frame and drag the oval up.**

   Flash converts the twelfth frame to a keyframe. The oval changes direction at this point and travels in a straight line unless you modify the path between keyframes.

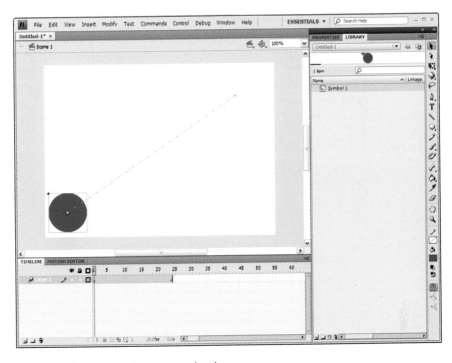

Figure 2-2: Creating a motion tween animation.

8. **Select the Selection tool.**

    You use this tool to modify the motion tween path.

9. **Move the cursor toward the bottom segment of the path.**

    When a curved line appears under the cursor, it's your notification that you can curve the motion path.

10. **Click and drag to curve the path.**

11. **Repeat Steps 9 and 10 for the upper segment of the path.**

    The motion path should resemble the one shown in Figure 2-3.

12. **Press Ctrl+Enter (Windows) or ⌘+Return (Mac) to preview the animation in another window.**

    Flash publishes the animation as an SWF movie and plays it in another window over and over and over and — the movie continues *looping* until you press Esc. To prevent this from happening when you publish your file for public consumption, you have to add some ActionScript, which we cover in Book IV.

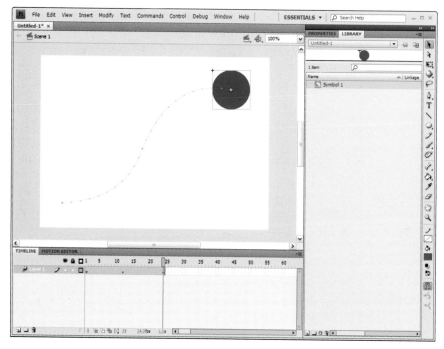

Figure 2-3: This animation is not on the straight and narrow.

You can create a motion tween animation inside a movie clip. When you do this, it occupies only a single frame on the Timeline, and you can use it wherever it's needed in your Flash project. (Talk about your reusable animations!)

After creating a motion tween animation, you can tweak the animation with the Motion Editor or Property inspector. The sophisticated Motion Editor feature gives you more control over your animations than was possible in previous versions of Flash. (Like the proverbial well, this subject is deep.) We cover the Motion Editor and other ways you can tweak your motion tween animations in Chapter 4 of this minibook.

Building a Shape Tween Animation

Another form of animation you can create in Flash is a shape tween animation. You supply the keyframes and the shapes, and Flash morphs one shape into another on the in-between frames. (It's a shame that you can't morph images in Flash — what better way to get even with a significant other who turned into a significant nothing?) To create a shape tween animation in Flash, follow these steps:

1. **Create a shape on a keyframe.**

   When you create a shape tween animation, you cannot use a symbol. The shape must be created with one of the object drawing tools. For the purpose of this exercise, create a rectangle with the Rectangle Primitive tool.

2. **Select a blank frame and then press F7 to create a blank keyframe.**

   The number of frames between the first keyframe and the blank keyframe determines the length of the animation. With a default frame rate of 24 frames per second (fps), a 48-frame animation lasts for two seconds.

3. **With the blank keyframe still selected, create another shape.**

   For the purpose of this exercise, create an oval using the Oval Primitive tool. The shape doesn't need to be in the same size or in the same position. With a shape tween animation, one shape morphs into another and moves.

4. **Click a frame between the keyframes and then choose Insert⇔Shape Tween.**

   Alternatively, you can right-click (Windows) or Ctrl+click (Mac) and choose Shape Tween from the context menu. After using either method, the in-between frames become green, and an arrow appears between keyframes (see Figure 2-4).

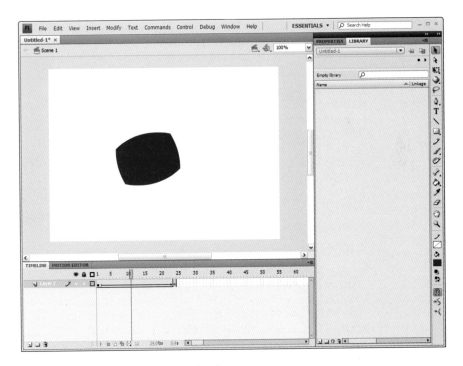

Figure 2-4: Creating a shape tween animation.

5. **Drag the playhead to preview your animation.**

   One shape morphs smoothly into the other.

In most instances, Flash does the math correctly, and you have an outstanding shape tween animation. We recommend against trying to tween a shape with negative space (a hole, if you will), which can cause undesirable results. However, if you're bound and determined to create a complex shape tween animation, shape hints can be added to show Flash which part of the first shape should morph into which part of the second shape. We cover tweaking an animation with shape hints in Chapter 4 of this minibook.

Reversing an Animation

Sometimes, you may need to have an animation reverse itself. For example, you can create a motion tween animation in which an object gently arcs in a direction from the upper-left to the lower-right of the Stage and then reverses direction. You can do the same thing for a shape tween animation: Have an object morph to another shape and then unmorph itself. It's easier than you think. Follow these steps:

1. **Create a motion tween or shape tween animation as outlined earlier in this chapter.**

   What? You didn't read the previous sections? If you don't know the new and much easier way of creating motion tween and shape tween animations, we suggest that you flip back a page or two where we show you how much easier it is in Flash CS4.

2. **Select the first keyframe of the animation, and then Shift+click the last keyframe of the animation.**

   You've selected the enter animation.

3. **Right-click (Windows) or Ctrl+click (Mac) and then choose Copy Frames from the context menu.**

4. **Select the blank frame after the last keyframe in your animation, right-click (Windows) or Ctrl+click (Mac), and then choose Paste Frames from the context menu.**

   Flash pastes all frames from the animation to the Timeline.

5. **Select the first keyframe of the frames you just pasted, and then Shift+click the last keyframe of the frames you just pasted.**

   The pasted frames are selected.

6. **Right-click (Windows) or Ctrl+click (Mac) and choose Reverse Keyframes from the context menu.**

   It doesn't look like anything has happened. To see the results of your handiwork, you have to preview the animation.

Going retro

Flash motion tweening seems to have been around forever. In the Jurassic period before Flash CS4, you had to create a symbol and then create keyframes and apply the motion tween. Flash CS4 makes it easy for anyone to create a motion tween animation. However, if you like the old way of creating a motion tween, you're in luck. After performing the preliminary steps of creating the symbol and keyframes, position the cursor on an in-between frame and then choose Insert⇨Classic Tween. We like the new way better because you produce a motion path that you can edit. Speaking of motion paths, you can also use the old method of animating a symbol along a path. After creating your classic motion tween, right-click (Windows) or Ctrl+click (Mac) the layer on which you created the classic tween and choose Create Classic Guide from the context menu. After you invoke the command, Flash creates a classic motion guide layer, just like the ones we knew and loved in previous versions of Flash. To finish the animation, you need to create a path on that layer, align your symbol to the start of the path on the first frame of the animation, and then align your object to the end of the path on the final frame of the animation. That's way too much work, as far as we're concerned. We tried the new way and we like it. But you know what they say: "Different strokes for different folks."

7. **Press Ctrl+Enter (Windows) or ⌘+Return (Mac).**

   Flash publishes the movie as an SWF file and plays it in another window. Your animation goes from Point A to Point B and then to Point A again.

To reverse the order in which a motion tween animation plays, select the frame span, right-click (Windows) or Ctrl+click (Mac), and choose Reverse Keyframes from the context menu. After you invoke this menu command, the last keyframe becomes the first keyframe and vice versa.

Simulating 3D Animation

Maybe some future version of Flash will be 3D, but true 3D isn't available in Flash CS4. However, the application has taken a quantum leap because now you can simulate 3D using the 3D Translation tool and the 3D Rotation tool. The first tool is used to make it appear as though an object is closer to or farther from the viewer during the course of an animation. The 3D Rotation tool can be used to make it appear as though an object is spinning through space during the course of an animation. These new tools are useful additions to an animator's arsenal. Combine the tools in the same animation and you get something way cool.

Using the 3D Rotation tool

The 3D Rotation tool makes it possible for you to create animations where objects look like they're spinning in space. As with a regular 3D spinning top, you can use the tool to make an object appear as though it's spinning on the X (top to bottom), Y (left to right), or Z (front to back) axis. To use the 3D Rotation tool, follow these steps:

1. **Create a motion tween animation with three or four keyframes.**

   For the skinny on how to create a motion tween animation, refer to the "Making a Motion Tween Animation" section, earlier in this chapter.

2. **Select the second keyframe, and then select the 3D Rotation tool.**

   Okay, you can select the first keyframe, but we want you to see how cool this tool is by comparing the shape on the first keyframe to the second keyframe.

3. **Click the object.**

   Three rings appear around the object (see Figure 2-5): a red ring, which controls rotation around the X axis, a green ring, which controls rotation around the Y axis, and a blue ring, which controls rotation around the Z axis.

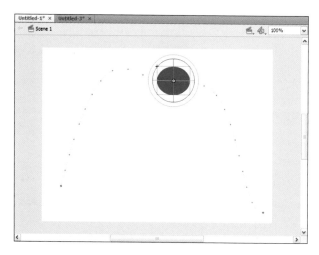

Figure 2-5: What goes up must come down. Spinnin' wheel, spinnin' round.

4. **Click and drag your favorite color.**

   The object spins about the associated axis.

5. **Click and drag other rings to rotate along the other axes.**

   The tool gets addictive — use it with discretion. You never know whether viewers might be susceptible to motion sickness.

6. **Repeat Steps 4 and 5 on the other keyframes however you want.**

   With a bit of experimentation, you create some interesting results by using this tool. Use it in conjunction with the 3D Translation tool to amaze your friends and the viewers of your Flash animations.

Using the 3D Translation tool

The 3D Translation tool makes it possible for you to create an animation that looks like an object is traveling toward and away from you during the course of the animation. Imagine creating a symbol that looks like the *Enterprise* and then creating a complex motion tween animation where the ship is bobbing and weaving between planets. Then use the 3D translation tool to make the ship appear to be at different distances from the viewer during the course of the animation. Put a reasonable facsimile of your favorite captain at the helm — we vote for Picard.

To use the 3D Translation tool, follow these steps:

1. **Create a motion tween animation with three or four keyframes.**

   For the skinny on how to create a motion tween animation, refer to the "Making a Motion Tween Animation" section, earlier in this chapter.

2. **Select the second keyframe, and then select the 3D Translation tool.**

3. **Click the object.**

   A red and green arrow appear from the center of the object (see Figure 2-6). The red arrow controls motion along the Y axis (from left to right), and the green arrow controls motion along the Y axis (from top to bottom). You can control motion on both axes with the Selection tool. The 3D Translation tool has another axis, which is Z (from front to back).

4. **Move the cursor over the center dot until a small *z* appears.**

   You can now make the object appear closer to or farther away from you.

5. **Drag left to make the object appear closer, and drag right to make it appear farther away.**

6. **Repeat Steps 3 through 5 after selecting the object on other keyframes.**

   If you want, use the other arrows to move the object along the X and Y axes. When you do so, the motion path is redrawn to reflect your changes.

7. **Press Enter or Return to preview the animation.**

   "I canna hold Warp Six, Cap'n; the reactor's gonna blow."

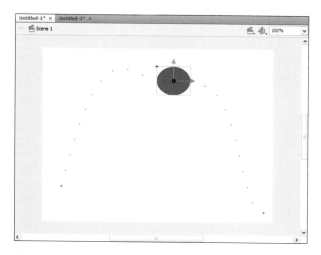

Figure 2-6: Say what? 3D in Flash! Way kewl.

Animating with the Spray Brush Tool

When you use the Spray Brush tool, you can fill it full of symbols and spray them at Will, if you have Mr. Robinson (in danger or not) in your Flash project. If you load the Spray Brush with a movie clip symbol of an animation, you have the basis of a cool animation. To animate with the Spray Brush tool, follow these steps:

1. **Create a Movie Clip symbol.**

    If you're not sure how to create a movie clip, place a bookmark here (we would appreciate it if you didn't dog-ear the corner of the page) and check out Book II, Chapter 4.

2. **Create an animation.**

    A shape tween or motion tween animation works equally well with this tool. You can also create an animation using an effect in the Property inspector. For example, you can use the Alpha effect on an object, like a star you create with the Polystar tool. Create an animation with three keyframes. On the first and third keyframes, set the Alpha value to zero and leave the middle frame at 100 percent. The resulting animation looks like a flashing star.

3. **Select the Spray Brush tool.**

4. **In the Symbol section of the Property inspector, click Edit.**

    The Swap Symbol dialog box appears (see Figure 2-7).

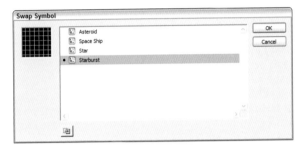

Figure 2-7: Swap symbols to load the Spray Brush tool.

5. **Select the desired symbol and click OK.**

   The Spray Brush tool is locked and loaded.

6. **Click the tool wherever you want in order to sprinkle the animation into your project.**

Creating an Inverse Kinematics (IK) Animation

A cool new feature of Flash CS4 is the ability to create an inverse kinematics animation. If you've ever worked with 3D applications, you know what an inverse kinematics animation is. If you aren't familiar with 3D, think about how your body moves. You have a skeleton of bones that are connected at joints. The joint has a range of motion. For example, unless you're a cast member of a horror movie, your neck has a range of motion of 180 degrees. Bones also work in unison. When you move your hand, the connected bones move as well. This is exactly what inverse kinematics is. You use the Bones tool to create an inverse kinematics chain and then specify the range of motion for each bone. When you drag a bone that's a child of another bone, the parent moves. This is just another shocking case where the child has control over the parent, which proves that it pays not to grow up when you grow older. In the upcoming sections, we show you how to create an inverse kinematics animation.

Creating the IK chain minus the daisies

When you create an IK animation, you use the Bones tool to create a skeleton for the object or symbols that are part of your animation. When you use the tool, you drag out the bones for the skeleton. The first bone you create is the parent for the following bones you create. Each subsequent bone in the chain is the parent of the next bone. You animate the chain by dragging a child to move the parent and all bones upstream. To create an IK chain, follow these steps:

1. **Select the object to which you want to add an IK chain.**

2. **Select the Bones tool, which looks like a dog bone.**

3. **Click where you want to position the head of the first bone, and then drag to determine the length of the bone.**

   When you create a bone, Flash automatically adds an armature layer.

4. **Release the mouse button when the bone is the length you want.**

   Be as precise as you can when creating the bones. This is the first version of IK in Flash, and there's no way to change the length of a bone after it's created. It may be beneficial to add guides as a visual reference where you want each bone to end.

5. **Click and drag to create the next bone.**

   Continue in this manner until you've created the skeleton for your shape. Figure 2-8 shows a finger created with the Oval tool and a bit of tweaking. The Bones tool was used to create a skeleton for the finger.

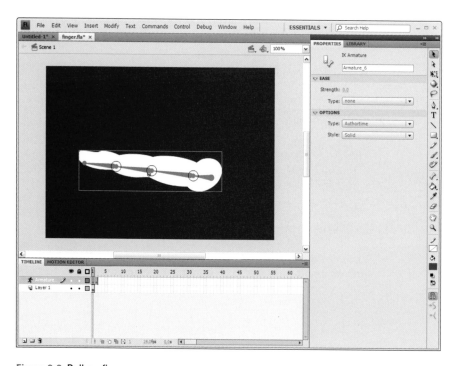

Figure 2-8: Pull my finger.

You can also create an IK chain with symbols. Create a Movie Clip symbol for each part of your IK chain and then use the Bones tool to create the skeleton as outlined in the previous steps. The only weird thing you'll notice is you can't see the last bone in the IK chain. Oh well, this is the first time we've had inverse kinematics in Flash.

You can change the way bones are displayed by selecting the armature layer and choose an option from the Style drop-down menu in the Options section of the Property inspector. You can display the bones on the armature by using one of the following styles: Solid, Wire, or Line.

Constraining the bones

When you create an IK chain, each bone rotates 360 degrees by default. If you're going to create realistic animations, you know that will never fly. You can, however, change this situation by constraining the bone. You can constrain the rotation of a bone, and constrain movement along the X and Y axes. You can also disable rotation or movement along the X and Y axes. To constrain bones in an IK chain, follow these steps:

1. **Using the Selection tool, select the first bone in the chain.**

   The Property inspector reconfigures to display options for constraining a bone (see Figure 2-9).

Figure 2-9: It's time to put a constraining order on this bone.

Book III
Chapter 2

Creating a Flash Animation

2. **Accept the default Speed value, or use the scrubby slider to specify a different speed.**

   You can also click the current value and enter a different value. The Speed value determines how quickly the bone moves when a child is moved. If you want the bone to lag behind a bit, specify a slower speed. If you specify a speed of 0, the bone doesn't move.

3. **In the Joint Rotation area, modify the following options:**

   - *Enable:* Joint rotation is enabled by default. Deselect this option, and the bone cannot rotate and instead acts an anchor.

   - *Constrain:* Enable this option and the Min and Max options become available. Use the scrubby slider to constrain the minimum and maximum angle to which the bone can rotate. For example, if you were constraining rotation for a bone that will function as a forearm, the minimum angle would be 0 (zero), and the maximum angle would be about 90 because the human forearm has approximately a 90-degree range of motion unless you're double-jointed. When you constrain rotation, an icon appears at the head of the bone and is a graphical representation of how far the bone can rotate in each direction.

4. **Specify translation options in the Joint: X Translation and Joint: Y Translation sections.**

   These options determine whether the bone can move from left to right (X Translation) or up and down (Y Translation). You have the following options:

   - *Enable:* Choose this option to enable movement along the applicable axis. For example, if you were animating a leg, the bone you create for the foot would be able to move forward and backward with minimal rotation. When you enable this option for the X axis, a horizontal line with two arrows appears at the head of the bone. If you enable this option for the Y axis, a vertical line with two arrows appears at the head of the bone.

   - *Constrain:* Enable this option to constrain motion along the applicable axis. When you choose this option, the Min and Max options are available. Use the scrubby slider to constrain the minimum and maximum range of motion that the object has along the applicable axis. The Min value for the X axis determines the range of motion to the left, and the Max value determines the range of motion to the right. The Min value of the Y axis determines the range of motion in a downward direction, and the Max value determines the range of motion in an upward direction.

Use the arrow keys at the top of the Property inspector to navigate from one bone to the next.

Creating the animation

After you create the IK chain and constrain the bones, you're ready to animate the puppy, or whatever you decided to animate. All you need to do is create a couple of keyframes and tug a bone or two, and Flash fills in the frames between the keyframes. To get a move on with your IK chain, follow these steps:

1. **Select the Armature layer.**

   If you have a lot of layers in your project, you may find it beneficial to lock the layers not directly associated with your IK animation.

2. **Click the frame where you want a change to occur and then press F6.**

   This step creates a keyframe.

3. **Click a bone and drag it.**

   It's alive — err, we mean, the bone moves.

4. **Move the other bones as needed.**

   Press the Shift key to constrain motion to the selected bone. This option comes in handy when you want to simulate motion, such as the second joint of a finger bending without affecting the first joint. Figure 2-10 shows a bent finger ready to point at something.

5. **Continue adding keyframes and moving bones as needed to finish your animation.**

**Book III
Chapter 2**

**Creating a Flash
Animation**

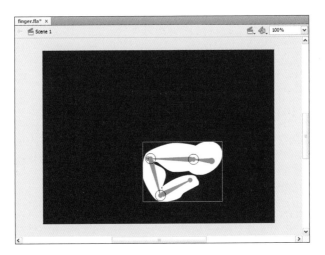

Figure 2-10: Let me make my point perfectly clear.

Using the Bind tool

In a perfect world, Flash would know which points to connect to which bones. But Flash is a computer application. Flash employs, at best, a scientific wild guess when interpolating which points should move when a bone is moved. If your animation isn't playing as expected, you need the help of the Bind tool. To use the Bind tool, follow these steps:

1. **Select the Bind tool and then click the bone that needs to be edited —** *unbound,* **if you will.**

   The points influenced by the bone are highlighted in yellow. Points that are connected to more than one bone are designated as triangles (see Figure 2-11).

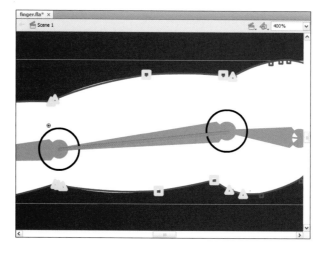

Figure 2-11: Some of these points are bound to be changed by the Bind tool.

2. **To prevent a point from being influenced by a bone, Alt+drag (Windows) or Option+drag (Mac) the point to whichever bone you want.**

   The point is highlighted in red. If the point was previously influenced by more than one bone, the icon changes from a triangle to a rectangle.

3. **To determine which bone influences a point, select it with the Bind tool and then Shift+drag it to the bone you want.**

   The modified point is highlighted in red. If the point was previously influenced by only one bone, its icon changes to a triangle.

Chapter 3: Animating Text

As authors, text is near and dear to our hearts. Without text, there wouldn't be books, and without books, there wouldn't be authors, which wouldn't be much fun for us. Dummies authors like to have fun with words, which means that we also like to play with text. So whenever we're writing about an application such as Flash, it's a no-brainer to create some flashy text about flashy techniques that animate text. If that's too much Flash for you, we'll excuse you while you catch your breath. Ah, you're back. Get ready to have some fun animating text.

Creating Typewriter Text

Believe it or not, people used to use a device known as a typewriter to write things like letters and books. It had no spell check. And it had no cut-and-paste feature. If you made a mistake, you dabbed on some correction fluid, waited for it to dry, and then typed again. If you remember typewriters (Doug still has one), we're sure that you welcome the power of the computer and the word processor. But if you're creating a Flash Web site for an author, for example, and you want to make it look like his name is being typed, you've come to the right chapter in this book. In this section, we show you how to create an animation that appears as though each word was typed. Follow these steps:

1. **Create a block of static text.**

   Choose a font type, size, and color to suit your project. Because we're authors, we're partial to the Courier font because it *looks* like it was created by a typewriter.

2. **Select the text and then choose Modify⇨Break Apart.**

   The text block is divided into individual, selectable letters.

3. **With the text still selected, choose Modify⇨Timeline⇨Distribute to Layers.**

   Flash creates a separate layer for each letter, and each layer is named for the letter (see Figure 3-1).

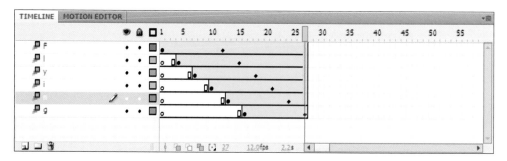

Figure 3-1: Distributed to layers again.

4. **Delete Layer 1.**

   It contains all the letters on the layers just created by the Distribute to Layers command. Therefore, you don't need it any more.

5. **Select the keyframe in the second layer and drag it one frame to the right.**

   Flash creates a blank keyframe in the first frame and moves the keyframe to the second frame.

6. **Select the keyframe on the third layer and drag it two frames to the right.**

   Starting to get the picture? You're adding an additional space between each keyframe to make the text look like it's being typed one letter at a time.

7. **Continue moving the keyframe for each letter, as outlined in Steps 1 through 6.**

8. **Select the blank frame to the right of the keyframe in the second-to-last layer, and then Shift+click the same frame in the first layer.**

   You've selected the same frame in all layers.

9. **Press F5.**

   This keyboard shortcut adds enough frames to display all letters until the end of the animation. If you didn't add the frames, each letter would disappear as soon as the next one appears. Your Timeline should resemble the one shown in Figure 3-2.

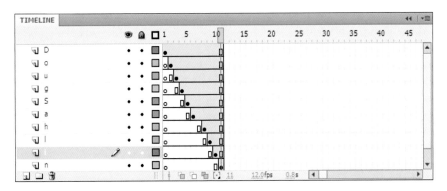

Figure 3-2: The typewriter text Timeline.

10. **Press Ctrl+Enter (Windows) or ⌘+Enter (Mac).**

Flash displays the animation in another window (see Figure 3-3). The only thing missing is the sound of a typewriter. If you like this technique and want to add some sound, take a look at Book V, Chapter 2, where we show you how to add sound to a Flash project.

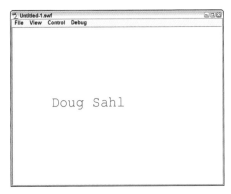

Figure 3-3: It's the old hunt-and-peck animation.

Creating Flying Text

Cool animation isn't reserved for graphical objects. When you create static text, you can use motion tweening to animate text. Of course, when you create a motion tween animation, it must be on its own layer, which is easily done with the Distribute to Layers command. If you have a lot of letters to animate, you may think that this task is difficult, but it's not. Follow along with us and we'll show you how to create an animation where text flies into the scene. Follow these steps:

1. **Use the Text tool to create a block of static text.**

   Create the text off the Stage. The effect you're creating has the text flying in from every direction.

2. **With the text still selected, choose Modify⇨Break Apart.**

   Flash breaks the block of text into individual letters that you can animate.

3. **Modify⇨Timeline⇨Distribute to Layers.**

   Flash creates a separate layer for each letter.

4. **Select Layer 1 and drag it to the Delete icon.**

   You no longer need this layer because each letter is on its own layer.

5. **Select the first frame of the first layer, and then Shift+click the first frame of the last layer.**

   You've selected the first frame in all layers.

6. **Right-click (Windows) or Ctrl+click (Mac), and choose Create Motion Tween from the context menu.**

   Flash adds 11 frames to each layer's timeline. The background is blue, indicating that a motion tween animation can be created by changing the position of the object in the last frame.

7. **Move the playhead to the last frame.**

8. **Using the Selection tool, move the letters to the position where you want them to stop.**

   Flash adds a keyframe to the twelfth frame of each layer.

9. **Move the playhead to the first frame.**

10. **Using the Selection tool, move each letter to a different position.**

    The letters "fly in" from the position to which you move them. Make sure that you truly jumble the position of the letters and vary the distance they have to travel. Your goal is to create some visual eye candy.

11. **Select an individual letter.**

    The letter's frame span is selected, and you can see its motion path.

12. **Move the cursor toward the motion path.**

    When the cursor changes to a pointing arrow with a curve beneath it, you can bend the motion path into a graceful curve.

13. **Click and bend the motion path into a graceful curve (see Figure 3-4).**

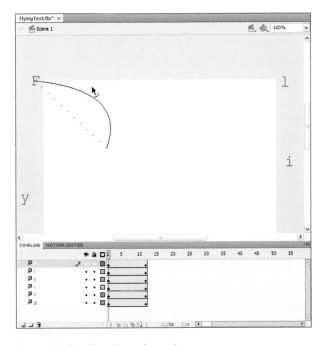

Figure 3-4: Bending the motion path.

14. **Bend the motion paths for the other letters.**

    Bend the paths in different directions to make each animation look random.

15. **Select the frame span in the second layer, and drag it a couple of frames to the right.**

    The goal is to have the letters fly in at different times. Moving the frame span to the right causes the second letter to fly in after the first.

16. **Select the frame span in the third layer, and drag it a couple of frames to the right of the second layer.**

    Your Timeline should resemble Figure 3-5.

17. **Repeat Step 16 for the remaining layers in your animation.**

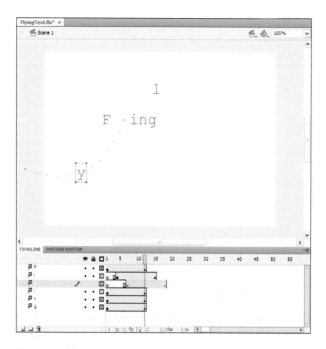

Figure 3-5: No letter will fly before its time.

18. **Select the blank frame directly above the last keyframe in the bottom layer.**

19. **Shift+click the same frame in the first layer and then press F5.**

    Flash adds enough frames to display each letter for the duration of the animation (see Figure 3-6).

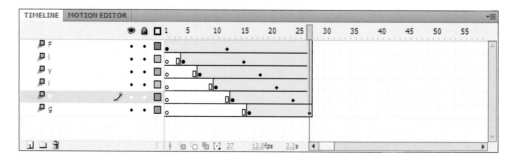

Figure 3-6: Adding enough frames to display each letter for the entire animation.

20. Press Ctrl+Enter (Windows) or ⌘+Enter (Mac).

Flash publishes the project as an SWF file and plays it in another window (see Figure 3-7). The animation plays repeatedly, which means that you need to add some ActionScript to stop the animation.

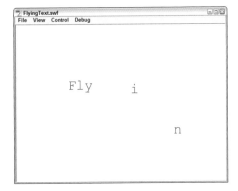

Figure 3-7: Is it a flock of seagulls? No. It's flying letters.

**Book III
Chapter 3**

Animating Text

You can modify the animation by adding keyframes and then moving the letters to a different position. Imagine having the letters fly in and then pause before flying out to different directions. Your only limitation is your imagination. When you have some spare time, experiment with different ways to animate text. If you don't have any spare time, check out *Successful Time Management For Dummies,* by Dirk Zeller (Wiley Publishing).

When you create a text animation, it doesn't have to be on the main Timeline. You can create a Movie Clip symbol for your animation. When you create an instance of a movie clip, it occupies only one frame on the Timeline.

Chapter 4: Advanced Animation Techniques

In This Chapter

- ↙ **Using motion presets**
- ↙ **Manually editing motion paths**
- ↙ **Editing animations**
- ↙ **Copying motion**
- ↙ **Using visual aids**

*I*n Flash CS4, animation took a quantum leap forward. In addition to changing the manner in which you create animation, the designers of Flash gave animators some bells and whistles that they can use to create sophisticated animations. New to Flash CS4 is the Motion Presets panel. The panel has some impressive presets that enable you to take your animations to the next level. And, if you create an animation of your own that you want to use again, you can add it to the panel.

The new Motion Editor is another tool you can use to create a sophisticated animation. From within the Motion Editor, you can control all phases of the animation, including property changes. You can also manually edit a motion path using the Subselection tool. You can even copy motion and apply it to other objects in your Flash project. If you prefer shape tween animations (also known as *morphing*), there's something for you in this chapter as well. In this chapter, we show you some advanced animation techniques and show you how to edit your animations.

Using Motion Presets

The Motion Presets panel is a welcome new addition to Flash CS4. If you're not the best animator in the world, you can apply a preset from the Motion Presets panel to an object in the workspace and — quicker than you can blink an eye — Flash does all the heavy lifting. If you're a good animator, or maybe even an expert one, you can use one of the presets as a starting point for your own animation. To use a motion preset, follow these steps:

1. **Create an object on the Stage.**

   Use your favorite drawing tool to create the object. You don't have to convert it to a symbol; Flash does that for you. Alternatively, you can use a symbol from the document library.

2. **Choose Window⇨Motion Presets.**

   The Motion Presets panel appears. At this stage, it's ho-hum. In fact, you might say it's boring. Read on.

3. **Click the Motion Presets folder.**

   Yikes! — look at all those presets.

4. **Select a preset.**

   A preview of the animation plays in the panel (see Figure 4-1).

5. **When you find an animation you like, right-click (Windows) or Ctrl+click (Mac) and choose an option from the context menu.**

   Choose Apply at Current Location to apply the motion preset from the selected keyframe forward, or choose End at Current Location to create the last frame of the animation at the current keyframe.

6. **Press Ctrl+Enter (Windows) or ⌘+Enter (Mac).**

   Your animation plays in another window.

Creating a motion preset

When you create a cool animation, one that you want to use on other projects or share with or sell to other Flash users, you can easily do so. To create a motion preset, follow these steps:

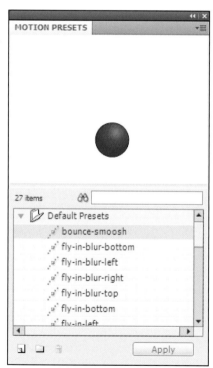

Figure 4-1: Follow the bouncing ball.

1. **Select the frame span that contains the animation you want to save as a preset.**

2. **Right-click (Windows) or Ctrl+click (Mac) and choose Save as Motion Preset.**

   The Save as Preset dialog box appears.

3. **Enter a name for the preset and click OK.**

   Make sure that you give the preset a meaningful name that reflects what the animation does to an object; for example, Exit Stage Left. After you save the preset, it appears in the Custom Presets folder of the Motion Presets panel.

Managing motion presets

You've got presets; lots of presets. As you gain experience as a Flash animator, you may find that some of the old presets you created are lame and should be evicted from the Motion Presets panel. You may also find that the name you gave to the animation isn't useful and should be changed. Or, you may find that you're scrolling through way too many presets to find the one you want and you need to use feng shui on the panel or call in a professional organizer. We're pleased to inform you that it's not nearly that difficult if you follow these steps:

1. **Choose Window⇨Motion Presets.**

   The Motion Presets panel opens.

2. **Open the Motion Presets Options menu by clicking the icon in the upper-right corner of the panel, and choose one of the following commands:**

   - *Import:* Imports a Motion Preset File in the XML format. You use this command to import a motion preset that a fellow Flash user has exported.

   - *Export:* Exports a selected preset as a motion preset file in the XML format. You use this command to share a motion preset with a fellow Flash user who can then use the Import command mentioned in the preceding bullet to import the preset into her Motion Presets panel.

   - *Rename:* Renames a custom preset. You cannot rename one of the default Flash motion presets.

   - *New Folder:* Creates a new folder in the Motion Presets panel. This option comes in handy when the panel overfloweth or you're using this copy of Flash with another user and you want to keep matching (or even his and hers) preset folders.

   - *Remove:* Removes a custom preset from the Motion Presets panel. You cannot remove a default Flash preset.

   - *Save:* Saves the selected frame span as a custom motion preset.

Manually Editing a Motion Path

When you create a motion tween animation, you can bend the path with the Selection tool, as noted in Chapter 2 of this minibook. Because a motion path has a point for each keyframe, you can manually edit the points with the Subselection tool. To edit a motion path manually, follow these steps:

1. **Select the Subselection tool.**

   It's the second tool on the toolbar.

2. **Click a point on the path.**

   The Bezier handles for all points are displayed (see Figure 4-2).

3. **Drag the Bezier handles to change the motion path.**

   Selecting a Bezier handle can be tricky. When the cursor for the Subselection tool becomes a solid arrow with no tail, you can click and drag one tangent handle to reshape the curve. If you Alt+click (Windows) or Option+click (Mac), the tool affects only the selected tangent handle. You can move a handle up and down to reshape the curve or the path, to the right to increase the length of the handle (which creates a gently flowing curve), or to the left to decrease the length of the handle (which creates a sharp curve).

4. **Move the tool toward a point.**

   When an unfilled square appears below the tool, click and drag the point to a different position.

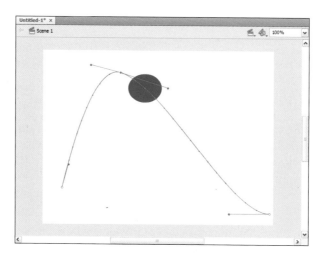

Figure 4-2: Manually editing a motion path.

5. Move the tool toward the path.

When you see a filled square beneath the tool, click and drag to move the path to a different location.

You can also select a path with the Selection tool and then drag it to a different location.

Editing Motion Tween Animations

Motion tween animations may not be the greatest thing since sliced bread, but they certainly beat creating animations frame-by-frame. After creating a motion tween animation, you can edit the animation to perfection. In the following sections, we show you techniques you can use to create the animation exactly the way you want it.

Fine-tuning the animation

Sometimes you create an animation, but it's too slow or too fast. And then at other times, you want the animation to start slowly and end quickly. Perhaps you even want the object to rotate a time or two during the course of the animation. The following subsections show you how to change the timing of the animation and edit the animation in the Property inspector.

Changing the timing of an animation

Does your animation fly by like a Jumpin' Jack Flash, or is it as slow as molasses flowing uphill? If your animation has either problem, you can change the timing of an animation by doing one of the following:

- **Move the cursor toward the last frame in the animation.** When it becomes a line with two arrows, click and drag to the right to increase the duration of the animation, or drag to the left to decrease it.

- **Ctrl+click (Windows) or ⌘+click (Mac) a frame between keyframes, and then press F5 to add a frame.** This action increases the duration of the animation. Press Shift+F5 to remove a frame, thereby decreasing the duration of the animation. You can also use the keyboard shortcut to select a single frame and then drag to select additional frames. Press F5 to add the same number of frames you selected, or press Shift+F5 to remove the same amount of frames you selected.

Editing an animation in the Property inspector

The new motion tween animation truly simplifies your life as a Flash animator. After you create the animation on the Stage, you can do several things to fine-tune it in the Property inspector. After creating an animation, follow these steps:

1. **Select the object you're animating.**

2. **Click Properties in the panel dock to open the Property inspector.**

   If you modified the workspace or are using a workspace that doesn't display the Property inspector, choose Window⇨Properties. Figure 4-3 shows the Property inspector after selecting the path for a motion tween.

3. **In the Ease section, drag the scrubby slider to set a value.**

   Drag the slider to the left to specify a negative value. Negative values cause the animation to start slowly and end quickly. It's the equivalent of a car accelerating from a dead stop. Drag the slider to the right to specify a positive value. This action causes the animation to start quickly and end slowly, like a car stopping for a light. The default value of 0 gives you constant speed throughout the animation.

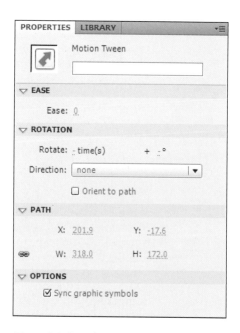

Figure 4-3: A motion path has properties you can modify.

4. **(Optional) Drag the Rotation scrubby slider.**

   If you enable this option, the object rotates along the path. Rather than drag the scrubby slider, you can click inside the field and enter a value.

5. **To add rotation to the object, drag the plus sign (+) scrubby slider.**

   This step specifies the number of degrees to be added to the object's rotation. In other words, if you specify 1 for the number of times the object rotates and specify 90 for this value, the object makes one complete rotation plus 90 degrees.

6. **If you enabled rotation, choose an option from the Direction drop-down menu.**

   This step is easy. The animated object can either rotate clockwise (CW) or counterclockwise (CCW). If you choose None, the object doesn't rotate and the value you specified in the Rotation section reverts to the default value of 0 (zero).

7. **Select the Orient to Path option if you haven't enabled rotation.**

   When you choose this option and you have a curved motion path, Flash aligns the object to the path. When the animation plays, the object rotates to maintain its original orientation to the path.

8. **In the Path section, use the scrubby sliders to change the X and Y values.**

   This step moves the motion path. Changing the X value moves the path horizontally, and changing the Y value moves the path vertically.

9. **In the Path section, use the scrubby sliders to change the W and H values.**

   This step changes the width and height of the motion path. The path is resized proportionately by default. Click the chain icon to change the icon to a broken link, and you can then resize each value independently of the other.

10. **In the Options section, accept the Sync Graphic Symbols option or select the check box to disable it.**

    This option synchronizes the timeline of a symbol with the main Timeline.

This set of steps shows you the options you have for the path, but there's much more you can do to a motion tween animation. Select the object you're tweening, and a different set of options appear in the Property inspector. The following steps show you how to modify the object:

1. **Select the object you're animating.**

   The Property inspector dons another mask, showing you the options available for modifying the object that's being animated (see Figure 4-4).

Figure 4-4: And now you get to modify the object you're animating.

2. **Drag the playhead to navigate to the point in the animation where you want a change to occur.**

3. **In the Position and Size section, drag the scrubby sliders to modify the X and Y values.**

   These values determine where the object is at this point in the animation. The *X value* determines where the center of the object is along the horizontal axis, and the *Y value* determines where the center of the object is along the vertical axis. Remember that the X and Y values for the upper-left corner of the Stage are 0 (zero).

4. **Use the scrubby sliders to modify the W and H values.**

   These values determine the width and height of the object at this point in the animation. The object is resized proportionately by default. Click the chain icon to change it to a broken link, and you can then resize each value independently of the other.

5. **In the 3D Position and View section, drag the scrubby sliders to change the X, Y, and Z values.**

   The X value determines the position of the object from left to right, the Y value determines the position from top to bottom, and the Z value determines the value from front to back. In essence, these values mimic a 3D animation. The Z value varies the size of the object to make it appear as though it's closer to or farther from the viewer at this point in the animation.

   Flash CS4 doesn't create keyframes when you change a property. You do, however, see a diamond icon on the Timeline when you change a property on a frame.

6. **Drag the scrubby slider to modify the perspective angle.**

   This value changes the apparent perspective of the object for the entire animation. Higher values severely distort the perspective of the object and can lead to some unpredictable results. Experiment with this value until you see something you like.

7. **Drag the scrubby sliders to change the X and Y vanishing point values.**

   These values stay constant for the entire animation. The X value determines the vanishing point relative to the horizontal axis, and the Y value determines the vanishing point relative to the vertical axis.

8. **Choose an option from the Color Effect drop-down menu.**

   This option applies a color effect at this point in the animation. You can create an interesting animation by applying a color effect, such as Alpha at the start of your animation. Set the Alpha value to 0 at the start of the animation and 100 at the end of the animation. The object looks like it's appearing out of thin air.

Introducing the Motion Editor

In Flash CS3, you had the option to create a custom ease. In Flash CS4, you have more control over your animations, thanks to the addition of the Motion Editor. If you've used Adobe After Effects, the Motion Editor should look familiar to you. In a nutshell, it enables you to control every facet of your animation, including applying a custom tween. We show you how to use the animation powerhouse now:

1. **Create a motion tween animation.**

   We go out on a limb here and assume that, because you're reading this section, you know how to create a motion tween animation. If not, check out Chapter 2 of this minibook, where we cover motion tweens, shape tweens, and all tweens in between.

2. **Open the Motion Editor.**

   The Motion Editor's default spot in the workspace is at the bottom of the workspace, next to the Timeline. Click its title to open it. If you're working in a different workspace or have created a custom one that doesn't display the Motion Editor by default, choose Window➪Motion Editor. The Motion Editor in all its glory is shown in Figure 4-5. Notice that there's a section for each motion parameter you can modify. Drag the scrollbar to navigate to the hidden ones.

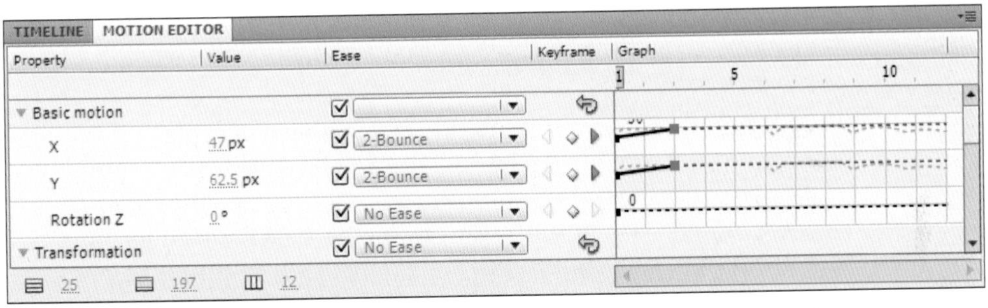

**Book III
Chapter 4**

Advanced Animation
Techniques

Figure 4-5: Yikes — the Motion Editor is a busy place.

3. **At the bottom of the interface, you find three icons. You use them to change the motion editor:**

   - *Graph Size:* Drag the scrubby slider to change the height of each graph. The option to increase graph height comes in handy when you're editing a complex animation with lots of changes on the Timeline.

- *Expanded Graph Size:* Drag the scrubby slider to set the height of the graph from the default graph size value explained in the preceding bullet. After changing this option, when you select a parameter such as X or Y in the Basic Motion section, the graph for that parameter expands to this value. You can use a relatively large value to gain better control when editing the Timeline for that parameter.

- *Viewable Frames:* Drag the scrubby slider to change the number of frames displayed in the Motion Editor.

4. **Navigate to the section you want to modify.**

   You can modify these sections:

   - *Basic Motion:* Change motion on the X and Y axes and rotate the object on the Z axis.

   - *Transformation:* Skew the object along the X and Y axes and scale the width (Scale X) and Height (Scale Y); change a color effect; change filters that have been applied to the object; and specify which ease options are available for the parameters that are animated. Note that each parameter has a check box that gives you the option of enabling or disabling animation for that parameter.

5. **In the Basic Motion and Transformation sections, you can click the curved arrow to the right of the section to reset values.**

   When you reset values for a section, any changes that have been applied to the Timelines in that section are removed.

6. **Choose an easing option from a parameter's easing drop-down menu, to the right of the check mark.**

   You can add easing options to the menu, as we explain in this step list.

7. **Drag the playhead to a frame on the Timeline where you want to change a parameter.**

   The playhead is identical to the one on the main Flash Timeline.

8. **To add a keyframe for a parameter, right-click (Windows) or Ctrl+click (Mac) and choose Add Keyframe from the context menu.**

   A keyframe on the Motion Editor Timeline is signified by a filled square.

9. **Change the value of the parameter.**

   You can change the parameter by dragging the keyframe up or down. We prefer using the scrubby slider next to the current value or clicking the current value and manually entering the value because it's more accurate.

10. **Add additional keyframes as needed.**

    When you have multiple keyframes on a Timeline, the arrow keys to the right of the Ease drop-down menu can be used. These arrows enable you to navigate to the next or previous keyframe. If you navigate to a frame on which there's no keyframe, click the spot between the arrows to add a keyframe. If you navigate to a frame on which there's a keyframe, a beige diamond appears between the arrows. Click the diamond to remove the keyframes for the parameter you're editing from the frame on which you parked the playhead.

11. **To add a color effect to the animation, click the plus sign (+) icon to the right of the Color Effect section.**

    When you add a color effect to the animation, you can set the value on the first keyframe and it remains constant throughout the course of the animation, or you can create a keyframe further into the animation and specify the value at that point. When you choose the latter method, the default value is applied to the first frame. After choosing a color effect, add keyframes and modify the values at each keyframe.

12. **To add a filter to the animation, click the plus sign (+) icon to the right of the Filter title.**

    You can apply multiple filters to an animation. After choosing filters, add keyframes and modify the values at each keyframe and then choose a filter from the drop-down menu.

13. **To remove a filter or color effect from the animation, click the minus sign (–) icon to the right of the Color Effect or Filters section.**

    After you click the minus sign, a menu appears, showing the color effect or filters that have been applied to the animation. Select the filter or color effect you want to remove.

14. **To add more eases to the animation, click the plus sign (+) to the right of the Eases title and choose an ease method from the drop-down menu.**

    When you select an ease, a graphical representation of the ease appears to the right of its name. As they say, a picture is worth a thousand words, so we save several thousand and let the graphs do what the designers of Flash intended — show you what the ease looks like.

15. **Modify the number of iterations of the ease.**

    If you choose an ease, such as Bounce or Sawtooth Wave, a value appears to the right of the name. For example, the default option for the Bounce ease causes the object to bounce four times. Use the scrubby slider to change the value, or click the current value and enter your own.

**Book III
Chapter 4**

**Advanced Animation
Techniques**

Figure 4-6 shows the Motion Editor after several parameters have been modified and three eases have been selected. Notice the Bezier handles on the Sawtooth Timeline. You can use these handles to modify the way the transition eases from one keyframe to the next. Each keyframe also has a context menu, which is also displayed in Figure 4-6. For the purpose of this animation, the Motion Editor has been undocked from the Timeline, which isn't a bad idea if you have a busy animation and have enough monitor real estate to view the Motion Editor and the Stage at the same time.

You can create a custom ease by choosing Custom from the Eases menu. Add keyframes to the Timeline to specify where the motion change takes place. Each keyframe has a Bezier point with handles. The first and last keyframe have one tangent handle. Drag the handles for each keyframe to define the custom ease, and then choose the parameters to which it will be applied.

If you're editing a motion tween animation and you decide that you want to animate a different symbol, select the first keyframe of the animation and drop a symbol from the document library onto the symbol you want to replace. Flash displays a dialog box asking whether you want to replace the symbol. Click Next to complete the swap.

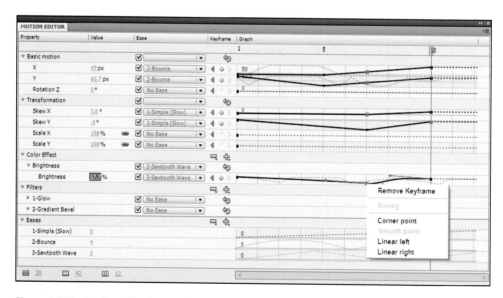

Figure 4-6: The Motion Editor is an animator's best friend.

Understanding nonroving and roving keyframes

When you create a motion tween animation and change an object's position on a specific keyframe, Flash applies the change at that keyframe. For example, if you create a 12-frame animation and on the eighth frame move the object, Flash adds a keyframe to the Timeline to note the change. When the animation plays, the object travels from Point A to Point B in 8 frames and then travels from Point B to Point C in 4 frames. If the distance from Point A to Point B is long and the distance from Point B to Point C is short, the first part of the animation proceeds slowly and then speeds up. When this scenario occurs, the object moves from Point A to Point B in a linear fashion, and then from Point B to Point C in a linear fashion. This process is known as an animation with nonroving keyframes (see Figure 4-7). Notice how much closer the points are on the final curve of the animation.

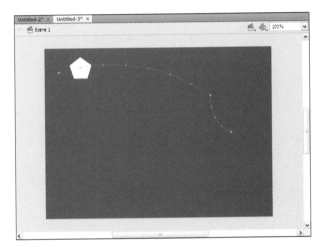

Figure 4-7: A motion tween animation with nonroving frames.

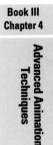

If you prefer to have a linear animation, you can do so if you switch the animation to roving frames. When you create a motion tween animation with roving keyframes and change the duration of the animation, the keyframes rove the motion path to create an animation that's perfectly linear from beginning to end. To change to roving keyframes, right-click (Windows) or Ctrl+click (Mac) the motion path and choose Motion Path⇨Switch Keyframes to Roving. Figure 4-8 shows the same motion path as in Figure 4-7 with roving keyframes. Notice that the dots that signify the in-between frames are evenly spaced. In fact, there isn't an in-between frame when the object changes direction. If, after previewing the animation, you decide to switch back, right-click (Windows) or Ctrl+click (Mac) the motion path and choose Motion Path⇨Switch Keyframes to Non-roving.

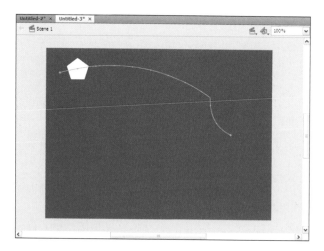

Figure 4-8: These frames were made for roving, and that's just what they'll do.

Copying Motion

Animation is fun. If you create a complex animation, though, with lots of key-frames and lots of changes in the Motion Editor, the chances of your duplicating the animation are nil unless you created the animation in a Movie Clip symbol. But if you didn't and you decide that what's cool for one object is cool for several more, you can replicate the animation blow by blow, keyframe by keyframe. You can do this by using a command or by using ActionScript as discussed in the following sections.

Using the Copy Motion command

It's Friday afternoon and you're thinking about a wonderful weekend not spent in front of a computer monitor when your favorite client (the one you nicknamed PITA) calls and tells you that the roller-coaster text animation you created for a word needs to be duplicated for two other words. In other words, the second word slides down the slippery slope a second or so after the first, and then the third follows the second. And you think "Yikes. No way." But there is a way. Follow these steps:

1. **Select the first keyframe of the animation you want to duplicate, and in the Property inspector, note the X and Y coordinates of the object.**

   This step is necessary only if you want the duplicated animation to start from the same spot.

2. **Right-click (Windows) or Ctrl+click (Mac) the first layer, and choose Insert Layer from the context menu.**

   Flash creates a new layer.

3. **Select the frame where you want the second animation to start and then press F6.**

   A keyframe is born.

4. **Create the object that you want to follow the first.**

   If you want the object to begin moving from exactly the same point, open the Property inspector and change the object's X and Y values to the same values you noted in Step 1. If you don't do this, the object has an identical motion path but starts from a different position. Sometimes that's just what you need, but in this scenario, you want the objects starting from the same place.

5. **In the first layer, right-click (Windows) or Ctrl+click (Mac) the motion path and choose Copy Motion from the context menu.**

6. **In the second layer, right-click (Windows) or Ctrl+click (Mac) the object and then choose Paste Motion from the context menu.**

   Like magic, a motion path is attached to the object.

7. **Repeat Steps 2 through 7 for other objects to which you want to apply the same animation.**

   Figure 4-9 shows three words that follow the same path, thanks to the Copy Motion command.

Figure 4-9: Follow the leader.

Copying motion using ActionScript

What happens when you create a cool animation and you want to use it with several instances of an object already on the Stage and on the same layer?

It's child's play — ActionScript to the rescue. We know what you're thinking: The ActionScript chapter hasn't happened yet. But you don't need to know much about ActionScript. All you need to do is name your symbol instances, use a command, and Flash does the rest. Follow these steps:

1. **Select a symbol instance that you want to animate with ActionScript.**

2. **Open the Property inspector.**

3. **In the Property inspector, give the symbol instance a name.**

   If the symbol instance is a graphic, choose Movie Clip from the Type drop-down menu to convert the symbol from a graphic to a movie clip. You can give a symbol instance any name you want, but don't use any special characters or spaces. For more information on naming symbol instances, see Book V.

4. **Choose Window➪Actions.**

   The Actions panel appears.

5. **Click the keyframe where you want the animation to start.**

   Alternatively, create a new keyframe where you want the animation to start.

6. **In the Actions panel, right-click (Windows) or Ctrl+click (Mac) and choose Paste from the context menu.**

   The Actions panel is filled with copious amounts of ActionScript that only a geek can understand (see Figure 4-10).

Figure 4-10: Do what?

7. Scroll to the next-to-the-last line of ActionScript.

The number of lines varies depending on the complexity of your animation. If you have lots of changes in your animation, you have a lot of code. The last line of code in this case is a curly brace. You're modifying the line of code before that.

8. Delete the two forward slashes at the start of the line.

Forward slashes indicate that the code is a comment. Some developers, including the fine folks at Adobe, comment a line of code that will turn into instructions when the forward slashes are deleted.

9. Select the text *<instance name goes here>* and replace it with the instance name you created in Step 3.

Figure 4-11 shows the modified ActionScript.

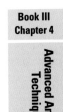

```
ACTIONS - FRAME
                                                        Script Assist
1    import fl.motion.AnimatorFactory;
2    import fl.motion.MotionBase;
3    import flash.filters.*;
4    import flash.geom.Point;
5    var __motion_Symbol1_2:MotionBase;
6    if(__motion_Symbol1_2 == null) {
7        import fl.motion.Motion;
8        __motion_Symbol1_2 = new Motion();
9        __motion_Symbol1_2.duration = 12;
10
11       // The following calls to addPropertyArray assign data values
12       // for each tweened property. There is one value in the Array
13       // for every frame in the tween, or fewer if the last value
14       // remains the same for the rest of the frames.
15       __motion_Symbol1_2.addPropertyArray("x", [0,46.4918,92.7691,138.201,182.027,223.57,262.175,297.476,329.31
16       __motion_Symbol1_2.addPropertyArray("y", [0,0.00185931,4.78771,14.8344,30.3782,51.3647,77.3603,107.703,1.
17       __motion_Symbol1_2.addPropertyArray("scaleX", [1.00]);
18       __motion_Symbol1_2.addPropertyArray("scaleY", [1.00]);
19       __motion_Symbol1_2.addPropertyArray("skewX", [0]);
20       __motion_Symbol1_2.addPropertyArray("skewY", [0]);
21       __motion_Symbol1_2.addPropertyArray("rotationConcat", [0]);
22       __motion_Symbol1_2.addPropertyArray("blendMode", ["normal"]);
23
24       // Create an AnimatorFactory instance, which will manage
25       // targets for its corresponding Motion.
26       var __animFactory_Symbol1_2:AnimatorFactory = new AnimatorFactory(__motion_Symbol1_2);
27       __animFactory_Symbol1_2.transformationPoint = new Point(0.500000, 0.500000);
28
29       // Call the addTarget function on the AnimatorFactory
30       // instance to target a DisplayObject with this Motion.
31       __animFactory_Symbol1_2.addTarget(Moe);
32   }
33
Layer 2 : 1
Line 31 of 33, Col 43
```

Figure 4-11: Cut and paste is simply mah-velous, dahlink.

10. Press Ctrl+Enter (Windows) or ⌘+Enter (Mac).

The ActionScript you pasted into the frame has the symbol instance jumping through hoops.

**Book III
Chapter 4**

**Advanced Animation
Techniques**

Editing a Shape Tween Animation

If you up the ante on a shape tween animation and have the sublime morph into the cor blimey, you may have a problem on your hands. If the shapes aren't simple, Flash may have a tough time doing the math, and Zippy the Wonder Rectangle doesn't morph into Zippy the Wonder Star in a predictable manner. When you create a shape tween animation, your audience should have a clue what the final shape will look like during the transition period from one keyframe to the next. If the in-between frames look like Heinz 57 pixels, you have to lend Flash a helping hand in the way of shape hints. To find out all about them, follow these steps:

1. **Create a shape tween animation.**

2. **Drag the playhead across the frames of the animation.**

   Pay special attention to the shapes on the in-between frames. Figure 4-12 shows a blob of pixels that's supposed to be a 5-pointed star morphing into a triangle. This shape is difficult for Flash to calculate because of the difference in the number of sides for each shape. When you have a difficult shape tween, look for common elements between the two shapes. In our scenario, the triangle has three points. Look for three points on the star that form a similar shape.

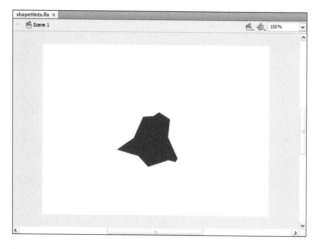

Figure 4-12: Say what?

3. **Select the first keyframe in your animation, select the object, and then choose Modify⇨Shape⇨Add Shape Hint.**

   Flash places in the middle of the shape a small red dot with a lowercase letter *a* in its center. You can't see it, but a red dot with a lowercase a in its center has been placed in the center of the second object. You use the letters as a guideline when placing shape hints on each object. Shape Hint *a* on the first object morphs into Shape Hint *a* on the second object.

4. **Drag the shape hint to the location you want.**

   If you examine both objects for similarities, you know where to place the shape hint. You should place it on something that Flash can recognize, such as the point where two lines intersect.

5. **Choose Modify⇨Shape⇨Add Shape Hint.**

   Flash places in the center of the first object a small red dot with a lowercase *b* and in the center of the second object.

6. **Drag the second shape hint to the location you want.**

   Shape hints work best when you arrange them in counterclockwise order.

7. **Continue adding shape hints as needed.**

   At the risk of being redundant, let us say that you'll know how many shape hints you need after examining the shapes for similarities and examining the animation on the in-between frames before adding shape hints.

8. **Click the last keyframe in the animation.**

   In the center of the shape, you find a pile of shape hints; the same as the number of shape hints in the first object. The last shape hint is on top.

9. **Arrange the shape hints on the second shape.**

   Remember to arrange the shape hints in counterclockwise order. As you move the shape hints to their respective points on the second object, they turn green, and the shape hints on the first object turn orange, which is Flash telling you that it can create a decent shape tween animation. Figure 4-13 shows the triangle in the animation with shape hints applied.

10. **Drag the playhead to preview the shapes on the in-between frames.**

    Figure 4-14 shows the in-between frames for the shape tween animation of a star morphing into a triangle. The viewer has a good idea of the shape that will appear at the end of the animation. Compare this object to the gnarly-looking one shown in Figure 4-11.

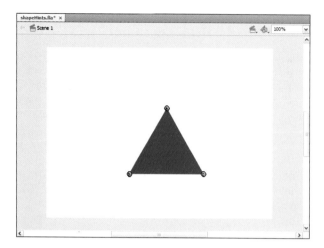

Figure 4-13: We're here to give Flash a helping hand. That's our lot in life.

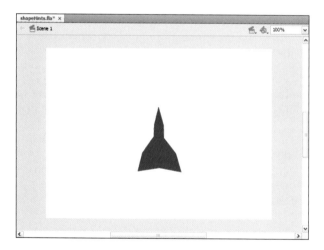

Figure 4-14: Shape hints come to the rescue again.

Editing Multiple Frames and Other Delights

When you're working with a frame-by-frame animation, the option to edit multiple frames can save you a lot of time. At other times, you might want to see what's happening on the other frames in your animation. That's when you call in the onion skins. Sometimes you need both features at the same time. If we've piqued your curiosity, please read on.

Using onion skins

Onion skins make it possible for you to see what your animation looks like on other frames. When you enable the Onion Skins option, Flash displays a lower-opacity version of the shapes on the in-between frames of a motion tween or shape tween, which shows you how the shapes on the in-between frames will be drawn and where they appear on the Stage. If you don't like what you see on a motion tween, you can modify the motion path and immediately see the results. If you're editing a shape tween animation, the onion skins on the in-between frames show you how the object morphs from Shape A to Shape B. You can view onion skins as outlines or as lower-opacity renditions of the shape as it appears on that frame. To enable onion skins, click the second icon on the bottom of the Timeline panel. To enable onion skin outlines, click the third icon at the bottom of the Timeline panel.

Figure 4-15 shows an animation after onion skins have been enabled. The default option shows only two frames on either side of the selected frames. You can change this option by dragging the hollow dots at the end of the onion skin markers that look like black braces at the end of the onion skin frame span, which is designated in dark gray on the Timeline.

You can change the manner in which onion skins are displayed by clicking the Modify Onion Markers icon at the bottom of the Timeline panel. This action opens a menu that gives you the option to display onion skin markers, anchor the onion skins to the selected frame, and specify the number of frames to which onion skins are applied.

Editing multiple frames

The option to edit multiple frames comes in handy when you need to fine-tune a classic motion tween or classic shape tween animation. When you enable the editing of multiple frames, you can select an object on any keyframe and change its position or size, for example. Used in conjunction with onion skins, it's a powerful one-touch punch that helps you finish your editing in record time. To enable the editing of multiple frames, click the

Book III
Chapter 4

Advanced Animation Techniques

Edit Multiple Frames icon at the bottom of the Timeline. Figure 4-16 shows a shape tween animation with the Edit Multiple Frames option enabled. Notice that both shapes are displayed as though they were on the same frame even though the playhead is parked on an in-between frame. Each shape can be edited from this frame or from any frame in the marked span.

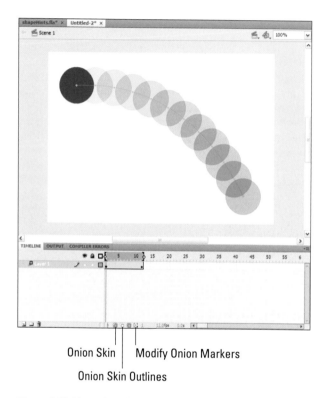

Onion Skin   Modify Onion Markers

Onion Skin Outlines

Figure 4-15: Use onion skins when your animation drives you to tears.

When you work with a shape or motion tween animation created with the new paradigm, viewing multiple frames is useful. However, you can edit only the object on the first keyframe in a motion tween animation and then edit the path. Using the new method of creating a shape tween, you can edit the object on the first and last keyframe.

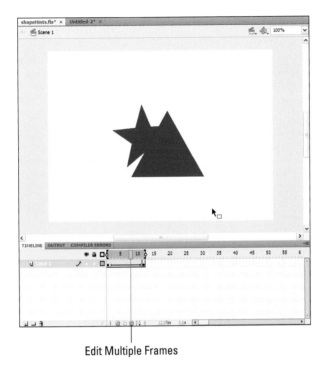

Edit Multiple Frames

Figure 4-16: Editing multiple frames is a powerful option.

Book IV
Adding ActionScript 3.0 Magic

The 5th Wave   By Rich Tennant

"See? I created a little felon figure that runs around our Web site hiding behind banner ads. On the last page, our logo puts him in a non-lethal choke hold and brings him back to the home page."

*A*ctionScript 3.0 gives you total control over what you want to happen on the stage. Long gone are the days when all ActionScript could do was start and stop an animation. You can now do everything from create shapes dynamically to load animated movie clips on the fly.

Book IV shows you how to harness the power of ActionScript 3.0 using both the Timeline and the external ActionScript files. You can drag images across the stage, dynamically use text to respond to user actions, use the new Vector class to draw images and store and retrieve data, and much, much more. This is Flash with a power boost!

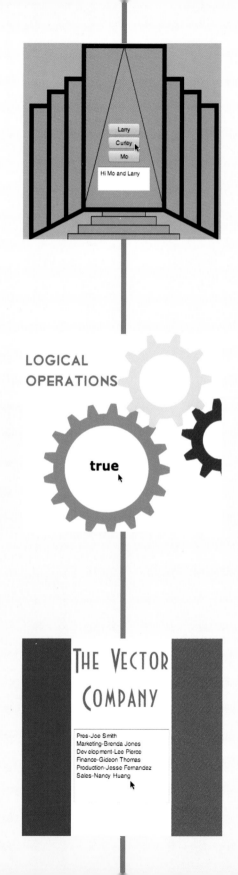

Chapter 1: Who's Afraid of the Big Bad ActionScript 3.0?

In This Chapter

- Understanding old and new ActionScript
- Working on the Timeline
- Writing scripts
- Using event listeners
- Capturing mouse events
- Creating functions for buttons
- Controlling movie clips

ActionScript in Flash began as a way to control the Timeline of a Flash movie. Buttons, movie clips, and keyframes could all contain little bits of script. For example, you could assign a `gotoAndStop(12)` statement to a button so that when that button is pressed, the playhead would move to Frame 12 and stop. Usually, the targets of the script were keyframes where new content would appear. The downside of this method is that each button required its own script, and as application sizes grew, so too did the complexity of working with all those little scripts.

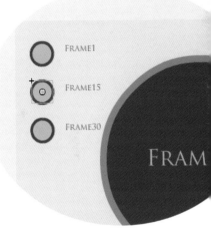

With each new version of Flash, ActionScript improved, but nowhere near as dramatically as with ActionScript 3.0, where the language has been revised from top to bottom.

So that you can write more powerful ActionScript, Adobe modeled the latest release of ActionScript similar to other programming languages. Yes, we said the ugly word: programming. But before you run off and jump into cauldron of boiling oil as a pleasant alternative to programming, in this chapter we show what you can do with ActionScript 3.0 and (we hope!) convince you to give the latest version a try.

Vive la Différence: New versus Old ActionScript

The new ActionScript 3.0 is based on a standard with the rather drab moniker ECMAScript Revision 4.

Standardizing the language increases both stability and familiarity, so you don't have to learn the language all over again each time a new version of Flash is released. The following sections give you the lowdown on some of the basic features of the new, improved ActionScript and how they've changed from previous versions.

Button scripts

ActionScript 3.0 can be used in conjunction with buttons and movement on the Timeline, but things are done differently. If you're an old hand with ActionScript, it might help to review some of the differences. If you're new to Flash and ActionScript, ignore the old way of using ActionScript and just concentrate on the new way.

The old way of working with buttons and ActionScript was to select a button and in the Actions Panel write something like the following:

```
on(release) {
    gotoAndStop(5);
}
```

Because the ActionScript was written on the button, you didn't have to reference the button name. It was simple, but with several buttons spread throughout an application at different levels and positions on the Timeline, debugging each individual button could quickly become a nightmare.

With ActionScript 3.0, the reference to a button is to the button instance name, where an *instance* is just the name you give to a button. For example, the name *myButton* uniquely identifies a button and differentiates it from every other button instance.

All button instance names must be unique so that you can tell one from the other.

You give a button an instance name by selecting the button and typing the name of the button in the Properties panel. (Figure 1-1, a little later in this chapter, shows the instance name of the button in the Properties panel.)

Mouse events

When you want a button to do something, first you assign it an *event handler,* which for a button can be several different actions, just as with the old ActionScript. However, because the events are actions taken using the mouse, the event handler is some kind of `MouseEvent`. The following mouse events are available:

CLICK

DOUBLE_CLICK

MOUSE_DOWN

MOUSE_MOVE

MOUSE_OUT

MOUSE_OVER

MOUSE_UP

MOUSE_WHEEL

ROLL_OUT

ROLL_OVER

As you can see, they're expressed in ALL CAPS; this is because they're constants that don't change in value. So, a CLICK is always a mouse click by the user and nothing else. Just say "Play it again, Sam:" A CLICK is just a CLICK, a mouse is just a mouse. These fundamental concepts apply as the Timeline goes by.

Also, MouseEvent constants are fairly self-explanatory. For example, a DOUBLE-CLICK means that the button is double-clicked, and a ROLL_OVER occurs when the mouse is rolled over the button.

Listen up! Adding event listeners to buttons

We human beings listen for all kinds of events every day, practically all day. You listen for your cell phone or doorbell to ring or for the dog to bark or a baby to cry. With ActionScript 3.0, you do the same thing. When *this event* occurs, the event listener is basically telling the rest of the code, "Listen up! do something!" The generic format for writing an event listener is

```
myButton.addEventListener(MouseEvent.EVENT, function);
```

This line of code needs one of the ten mouse events listed in the previous section. Likewise, the function that it calls can be any kind of function allowable in ActionScript 3.0; for example:

```
btnTxt.addEventListener(MouseEvent.CLICK, launchShip);
```

Imagine that a doorbell is the button, the wiring of the doorbell to the chimes adds the event listener, the particular sound made by the chimes is the event ("ding, dong!"), and the function (answering the door) is the action taken when the doorbell rings. Figure 1-1 illustrates this relationship.

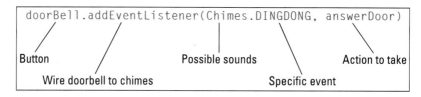

Figure 1-1: The relationship between the even listener, event, and action.

Functions for buttons

You need to add a function in order to do something. Further details about ActionScript 3.0 functions are discussed in Chapters 2 and 5 of this minibook, but for now, we describe a simple one just to get you started. An ActionScript 3.0 function is made up of the word *function;* a function *name; parameters*, if any; and *statements* telling the application what to do. Functions also have a return type, consisting of either the data type returned or void, which means that nothing is returned. (Think of a *return* as a value that the function generates, just like a value in a variable.) Sometimes when the function returns nothing, the return type is omitted. With buttons, you always need an event parameter that provides a variable with the event type. For example, the following code shows a function that tells the application to go to Frame 10 and stop:

```
function launchShip(e:MouseEvent):void
{
    gotoAndStop(10);
}
```

Figure 1-2 shows all the different parts of the function used by the button.

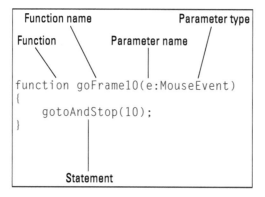

Figure 1-2: The parts of a function.

In looking at the parts of a function, they're pretty simple. You might think of them as instructions you give to a small child. You lay out the instructions in detail. First, you tell the child that you're giving him an instruction (function) and the name of the task (coming to dinner.) The parameters represent the event that initiates the action (immediately), and the statements are further instructions (sit down, don't play with your food, and eat your vegetables). It might look like this:

```
function comeToDinner(yell:MomInstruction)
{
    sit down;
    don't play with your food;
    eat your vegetables;
}
```

The extent to which you imagine functions as a set of instructions — an instruction package — the more sense they make.

Bossing around movie clip scripts

As you may know from working with Flash movies, the main stage or Timeline is just one big movie clip. So writing movie clip scripts is just a matter of selecting keyframes on a movie clip's Timeline and adding code in the Actions panel. However, we don't have you write much code on movie clips' Timelines because it's not only an easy way to get tangled up and make a mess but also bad form. That's because it hides the code from the main program, and you'll play *Where's Waldo* trying to find out which movie clips have embedded code. Essentially, you need a way to order movie clips around. With buttons as a user interface, the code needs to indicate which movie clip is being sent an instruction. Keeping all your code in one place makes life a lot easier, and the only code that's in the movie clips is a `stop()` statement in the first frame.

You might be thinking, if you build a sophisticated movie clip with lots of different places to stop, that you need lots of `stop()` statements in the movie clips. It isn't true. Suppose that your movie clip has 50 places with 50 different keyframes where the user should be able to stop. The magic method is

```
gotoAndStop(n);
```

You can not only direct a movie clip's Timeline to stop at a keyframe (n) but also have it stop at any frame. All you need is to address the movie clip's instance name and use the magic method. For example,

```
froggy.gotoAndStop(23);
```

instructs a movie clip with the instance name `froggy` to hop over to Frame 23 and stop.

You're not confined to using Timeline commands. You can use any of the MovieClip class methods or properties that you want. Figure 1-3 gives you an idea of the large number of methods that are available. Just select the MovieClip class in the Actions panel and click the Methods or Properties directory.

Figure 1-3: The Actions panel displaying a MovieClip's methods.

To find the MovieClip class, you need to first locate the directory (or package) it's in. Take a look in the `flash.display` directory.

Experiment with some of the different methods besides `gotoAndStop()`, and notice that you already used `addEventListener()`, another MovieClip method. After you experiment with several methods, open the Properties directory and see what trouble you can cause. (Just kidding.) For example, the following examples show the use of different MovieClip properties with a movie clip instance, myClip:

```
myClip.x=200; // Horizontal position on screen
myClip.y=150; // Vertical position on screen
myClip.rotation=33; // Tilt to 33 degree angle
```

Go ahead and experiment with different properties until you get the hang of it.

Movin' On the Timeline

After you have an idea of what you can do, we show you how to use that knowledge to put together something practical; for example, an application that lets the user control the Timeline.

The following steps walk you through the project using buttons, keyframes, simple graphics and ActionScript 3.0 that holds the whole thing together:

1. **Open a new Flash file (ActionScript 3.0), give the file a name, name the layer, and then save the file.**

   Our example uses three different pages located on three different keyframes. The ones we use in this example are just big circles, but they could be different product or services descriptions, steps in a project, descriptions of different people in a company, or any other endless number of possibilities.

   In the example, we saved it as `TimeLine.fla` and named the layer `actions`.

2. **Click on a frame and press the F5 key.**

   We clicked on Frame 30 and pressed F5, which creates 30 frames.

3. **Create two more layers and position them below the Actions layer.**

   We named the layers `Controls` and `Timeline`, as shown in Figure 1-4.

4. **Select the Timeline layer and add the keyframes you want by selecting each frame you want to add content to individually and pressing F6.**

   We added keyframes at Frames 15 and 30.

5. **Click on the first frame of the Timeline layer and add whatever content you want to the frames.**

   We drew a circle and, in the middle of the circle, typed `Frame 1` using the Text tool set to Static Text. We did the same thing in Frames 15 and 30, typing the names `Frame 15` and `Frame 30`, respectively. Figure 1-4 shows how Frame 30 looks.

6. **Lock the layer.**

7. **To create a button, click on a frame and add an image to it, if it doesn't already have one.**

   This image is the visual button that users expect to click. We clicked the first frame of the Controls layer and drew a circle with the dimensions (W=32.5 and H=32.5). The numbers represent the number of pixels, but all you see in the Properties panel are the numbers associated with W and H — W(idth) and H(eight).

**Book IV
Chapter 1**

**Who's Afraid
of the Big Bad
ActionScript 3.0?**

Figure 1-4: An instance name of a selected button being added in Properties panel.

8. **Select the image and press F8.**

   The Convert to Symbol dialog box appears.

   We selected the circle (including the stroke line) and pressed F8 to create a symbol.

9. **Select Button as the type, type a name for the button, and then click OK.**

   We named ours Btn.

10. **Make as many buttons as you want and click a button.**

    The Properties panel appears.

    For this example, we made two copies of the button, lined them up vertically (as shown earlier, in Figure 1-1), and selected the top button.

11. **Type a name for the button's instance name and do the same for any other buttons, if you have more than one.**

    We named our buttons not very imaginatively but short, sweet, and obvious: btn1, btn2 (refer to Figure 1-4), and btn3.

12. **Add content to the frames that the buttons will target and then lock the layer.**

We used the Text tool set to Static Text and then typed Frame 1 next to the first button and Frame 15 and Frame 30 next to the second and third buttons, respectively (refer to Figure 1-4).

13. Click the first frame of the Actions layer, open the Actions panel, and add a script similar to the following. Change the italicized text and add or delete lines as necessary, depending on the number of buttons you have, their names, and which frames you used:

```
stop();

//Add event listeners to buttons
btn1.addEventListener(MouseEvent.CLICK,go01);
btn2.addEventListener(MouseEvent.CLICK,go15);
btn3.addEventListener(MouseEvent.CLICK,go30);

//Functions for buttons
function go01(e:MouseEvent):void
{
    gotoAndStop(1);
}
function go15(e:MouseEvent):void
{
    gotoAndStop(15);
}
function go30(e:MouseEvent):void
{
    gotoAndStop(30);
}
```

You might be wondering what `:void` means in the functions. That term tells the compiler not to expect anything to be returned. If you want a value returned, you enter the type (such as `String` or `Number`) rather than `void`.

14. After you complete the script, lock the layer and test the movie by pressing Ctrl+Enter (or ⌘+Return on the Mac).

If everything is working correctly, your movie plays.

If you followed our example (download it at www.dummies.com/flashallinone), you see that as you press each button, a different circle appears, indicating the appropriate frame. You have total control over the Timeline, and users can select where on the Timeline to position the playhead. Of course, users never see the playhead. All they see is different information arranged so that it's easy to find, and you managed to create three pages from a single page.

If you use the Timeline as a means of moving to different sets of information in your application, your application can accumulate a large number of bytes in the size of the SWF file. For smaller projects with just a few images or a little text, it works fine. In Chapter 2 of this minibook, you see an alternative to using the Timeline. Rather than create giant SWF files, you just bring in what you need, when you need it, and still just use one page.

Controlling Movie Clip Timelines

After you know how to control a Timeline using ActionScript 3.0, you can see how to control another movie clip's Timeline. Keep in mind that the task we show you in the preceding section only moves the playhead on the main Timeline, What you do in this section is move the playhead on a different movie clip's Timeline.

Suppose that you have created an animation that you want to execute only when directed to do so by the user. You can have bouncing balls, dancing bears, and juggling jugglers if you want, all animated and ready to go. However, you only want the balls to bounce, bears to dance, and jugglers to juggle when the user so directs. You can add a lot of stop() statements to different positions on a Timeline of a movie clip to help to control the flow, but to do so adds an unacceptable level of clutter.

Clutter in an application is a slippery slope to chaos, wringing of hands, and gnashing of teeth. The bigger the application, the more problems you encounter. Therefore, the only ActionScript in the movie clip is a single stop() statement in the first frame of the Timeline.

Now we show you how to do something interesting with a movie clip and ActionScript.

The following application uses three instances of a single movie clip. The movie clip represents a glass that fills up using a shape tween. Four buttons control the glasses and the tween in the movie clip. The following instructions step you through the process:

1. **Open a new Flash file (ActionScript 3.0), name it, save it under the name you want, and then name the layer.**

   We saved our file as McTimeLine.fla and named the layer actions.

2. **Choose Insert⇨New Symbol.**

   The Create New Symbol dialog box appears.

3. **Type the name for the symbol, select Movie Clip for the type of symbol, and then click OK.**

   The Symbol Editor appears, where you can create your movie clip as though you're working on the main Timeline.

   We typed Cup for the name.

4. **In Symbol Editor mode, name the layer and type the stop(); statement in the Actions panel (as shown in Figure 1-5).**

   We named the layer action.

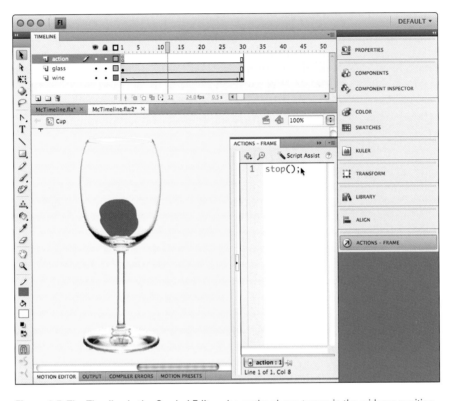

Figure 1-5: The Timeline in the Symbol Editor shows the shape tween in the midway position.

5. **Click on a frame and press the F5 key to add frames from Frame 1 all the way out to your chosen frame. Then lock the action layer.**

We chose to add frames out to Frame 30 and then locked our `action` layer.

6. **Add at least one more layer beneath the `action` layer, name the new layers, and lock them.**

Our example adds two more layers beneath the `actions` layer and names them `glass` and `wine`, respectively (refer to Figure 1-5); we locked only the `wine` layer.

7. **Select a layer where you want your image and draw or paste an image on the Stage.**

We selected the glass layer and pasted an image of a glass on the Stage. We used a large (roughly 70 x 400) image to make it easier to create a shape tween of liquid being added in the next step. After we finished, we locked the glass layer.

Book IV
Chapter 1

Who's Afraid
of the Big Bad
ActionScript 3.0?

8. **Unlock the layer you plan to use, select it, and use the Paint tool to add drawings to be tweened.**

   We unlocked the `wine` layer, and using the Paint tool, brushed a small burgundy-colored (#8E3557) dab at the bottom of the glass. This makes it look as though just a small bit of wine remains.

9. **Click on the frame where you want the tween to end and press the F6 key to add a keyframe. Expand the painted image to the size you want at the end of the tween.**

   We selected Frame 30 on the `wine` layer to add a keyframe. Using the Paint tool, we filled in the area so that the entire glass is burgundy colored. You can expand the initial paint dab using one of the selection tools or just paint using the Paint tool to fill it up. The largest glass in Figure 1-7 (later in the chapter) shows what the filled glass should look like.

10. **Click on the first frame of the current layer and right+click the mouse (or Ctrl+click on the Mac) to open the context menu. When the context menu opens select Create Shape Tween. To check whether the tween is working as intended, drag the playhead back and forth on the Timeline.**

    We selected the `wine` layer. The arrow with a green background on the `wine` layer told us that we had successfully created a shape tween. If everything is working correctly, save all files and then click the Scene 1 icon to close the Symbol Editor and open the main Timeline.

11. **In the main Timeline, add three layers and provide names for them.**

    We named the layers `buttons`, `glasses`, and `table`, placing them below the `actions` layer, as shown in Figure 1-6. Then we locked all layers except the `table` layer. In the upper-right corner, we added a rectangle that serves as a "table" on which to place the wine glasses. After it was completed, we locked the table layer.

12. **Prepare to add your movie clips above the background layer by unlocking the layer and locking the others. Drag your movie clips from the Library panel to the Stage and use the tools to modify them.**

    We selected the `glasses` layer and dragged three instances of the Cup movie clip from the Library panel to the table area, as shown in Figure 1-6. We resized the Cup instances using the Free Transform tool.

13. **Select each movie clips object, and in the Properties panel, provide each one with a unique instance name in the Instance window.**

    We selected each of the Cup instances and in the Instance name window in the Properties panel, named them `glass1`, `glass2`, and `glass3`. This step is crucial because ActionScript uses those names to reference each instance. We locked the glass layer when we finished.

14. **Unlock and select the layer where you plan to place your buttons. Use the Oval tool to draw an image on the Stage that you will transform into a button. Then select the image and press F8 to open the Convert to Symbol dialog box and select Button as the type. Finally, provide a name for the symbol and click OK.**

We used the `buttons` layer (no surprise there). Using the Oval tool, we drew a simple circle for our button shape and named it `fill`. When you click one of these buttons, it *fills* the glass — we probably could have named it Phil.

15. **Drag button instances from the Library panel to the Stage and arrange them as you want them to appear. Then select each button and provide each one with a unique instance name in the Properties panel.**

We made a total of four buttons and arranged them vertically, as shown in Figure 1-6. Then, in a fit of creativity, we named the buttons btn1, btn2, btn3, and btn4, respectively, from top to bottom.

16. **Add static text labels to the buttons. Then lock the layer when you're finished.**

Figure 1-6 shows the labels we used for the buttons, ordering from top to bottom, Full, Half, Third, and Down the Hatch.

17. **Click the first frame of the actions layer, open the Actions panel and add the ActionScript. Then save the file.**

We used the following code:

```
//Buttons
btn1.addEventListener(MouseEvent.CLICK,full);
btn2.addEventListener(MouseEvent.CLICK,half);
btn3.addEventListener(MouseEvent.CLICK,third);
btn4.addEventListener(MouseEvent.CLICK,empty);
//Button Functions
function full(e:MouseEvent):void
{
    glass1.gotoAndStop(30);
}

function half(e:MouseEvent):void
{
    glass2.gotoAndStop(15);
}

function third(e:MouseEvent):void
{
    glass3.gotoAndStop(10);
}

function empty(e:MouseEvent):void
```

```
{
    glass1.gotoAndStop(1);
    glass1.rotation=90;
    glass1.x=450,glass1.y=200;
    glass2.gotoAndStop(1);
    glass3.gotoAndStop(1);
\}
```

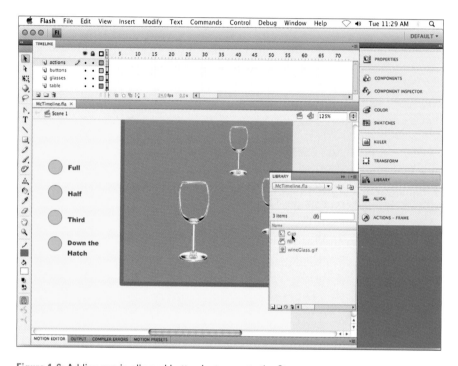

Figure 1-6: Adding movie clip and button instances to the Stage.

18. Test the application by pressing Ctrl+Enter (or ⌘+Return on the Mac).

After the application has launched, click the different buttons. You see the glasses filled at different levels after clicking the top three buttons, as shown in Figure 1-7.

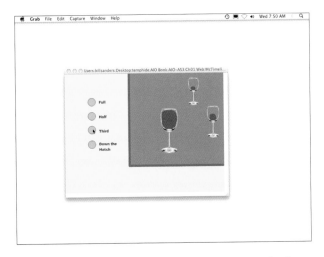

Figure 1-7: ActionScript controls the tweens in the movie clips.

When you press the Down the Hatch button, all glasses are emptied, and one falls on its side. They're emptied by moving the playhead to the first frame, and the glass tipped over had its rotation changed.

Chapter 2: Working Off the Timeline with Symbol and Component Classes

In This Chapter

✓ Working off the Timeline

✓ Writing programs in ActionScript files

✓ Inserting comments in code

✓ Using clip code

✓ Creating a class

✓ Using a symbol button in a class

✓ Addressing classes and instances on the Stage

✓ Using user interface (UI) component classes

✓ Constructing list events

Designers and developers have long been accustomed to the idea of using clip art in their work. Clip art includes ready-made drawings and photographs that can be used copyright-free in everything from printed flyers to images used in Flash applications.

You don't have to be an artist or a designer to use clip art, but you have to have a sense of design in terms of where to place it. (Yes, you can create *ugly* designs if you put clip art in the wrong surroundings!) Likewise, using code, you can cut and paste chunks of ActionScript code like clip art, but rather than artwork, it's just code. That's all we mean by *clip code* — it's just a chunk of code that you can cut and paste and that does something. To get started working with ActionScript 3.0 off the Timeline, you may have to think of some of the codes as clip code: You may not understand all of it at first, but if you know where to put it, it can accomplish just what you want. Coding "off the Timeline" means that you write ActionScript in separate (ActionScript) files rather than in the Actions panel associated with a keyframe on the Timeline.

Breaking the Timeline Habit

Having code scattered throughout keyframes in a Flash application multiplies exponentially the chance of experiencing a disaster every time you add a new keyframe with code attached. Changing code makes an even bigger mess, so we show you how to use the available tools in Flash CS4 and ActionScript 3.0 to start working without having to rely on code embedded in the Timeline.

Forming a tag team with ActionScript and a Flash file

Before you begin creating applications with ActionScript 3.0, you must to consider two basic concepts: class and object. An easy way to think of these two concepts is in terms of a *template* for a class and an *actual use* of the template for an object. For example, Flash CS4 lets you open the Advertising template named Banner. That template is similar to a class — it's the general outline. Some templates are rich and complex, and others, like the Banner template, are quite simple. When you use the banner template to create a banner for your company, *Acme Flash Developers*, for example, that's analogous to an object.

Rather than have you develop programs using the Actions panel, we show you how to use another method that doesn't use the Timeline. Flash files are used in conjunction with ActionScript files. The Flash file provides the Stage for any graphics and symbols you want to create and access ActionScript by a reference to a class name. That class name is embedded in the ActionScript file. Figure 2-1 illustrates this method of working with dual files.

With a Flash file open, you just type the class name in the Properties panel. Then you use that name for the class you create in the ActionScript file. Most classes begin with these lines:

```
package
{
    class ClassName
    {
        function ClassName()
        {
```

The `package` statement may be followed by the name of a folder where you have stored other classes. No matter what, you start your class definition with `package`. Following a curly brace (`{`), type the `class` statement followed by the name of the class and another curly brace (`{`). After the second curly brace (`{`), add a constructor function, which typically has the same name as the class. The *constructor* function contains the main statements that can call other functions (methods) in the class and construct objects from other classes or assign values to properties.

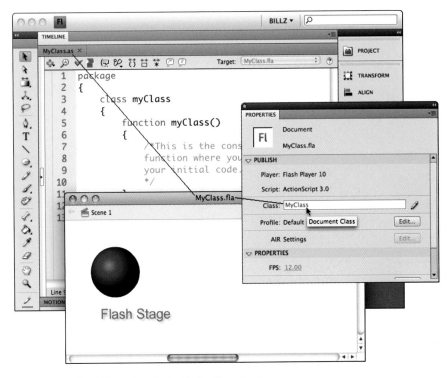

Figure 2-1: A Flash file and an ActionScript file with class.

When you create a class in ActionScript 3.0, your class generally inherits from another class that has all the necessary methods, events, and properties you need in order to display objects on the Stage. More likely than not, you use the Sprite or MovieClip class as a basis for your new class. We prefer using the Sprite class because we don't need the Timeline for most projects, and the files are a bit smaller. To inherit a class, ActionScript 3.0 uses the `extends` statement. Furthermore, to use the Sprite class in addition to most other classes, the other classes need to be imported from the appropriate package. For example, the Sprite class is imported using the following line:

```
import flash.display.Sprite;
```

All imports generally begin with either `flash` or `fl`. The `flash` packages contain the bulk of ActionScript classes, and `fl` packages contain components such as buttons and lists. As you can see in Book VII, Chapter 2, components are treated just like classes in that they have properties, methods, and events that you can address with code.

Book IV
Chapter 2

Working Off
the Timeline with
Symbol and
Component Classes

Comments and clip code

In a computer program, *comments* are lines of code that are used to remind the developer what the code is used for or to suggest alternatives. You usually see comments embedded within lines of code. A single comment is prefaced by double slashes (//). In our example, the following line reminds the developer that the color red is used:

```
//0xcc0000 is a medium dark red
```

Sometimes, comments are used to add a title or description at the beginning of a code set. At other times, comments are quite long, and rather than place double slashes at the beginning of every line, the developer uses /* to begin a block of comments and */ to end the block. For example, the following block reminds the developer that different options are available for text styling:

```
/* Instead of using the default serif
font, try a sans serif font, such as
Arial or Verdana. Also, consider
changing the background color to make
it stand out more.
*/
```

Comments are important for making code easier to understand for developers — and for the people they work with. Comments help explain what's going on in a program. In this book, you see some comments, but because most of the code is described in the text, comments in the code are minimal. Seeing the flow of the code is important, and sometimes comments can get in the way of seeing that flow. So, because you're finding out how to use ActionScript 3.0, we decided not to put too many comments in the code.

The first piece of clip code is something you can cut and paste into most of your classes. It's a class template that you see repeatedly in this book. You can save the template in an ActionScript file named ClassStarter and just load it up and then use the Save As command to save it as the name of the current class:

```
//Class Starter
package
{
    import flash.display.Sprite
    /*Declare private variables
    here */
    public class ClassName extends Sprite
    {
        public function ClassName()
        {
            //Add statements here
        }
    }}
```

The world's simplest class

In this section, we show you a simple class, and then we show you how to build a class that displays text in the Output panel using the `trace()` statement. Follow these steps:

1. **Open a new Flash (ActionScript 3.0) file, and in the Properties panel, type a name for the class in the Class window and then save the file.**

   You see a warning message that the file wasn't found, but don't worry about that. The next step creates the necessary file.

   We named our class `SimpleClass`, as shown in Figure 2-2. We then saved the file as `SimpleClass.fla`.

Figure 2-2: Setting the Document class in a Flash file.

2. **Open a new ActionScript file and save it in the same folder as the file you created in Step 1.**

   We named our file `SimpleClass.as` and saved it in the same folder as `SimpleClass.fla`.

3. **Open the ClassStarter clip code file and copy the contents to the Clipboard.**

   You can download ClassStarter from this book's companion Web site at `www.dummies.com/go/flashallinone`.

Book IV
Chapter 2

Working Off
the Timeline with
Symbol and
Component Classes

You can copy by choosing Edit➪Select All and then Edit➪Copy or by pressing Ctrl+A (Windows) or ⌘+A (Mac) to select all the code and then Ctrl+C (Windows) or ⌘+C (Mac) to copy it.

4. **Open the file you created in Step 1 (again, we named ours SimpleClass.as) and paste the ClassStarter code into the file.**

   You can paste by choosing Edit➪Paste or by pressing Ctrl+V (Windows) or ⌘+V (Mac).

5. **Edit the code so that it appears as the following and then save the file:**

   ```
   //Simple class
   package
   {
       import flash.display.Sprite

       public class SimpleClass extends Sprite
       {
           public function SimpleClass()
           {
               trace("Simple class--hello world");
           }
       }
   }
   ```

   As you can see, all you had to change was the name of the class from ClassName to SimpleClass (or whatever name you chose) and add the trace statement. (The changes are highlighted in bold.)

6. **Test the application as you would test any Flash file by pressing Ctrl+Enter (Windows) or ⌘+Return (Mac).**

   If all the code is entered correctly in the Output panel, you see the text Simple class--hello world (refer to the bottom of Figure 2-2).

Making a MovieClip class in Flash

During all the time you're creating movie clips, you're creating new *classes*. Each movie clip can be treated as a class by simply opening the Symbol Properties dialog box and selecting the Export for ActionScript check box, as shown in Figure 2-3.

In this application, you don't place any items on the Stage in the Flash (FLA) file. Instead, you use the code in the ActionScript file to do it for you. To use code to place the movie clip on the Stage, you use a *display list,* which lists everything displayed on the Stage. You don't see the list, but ActionScript keeps it for you. Using the statement addChild(objName), you add objects to the Stage (and the display list). Using the x and y properties of the MovieClip class, you can put the movie clip object anywhere you want on the Stage. The most recently added objects overlap the earlier objects. However, using `addChildAt(objName, index)`, you can specify the index level. Higher index values overlap lower index values. Likewise, using the `rotation` property, you can angle it any way you want.

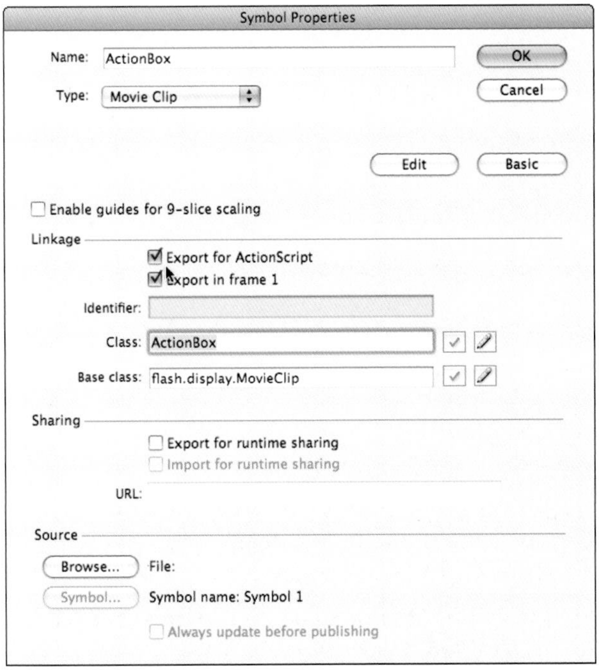

Figure 2-3: Exporting a movie clip class for ActionScript.

The next project shows you how easily you can create a class just by working on a movie clip on the Stage. (And you didn't think you could make a class!) Follow these steps:

1. **Open a new Flash (ActionScript 3.0) file, add a class name for the application in the Class window in the Properties panel and save it.**

   You see that pesky alert box telling you that the class doesn't exist; just ignore it.

   We named our class `MCaction` and named the file `MCaction.fla`.

2. **Choose Insert⇨New Symbol to open the Symbol Editor.**

3. **When the Create New Symbol box appears, type a name for the symbol, select MovieClip for the type, and select the Export for ActionScript check box. Click OK when you're finished.**

Book IV
Chapter 2

Working Off
the Timeline with
Symbol and
Component Classes

We named our symbol ActionBox.

The Export in Frame 1 check box is automatically selected. (In case you don't see it, click the Advanced button to display the advanced options.)

4. **Draw a 150 x 100 rectangle using the Rectangle tool at the 0,0 point in the Symbol Editor.**

The 0,0 point represents the little crosshair (+) that appears when you open the Symbol Editor.

5. **(Optional) You can add tweens, inverse kinematics (IK), additional frames, or anything else that you would add to any other movie clip.**

Figure 2-4 shows a movie clip that's loaded, containing an IK and some shape tweens that reverse the rectangle's fill and stroke colors.

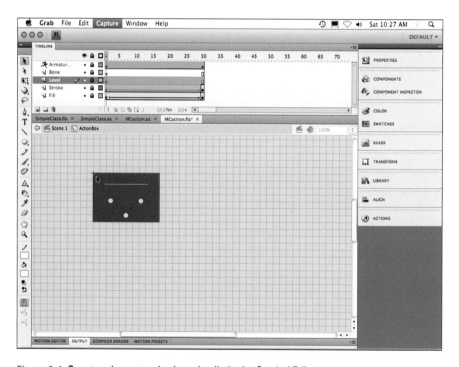

Figure 2-4: Constructing a standard movie clip in the Symbol Editor.

6. **After you finish the movie clip, click Scene 1 and save the FLA file again.**

Do not place a copy of the movie clip on the Stage. The Stage should be blank, and the movie clip should be visible in the Library panel. All the placement is done by ActionScript, and if you leave any movie clips on the Stage, they may overlap the ones created dynamically by ActionScript.

7. Open a new ActionScript file and save it in the same folder as the file you created back in Step 1.

We named ours `MCaction.as` and saved it in the same folder as the `MCaction.fla` file.

8. Add the following script to the ActionScript file and then save the file:

```
package
{
    import flash.display.MovieClip;

    public class MCaction extends MovieClip
    {
        private var ab1:ActionBox;
        private var ab2:ActionBox;

        public function MCaction()
        {
            ab1=new ActionBox();
            addChild(ab1);
            ab1.x=150, ab1.y=150;
            ab1.rotation=33;

            ab2=new ActionBox();
            addChild(ab2);
            ab2.x=200, ab2.y=165;
            ab2.rotation=-30;
        }
    }
}
```

The `public` and `private` statements are access statements. If a variable is defined using a `private` access statement, it can be used only by elements in the same class. The `public` access statements are the default option, but adding them helps to remind you that they're public.

9. Save the file and then test the application by pressing Ctrl+Enter (Windows) or ⌘+Return (Mac).

You see the two movie clips on the Stage, one slightly overlapping the other, as shown in Figure 2-5. They're two instances (objects) of the `ActionBox()` class. Because a movie clip is involved, the class inherits (extends) from the MovieClip class rather than from the Sprite class.

Book IV
Chapter 2

Working Off
the Timeline with
Symbol and
Component Classes

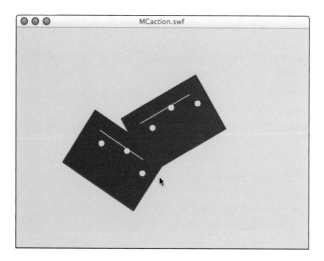

Figure 2-5: Movie clips sent to the Stage.

Buttons and text fields: A tale of two objects

After you realize that you can treat a movie clip symbol as a class, why not treat a button symbol and a text field in the same way? You can make a button symbol and export it for ActionScript, just as you can do with a movie clip. The button symbol is based on the SimpleButton class. However, a text field has a different story. A text field, as you might recall, isn't one of the symbol options. You create it by using the Text tool. Then you decide whether the text is Input, Dynamic, or Static, depending on the task. (The different types of text fields are introduced in Book II, Chapter 3.) Nevertheless, ActionScript has a TextField class that you can dynamically create.

Follow these steps to create a button class by using standard drawing tools and to create different kinds of text fields using only code:

1. **Open a new Flash (ActionScript 3.0) file and save it.**

   We saved ours as `TextMove.fla`.

2. **Open the Properties panel, and in the Class window, type** TextMove.

3. **Create a few layers, name them, and save the file.**

   We created three layers with the names Labels, Oval, and Lines, from top to bottom, respectively.

   Add a dark background or use the one shown in Figure 2-6 so that the light-colored text used by the dynamically created output text field is visible.

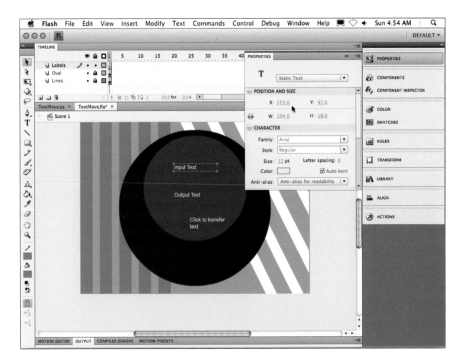

Figure 2-6: The label position on the Stage in the Properties panel.

4. **Choose Insert⇨New Symbol to open the Symbol Editor.**

   The Create New Symbol box appears.

5. **Type a name for the symbol, select Button for the type, and select the Export for ActionScript check box.**

   We named our symbol Btn.

   The Export in Frame 1 check box is automatically selected. If you don't see the check box, click on the Advanced button to display the advanced options.

6. **Draw a circle that has a 29-point diameter (W=29, H=29) using the Oval tool at the 0,0 point in the Symbol Editor.**

   The 0,0 point is represented by the little crosshair (+), in the middle of the page, that appears when you open the Symbol Editor.

7. **(Optional) Add varying state conditions in the special Button Timeline by adding keyframes and different shapes or colors to the button object; when you're finished, click on the Scene 1 icon to close the Symbol Editor.**

**Book IV
Chapter 2**

**Working Off
the Timeline with
Symbol and
Component Classes**

8. **Back on the main Timeline, add the following text to the Labels layer by using the Text tool set to Static Text. (See Book II, Chapter 3 for a refresher on how to add static text with the Text tool.) Use the Properties panel to create the precise x and y values.**

   - *Input Text:* x=223, y=97

   - *Output Text:* x=223, y=161

   - *Click to transfer text:* x=260, y=219

   Figure 2-6 shows the first label's information in the Properties window.

9. **Save the file.**

If you're a designer, add the text where you think it looks best and make a note of the x and y positions by selecting the objects and checking the Properties panel. Likewise, you can add Input and Dynamic text fields and align them with the labels. Make a note of the Input and Dynamic text fields and remove them from the Stage. Then when you're entering the code that includes the x and y positions of the Input and Dynamic text fields, everything looks the way you intended.

10. **Open a new ActionScript file and save it in the same folder as the file you created in Step 1.**

    We saved our file as `TextMove.as` in the same folder as the `TextMove.fla` file.

11. **Add the following script to the ActionScript file:**

```
package
{
    import flash.display.Sprite;
    import flash.events.MouseEvent;
    import flash.text.TextField;
    import flash.text.TextFieldType;

    public class TextMove extends Sprite
    {
        private var btn:Btn;
        private var inputTxt:TextField;
        private var outputTxt:TextField;

        public function TextMove()
        {
            //Button
            btn=new Btn();
            addChild(btn);
            btn.x=216,btn.y=220;
            btn.addEventListener(MouseEvent.CLICK, moveText);
            //Input Text Field
            inputTxt=new TextField();
            inputTxt.width=86,inputTxt.height=18;
            inputTxt.x=223,inputTxt.y=66;
            inputTxt.background=true;
            inputTxt.border=true;
            inputTxt.type=TextFieldType.INPUT;
            addChild(inputTxt);
```

```
        //Dynamic Text Field
        outputTxt=new TextField ();
        outputTxt.textColor=0xDDDCC5;
        outputTxt.type=TextFieldType.DYNAMIC;
        outputTxt.x=223,outputTxt.y=128;
        addChild(outputTxt);
    }
    private function moveText(e:MouseEvent):void
    {
        outputTxt.text="Hi, "+inputTxt.text+"!";
    }
  }
}
```

12. **Save the file and test it by pressing Ctrl+Enter (Windows) or ⌘+Return (Mac).**

    Figure 2-7 shows that `All in One` has been entered in the Input text field and that `Hi, All in One!` now appears in the Output text field.

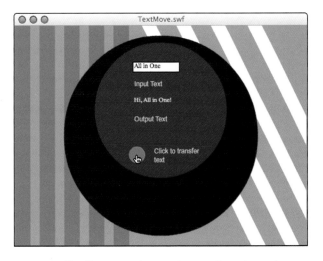

Figure 2-7: Sending text and a greeting to a dynamic text box.

Code and Design Made Easy

In case the idea of creating all your class-based objects in code is just too much for you, you can mix code with objects you place on the Stage. You may already know this if you read Chapter 1, but in that chapter, we use the Actions panel and not classes. In this section, we show you what you need to do to write classes that can reference an object on the Stage.

Book IV
Chapter 2

**Working Off
the Timeline with
Symbol and
Component Classes**

Going back to instance names

The good news about using objects created on the Stage is that you simply give the object an *instance name*, as we mention in Chapter 1. The display list holds the order that you put objects on the Stage and not the order that you instantiate them in code. You don't have to declare or instantiate objects in code that you place on the Stage, but you do have to give each one an instance name. Furthermore, because you're using symbols, you need not select the Export for ActionScript check box.

This process sounds easy if you're used to working on the Stage. The only drawback is that you cannot see the instance names of the objects unless they're selected and the Properties panel is open. So, when you're writing your code, you need to remember the instances names.

 If you choose to give objects instance names on the Stage, you might want to add the instance names in sections of your program that are *commented out* — they're nonrunning sections of code in comment lines or tags. (*Nonrunning* code refers to comments in the code that are not executed when the program runs.)That way, you can have the instance (object) names right in front of you while you're entering ActionScript.

Easy application and easy objects

To see how the mixed-code-and-symbol approach works, we devised a simple application that sends different text to two dynamic text boxes. Using two buttons that you create on the Stage, along with the two text fields, also created on the Stage, you use the instance names to send each text box a message. The following steps show you how:

1. **Open a new Flash (ActionScript 3.0) file and open the Properties panel from the dock or from the Windows menu. Type a class name in the Class window and save the file.**

   We named our class OnStage and saved the file as OnStage.fla.

2. **Draw a circle, select it, choose Modify⇨Convert to Symbol (press F8) to open the Convert to Symbol dialog box, select Button as the type, type a name for the symbol, and click OK.**

   We typed Btn for the symbol name.

3. **Make a copy of the button symbol and place it on the Stage.**

   You now have two buttons on the Stage.

4. **Select the first button and open the Properties panel from the dock or by choosing Windows⇨Properties from the menu bar. Give the button an instance name, and then do the same for the second button.**

   We named our buttons btn1 and btn2.

5. **Select the Text tool and click on the Stage.**

6. **In the Properties panel, select the font you want and set the Text type to Dynamic in the pop-up menu at the top of the Properties panel.**

7. **Give the text field an instance name, copy the text field on the Stage, and give it a different instance name.**

   We named our instances `txt1` and `txt2`, respectively.

   Use a different size, color, and font type for the two different text fields so that you can see the difference in the text when you launch the program.

8. **Save the file.**

   Figure 2-8 shows an example of two text fields and buttons on the Stage.

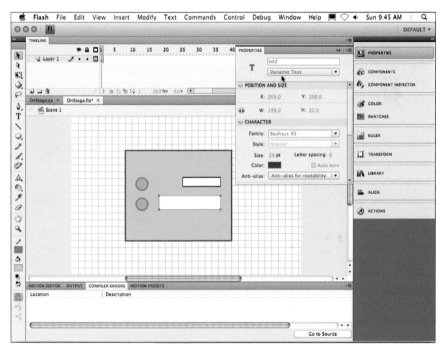

Figure 2-8: Two button instances and two text field instances on the Stage.

9. **Open a new ActionScript file, name it, and save it in the same folder in which you saved the file you created in Step 1.**

   We named our file `OnStage.as` and saved it in the same folder as `OnStage.fla`.

Book IV
Chapter 2

Working Off
the Timeline with
Symbol and
Component Classes

Add the following script to the ActionScript file:

```
package
{
    import flash.events.MouseEvent;
    import flash.display.Sprite;
    {
        public class OnStage extends Sprite
        {
         public function OnStage()
         {
    btn1.addEventListener(MouseEvent.CLICK, showTxt1);
    btn2.addEventListener(MouseEvent.CLICK, showTxt2);
         }
            private function showTxt1(e:MouseEvent)
            {
                txt1.text="This is txt1";
            }
            private function showTxt2(e:MouseEvent)
            {
                txt2.text="This is txt2";
            }
        }
    }
}
```

10. **Save the file and test it by pressing Ctrl+Enter (Windows) or ⌘+ Return (Mac).**

You should see the text moving directly into the designated text field when the buttons are clicked, as shown in Figure 2-9.

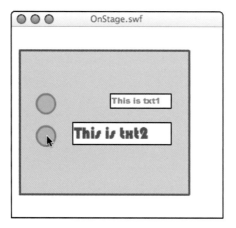

Figure 2-9: ActionScript content in two text fields.

The Simple Power of User Interface (UI) Component Classes

For the most part, a *component* is nothing more (or less) than a fancy movie clip. You know that you can work with movie clips, so it follows that you should be able to work with components. Elementary, my dear Watson!

After you exhaust the logical deductions we tackle in this book, consider the advantages you have in using components. In Book VI, you see plenty of examples of using video components, so in this section, we focus only on UI components.

For the most part, components have more properties and methods than noncomponent symbols, such as the movie clips and buttons, which means that it's easier to add content to a UI component. For example, if you create a button, you cannot dynamically label it (without a lot of extra work), nor can you easily change its other properties. With the Component button, you can easily label it or change it.

Choosing from a list

A handy user interface in most applications is a list. Users can see the selections in the List component and choose what they want by simply clicking the appropriate choice. To illustrate how a list might be used and indicate which ActionScript to use with it, this next Flash application uses both a list and some TextArea components. After a user selects a name from the List UI, a quote from that name appears in the TextArea.

List events

In the next Flash application, you let the user click a name in the List component, and a quote from that person then appears in the TextArea component. So you have to listen for a click on a *list item* — one of the selections in the list. The particular event handler looks like this:

```
list.addEventListener(ListEvent.ITEM_CLICK,handler);
```

The preceding line shows essentially the same kind of listener you see on buttons. However, rather than a MouseEvent, it's a ListEvent. The event is an ITEM_CLICK rather than a CLICK. Otherwise, though, it uses exactly the same logic.

Book IV
Chapter 2

Working Off
the Timeline with
Symbol and
Component Classes

List data

To be able to select from a List component, you need to put something in the List. Using the Component inspector, you add both a label and some data. The label becomes what you see, and the data is a value (numeric or string) associated with the label. All you need is some kind of abbreviated code — initials, for example — to determine which quote to display. For example, for Dorothy Parker, you can use dp. However, for Homer, you can use hom (because, like Madonna and Cher, Homer has only one name). Figure 2-10 shows the names in the label and the data. (Whatever value you place in the label row becomes the name that appears in the selected row.)

Figure 2-10: Adding content to the List component.

To get the data out of the list box, you must capture the event property. The ListEvent class has item.label and item.data properties. Using the item.data properties, you use a switch statement to determine which item has been clicked. (The switch statement is explained in detail in Chapter 4 of this minibook.) Here, switch is a clip code that you can cut, paste, and edit, and it determines which of several choices have been made:

```
private var choice:String;
private var choiceNum:Number;
. . .
choice="choiceB";
switch(choice)
{
    case "choiceA" :
        //Do A;
        break;

    case "choiceB" :
        //Do B;
        break;

    case "choiceC" :
        //Do C;
        break;
}
```

The `switch` clip code can be expanded (to the limit of the computer and the language) to add as many choices as you want. The `choice` variable can be a string or a number. The numeric variable `choiceNum` in the clip code is used where the data is numeric.

Don't quote me!

The application in this section shows how to use components on the Stage with class references through an ActionScript 3.0 user class. Creating the application in the following steps requires only two components on the Stage:

1. **Open a new Flash (ActionScript 3.0) file and save it.**

   We saved ours as `AutoQuote.fla`.

2. **Open the Properties panel from the dock or by choosing Windows⇨Properties from the menu bar. In the Property panel's Class window, type** AutoQuote **and save the file.**

   Ignore the error message that informs you that no such class exists.

3. **Open the Components panel from the dock or by choosing Windows⇨Components from the menu bar. Drag some components from the Components panel to the Stage or double-click the components for them to jump to the Stage. Position the components on the Stage by dragging them. Select the components you want to change and make the changes in the Properties panel.**

   We dragged one List and one TextArea component to the Stage, placing the List component directly above the TextArea component. (Figure 2-11 shows where we placed them.) We changed the size of the List component to 150 x 100 and the TextArea to 300 x 150 by using the Properties panel. The two components were then center-aligned to the Stage using the Align panel.

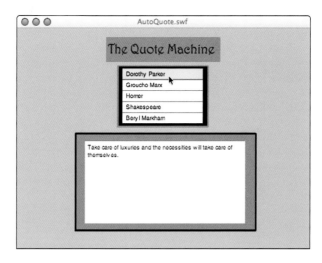

Figure 2-11: Displaying a quote from the selected item in the List component.

4. **Select each component, and in the Properties panel enter the instance name for the component.**

   We named the List component `list` and the TextArea component `output`.

5. **Open the Component inspector and click on the dataProvider magnifying glass icon.**

   This step opens a box named `Dialog`, where you can enter the information for the list box.

6. **Click on the plus sign icon (+) and enter the label and data information.**

   Here's our example:

   - Label: Dorothy Parker: Data: dp
   - Label: Groucho Marx: Data: gm
   - Label: Homer: Data: hom
   - Label: Shakespeare: Data: ws
   - Label: Beryl Markham: Data: bm

   When you finish, you should see the label names you entered in your List component on the Stage. Save the file.

7. **Open a new ActionScript file and save it.**

   We saved ours as `AutoQuote.as`.

Add the following code in the file and save the file again:

```
package
{
    import flash.display.Sprite;
    import fl.events.ListEvent;

    public class AutoQuote extends Sprite
    {
        private var choice:String;
        private var dorothy:String;
        private var groucho:String;
        private var homer:String;
        private var shake:String;
        private var beryl:String;

        public function AutoQuote()
        {
            //Quotes
            dorothy="Take care of luxuries and ";
            dorothy+="the necessities will take ";
            dorothy+="care of themselves.";
            //
            groucho="Those are my principles, ";
            groucho+="and if you don't like them";
            groucho+="... well, I have others.";
            //
            homer="A generation of men is like ";
            homer+="a generation of leaves; ";
            homer+="the wind scatters some leaves ";
            homer+="upon the ground, while others ";
            homer+="the burgeoning wood brings forth";
            homer+="--and the season of spring comes on.";

            homer+="So of men one generation springs";
            homer+="forth and another ceases.";
            //
            shake="For I have neither wit, ";
            shake+="nor words, nor worth,";
            shake+="\nAction, nor utterance, ";
            shake+="nor the power of speech,";
            shake+="\nTo stir men's blood: ";
            shake+="I only speak right on;";
            shake+="\nI tell you that which ";
            shake+="you yourselves do know;";
            //
            beryl="You can live a lifetime ";
            beryl+="and, at the end of it,";
            beryl+=" know more about other people ";
            beryl+="than you know about yourself";

            list.addEventListener(ListEvent.ITEM_CLICK, sendSelect);
        }
        private function sendSelect(e:ListEvent)
        {
            choice=e.item.data;
            switch (choice)
            {
                case "dp" :
                    output.text=dorothy;
                    break;
```

Book IV
Chapter 2

**Working Off
the Timeline with
Symbol and
Component Classes**

```
                   case "gm" :
                        output.text=groucho;
                        break;

                   case "hom" :
                        output.text=homer;
                        break;

                   case "ws" :
                        output.text=shake;
                        break;

                   case "bm" :
                        output.text=beryl;
                        break;
              }
         }
      }
   }
```

It's easier to read the code in a long string if you use the += compound operator. It adds each new part of the string to the whole while letting you see what you're writing.

Wherever you want a line break in a string of text, use the \n character.

When you test the application, you can click any of the names in the list and display the associated quote in the TextArea component. If your text is a long quote that's overruns the space provided, a scroll bar appears automatically so that you can scroll and read the entire text. Figure 2-11 shows an example of what you see.

Chapter 3: Formal Features and Structures

In This Chapter

↙ **Checking out basic ActionScript 3.0 structure**

↙ **Typing data**

↙ **Adding instance names for stage objects**

↙ **Using components in the Library panel**

↙ **Ogling variables, constants, and objects**

↙ **Importing packages**

↙ **Setting access**

↙ **Working with operators**

↙ **Commenting and uncommenting code**

↙ **Understanding logical operations**

U p to this point in this book we really haven't discussed the general features of ActionScript 3.0. Usually, discussions of the new ActionScript begin with explanations of all of the different parts and structures. Thus far we've decided to choose the road less traveled and discussed several key features and structures and asked you to use *clip code* with the promise that everything will be explained in good time. Well, now is that *good time*, and so in this chapter we'll explore the groundwork for the code we've been using in earlier chapters. By understanding the structures and features, you will become less dependent on clip code and can start developing your own code to create whatever you want.

Checkin' Out the Basics: "My, My, 1 Declare!"

One of the most important basic structures in ActionScript is the *variable*, which is simply a temporary storage place where you can put data. To make life interesting, the data within a variable can change. For example, suppose you have a variable that stores the current temperature — tempNow. As the day passes, the temperature might be hot and then later cool off, and the temperature changes. So, the first time we look, tempNow might be 95, and at another time it might be 68. In this case, the variable's value has changed (from 95 to 68) but we're still using the same variable.

Often, we will use different properties of a class to store information that changes, and so you can think of *class properties* as variables that belong to the class.

You are soooo not my type!

In early versions of ActionScript, the variables were sometimes considered *smart*, which meant that you could put any kind of data you wanted into a variable. For example, a variable smartyPants could have number or string values (as defined in the next section) and so the following sequence was perfectly acceptable:

```
smartyPants = 55;
trace(smartyPants);
smartyPants = "fifty-five";
trace(smartyPants);
```

You *cannot* do this in ActionScript 3.0. To make the code run better and faster, every variable now has a *type*. When you declare a variable, you enter a type to indicate what kind of data it can hold. Depending on what you want to do and which type (or types) you use. Think of String types as text and Number types as plain old numbers. For example, if you want to keep track of purchases and add them up, you would want a Number type; however, if you want to store the names of your friends, you would use a String type.

Figure 3-1 shows the basic structure of a command that declares a variable and assigns it a value.

You do not need to assign a value to a variable when you declare it. All you need to declare a variable is indicate that it is a variable with var, give it a name (such as myVar) and indicate the variable type by placing a colon (:) followed by the data type (type). The following examples show some different types of variables you may declare and assign values:

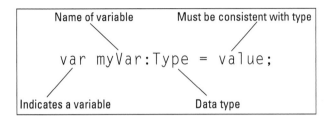

Figure 3-1: Declaring a variable and assigning a value.

```
var bestFriend:String;
var crowdSize:int;
var averageWeight:Number;
var favColor:uint;
```

All of the above variables have fairly general types:

- A *string* is any kind of expression enclosed in quotation marks (`"string"`). Usually, a string is used where the variable stores a description or label. For example, the address `123 Elm Street` is a string even though it contains numbers.

    The numbers in an address or a phone number are really *identifiers* and cannot perform like numbers. If you add two addresses, you'll find that you do not get the sum of the two!

    When working with strings, be careful if you copy and paste a program from a word processor or PDF file. Sometimes, *smart quotes* are used. Smart quotes are either opening (") or closing (") quotes and are not recognized by ActionScript. You need the straight quotes (" ") that are identical for opening and closing a string.

- Numbers, even simple ones, are a little trickier. Three different numeric types are used: `int` (integer), `uint` (unsigned integer), and `Number` (real number.) An integer is any whole number, be it positive or negative. If your integers are all *positive*, use unsigned integers. Finally, real numbers are *floating point numbers* that can have fractions. They're called *real* because they can have fractions, and *floating point* because the decimal point can change places (float). (Unreal numbers are what you put on your expense account!)

We will be using *type* differently than usual. Expressions such as *typing a variable* or *an object has been typed as a Button* aren't talking about someone pounding away on a keyboard; rather, *typed* refers to what type a variable or object has been declared.

Typing on the Stage

So far in this minibook, you've created *instances* () of Buttons and MovieClips on the Stage using the tools available in Flash CS4 for drawing.

When you use Flash tools to create objects on the stage and provide them instance names in the Properties panel, you are, in effect, declaring and typing them. Therefore, you don't have to do it again, nor do you need to import Button or MovieClip objects when created on the stage — it's done automatically. Likewise, when using the different UI components, once they have been declared on the stage using the Properties panel, you need not type them or import their base class. That's also done automatically when you put an instance name in the Properties panel.

Using components in the Library

Say you want to dynamically create user interface (UI) buttons on the stage with different buttons being available in different contexts: In one context, you want five buttons, and in another you only want three. If you create five buttons on the stage, you can reduce the number from five to three by making two of them invisible. However, doing so will force you to rename labels and perform other chores that may be more trouble than using ActionScript.

To make objects more flexible when you create them on the stage, place them in the Library panel. For example, if you place a `Button` component in the Library but do not have it on the stage, you can access it by code. You have to import the Button class *and* place a UI button in the Library panel. Here's an outline of the procedure:

1. **Place a UI in the library.**
2. **Import the UI object in the code.**
3. **Declare an instance.**
4. **Instantiate an instance.**
5. **Add the instance to the display.**

As an example, the following code shows Steps 2 through 5. (We assume that the UI component has already been placed in the Library, as mentioned in Step 1.) Note that the lines in boldface correspond with Steps 2 through 5 in the preceding list, respectively:

```
package
{
    import flash.display.Sprite;
    import fl.controls.Button; //Import

    public class TestBench extends Sprite
    {
        private var btnUI:Button; //Declare

        public function TestBench()
        {
            btnUI=new Button(); //Instantiate
            btnUI.label="UI for You!";
            btnUI.x=150, btnUI.y=200;
            addChild(btnUI); //Add to display list
        }
    }
}
```

If you make any changes to the UI component, such as color, shape, or size, those changes will be seen when the component is placed on the stage. You can also use ActionScript to make changes.

Even though a component is in the library, you need to provide a way to reference each instance of the component. You cannot use the Properties panel, because the component needs to be on the Stage. All you have to do is to use a name when you declare it so that the instance name will be created just as any other variable would be.

Variables, constants, and objects

When creating a variable or object, use the `var` statement.

When you create a *constant* (a value that does not change), you use the `const` statement. Because both variables and objects have been discussed, let's look at constants.

Like the name implies, constants do not vary. Certain things are immutable such as the value of `pi`, the freezing point of water (32 °F/0 °C) and water's boiling point (212 °F/100 °C). Once you assign a value to a constant, you cannot change it. Also, by convention, constants are written in ALL CAPS to help you remember they're constants and not variables.

In the following code, you'll see how constants differ from variables and object properties. Once you declare and assign a value to a constant, any re-assignment of a value results in an error.

```
const FREEZE:uint= 32;
trace(FREEZE);
FREEZE= 55; // causes error
trace(FREEZE);
```

You'll get the following error message:

```
1049: Illegal assignment to a variable specified as constant.
```

That's exactly what you want to happen with a constant. Any change in the constant's value means it is varying (like a variable) and it's not supposed to do that.

Types that need importing

One of the ongoing learning experiences in ActionScript 3.0 is knowing when to load a class you want to use. Rather than learning all of the classes that require you to load a package that includes the class, it's easier to just learn what classes you do *not* need to import. These are the *top-level* classes that are packaged with Flash CS4 ActionScript 3.0.

If you don't see the object class you wish to import in Table 3-1, plan on using the import statement.

Table 3-1	Top-Level Classes	
ArgumentError	arguments	Array
Boolean	Class	Date
DefinitionError	Error	EvalError
Function	int	Math
Namespace	Number	Object
QName	RangeError	ReferenceError
RegExp	SecurityError	String
SyntaxError	TypeError	uint
URIError	Vector	VerifyError
XML	XMLList	

The import statement itself is similar whether you're importing classes or components. (Okay, okay, components *are classes,* but it helps to differentiate them for now.) Figure 3-2 shows the format for importing classes and components.

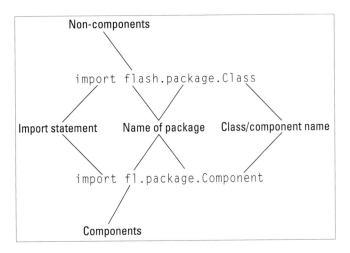

Figure 3-2: Importing classes and components.

As a rule, components are in the fl.* packages and the non-components are in the flash.* packages. However, to make your life more interesting, Adobe also includes in the fl.* package, a class for Multilanguage text (fl.lang), ActionScript 3.0 Motion classes (fl.motion), and one for Tween and Transition classes (fl.transitions).

Use the asterisk (*) as a wildcard character to allow you to quickly download multiple files with names that begin identically and end differently. So a reference to flash.media.* means that everything in the flash.media package that begins with flash.media.* will be either imported or referenced.

Don't use the asterisk (*) wildcard for importing a package unless you know you will be using everything (or almost everything) in the package. If you only need the Video class in the flash.media package, for example, using the wildcard would load up nine unnecessary classes, adding unnecessary size (bulk!) to the file and giving the loading and processing more work to do.

To know which class belongs to which package, say that you have flash. display, flash.text, flash.net, and other flash.this-and-that packages. If you want to create a MovieClip object, you should first know the correct package to import, but none of the flash.* package names seem to have anything to do with the MovieClip class based on the package name.

Rather than trying to memorize all the classes in all the packages in the *ActionScript 3.0 Language and Components Reference* (which comes with Flash CS4), start with just a few and then learn the rest later as you use them. The following packages have most of what you need:

- ⮞ **flash.display:** In this package you will find most of the classes that are commonly used in Flash. Included are the MovieClip, SimpleButton, Sprite, Loader and many of the graphic classes.

- ⮞ **flash.text:** As the name implies, this package holds classes for text, fonts and types of text fields.

- ⮞ **flash.media:** When working with sound and video, this package has the classes you need.

- ⮞ **flash.net:** While you will find expected classes like NetConnection and NetStream in this package, you will also find the classes you need to link to other Web pages.

- ⮞ **flash.events:** You may overlook this package, but this is where you will find the events you need for a wide assortment of classes that use events to trigger methods. The MouseEvent class is one widely used example.

- ⮞ **fl.controls:** The UI components can be found in this package.

Forget memorizing all of this. Don't waste your time! As soon as you type the `import flash` statement and add a period, a pop-up menu appears and shows you the available options. (This is *code hinting!* Hint, hint.) Likewise, when you select an available package from the list and add a period, the next level appears with the classes contained therein. So, instead of trying to memorize everything, just start using the packages and classes that you know, and with use you'll learn the others. Figure 3-3 shows some of the classes found in the `flash.display` package.

Figure 3-3: Using pop-up menus to find which class you need.

Access denied! Setting access

Another statement type that you will see is an *access modifier*. Access modifiers determine what other objects can access variables, constants, and functions (methods). Unless otherwise stated, constants, variables and methods are available to other classes — public access, meaning that any other class can use the element. The problem with such open access is that the same variable may be given conflicting values. Likewise, different parameters may be assigned to a method when that's not really what you want.

If you ever find yourself at a gathering where programmers are serious about their craft (also know as a flock of geeks . . . or would that be a gaggle?), you will hear the term *encapsulation*, one of the foundations of object oriented programming (OOP). You definitely should understand what it means. When programming with objects, you can think in terms of larger parts that can have several variables (properties) and functions (methods).

Think of your automobile as an object with lots of parts (properties and methods) that make up the car. You have control over access to your car because it is *encapsulated* — self-contained. If your car were not private — that is, if it had no locks and key — anyone could use it. In programming, the same is true. An encapsulated object restricts access to its properties and methods just like you restrict access to your car. In the same way that you can own your car, and the car "owns" its various parts, encapsulated elements in your class help to maintain the *object character* of your program. (Think of an object character as an object in its own right instead of a collection of parts.)

The following list briefly describes the main access modifiers:

- ✔ **public:** Any other class can access and use the object. For the most part, you want your classes and construction functions to be public. Also, if you have methods you want to be able to be used when implemented by another class, the methods should be given public access.

- ✔ **private:** Only members of the same class can access this object. (Remember your car!)

- ✔ **protected:** Only members of the same class or inherited from the same class can use the method or property.

To demonstrate how to use these access modifiers, check out the following two classes. The first class, TestBench, has three different methods, one each for private, protected, and public access modifiers. Both the private and protected methods can be called from the TestBench class. All private, protected, and public methods can be called from the class of origin. However, only the public methods can be called from an outside class. So, in the TestBench class, we called the private and protected method. The following listing shows this. (You can create this listing in an ActionScript file saved as something like TestBench.as.)

```
package
{
    import flash.display.Sprite;

    public class TestBench extends Sprite
    {
        private var privMsg:String;
        private var protecMsg:String;

        public function TestBench()
```

```
    {
        privMsg="This is exclusive...";
        priv(privMsg);

        protecMsg="This 's extended to children...";
        protec(protecMsg);
    }
    private function priv(msg:String):void
    {
        trace(msg);
    }
    public function pub(msg:String):void
    {
        trace(msg);
    }
    protected function protec(msg:String):void
    {
        trace(msg);
    }
    }
}
```

To call the public method and illustrate how it can be used, we created a second class, `PubPriv`. All this class does is create (programmers say *instantiate*) an instance of the TestBench class and invoke the `pub()` method. The following listing shows the code for this simple chore. (Create this listing in an ActionScript file saved as `PubPriv.as`.)

```
package
{
    import flash.display.Sprite;

    public class PubPriv extends Sprite
    {
        private var tb:TestBench;
        private var outMsg:String;

        public function PubPriv()
        {
            tb=new TestBench();
            outMsg="Greetings from another class!"
            tb.pub(outMsg);
            //tb.priv("private");
            //tb.protec("protected");
        }
    }
}
```

To test these two classes, you can create a `PubPriv.fla` file using the `PubPriv` as a class reference in the Properties panel. Save it in the same folder as the `TestBench.as` file.

You do not need a `TestBench.fla` file because you can use any FLA file to contain the name of the class you will be using.

Be sure to place all the files in the same folder and then load `PubPriv.fla` and test it. You see the following lines in the Output panel:

```
This is exclusive...
This is extended to children...
Greetings from another class!
```

The first two lines are generated by the TestBench class because it's the only one with access to the private and protected methods. The third line is generated by the PubPriv class. It uses the `pub()` method, adding a string literal (actual text, like "hello!") in the parameters.

Note that two lines in the PubPriv class have been commented out.

```
//tb.priv("private");
//tb.protec("protected");
```

After testing the application, uncomment the lines (that is, remove the slashes `//`), save it, and try it again. You'll get error messages because you attempted to launch functions with limited access (private and protected.) Because the PubPriv class is a different one than the one where the methods are created (TestBench) and it is not derived from (that is, it does not extend) TestBench, it has access to neither private nor protected methods in that class.

Operators: Assign, Compare, and Do the Math

ActionScript 3.0 has a wide range of operators, some of which we've used. For example, we've used the equal sign (=) operator to assign values to variables and we've used the plus sign (+) to perform addition as well as *concatenate* (combine) strings. Some operators have been compound, such as the plus equal (+=) used to add the existing string with a newly added one.

Operator? Operator?

Now it's time for a general overview of three types of operators we'll be using. Table 3-2 shows the main operators used in math, comparison, logical, and assignment operations.

Table 3-2		Operators
Symbol	**Name**	**Action**
+	Addition	Adds numbers
--	Decrement	Subtracts 1 from current value
/	Division	Divides one number by another
++	Increment	Adds 1 to current value
%	Modulo	Returns remainder in division
*	Multiplication	Multiplies numbers
-	Subtraction	Subtracts numbers
+=	Add/assign	Adds current value to new value
/=	Divide/assign	Divides current value by second value
%=	Modulo/assign	Shows modulo of current value divided by second value
*=	Multiply/assign	Shows product of current value multiplied by second
-=	Subtract/assign	Shows result of current value minus second value
Assignment		
=	Assignment	Assigns value to object property, variable, or array element
Comment Operators		
//	Comment	Sets line to a comment
/* */	Block comment	Provides block for comments
Comparison Operators		
==	Equality	Tests for expression equality
>	Greater than	Tests for left expression being greater than right expression
>=	Greater than or equal to	Tests for left expression being greater than or equal to right expression
!=	Inequality	Tests for inequality to right expression
<=	Less than or equal to	Tests for left expression being less than or equal to right expression
===	Strict equality	Tests for left expression being equal to right expression and the same data type
!==	Strict inequality	Tests for left expression being unequal to right expression and a different data type

Symbol	Name	Action
Logical		
&&	Logical AND	Returns true if values for left and right expressions are both true. Otherwise returns false.
&&=	Logical AND assignment	Assigns true if values for left and right expressions are *both* true. Otherwise assigns false.
!	Logical NOT	Tests for expression false. If it is NOT true, it returns a true.
||	Logical OR	Returns true if either value for left or right expressions are true. Otherwise returns false.
||=	Logical OR assignment	Assigns true if either value for left or right expressions are true. Otherwise assigns false.

As you can see, we've already used a number of the operators. In Chapter 4 of this minibook, we examine the basic structures of ActionScript 3.0 and more of its operators.

A *Sheffer stroke* or *vertical bar symbol* (|) is often called a *pipe*, and the two vertical bars comprise a *double pipe*. We'll use the term *pipe* because it sounds cooler than a Sheffer stroke or vertical bar symbol.

Elementary logic, my dear Watson

In this section, we give you examples of comparison and logical operators. Comparison operators compare two values and decide if they're different or the same. Logical operators examine *expressions* (code with operators) to see if they are true or false. The results of the comparison are *(evaluate to)* either true or false.

This next little program does a number of logical comparisons (compares expressions to see if they're true or false) so that you can get an idea of how they work. Because the outcomes can only be true or false, we use a Boolean type. In this application, one Boolean variable name logicalResult will always be true or false. All you have to do is to compare two expressions and evaluate their outcomes. This sample application is designed for you to use as a logical test bench. Go ahead and try out different combinations of logical expressions and see if you can get to the point where you are no longer surprised by the outcome. You'll be using them a good deal in the next chapter.

The following steps show how to create the application:

1. **Open a new Flash (ActionScript 3.0) file, name it, and save it (we saved it as `Logic.fla`).**

2. **Open the Properties panel by selecting Window⇨Properties from the menu bar (Ctrl+F3 in Windows or ⌘+F3 on the Mac) and enter the class name (we used `Logic`).**

Everyone knows that when you start thinking logically, the gears begin to spin. Well, you can add spinning gears to the application for an added flair. Follow these steps to do so:

a. **Add some frames to the existing layer, name it Label, and add a static text label.**

   We added 40 frames to have some room to work with and named it `Logical Operations`.

b. **Add one or more layers depending on how many gears you want.**

   We created three and named them `Gear1`, `Gear2`, and `Gear3`.

c. **In each layer, add a movie clip shaped like a gear.**

   See Figure 3-4 to give you an idea.

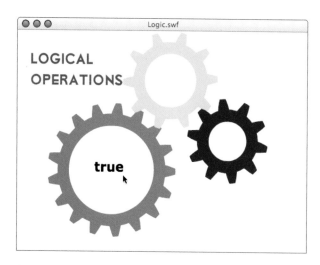

Figure 3-4: Add a movie clip shaped like a gear.

d. **Select the first frame of one of the layers, right-click it (or Ctrl+click on the Mac), and choose Create Motion Tween.**

e. **Then click into your last frame (ours is Frame 40) and choose Insert⇨Timeline⇨Keyframe (or press F6) to add a keyframe.**

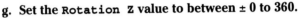

f. **With the keyframe in Frame 40 selected, open the Motion Editor by choosing Window⇨Motion Editor, and open the Basic motion selection by clicking the little arrow.**

g. **Set the `Rotation z` value to between ± 0 to 360.**

A negative value rotates to the left and a positive value rotates to the right. Higher values make the rotation faster.

h. **Repeat the process for the layers with gears in them (in this case, the `Gear2` and `Gear3` layers) and save the file.**

3. **Open a new ActionScript file and save it in the same folder as the file you created in Step 1.**

We named ours `Logic.as` and saved it in the same folder as we saved the `Logic.fla` file back in Step 1.

4. **Add the following script and save it again.**

```
package
{
    import flash.display.Sprite;
    import flash.text.TextField;
    import flash.text.TextFormat;

    public class Logic extends Sprite
    {
        private var outcome:TextField;
        private var textFormat:TextFormat;
        private var exp1:String;
        private var exp2:String;
        private var logicalResult:Boolean;

        public function Logic()
        {
        exp1="up";
          exp2="down";
          //Logical expressions
          logicalResult= !(exp1==exp2);
          //logicalResult=(exp1=="up" && exp2=="up");
          //logicalResult=(exp1=="up" || exp2=="up");
          //logicalResult=(exp1=="up" && exp2=="down");
          //logicalResult= !(exp1!=exp2);
          //logicalResult=(exp1===exp2);

          doFormat("Verdana");
          doTextField();
        }
        private function doFormat(txFont:String)
        {
          textFormat=new TextFormat();
          textFormat.bold=true;
          textFormat.font=txFont;
          textFormat.size=24;
        }
```

```
private function doTextField()
{
  outcome=new TextField  ();
  outcome.x=145,outcome.y=230;
  outcome.defaultTextFormat=textFormat;
  outcome.text=logicalResult.toString();
  addChild(outcome);
}
}
}
```

5. **Remove comment operators from the different values assigned the Boolean variable logicalResult and save it again.**

   Whenever you un-comment one of the lines, add the comment operators to all others.

6. **Choose Control⇨Play (press Ctrl+Enter in Windows or ⌘+Return on the Mac) to test the program by trying out the different logicalResult values.**

If you recall in English class where you were warned *never* to use double negatives, you'll understand better what's going on in the logic. The negative operator (!) can be used with other results with the consequence that you will end up with an unexpected true or false. If you say (or think), "Hmmm, the two expressions are not equal, and if I say that they are not *not* equal, that would be `false`." For the most part, it's a good idea to avoid double negatives in your logical operations to reduce confusion. However, unlike your English teacher, ActionScript 3.0 is perfectly willing to accept double negatives and generate results reflecting their logic.

Experiment with the program with logical operators to see the different results. Such experimentation will help you understand how they work and give you some ideas for using them.

Chapter 4: Making Decisions . . . and Repeating Yourself

In This Chapter

Computer programs can make decisions by comparing different sets of information. In Flash CS4, this can be important for applications where more than one alternative is available to the user. Likewise, your computer can process repeated chores so that you only have to write a little code and you can repeat it using loop structures.

In this chapter, we explore the main applied structures of ActionScript 3.0 and also a special kind of object called an array, in which you can store all kinds of elements in a single object. You can use these structures with different functions you can create. Some of the features in this chapter may be familiar from other chapters, but in this chapter we go into more depth.

On One Condition! (Or, Maybe More than One): Conditional Statements

At its base, the *conditional statement* in ActionScript 3.0 works very much like everyday decisions, such as what to wear, what to read, where to go, and what to do. In all these decisions are conditions. For example, in deciding what to wear, you may have a situation where you don't know whether it is going to rain or not rain. So, you may have the following decision:

> *If it's going to rain, I'll wear my raincoat. Otherwise, I'll wear a light windbreaker.*

The two conditions are rain and no rain, and depending on which of those conditions occurs, you make one choice or the other. So, when considering conditional statements in ActionScript 3.0, keep in mind that they work just like you think they do.

The `if` statement

The most basic conditional statement is the `if` statement. If you're making a game, for example, you may need to check to see whether the player has met whichever condition ends the game. Also, if the game is over, you need to find out whether the player won or lost. If the player won, she sees a banner declaring "You won!," but if she lost, she sees a different banner, "Better luck next time." Figure 4-1 shows the structure of an `if` statement.

In Chapter 3 of this minibook, we discuss Boolean variables, which can have only the values `true` or `false`. As you can see in Figure 4-1, the condition `x > 50` has a Boolean result. Either `x` is going to be greater than 50 or it is not. If `x` is greater than 50, the result is `true`; otherwise, the result is `false`.

To help you visualize the concept, suppose you are pre-screening candidates for a job. You want to select a candidate who knows either ActionScript 3.0 or object oriented programming. You could write a statement such as

Structure
```
if(condition == true)
{
    //statements
}
```
Example
```
if(x > 50)
{
    output.text="Winner!";
}
```

Figure 4-1: The structure of an `if` statement.

```
if(candQ1 == knowsAS3 || candQ2 == knowsOOP)
{
    hire();
}
```

Now suppose you have a deep and talented candidate pool and decide that you want someone who knows ActionScript 3.0 and knows how to design sites in Flash. Such a person would be an even better candidate:

```
if(candQ1 == knowsAS3 && candQ3 == knowsDesign)
{
    hire();
}
```

In the first conditional statement, if either condition is true, the result is `true`. However, in the second condition, both conditions in the expression must be true to result in `true`. Otherwise, the result is `false`.

 When using logical operators for AND (`&&`) and OR (`||`), remember that you must have two complete expressions separated by a logical operator. If you type `if(depth > 6 && < 20)`, you'll encounter an error. The variable `depth` must be restated after the `&&` operator. Typing `if(depth > 6 && depth < 20)` instead correctly lists both conditions.

The `else` clause

The `else` clause in an `if` statement allows you to have more than one option. In other words, "if X is true, do Y, else, do Z." Figure 4-2 shows the basic structure in the context of an `if` statement.

Using the `if` statement together with the `else` clause, you have more options. To get a grip on what you can do with the `if..else` statement, this next application is a simple interaction that keeps looking to see if the game is over. If the game is not over, it outputs the number of times you have clicked the button. When you get to 10, it tells you that the game is over and disables the button. The following steps show you how to get it up and running:

The else clause
```
if(condition)
{
        //Do this
}
else
{
        //Do that
}
```

Figure 4-2: The structure of the `else` clause.

---

1. **Open a new Flash (ActionScript 3.0) file and save it.**

   We saved ours as `SimpleIf.fla`.

2. **In the Property inspector, enter the name for the class and save the file again.**

   We named ours `SimpleIf`.

   You can open the Property inspector by choosing Window➪Properties (or pressing Ctrl+F3 in Windows or ⌘+F3 on the Mac).

   Optionally, you can decorate the Stage as shown in Figure 4-3. The button and text output fields are dynamically added by the code, so don't add them on the Stage using Flash tools. If you do so, save the file when you're done.

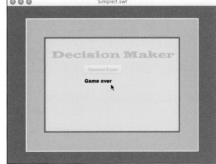

Figure 4-3: Using the `if..else` statement to determine the end of the game.

3. **Open the Components panel by choosing Window⇨Components (or pressing Ctrl+F7 in Windows or ⌘+F7 on the Mac). Drag a Button component to the Stage and delete it.**

   You now have a Button component stored in the library.

4. **Open a new ActionScript file and save it in the same folder as the `Simple.fla` file.**

   We named ours `SimpleIf.as` and saved it in the same folder as the `Simple.fla` file.

5. **Add the following code and save the file again:**

```
package
{
    import fl.controls.Button;
    import flash.display.Sprite;
    import flash.text.TextField;
    import flash.text.TextFormat;
    import flash.events.MouseEvent;

    public class SimpleIf extends Sprite
    {
        private var btn:Button;
        private var scoreBoard:TextField;
        private var styleBoard:TextFormat;
        private var addClick:uint;

        public function SimpleIf()
        {
            btn=new Button ();
            btn.addEventListener(MouseEvent.CLICK,addScore);
            btn.x=200;btn.y=150;
            btn.label="Click to Play";
            addChild(btn);
            //Add text field
            scoreBoard=new TextField();
```

```
                 scoreBoard.x=200;
                 scoreBoard.y=180;
                 addChild(scoreBoard);
                 //Add text format class
                 styleBoard=new TextFormat();
                 styleBoard.font="Arial Black";
                 scoreBoard.defaultTextFormat=styleBoard;
             }
             private function addScore(e:MouseEvent):void
             {
                 addClick++;
                 if (addClick>=10)
                 {
                    scoreBoard.text="Game over";
                    btn.label="Disabled Button";
                    btn.enabled=false;
                 }
                 else
                 {
                    scoreBoard.text="Clicks ="+addClick;
                 }
             }
        }
    }
```

6. Test the application by choosing Control⊏⟩Test (or pressing Ctrl+Enter in Windows or ⌘+Return on the Mac).

You will see that the program adds new values to the output each time you click the button. When you click it for the tenth time, the button is disabled and the Game Over sign appears. Figure 4-3 shows what you'll see before the count reaches 10; on the left, you can see what it looks like after the count has reached 10. By disabling the button, the user cannot add more values than the game allows.

The addClick in the preceding variable is an unsigned integer (uint). Notice that while it is declared, it is created *(instantiated)* by the add-assign (++) compound operator, which is perfectly legal because it adds a value of one to a value of *undefined*. With each click, the add-assign operator adds one to its value to be evaluated by the conditional statement.

Let's do the switch!

With one or two outcomes, the if statement with the else clause works fine. However, when you have several different conditions and need to deal with several outcomes, you need to be able to handle them all. Thanks to the switch statement, you can use several different condition states and deal with each case appropriately.

Although we first mentioned the switch statement in Chapter 2 of this mini-book, Figure 4-4 shows the structure of the switch statement in a bit more detail.

**Book IV
Chapter 4**

**Making Decisions . . .
and Repeating Yourself**

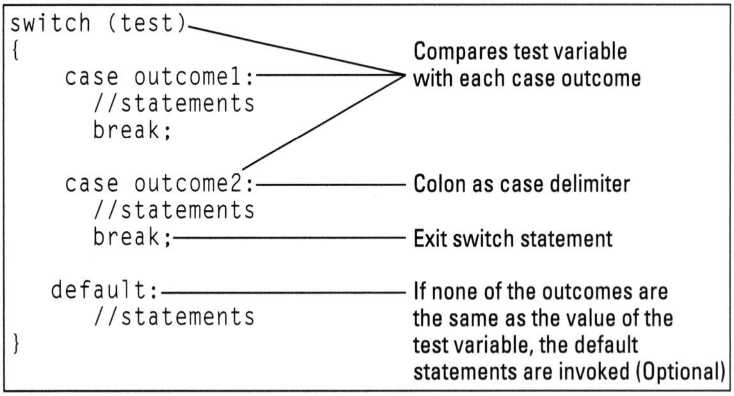

```
switch (test)
{
    case outcome1:
        //statements
        break;

    case outcome2:
        //statements
        break;

    default:
        //statements
}
```

Compares test variable with each case outcome

Colon as case delimiter

Exit switch statement

If none of the outcomes are the same as the value of the test variable, the default statements are invoked (Optional)

Figure 4-4: The structure of the `switch` statement.

The logic of the `switch` statement is different from the `if` statement. With the `if` statement, you use a Boolean (true or false) condition. With the `switch` statement, a test value is compared with several different `case` values. If the values are equal, the statements in the case are invoked. Using the `break` statement (after the other `case` statements are launched) moves the program to the next statement.

In this next example, we'll create a program with three choices in three different buttons — Larry, Curley, and Mo. With a few exceptions, when we've assigned an event listener to a button, we've used different functions for each button. However, in this application all of the listeners call the same function. By using the `target` and `label` information passed when the button is clicked, we can store that information in a variable and then use that variable as the test variable in the `switch` statement. The following line uses a string variable named `decide` to store the target (instance name):

```
decide=e.target.label;
```

The `e` is the instance name of the mouse event passed in a parameter in this line:

```
private function choose(e:MouseEvent)
```

So, if you've been wondering what the event parameter is, now you know! The following steps show how to create the full application:

1. **Open a new Flash (ActionScript 3.0) file and save it.**

   We named ours `Switch.fla`.

2. **In the Property inspector, enter the name for the class.**

   We named ours `Switch`.

   You can open the Property inspector by choosing Window⇨Properties (or pressing Ctrl+F3 in Windows or ⌘+F3 on the Mac).

3. **Place a `Button` and `TextArea` component in the Library that will instantiate with code and save the file again.**

   You can place a component on the stage and then delete it to automatically place it in the library. However, don't leave the components on the Stage, or else they will conflict with the components being placed on the Stage by the program. If you want, you can decorate the Stage, as shown in Figure 4-5, or use your own design.

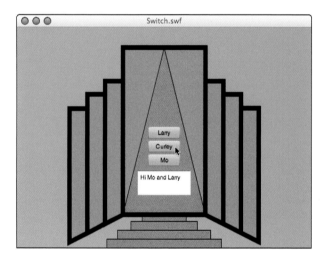

Figure 4-5: Using button information and the `switch` statement.

4. **Open a new ActionScript file and save it as in the same folder as the file you created in Step 1.**

   We named our file `Switch.as` and saved it in the same folder as we saved the `Switch.fla` file.

5. **Add the following code and save the file again:**

   ```
   package
   {
       import flash.display.Sprite;
       import flash.events.MouseEvent;
       import fl.controls.Button;
       import fl.controls.TextArea;
   ```

```
public class Switch extends Sprite
{
    private var larry:Button;
    private var curley:Button;
    private var mo:Button;
    private var showMe:TextArea;
    private var decide:String;

    public function Switch()
    {
        larry=new Button ();
        larry.x=245,larry.y=180;
        larry.label="Larry";
        larry.addEventListener(MouseEvent.CLICK,choose);
        larry.width=60;
        addChild(larry);
        curley=new Button ();
        curley.x=245,curley.y=205;
        curley.label="Curley";
        curley.addEventListener(MouseEvent.CLICK,choose);
        curley.width=60;
        addChild(curley);
        mo=new Button ();
        mo.x=245,mo.y=230;
        mo.label="Mo";
        mo.addEventListener(MouseEvent.CLICK,choose);
        mo.width=60;
        addChild(mo);
        showMe=new TextArea ();
        showMe.x=225,showMe.y=260;
        addChild(showMe);
    }

    private function choose(e:MouseEvent)
    {
        decide=e.target.label;
        switch(decide)
        {
            case "Larry" :
                showMe.text="Hi Mo and Curley";
                break;

            case "Curley" :
                showMe.text="Hi Mo and Larry";
                break;

            case "Mo" :
                showMe.text="Hi Larry and Curley";
                break;
        }
    }
}
}
```

6. **Test the application by choosing Control⇨Test (or pressing Ctrl+Enter in Windows or ⌘+Return on the Mac).**

You will see that as you click on each name, a greeting to the other two characters appears in the TextArea component. Figure 4-5 shows what you can expect to see.

As you can see when you test the application, all of the responses are from the single `choose()` method (function). This should give you some ideas for using the `switch` statement when you have several buttons but only want to use a single method for an event handler.

Let the Looping Computer Do the Work

When you have a repeated set of tasks, instead of writing multiple statements to handle the same task, ActionScript 3.0 allows you to write a single loop statement with the task inside the loop and repeat the same task again and again. ActionScript 3.0 has the following types of loops:

- ✔ `for`
- ✔ `for..in`
- ✔ `for each..in`
- ✔ `while`
- ✔ `do..while`

Each of these loops has a different purpose. In the following sections, we show you each one in turn and provide a small example of using each. A bit later on in the section on arrays, we show you more uses for loops.

The `for` loop

The `for` loop is the most common loop. With it, you can specify a starting point, an end condition (what will make it stop), and an increment (increase value) or decrement (decrease value). The basic structure is

```
for(begin , end_condition, value_change)
```

For example, the following loop begins at 0, ends if the value is less than 10, and increments by 1 with each iteration through the loop:

```
for( var lv:uint = 0; lv < 10; lv++)
```

The loop variable (`lv`) has a value of 0 the first time through the loop, a value of 1 the second time, 2 the third time, and so forth until it reaches 10 and stops the iterations. You will often see the term *iterate* when dealing with loops of all types; an *iteration* refers to a single time through the loop.

The following example shows the value of the loop variable (`ele`) incremented as it goes through the loop. Follow these steps to set it up:

1. **Open a new Flash (ActionScript 3.0) file and save it.**

   We saved ours as `Loopy.fla`.

2. **In the Property inspector, enter the name for the class.**

   We named our class `Loopy`.

   You can open the Property inspector by choosing Window⇨Properties.

3. **Choose Window⇨Components to open the Components panel and drag a TextArea component to the Stage. Then save the file.**

   This action automatically places the component and supporting files in the library that you will instantiate with code.

   Delete the component from the Stage so that it does not conflict with the components placed on the Stage dynamically with ActionScript.

4. **Open a new ActionScript file and save it in the same folder as the file you created in Step 1.**

   We named our file `Loopy.as` and saved it in the same folder as the `Loopy.fla` file.

5. **Add the following code and save the file again:**

   ```
   package
   {
       import flash.display.Sprite;
       import fl.controls.TextArea;

       public class Loopy extends Sprite
       {
           private var showLoop:TextArea;

           public function Loopy()
           {
               showLoop=new TextArea();
               showLoop.x=150,showLoop.y=100;
               showLoop.height=150;
               showLoop.width=50;
               addChild(showLoop);

               for (var ele:uint =1; ele < 11; ele++)
               {
                 showLoop.appendText(ele.toString()+"\n");
               }
           }
       }
   }
   ```

6. **Test the program.**

   When you test it, you will see the output neatly presented in the elongated TextArea component.

   Keep this loop in mind whenever you encounter a situation where you need to repeat a task a given number of times.

The foreign . . . er, `for..in` loop

Sometimes you have no idea how many times you have to loop through an object or list to get everything out that's in the object. In these cases, the simple `for` loop isn't much help, in which case you use the `for..in` loop, which keeps iterating until all elements in the object are accounted for. The `for..in` loop has the following structure:

```
for(var property in object)
```

When dealing with objects, you can add just about anything as a property. Suppose that you're making a Flash site for a musical trio made up of a bass, guitar, and piano. You want the group to be flexible so that if a player is out sick or out of town, you can add another player. Also, you don't know whether the trio might decide to become a quartet or a duo. In this case, here comes the `for..in` loop to the rescue. The following steps show how:

1. **Open a new Flash (ActionScript 3.0) file and save it.**

   We saved ours as `Loopy2.fla`.

   All the loop examples use the same component: TextArea. You can save time if you use Save As and just save the files with a different name and Document name. For example, you could save `Loopy.fla` and `Loopy.as` as `Loopy2.fla` and `Loopy2.as`. Then just use the different code for each example and be sure to change the class name in the Property inspector.

2. **In the Property inspector, enter the name for the class.**

   We named our class `Loopy2`.

   To open the Property inspector, choose Window⇨Properties.

3. **Choose Window⇨Components to open the Components panel and drag a TextArea component to the Stage. Then save the file.**

   This action automatically places in the library the component and supporting files that you will instantiate with code.

   Delete the component from the Stage so that it does not conflict with the components placed on the Stage dynamically with ActionScript.

4. **Open a new ActionScript file and save it in the same folder as the file you created in Step 1.**

   We named ours `Loopy2.as` and saved it in the same folder as the `Loopy2.fla` file.

5. **Add the following code and save the file again:**

```
package
{
    import flash.display.Sprite;
    import fl.controls.TextArea;
```

```
public class Loopy2 extends Sprite
{
    private var showLoop:TextArea;
    private var obj:Object;

    public function Loopy2()
    {
        obj=new Object();
obj={Bass:"Joe",Piano:"Sheila",Guitar:"Harry"};
        showLoop=new TextArea ();
        showLoop.x=150,showLoop.y=100;
        showLoop.height=100;
        showLoop.width=150;
        addChild(showLoop);
        showLoop.text="The Loopy Trio\n";
        showLoop.appendText("-----------------\n");
        for (var prop in obj)
        {
showLoop.appendText(obj[prop]+" playing "+prop+"\n");
        }
    }
}
}
```

This example shows that you get both the static (unchanging) property (an instrument) and the dynamic (changing) property of the static property (one of the musicians). So, the piano can be played by Sheila one day and by Joe the next day — same piano, different players.

The `for each..in` *loop*

The `for each..in` loop was developed primarily for XML files with E4X. E4X is language support that allows access to XML from ECMAScript languages like ActionScript 3.0. If you're not familiar with XML, don't worry about it. The loop iterates through an object and targets only the *dynamic* elements of an object, including an XML object. It has the following format:

for each(var ele **in** object)

The `each` keyword simply tells the loop that only dynamic elements are to be brought out and all the static properties are ignored. This approach is probably more realistic because you're usually interested in the dynamic values anyway.

Because the loop was developed for XML, we'll loop through an XML object. The following steps show you how:

1. **Open a new Flash (ActionScript 3.0) file and save it.**

   We named ours `Loopy3.fla`.

2. **In the Property inspector, enter the name for the class.**

3. **In the Component panel, drag a TextArea component to the stage and delete it.**

This action places a component in the library, where ActionScript 3.0 can access it.

4. **Open a new ActionScript file and save it in the same folder as the file you created in Step 1.**

We named ours `Loopy3.as` and saved it in the same folder as the `Loopy3.fla` file.

5. **Add the following code and save the file again:**

```
package
{
    import flash.display.Sprite;
    import fl.controls.TextArea;

    public class Loopy3 extends Sprite
    {
        private var showLoop:TextArea;
        private var xmlFun:XML;

        public function Loopy3()
        {
            xmlFun=new XML();
            xmlFun=
            <dogs>
                <breed>Sheep Dog </breed>
                <breed>Swiss Mountain Dog </breed>
                <breed>Basset Hound </breed>
                <breed>English Springer Spaniel</breed>
            </dogs>;

            showLoop=new TextArea ();
            showLoop.x=150,showLoop.y=100;
            showLoop.height=100;
            showLoop.width=180;
            addChild(showLoop);
            showLoop.text="Dogs I know\n";
            showLoop.appendText("--------------\n");

            for each (var doggy in xmlFun.breed)
            {
                showLoop.appendText(doggy+"\n");
            }
        }
    }
}
```

6. **Test the program by choosing Control⇨Test (or pressing Ctrl+Enter in Windows or ⌘+Return on the Mac).**

Figure 4-6 shows what you can expect to see.

The for each..in loop was successful in extracting just the information that you want. If you decided to add more dog breeds to the XML file, the for each..in loop would get the additional information out for you.

Figure 4-6: Output of the for each..in loop to extract data from an XML file.

(Go ahead and add a Chihuahua to the XML breed list and watch him get extracted and displayed on the screen.)

The `while` and `do..while` loops

A `while` loop keeps looping until a certain condition is met. (You keep doing this until you get it right! Now do it again!) You need to know that the condition can be met; otherwise, you can get into an infinite loop that locks up the program. Figure 4-7 shows the general format for both types of loops.

The only difference between these two types of loops is that the `do..while` loop *always* iterates at least once, and the `while` loop stops before any iteration of the condition is met. The following example shows how each is set up and the identical outcomes they generate in the case where the first time through the loop, the stop condition is not met:

```
while loop
while(condition)
{
      //statements
}

do..while loop
do
{
      //statements
}
while (condition)
```

Figure 4-7: The structure of `while` and `do..while` loops.

1. **Open a new Flash (ActionScript 3.0) file and save it.**

   We saved ours as `Loopy4.fla`.

2. **Choose Window⇨Properties to open the Property inspector. In the Property inspector, enter the name for the class.**

   We named ours `Loopy4`.

3. **Choose Window⇨Components to open the Components panel and drag a TextArea component to the Stage.**

   This action places a component in the library, where ActionScript 3.0 can access it.

4. **Open a new ActionScript file and save it in the same folder as the file you created in Step 1.**

   We named ours `Loopy4.as` and saved it in the same folder as the `Loopy4.fla` file.

5. **Add the following code and save the file again:**

   ```
   package
   {
       import flash.display.Sprite;
       import fl.controls.TextArea;

       public class Loopy4 extends Sprite
       {
           private var showLoop:TextArea;
           private var endItAll:uint;
           private var iter:String;
   ```

```
public function Loopy4()
{
    showLoop=new TextArea ();
    showLoop.x=150,showLoop.y=50;
    showLoop.height=265;
    showLoop.width=120;
    addChild(showLoop);
    showLoop.text="A Tale of Two Loops\n";
    showLoop.appendText("---------------\n");
    showLoop.appendText("The while loop\n");
    endItAll=6;
    iter="Iteration=";

    while (endItAll !=0)
    {
        showLoop.appendText(iter+endItAll+"\n");
        endItAll--;
    }
    showLoop.appendText("\n");

    endItAll=6;
    showLoop.appendText("The do..while loop\n");
    do
    {
        showLoop.appendText(iter+endItAll+"\n");
        endItAll--;
    } while (endItAll !=0);
    }
  }
}
```

6. **Choose Control⇨Test to test the application.**

The outcomes should be identical to what you see in the figure on the left in Figure 4-8.

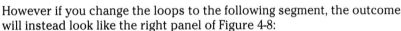

However if you change the loops to the following segment, the outcome will instead look like the right panel of Figure 4-8:

```
endItAll=20;
iter="Iteration=";

while (endItAll !=20)
{
    showLoop.appendText(iter+endItAll+"\n");
    //endItAll--;
}
showLoop.appendText("\n");

endItAll=20;
showLoop.appendText("The do..while loop\n");
do
{
    showLoop.appendText(iter+endItAll+"\n");
    //endItAll--;
} while (endItAll !=20)
```

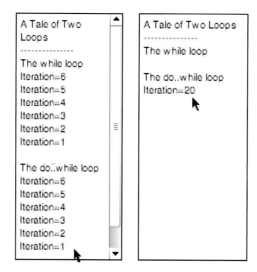

Figure 4-8: The `do..while` loop always has at least one iteration.

Instead of both loops generating the same values, the `do..while` loop has the condition at the bottom, so it generates a single iteration and the `while` loop generates nothing.

With the basic conditional and loop structures at your service, you have most of the structures you need to create programs that can make decisions and repeat processes without having to rewrite the same code repeatedly.

Chapter 5: Harnessing the Power of ActionScript 3.0

In This Chapter

- ✔ Creating arrays
- ✔ Pushing data to arrays
- ✔ Retrieving array elements with Pop
- ✔ Sorting arrays
- ✔ Introducing the Vector class
- ✔ Using string identifiers in Vector elements
- ✔ Incorporating the `Vector.forEach()` method
- ✔ Starting and stopping drag operations
- ✔ Drawing with ActionScript 3.0
- ✔ Creating triangles with vertices and indices

Too often, we hear Web designers and developers pine for the "good old days" when ActionScript consisted of just a few lines of code spread all over the place. Well, we disagree. ActionScript 3.0 has a learning curve for people accustomed to using previous versions, but the good thing about ActionScript 3.0 is that now that it has been retooled into a standardized, more efficient form, it will be around for a while, and, even though some changes will inevitably be made in future versions, you don't have to figure out how to use it from scratch every time a new version is released and you want to sit down to make the world's greatest Flash application.

In this chapter, we show you how to use grouping structures that corral more than a single element and give each one a unique value, and we tell you about arrays that have been included in several generations of ActionScript. Using arrays, you can easily have several values different types of data stored in the same place for ease of access. In addition, you see vectors, the brand-new type of grouping structure. As you will see, vectors are much like arrays, although they can be of different types, just like variables.

In this and the preceding chapters in this minibook, we only scratch the surface of ActionScript 3.0. In Book VI, you see lots more ActionScript 3.0 used with video.

All the code listings in this chapter are available for downloading from this book's companion Web site at www.dummies.com/go/flashallinone. Some code listings are long, so you may want to download the code to avoid making typing errors. Then you can make changes to create your own applications with the same structures.

Meet the Gang: Arrays

When you have several different elements organized in groups, you may need an *array*. In some respects, an array is just any other object with different properties. As you've seen, object properties can be numeric, Boolean, or character strings. The same is true with arrays.

Unlike a variable, an array isn't assigned a type. In programmer lingo, you would say instead that an array isn't *typed;* rather, an array *is* a type. When you create a variable, you include the data type. So, variable xray might be a string and variable stack might be a number. When you create an array, you add elements of any type you want — or you can just use literals. An *element* in an array is a unique member of the array — sort of like a member of a club with the array as the club. Each element can have its own value. A *literal* is an actual value, such as the number 2 or the string "hello".

Creating an array

When you create an array, you use the following format:

```
var myArray:Array;
myArray=new Array();
```

At the same time you create the array, you can include data within the parameters. For example, this line:

```
myArray=new Array(7, 30, "San Francisco");
```

creates an array with three elements: two numbers and a string. These are stored in elements with a zero-base numbering system using the following format:

```
myArray[0];
myArray[1];
myArray[2];
```

For example, the value of `myArray[1]` is `30`. You can pass that value to a variable or do whatever else you want do with it as you would a variable or literal. For example, the following chunk of code passes the third element to a string:

```
var song:String = "I left my heart in ";
song += myArray[2];
//song value = I left my heart in San Francisco
```

The important difference between strings and arrays is that both numbers and strings are added to the array. Variables can accept only a certain data type that is made when the variable is declared.

Getting pushy: Adding data to an array

Besides adding data to an array when you instantiate (create an instance of) the array, you can do it in other ways too. The easiest is just to keep adding elements with different numbers. For example, to add more elements to an array with three elements in it already, you could do the following:

```
myArray[3]="New York";
myArray[4]=22;
myArray[5]=false;
```

Keeping in mind that the array is zero-based, the three added elements give the array a new total of six elements.

In addition to assigning values to array elements (just like assigning values to variables), you can use the `push()` method. When you add elements to an array using the `push` statement, you place the most recent element on the top of the stack. For example, the following would add three elements to the array numbered `6,7,8` from left to right if added to the existing elements already in the array:

```
group.push("Apple",4,Math.PI);
```

Keep in mind that the `push()` method adds elements to the *top* of the array. Imagine one of those spring-load cafeteria tray containers, and that each tray is an array element. As you add more elements, they're simply added to the top.

pop() goes the element! Retrieving data from an array

Getting elements out of an array has several advantages over using variables to store data, the most important being that you can use a loop to numerically iterate through the array to extract all the values. Consider the difference between using an array with 100 elements and 100 variables that you're putting into a `TextArea` for output. First, in looking at variables, you would have to do something like the following:

```
myTA.appendText(wheels + "\n");
myTA.appendText(door + "\n");
myTA.appendText(radiator + "\n");
...
//On to the 100th variable
myTA.appendText(tailPipe + "\n");
```

You can imagine the amount of coding you would have to do for a quick variable inventory. With an array, all you need to do is to loop through the array and extract each element in turn using the following code:

```
for (var myEle in myArray)
{
    textArea.appendText(myArray[myEle]+"\n");
}
```

The `for..in` loop keeps on extracting element values until the array is empty. You can easily add or reduce the number of elements, but you need not change any code to send the code to an output.

Rather than iterate through a loop and selecting each element by a reference to the element number, you can also use the `pop()` method. The `pop()` method takes the top element off the array, makes it available, and then discards it. For example, this statement:

```
myVar = myArray.pop();
```

passes the value of the last element on the array to `myVar`. After the value is passed to the variable, the size of the array is reduced by 1.

You must remember that the `pop()` operation uses and removes the *last* element. So, if you want the first element, you're better off using `array[0]` rather than `pop()`.

You may be scratching your head wondering, "What would I *ever* do with an array using `pop()`?" If you have a large number of values you want to pass using an array, using the `pop()` method gets rid of the content as soon as you're finished using the information, which can help free up memory.

In case you're thinking of creating games with Flash CS4, you can keep a game crisp (running without delays) by keeping memory free.

Sorting with an array

The final topic we cover with arrays is the `sort()` method. By adding it with an array instance, you can sort (surprise!) all elements in the array. For example, this line:

```
myArray.sort();
```

sorts all contents in `ascending` order (from lowest to highest). To sort in `descending` order, all you have to do is to use the number 2 as a parameter. So, this line:

```
myArray.sort(2);
```

would begin with the highest value and go to the lowest. Using the ten most common American surnames (last names), let's take a look using the following chunk of code:

```
var myArray:Array;
myArray=new Array("Smith","Johnson","Williams");
myArray.push("Jones","Brown","Davis","Miller");
myArray.push("Wilson","Moore","Taylor");
myArray.sort();
for (var ww in myArray)
{
    trace(myArray[ww]);
}
```

The preceding code sorts the names alphabetically. If you change the line with the `sort()` method to the following:

```
myArray.sort(2);
```

all the names are instead listed in reverse alphabetical order.

Strings are case sensitive when it comes to sorting and capital letters come before lowercase letters. For example, if you change `Davis` to `davis`, it's sorted last using ascending order.

Array practice

Now that you have an idea of what you can do with arrays, this next application employs different kinds of content in addition to input and output. The following steps guide you through creating it:

1. **Open a new Flash (ActionScript 3.0) file and save it.**

   We named ours `ArraySample.fla`.

Book IV
Chapter 5

Harnessing
the Power of
ActionScript 3.0

2. **In the Class box in the Properties panel, enter the class name.**

   We named ours `ArraySample`.

   You can open the Property inspector by choosing Window➪Properties (or pressing Ctrl+F3 in Windows or ⌘+F3 on the Mac).

3. **Using the Text tool, position a static TextField on the Stage and add some content.**

   We positioned ours at X=100, Y=42, and using a 32-point graphic font, typed `Array Machine` and saved the file.

4. **Create a small shape to become a button and Choose Modify➪Convert to Symbol from the menu bar (or press F8) to open the Convert to Symbol dialog box.**

   We drew a circle with the Oval tool with a diameter of 32 (H=32, W=32).

5. **In the Convert to Symbol dialog box, select Button as the type and type a name for the button (we named ours Btn). Click the Export for ActionScript check box and click OK.**

6. **Select the button and press the Delete key to remove it from the Stage.**

   The button is preserved in the library.

7. **Drag a Label and TextArea component to the library.**

   Alternatively, you can drag the Label and TextArea components to the Stage and then delete them. This action places the components in the library.

   Depending on how you have your panels docked, it might be easier to drag components from the component panel to the Stage and then delete them. As soon as a component or symbol is placed on the Stage, one is automatically placed in the library.

8. **Open a new ActionScript file and save it in the same folder with the file you created in Step 1.**

   We named ours `ArraySample.as` and saved it in the same folder as the `ArraySample.fla` file.

9. **Add the following code and save the file again:**

```
package
{
    import flash.display.Sprite;
    import flash.events.MouseEvent;
    import fl.controls.Label;
    import fl.controls.TextArea;

    {
```

```
public class ArraySample extends Sprite
{
    private var group:Array;
    private var size:String;
    private var msg:String;
    private var btn:Btn; //From Library
    private var label:Label;//From Library
    private var textArea:TextArea; //From Library
    {
        public function ArraySample()
        {
            group=new Array(1,true,"Cow",66);
            group.push("Apple",4,Math.PI);

            label=new Label();
            label.x=100,label.y=80;
            label.width=250;
            msg="Press button to ";
            msg+="see array contents:";
            label.text=msg;
            addChild(label);

            textArea=new TextArea();
            textArea.width=150,textArea.height=200;
            textArea.x=100,textArea.y=140;
            addChild(textArea);

            btn=new Btn();
            btn.x=100,btn.y=100;
            btn.addEventListener(MouseEvent.CLICK,unpeel);
            addChild(btn);
        }

        private function unpeel(e:MouseEvent)
        {
            //group.sort();
            //for(var stuff:uint =0; stuff<7;stuff++)
            for (var stuff in group)
            {
                textArea.appendText(group[stuff]+"\n");
                //textArea.appendText(group.pop()+"\n");
            }

            size="This array has "+group.length +" elements."
            textArea.appendText(size);
        }
    }
}
}
}
```

10. **Test the file by choosing Control⇨Test (or pressing Ctrl+Enter in Windows or ⌘+Return on the Mac).**

    Figure 5-1 shows what you can expect to see the first time you test it, assuming that you used our examples to the letter.

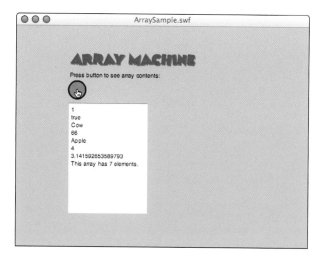

Figure 5-1: TextArea component displaying contents of array.

The lines in the `unpeel` function that are commented out are for testing the application using different methods. Begin by un-commenting (taking out `//` characters) the statement, `group.sort()`. Test it and see what you get. Next, change it to read, `group.sort(2)`. As you can see, numbers have lower values than strings, so `20000` always comes *before* `Aardvark` in an ascending sort. However, the opposite is true in a descending sort.

Next, change the `unpeel` function to the following:

```
private function unpeel(e:MouseEvent)
{
    for(var stuff:uint =0;  stuff<7;stuff++)
    {
        textArea.appendText(group.pop()+"\n");
    }
    size="This array has ";
    size+=group.length +" elements.";
    textArea.appendText(size);
}
```

Because you used the `pop()` method, the order is reversed and the size of the array is down to zero. The `for` loop was used to iterate through all the elements rather than the `for..in` loop because of the shrinking size of the array. With each iteration, the loop size changes and because the `for..in` loop uses the array size, some elements are always left out.

New in Flash CS4: Vectors

Vectors are close cousins to arrays and are newly introduced in ActionScript 3.0 with Flash CS4. A *vector* is something like an array, and most of the methods used with arrays are also available for vectors.

The main difference between the two is that vectors are *typed* and all items in a vector must be of a single declared type. The result is that vectors are much faster and more efficient than arrays. Adobe recommends that vectors be used rather than arrays wherever you're storing data of the same type in a single object.

To see how each one is set up, Figure 5-2 shows their structures along with an example (in blue) so that you can see the difference. You cannot add data to a vector when you instantiate it as you can with an array, and so in Figure 5-2, the opt1 and opt2 elements indicate the option of declaring an array and adding data at the same time and of different types.

```
Array
var myArray:Array;
myArray=new Array("opt1", opt2)

var myArray:Array;
myArray=new Array("Name",7, false);

Vector
var myVector:Vector.<T>;
myVector=new Vector.<T>(length,fixed)

var myVector:Vector.<String>;
myVector=new Vector.<String>(12, true);
```

Figure 5-2: Arrays and vectors.

One feature about vectors that you will find new is the use of arrow brackets (<>) for typing vectors. The <T> is a generic symbol used for type, and the type can be any ActionScript 3.0 type. So you might see <String>, <int>, <Number>, or any other type. Also, note that a dot (.) appears between Vector and the type (Vector.<String>).

Checking out non-numeric ID for vector elements

The first example shows how to set up a vector and to use string names as element identifiers. This means that you can name an element anything you want using quotes around a label, such as

```
myVector["alpha"]="A perfect day!";
myVector["beta"]="A beautiful night!";
```

You can do the same thing with arrays but Adobe recommends that you use an Object instance rather than an array. Doing so allows you to initialize your array with an object literal.

A vector is another alternative for creating groups of elements using string literals rather than numbers to identify the items in the vector. This next example provides a simple example:

1. **Open a new Flash (ActionScript 3.0) file and save it.**

   We named ours `VectorWork.fla`.

2. **In the Class box in the Properties panel, enter the class name and save the file again.**

   We used `VectorWork` as the class name.

3. **Drag a TextArea component into the library.**

   We *told* you it's in the library!

4. **Open a new ActionScript file and save it in the same folder as the file you created in Step 1.**

   We named ours `VectorWork.fla` and saved it in the same folder as `VectorWork.as`.

5. **Add the following script and save the file again:**

```
package
{
    import fl.controls.TextArea;
    import flash.display.Sprite;
    import fl.controls.ScrollPolicy;

    public class VectorWork extends Sprite
    {
        private var myAA: Vector.<String>;
        private var textArea:TextArea;
        private var cr:String;

        public function VectorWork()
        {
            myAA=new Vector.<String>(6,true);
            myAA["President"]="Pres-Joe Smith";
            myAA["VPm"]="Marketing-Brenda Jones";
            myAA["VPd"]="Development-Lee Pierce";
            myAA["VPf"]="Finance-Gideon Thomas";
            myAA["VPp"]="Production-Jesse Fernandez";
            myAA["VPs"]="Sales-Nancy Huang";

            textArea=new TextArea  ();
            textArea.x=188,textArea.y=160;
            textArea.width=175;
            textArea.height=130;
            textArea.verticalScrollPolicy=ScrollPolicy.OFF;
            addChild(textArea);
            putOut();
        }
        private function putOut()
        {
            cr="\n";
            textArea.appendText(myAA["President"] + cr );
            textArea.appendText(myAA["VPm"] + cr);
            textArea.appendText(myAA["VPd"] + cr);
            textArea.appendText(myAA["VPf"] + cr);
            textArea.appendText(myAA["VPp"] + cr);
            textArea.appendText(myAA["VPs"] + cr);
        }
    }
}
```

Note how the vector items were addressed. Each element is addressed by the element name and not by a number. For example, the vice president of finance has the item identifier `"VPf"` rather than any numeric value. If you attempt to use a number as an index to one of the elements, you find a return value of *undefined*.

6. **Choose Control⇨Test from the menu bar (Ctrl+Enter in Windows or ⌘+Return on the Mac) to test the application.**

Sometimes you do not want the scrollbar to appear — ever. Using the `ScrollPolicy` class, you can set it to `OFF`. Assign `ScrollPolicy.OFF` to the `verticalScrollPolicy` or `horizontalScrollPolicy` method to hide the scroll bar. (Alternatively, you can set it to `ON` or `AUTO`.)

Figure 5-3 shows the output you can expect to see when you test the application.

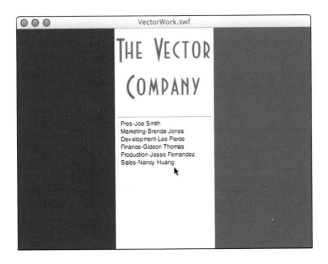

Figure 5-3: Output sent to TextArea from the Vector instance.

Using the `forEach()` *method*

Another unique feature of vectors is the `forEach()` method. From Chapter 4, you're familiar with the `for..each` loop, but the Vector class has a method that includes a loop! Figure 5-4 shows how to set up and use the special function used by the `forEach()` loop method. (Arrays also have a `forEach()` method.)

```
                       Function called
    Vector identifier                     Any object(default=null)
  myVec.forEach(fName, vecObj);                    Data type
  . . .                    Data type
  function fName(item:T, indent:int, vec:Vector.<T>):void
  {
        //Statements
  }
  veck.foreach(puller,null);
  . . .
  function puller(item:String index:int vect:Vector.<String>):void
  {
        trace(item);
  }
```

Figure 5-4: Using `Vector.forEach()`.

You do not need to know the name of vector elements using for each. All you need to do is provide the name of the first parameter set up in the function. (In the example, 'item' is the term used, but it could be any label.)

With this valuable new knowledge, let's see an example using the forNext() method. The following steps show you how:

1. **Choose New⇨Flash File (ActionScript 3.0) from the menu bar to open a new Flash (ActionScript 3.0) file and save it.**

   We saved ours as EachVector.fla.

2. **In the Class box in the Properties panel, enter a class name and save the file again.**

   We chose EachVector as the class name.

   You can decorate the Stage any way you want. Figure 5-5 shows a simple design using a dynamically created TextArea component.

3. **Drag a TextArea component into the library.**

4. **Open a new ActionScript file and save it in the same folder as the file you created in Step 1.**

5. **Add the script in the following listing and save the file again:**

```
package
{
    import flash.display.Sprite;
    import fl.controls.TextArea;

    public class EachVector extends Sprite
    {
        private var myVec:Vector.<String>;
        private var textArea:TextArea;

        public function EachVector()
        {
            textArea=new TextArea();
            textArea.x=210,textArea.y=150;
```

```
        textArea.width=130;
        textArea.height=100;
        addChild(textArea);

        myVec = new Vector.<String>;
        myVec.push("Sale Items\n",
                "--------------\n",
                "Flash Drives\n",
                "External Hard Drives\n",
                "DVD Drives\n",
                "Optical Drives");
        myVec.forEach(displayItems, null);
    }
    private function displayItems(item:String, index:uint,
        vec:Vector.<String>):void
    {
        textArea.appendText(item);
    }
  }
}
```

The forEach() method depends on the function that it calls having all the right parameters — an element type (item), a typed index (index:uint) and a vector type (String). Within that function, just type your statements in the ActionScript file. Note that in the example, the *item* is each and every element in the vector. We could have written the line as

```
textArea.appendText(myVec[index]);
```

and you would have had the same results. Figure 5-5 shows what you can expect to see.

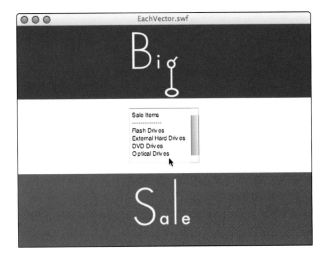

Figure 5-5: TextArea populated using forEach() method.

Look what the cat dragged in!

One fun feature for any Web page is a an object you can drag. Well, you can drag any movie clip or sprite you want by writing a little ActionScript. All you need to make a movie clip or sprite draggable is the startDrag() and stopDrag() methods. Follow these steps:

1. **Choose New⇨Flash File (ActionScript 3.0) from the menu bar to create a new FLA file.**

2. **Draw a shape to drag by using the Text tools and choose Modify⇨ Convert to Symbol from the menu bar (or press F8) to open the Convert to Symbol dialog box.**

   We made ours from a dark red rectangle and a static text label of "Drag Me!"

3. **Select Convert to a MovieClip, select the Export for ActionScript check box, and click OK.**

   We saved ours with the name DragRat.

4. **Delete copies of the movie clip from the Stage by selecting them and pressing the Delete key.**

   The movie clip is still in the library, however.

5. **In the Properties panel, type the class name and save the file.**

   We saved our file as Drag.fla.

6. **Create an ActionScript file and save it in the same folder as the file you created in Step 1.**

   We saved our file as Drag.as and saved it in the same folder as the Drag.fla file.

7. **Add the following code save the file again.**

```
package
{
    import flash.display.Sprite;
    import flash.events.MouseEvent;

    public class Drag extends Sprite
    {
        private var dragRat:DragRat;

        public function Drag()
        {
            dragRat=new DragRat();
            dragRat.x=200,dragRat.y=150;
            dragRat.addEventListener(MouseEvent.MOUSE_DOWN,
                ratDrag);
            dragRat.addEventListener(MouseEvent.MOUSE_UP, ratFree);
            addChild(dragRat);
        }
```

```
private function ratDrag(e:MouseEvent):void
{
        dragRat.startDrag();
}

private function ratFree(e:MouseEvent):void
{
        dragRat.stopDrag();
}
    }
}
```

8. **Test the program by choosing Control➪Test (or pressing Ctrl+Enter in Windows or ⌘+Return on the Mac).**

9. **If you used our files, place the mouse on the red rectangle and drag it around the Stage. Otherwise, test your application to see whether it does what you expected it to do.**

You can add the preceding code to any Sprite or MovieClip object that you want to be draggable. By copying and pasting the code to your own application, you don't have to reinvent the wheel every time you sit down to create an application that has draggable objects.

An Introduction to ActionScript Graphic Programming

Although most of your graphics work may be done with graphic tools in Flash, you can also program Flash graphics for dynamic rendering and total flexibility in your design. In this section, we get you started, but it's only the first step in a 1,000-mile trip!

Get in Shape!

The first class you need to consider is Shape. Along with Shape is the Graphics class. In fact, just about everything that Shape does with graphics is through the Shape.graphics property. Although a bit different from most implementations, the graphics property provides a Graphics object to be used as part of the Shape object. It makes all the drawing methods available to the Shape object. As a result, whenever you see Shape imported, you also see Graphics imported. The statements

```
var myShape:Shape=new Shape();
myShape.graphics.beginFill(0xaabbcc);
```

show how an instantiated Shape object works with the Graphics class through the graphics property and *not* a direct instance of the Graphics class. Don't lose any sleep over this structure; just remember that when you want a Shape, you need Graphics. (Or vice versa — take your choice.)

Simple rectangle

Let's start with a simple rectangle drawing. Here's what you need in any rectangle (pretend that you're using the Drawing tool):

- ✓ **Fill color:** beginFill(0xaabbcc);

- ✓ **Border stroke size and color:** lineStyle(3, 0xccbbaa);

- ✓ **X and Y & W and H:** drawRect(30, 30, 160, 120);

You need exactly the same elements with ActionScript 3.0 code. Beginning with a Shape object, you then use the `graphics` property to provide all the methods you need. The following example shows you how:

1. **Open a new Flash (ActionScript 3.0) file and save it.**

   We named ours `Rectangle.fla`.

   In the Class box in the Properties panel, enter the class name and save the file.

   We chose `Rectangle` as the class name.

2. **Open a new ActionScript file and save it in the same folder as the file you created in Step 1.**

   We saved ours as `Rectangle.as` in the same folder as the `Rectangle.fla` file.

3. **Add the following script and save the file again.**

```
package
{
    import flash.display.Sprite;
    import flash.display.Graphics;
    import flash.display.Shape;

    public class Rectangle extends Sprite
    {
        private var rec:Shape;

        public function Rectangle()
        {
            rec = new Shape();
            rec.graphics.beginFill(0x880000);
            rec.graphics.lineStyle(3, 0x008800);
            rec.graphics.drawRect(30, 30, 160, 120);
            rec.graphics.endFill();
            addChild(rec);
        }
    }
}
```

4. **Test the application.**

   You see a red rectangle with a green border in the upper-right portion of the Stage. So, really, all you're doing is drawing with code. Simple shapes are easy to create with code.

The image maker

To make image creation easier, you can create a class that can make circles, ellipses, rounded rectangles, and triangles. (The `createTriangles()` method is a new one that is a bit different, and we look at it a bit more later.) The class has methods that you can invoke from another class, and that's exactly what we plan to do. First, though, put `GraphicPlay` class together with the following steps:

1. **Open a new ActionScript file and save it.**

   We saved ours as `GraphicPlay.as`.

2. **Add the following script and save the file again.**

```
package
{
    import flash.display.Sprite;
    import flash.display.Graphics;
    import flash.display.Shape;

    public class GraphicPlay extends Sprite
    {
            private var circle:Shape;
            private var rndRec:Shape;
            private var elip:Shape;

            public function GraphicPlay()
            {
                //Constructor
            }
            public function doOval(
                    fill:uint,borW:Number,borC:uint,
                    px:Number,py:Number,r:Number):void
            {
              circle = new Shape();
              circle.graphics.beginFill(fill);
              circle.graphics.lineStyle(borW,borC);
              circle.graphics.drawCircle(px,py,r);
              circle.graphics.endFill();
              addChild(circle);
            }
            public function doRnd(
                        fill:uint,borW:Number,borC:uint,
                        px:Number,py:Number,rw:Number,rh:Number,
                        ew:Number):void
            {
              rndRec = new Shape();
              rndRec.graphics.beginFill(fill);
              rndRec.graphics.lineStyle(borW,borC);
              rndRec.graphics.drawRoundRect(px, py, rw,rh,ew);
              rndRec.graphics.endFill();
              addChild(rndRec);
            }
            public function doLips(
                            fill:uint,borW:Number,borC:uint,
                            px:Number,py:Number,rw:Number,
                            rh:Number):void

            {
```

**Book IV
Chapter 5**

**Harnessing
the Power of
ActionScript 3.0**

```
                    elip = new Shape();
                    elip.graphics.beginFill(fill);
                    elip.graphics.lineStyle(borW, borC);
                    elip.graphics.drawEllipse(px, py, rw, rh);
                    elip.graphics.endFill();
                    addChild(elip);
                }
                public function doTri(fill:uint,v1:Number,v2:Number,
                                      v3:Number,v4:Number,
                                      v5:Number,v6:Number):void
                {
                  graphics.beginFill(fill);
                  graphics.drawTriangles(Vector.<Number>
                                        ([v1,v2,v3,v4,v5,v6]));

                }
            }
        }
```

3. **Open a new Flash (ActionScript 3.0) file and save it in the same folder as the file you created in Step 1.**

   We named our file `UseGraphics.fla` and saved it in the same folder as `GraphicPlay.as`.

4. **In the Class box in the Properties panel, enter the class name.**

   We typed `UseGraphics` as the class name.

5. **Also in the Properties panel, provide a light gray background and save the file again.**

6. **Open a new ActionScript file and save it in the same folder as the file you created in Steps 1 and 3.**

   We named ours `UseGraphics.as` and saved it in the same folder as the `GraphicPlay.as` and `UseGraphics.fla` files.

7. **Add the following script and save the file again:**

```
package
{
        import flash.display.Sprite;

        public class UseGraphics extends Sprite
        {
            private var graphicPlay:GraphicPlay;

            public function UseGraphics()
            {
                graphicPlay=new GraphicPlay();
                addChild(graphicPlay);
                graphicPlay.doOval(0x800000,3,0x008000,150,100,20);
                graphicPlay.doRnd(0xffff00,3,0x000000,130,220,60,70,30);
                graphicPlay.doTri(0x000080,300,300,410,200,410,300);
                graphicPlay.doLips(0x008800,3,0x990099,280,80,130,88);
            }
        }
    }
```

8. Select the tab containing the FLA file and test the application.

Figure 5-6 shows what you can expect to see when you test the application.

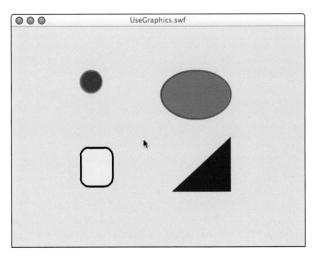

Figure 5-6: Dynamically created graphics.

Try changing the values in the parameters of the methods used in the UseGraphics application. In this way, you see that you have complete control over the graphics.

The triangle and the vector

The *triangle* represents a whole new way of dealing with graphics. It uses our friends the Vector and Graphics classes, but they're built-in so that you can use them without either the Shape class or the addChild() method to place graphics on the page.

Two kinds of vector parameters are used — vertices and indices. The drawTriangles() method expects the first set of numbers to be coordinates on the Stage and the second set to be indices referencing the coordinates. The indices are zero-based, just like you would expect in a Vector — the first coordinates are 0; the second, 1; and so on.

In thinking about the drawTriangles() method, first consider it to be a simple statement with two parameters:

```
graphics.drawTriangles(vertices, indices);
```

The *vertices* are coordinate pairs made of an x and a y position (such as 20,30). Each triangle needs at least three coordinates. So, at a minimum, the vertices are made up of six values representing three pairs of coordinates. The vertices are stored in a vector typed as a number. For example, the following vertices parameter shows three sets of coordinates:

```
Vector.<Number>([60,60, 160,60, 60,160])
```

You can create a simple triangle using just the vertices, but finding out how to use the vertices and indices together gives you a better idea of how to use this powerful new tool that will be the basis of 3D graphics in Flash.

Indices are integers pointing to the different coordinates. The first vector item in the indices points to the first pair. Being zero-based, the first index is 0. For example, if the first coordinate pair in the vertices list is 20,30, then 0 would point to the coordinate 20,30. The following line shows what you can expect to see in the second parameter in the drawTriangles() method:

```
Vector.<int>([0,2,1])
```

Essentially, that parameter tells the program to draw a triangle starting at coordinate 0, and then proceed to coordinate 2, and then to coordinate 1. When you put it all together, you get the full statement:

```
graphics.drawTriangles(
Vector.<Number>([60,60, 160,60, 60,160]),
Vector.<int>([0,2,1]));
```

At first glance, you might be thinking that the preceding looks a bit redundant, given that the first set of numbers does a dandy job of defining the coordinates. So why the second set? The reason for that is to reduce the number of references. Because you have only three coordinates, you're going to get the same triangle no matter what you do. However, if you add a fourth set of coordinates, you can draw a far wider range of triangles using only three indices for each triangle rather than six numbers. Figure 5-7 shows the relationship between vertices and indices.

In looking at Figure 5-7, you can see a green and red triangle overlapping one another. The indices 0,1, and 3 define the green triangle and the indices 1, 3, and 2 define the red triangle. If you trace those values with your finger, you can see how each comes to create a different triangle.

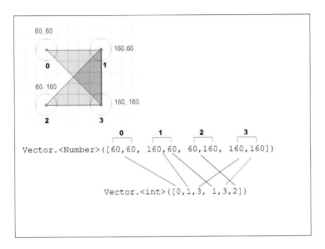

Figure 5-7: Vertices and indices define triangle paths.

Now, all that's left is to create an example that brings everything together. Follow these steps:

1. **Open a new Flash (ActionScript 3.0) file and save it.**

   We named ours `Triangle.fla`.

2. **In the Class box in the Properties panel, enter the class name and save the file again.**

   We used `Triangle` as the class name.

3. **Open a new ActionScript file and save it in the same folder as the file you created in Step 1.**

   We named ours `Triangle.as` and saved it in the same folder as the `Triangle.fla` file.

4. **Add the following script and save the file again:**

```
package
{
    import flash.display.Sprite;
    import flash.display.Graphics;

    public class Triangle extends Sprite
    {
        public function Triangle()
        {
            graphics.beginFill(0x800000);
            graphics.drawTriangles(
            Vector.<Number>([60,60, 160,60, 60,160, 160,160]),
            Vector.<int>([0,1,3, 1,3,2]));
        }
    }
}
```

Notice that the code has no Shape instances and doesn't require the addChild() method to place the images on the Stage. Figure 5-8 shows the hourglass image that you get. That's because *nothing* appears where the two triangles overlap. If you remove the first three or last three numbers in the indices parameter, you can see the single triangle for each.

Figure 5-8: An hourglass created by using triangles.

Book V

Working with Flash Audio

The 5th Wave — By Rich Tennant

SCREEEEEK...

"Is this really the best use of Flash animation on our e-commerce Web site? A bad wheel on the shopping cart icon that squeaks, wobbles, and pulls to the left?"

*W*hen you visit a full-fledged Flash Web site, sound is almost always present. Some sites greet you with background music, and other sites have buttons that make noises when you click them. Sound used with discretion is a useful addition to any Flash project. In this minibook, we show you how to incorporate sound into your projects. We discuss the supported sound formats and then show you how to sync sound to your projects and create noisy buttons to optimize your joyful noises for Flash. We also show you how to use ActionScript to load external sound files into a project.

Chapter 1: Understanding Web Audio

In This Chapter

- About Internet audio files
- Deciphering bit depth and data rate
- Audio hardware and software

Sound is everywhere on the Internet, and you can include sound in your Flash projects. If you're creating a Flash Web site for a music group, you can include background music or an audio player, for example, and add sounds to buttons. For example, if you're creating a Web site for a photographer, you can have a shutter-click sound play when a button is clicked. In this chapter, we discuss the sound file formats supported by Flash and introduce you to a couple of important concepts about sound. In case you will be recording your own material or editing material supplied by clients, we show you some hardware and software solutions.

Exploring Flash-Sanctioned Audio Formats

Flash supports many different sound formats. We don't profess to be experts when it comes to sound, but we do know enough to be dangerous, and more than enough to know the lowdown on sound for Flash. Do you need to be a sound expert to incorporate sound in your Flash movies? No. But it does help to know something about the different file formats, especially if you're dealing with clients who ask you to add sound to their Flash projects. When they do, you tell them which format you need it in. The following list briefly describes the sound formats supported by Flash:

- **WAV (*.wav):** A format that's compatible on the Windows and Macintosh operating platforms. (WAV is an abbreviation of WAVeform.) As a rule, sound in this format isn't compressed and is encoded with PCM (pulse-code-modulation). If you use a WAV file in a Flash project, you start with high-quality sound. This format is ideal if you're including background music that must be of high quality.

- ✔ **AIFF Sound (*.aif, *.aiff):** A format that can be used on both Windows and Mac operating systems. This sound file format (another one that usually isn't compressed) offers CD sound quality and is another good option for high-quality background music. (AIFF is an acronym for Audio Interchange File Format.)

- ✔ **Adobe Sound Document (*.asnd):** A file created by using the Adobe Soundbooth software. The user can specify the data rate and bit rate for the file. Flash CS4 has an option to edit a sound file in Adobe Soundbooth.

- ✔ **MP3 (*.mp3):** Officially known as MPEG-1 Level 3 but more commonly referred to as MP3. This sound format is commonly used for Internet sound and portable audio players. Sound in this format is compressed. The amount of compression (the data rate) determines the quality of the sound. This format is acceptable for a music background with a data rate of 128 Kbps and also works well for the spoken word. You can get good results with an MP3 recording of the spoken word with a data rate of 16 Kbps.

If you have QuickTime 4 or later installed, you can also import the following file formats into Flash:

- ✔ **Sound Designer 2 (*.sd2, Macintosh only):** A sound format developed for recording audio on Macintosh-based computers. This high-quality sound format is capable of recording CD-quality sound.

- ✔ **Sun Audio (*.au):** A sound format created by Sun Microsystems for Internet use. The file format is suitable for simple sounds and the spoken word, but not for music.

- ✔ **System 7 Sounds (Macintosh only):** Associated with the Mac OS7 operating system.

Understanding Bit Depths, Data Rates, and Sample Rates

Whenever sound is recorded, a bit depth and sample rate are chosen. When sound is compressed for playback, a bit depth and sample rate are also chosen. These factors determine the quality of the sound, and the resulting file size.

Bit depth determines the dynamic range and signal-to-noise ratio of a digital audio file. The dynamic range is the sound range in decibels that can be reproduced when the sound is played back. The human hearing range is approximately 100 decibels (dB). A 16-bit recording has a dynamic range of approximately 98 dB. The signal-to-noise ratio is the amount of noise that can be heard in soft passages. When you import a sound into Flash that has a high bit depth, you end up with a sound that has a wide dynamic range and a low signal-to-noise ratio.

Frequency, measured in hertz (Hz), is the number of cycles a waveform completes in one second. A frequency of I Hz plays 1 sound wave or cycle per second. The human range of hearing is from approximately 20 Hz to 20 kHz (20,000 Hz). A fellow named Harry Nyquist came up with the theory that the frequency needed to cover the range of human hearing is exactly double that range. A fudge factor of 10 percent was added, which brings the frequency to 44.1 kHz, the frequency commonly used to record CD-quality sound. TV audio is 48 kHz, and DVD-quality audio has a frequency of 96 kHz.

When you're choosing an audio file for a Flash project, the bit depth and frequency are quite important. If you're importing a sound file for background music, choose a 16-bit file with a 44.1 kHz frequency. If you're importing a simple sound for a button, you can get by with an 8-bit file with an 11 kHz frequency. For more complex sounds or a recording of the spoken voice, use an 8-bit file with a 22.5 kHz frequency. For music, use a 16-bit file with a 44.1 kHz frequency.

Data rate is a factor when a file is compressed into a format such as MP3. The *data rate,* also known as the *bit rate,* is the number of bits played back per second. A low bit rate produces a small file size at the expense of sound quality. For the spoken voice with no background music, a bit rate of 16 Kbps is acceptable, unless the person has a deep voice. FM radio quality is 96 Kbps, and near CD quality is 320 Kbps.

Stereo is something else to consider. Stereophonic sound consists of two channels, which plays back in the left and right speakers of a stereo sound system or a computer with a sound card that supports stereo. A stereo file is twice as large as a monophonic (one channel of sound) sound file.

If you're not sure about the frequency and bit depth of a sound file, launch Flash and choose File⇨Import to Library. After the file is imported to the document Library, select it, right-click (Windows) or Control+click (Macintosh), and then choose Properties. The properties of the sound file appear to the right of the waveform (see Figure 1-1).

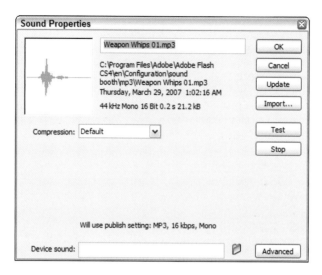

Figure 1-1: This sound file has properties.

Recording Hardware

If you record sound for your Flash productions or are considering recording sounds for your Flash production, you should buy the best microphone you can afford. Several microphone models operate from one of your computer's USB ports. This section presents a couple of solutions that will give you good sound quality without breaking the bank.

Zoom H2

The Zoom H2 (type **H2** in the Search box at `www.samsontech.com`) is a handheld recording powerhouse with four microphones in an incredibly small package. The device can record 16- or 24-bit sound files with a frequency of 96/48/44.1 kHz uncompressed in the WAV format or in the MP3 format with a sample rate of up to 320 Kbps. Users can change the sound format, frequency, and sample rate by using menu commands. Buttons on the front of the recorder enable users to switch microphone configurations. The unit can record a 90-degree pattern using two microphones from the front of the unit, which is ideal for recording your own voice; a 120-degree pattern using two microphones from the rear of the unit, ideal for recording a group of people; or four microphones for 360-degree surround sound. The sound quality is incredible.

The Zoom H2 also doubles as a USB microphone. Simply plug in the supplied USB cable to the microphone and use a menu command to connect the H2 as an audio input device, and you can use your computer recording software to record your voice or sounds. In fact, Doug has used the Zoom H2 to record podcasts. For field recordings, the unit uses SD (Secure Digital) memory cards. The unit ships with a 512MB SD card, earbuds, a small tripod, a windscreen, a USB cable, a power adapter, and a handle that can be used to connect the device to a microphone stand. As of this writing, the list price of the Zoom H2 (see Figure 1-2) is $199.

Figure 1-2: The Zoom H2 can be used for field and computer recordings.

Blue Snowball

Professional podcasters and radio personalities use condenser microphones to produce sweet, rich vocals. Most condenser microphones need phantom power to work. Blue Microphone's Snowball (see Figure 1-3) is white and round — just like a snowball — and is powered by your computer's USB port. The Snowball (click the Snowball link at the top of the page at www. bluemic.com) is a professional-quality condenser microphone.

It has two polar patterns — omnidi-rectional (360 degree) and cardioid — which records sound from the front of the microphone. The cardioid pattern is ideal if you're recording in an environment with background noise such as computer fans. There is also a cardioid pattern with a –10 dB attenuator if you're recording in a noisy environment. The microphone records 16-bit sound with a sample rate of 44.1 kHz. The microphone needs no drivers.

Connect the Snowball to a microphone stand using the thread mount at the bottom of the unit, connect the USB cord to the microphone, and then to your computer. It's as simple as that. The Snowball works with a Macintosh (OS X; USB 1.0 or 2.0; with a minimum of 64MB RAM) or on Windows (XP Home Edition or XP Professional; USB 1.0 or 2.0; with a minimum of 64MB RAM). The initial USB drivers for Windows Vista caused some problems with this microphone.

Figure 1-3: The Snowball condenser microphone is ideally suited for computer recording.

If you perform a Windows update, the microphone will work just fine. Doug uses the microphone with Vista to record his podcast. As of this writing, the Blue Snowball has a list price of $159.

Blue Snowflake

Blue Microphone's Snowflake is an ideal recording solution for road warriors. The Snowflake is small — toss it in your laptop case and it's readily available when you need to record on the road. The device can be placed flat on a desktop or clipped to most laptop computers. The Snowflake is a professional-quality condenser microphone in an incredibly small package.

The microphone has a cardioid pattern, which means that the device picks up sound in front of the microphone. The Snowflake records 16-bit sound with a sample rate of 44.1 kHz and needs no drivers. Connect the USB cable to the microphone and then to your computer, and you're ready to record. When you need to pack the microphone away, coil the USB cord, place it in the base, and close it. You can also separate the base and attach the microphone to a laptop computer (see Figure 1-4). This handy microphone is about the same size as a classic iPod and works with a Macintosh (OS X;

USB 1.0 or 2.0; with a minimum of 64MB RAM) or on Windows (Vista, XP Home Edition, or XP Professional; USB 1.0 or 2.0; with a minimum of 64MB RAM). For more information, visit www.bluemic.com and click the Snowflake link at the top of the page. As of this writing, the Blue Snowflake has a list price of $79.

Figure 1-4: The Snowflake, a road warrior's best friend.

Sound-Editing Software

After picking up a good microphone, you need software to capture your words of wisdom and the sounds you record. Sound-editing software is also useful when you need to edit files supplied by a client. In this section, we show you three applications we use: Adobe Audition, Sony Sound Forge, and Acid Music.

Adobe Audition

Adobe Audition (www.adobe.com/products/audition) is a full-featured professional recording and sound-editing application. You can record multiple tracks with the application, clean up existing audio, and edit your projects. The software features several options. You can work in multitrack mode or edit an individual track. The software has tools you use to analyze a sound and much more. You can also restore noisy and clipped files. Doug uses Audition to record and edit his podcast (www.pixelicious.info). The workspace (see Figure 1-5) is fairly intuitive if you've edited sound before. As of this writing, Adobe Audition lists for $349.

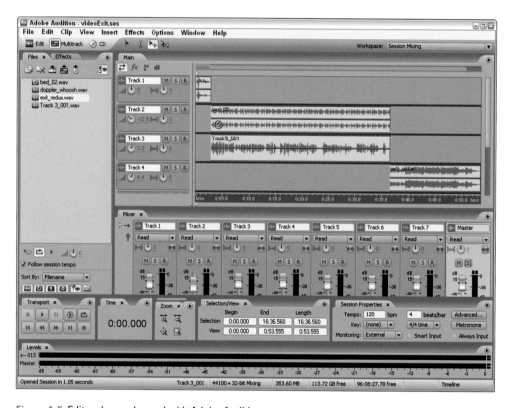

Figure 1-5: Edit and record sound with Adobe Audition.

Adobe Audition may be overkill for your needs. Adobe has another application, Sound Booth, that's targeted toward developers and designers with little or no experience in sound editing. The application is tailored for working with Flash and other Adobe applications. As of this writing, the application lists for $199.

When you record, make sure to use the VU meters that are available in most applications. When you record, make sure that the VU meters don't reach the red zone. If you do, the peak of the waveform is flat, which means that the sound is clipped and distorted.

Sony Sound Forge

Sony Sound Forge is another powerful sound-editing application. Sony Sound Forge 9.0 (www.sonycreativesoftware.com/soundforge) features multi-track editing. You can record, edit, restore old recordings, and do much more. As of this writing, Sony Sound Forge 9.0 retails for $299. If you don't need the option to record multiple tracks, Sony Sound Forge Audio Studio (`www.sonycreativesoftware.com/audiostudio`) may be the solution for you. As of this writing, the application sells for $54.95. Figure 1-6 shows the workspace for Sony Sound Forge 7.0.

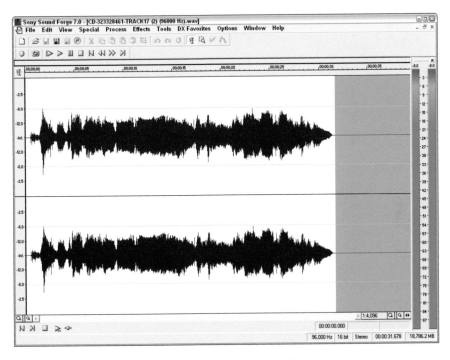

Figure 1-6: You can record, edit, and repair sound files with Sony Sound Forge.

Sony ACID Music Studio (Windows only)

The Sony ACID Music Studio (`www.sonycreativesoftware.com/music studio`) application enables you to create soundtracks using music sample loops. The application supports multiple tracks and recording. When you assemble a song in ACID, the loops seamlessly mix to create your soundtrack. If you have clients who can't create their own soundtracks and you have an ear for music, consider purchasing a copy of ACID Music Studio. The application ships with 3,000 sound loops that you can mix and match to create your own unique soundtracks. Doug uses Sony ACID to record background music for his podcast and Flash projects. Bill uses the Macintosh equivalent: GarageBand (`www.apple.com/ilife/garageband/`). As of this writing, Sony ACID Music Studio sells for $54.95. You can purchase additional loops for most musical instruments in a wide variety of genres from the Sony Web site (www.sony creativesoftware.com/loops).

If you're on a budget, check out a cross-platform application called Audacity (http://audacity.sourceforge.net). It's not the prettiest interface on the planet, but it does support multiple tracks and editing. There are also plug-ins that enable you to export the sound in the MP3 format (http://audacity.sourceforge.net/download/lame).

Chapter 2: Adding Sound to a Flash Production

*1*t seems like every Flash movie has sound in it. Flash sites have background music playing, and buttons make noise when they're clicked, for example. If you want sound in your Flash projects, you've come to the right place. In this chapter, we show you how to import audio, add audio to keyframes, and add audio to buttons. Last but not least, we show you how to use ActionScript to load a music soundtrack.

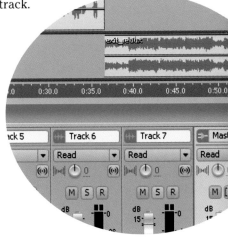

Importing Audio

If you want music in a Flash project, you have to import it — it's a Flash law. When you import music to a project, you can import it to the Stage or to the document library.

To import a sound to the document library:

1. **Choose File➪Import➪Import to Library.**

   The Import to Library dialog box appears (see Figure 2-1).

2. **Select the file you want to import.**

   You can import any sound file format supported by Flash. If you don't have your sound assets organized in their own folder, you can save time by choosing All Sound Formats from the Files of Type drop-down menu.

When you choose this option, only supported sound files are displayed in the dialog box. Alternatively, you can select a file format type from the Files of Type drop-down menu to display only those files.

3. **Select a file and then click OK.**

    The sound file is added to the document library.

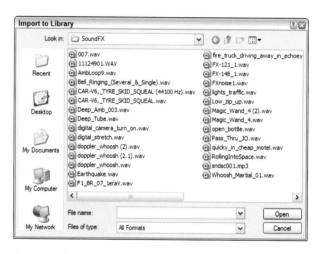

Figure 2-1: Importing a sound file to the document library.

To add a sound to the Stage, follow these steps:

1. **Select the keyframe where you want the sound to appear.**

    You can select a keyframe on the main Timeline, a Timeline for a movie clip you're creating, or the keyframe for a button you're creating. If you select a frame, Flash adds the sound to the previous keyframe.

2. **Choose File⇨Import⇨Import to Stage.**

    The Import dialog box appears (see Figure 2-2).

3. **Select the file you want to import.**

    You can import any sound file format supported by Flash.

4. **Select a file and then click OK.**

    The file is imported to your project, and a waveform appears in the key-frame (see Figure 2-3).

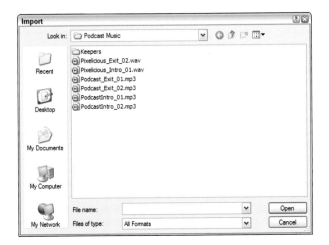

Figure 2-2: Importing a sound to the Stage.

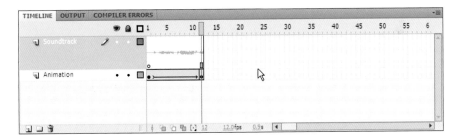

Figure 2-3: A sound imported to a keyframe.

Using Sound in a Project

After you add some sound files to the document library, it's time to put them
to work. You may think that you can just plop a sound file on the Timeline
and be done with it. But no, you have to tell Flash how to synch the sound
to the Timeline. Then you decide whether you want the sound to play more
than once or when you want it to stop, for example. It's not rocket science,
but if you've never done it, you've come to the right section of the book. In
the following sections, we show you how to use sound from the document
library, choose the proper method of synching the sound, and add sound
effects if you want them.

Adding a sound from the document library

Unless we're using ActionScript to load a sound file, we always add our sounds to the document library and then add them to the project. We find this method to be a better way to work than importing sounds to the Timeline when you suddenly remember that a sound is supposed to play on Keyframe 6. To add a sound from the document library to your project, follow these steps:

1. **Select the keyframe where you want the sound to appear.**

   You can select a keyframe on the main Timeline, on a Movie Clip symbol you're creating, or on a keyframe for a button you're creating. If you select a frame by mistake, Flash adds the sound to the previous keyframe.

2. **Open the Property inspector.**

   If the Property inspector isn't visible in the workspace, choose Window⇨Properties (see Figure 2-4).

3. **In the Sound section, select a file from the Name drop-down menu.**

   On this menu, you find a list of all sounds you've imported to the document library.

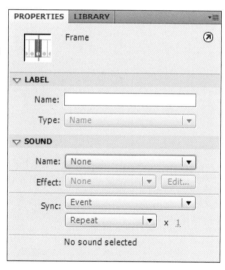

Figure 2-4: Adding a sound from the document library.

4. **Select an option from the Effect menu.**

   We cover effects in the "Adding Sound Effects" section of this chapter.

5. **Select an option from the Sync menu.**

   We cover these options in the "Synching sound" section, later in this chapter. After you add a sound to a keyframe, the sound's waveform appears on the Timeline.

Synching sound

After you add a sound to your project, you have to determine how Flash synchronizes the sound to the Timeline. You have several different options to consider. These options determine how the sound file plays in relation to your movie. To synchronize a sound, follow these steps:

1. **Add a sound to the Timeline from the document library or by importing a sound to the Stage.**

   If you jumped to this part of the chapter before reading anything else and you don't know how to add a sound to the Timeline, put on the brakes and read the earlier sections "Importing Audio" or "Adding a Sound from the document library."

2. **Choose one of the following options from the Sync drop-down menu:**

   - *Event:* Plays the sound when the keyframe is reached and plays the sound in its entirety. The sound plays again when the keyframe is triggered. This may cause a problem if you add the sound to the Timeline of a looping animation and the duration of the sound is longer than the duration of the animation. The sound plays again, even though the first instance of the sound hasn't stopped playing. This sync method is best suited for sounds that have a short duration, such as the sound you add to button keyframes.

   - *Start:* Starts the sound when the keyframe is reached. However, it doesn't play again if the keyframe is reached before the sound stops playing.

   - *Stop:* Stops the sound when the keyframe is reached. This option works well when you want a sound to stop on a given frame.

   - *Stream:* Starts playing the sound as soon as enough frames have downloaded into the viewer's Flash Player. This option causes the Flash Player to skip frames if the animation cannot keep up with the streaming sound. If an animation in the movie stops while the sound is playing, the sound stops too. A streaming sound stops playing if its duration exceeds the number of frames in the movie.

3. **Choose an option from the Sound Loop drop-down menu that's right below the Sync menu.**

   The default option, Repeat, enables you to determine how many times the sound plays. After choosing this option, drag the scrubby slider to determine how many times the sound plays, or click the current value and enter a different one. Alternatively, you can choose Loop from the menu and the sound loops infinitely. Looping isn't recommended for streaming sounds because it adds frames to the file to play the sound for the number of times you specify, which can significantly increase the file size.

Adding sound effects

By default, the sound plays out of both speakers. Can you say stereo? We knew you could. However, by adding a sound effect, you can have the sound play in the left channel or right channel, or cross the great divide from right to left, or vice versa. Intrigued? Follow these steps:

1. **Add a sound to the Timeline from the document library, or by importing a sound to the Stage.**

   If you don't know how to add a sound to the Timeline, read the earlier sections "Importing Audio" or "Adding a sound from the document library."

2. **Choose one of the following options from the Effect menu:**

   - *None:* The default option; applies no effect to the sound

   - *Left Channel:* Plays the sound in the left speaker of the host computer

   - *Right Channel:* Plays the sound in the right speaker of the host computer

   - *Fade to Right:* Gradually fades the sound to the right speaker of the host computer

   - *Fade to Left:* Gradually fades the sound to the left speaker of the host computer

   - *Fade In:* Gradually increases the volume of the sound through its duration

   - *Fade Out:* Gradually decreases the volume of the sound through its duration

   - *Custom:* Lets you tweak the sound to your liking. If you're a custom kind of person, check out Chapter 3 of this minibook.

Adding Sound to Buttons

Button sounds are quite common in Flash movies. You can have a sound play when a user pauses the cursor over the button or clicks the button. To add a sound to a button, follow these steps:

1. **Create a button.**

   We know — we haven't covered buttons yet. If you don't know how to create a button, please bookmark this page and check out the section in Book VII, Chapter 1, about creating buttons.

2. **Right-click (Windows) or Ctrl+click (Mac) and choose Add Layer from the context menu.**

   Flash creates a new layer. While you're at it, be neat and tidy. Double-click the current layer name to select it, and then enter **Sound**. Even on a simple two-layer Timeline, it pays to be tidy and label your layers.

3. **Select the Over keyframe if you want a sound to play whenever a user pauses the cursor over the button; or select the Down frame if you want a sound to play when the button is clicked.**

4. **Press F6 to create a keyframe.**

   You can have a sound play for both states. Just make sure that the sounds are short in duration.

5. **Open the Property inspector.**

6. **In the Sound section, choose a sound from the Name drop-down menu.**

   This menu shows every sound you imported into the document library. If you haven't imported any sounds, choose File➪Import to Stage and follow the prompts to select the file and open it.

7. **Accept the default Event option from the Sync menu.**

   Figure 2-5 shows the Timeline of a button to which a sound has been added to the Over state.

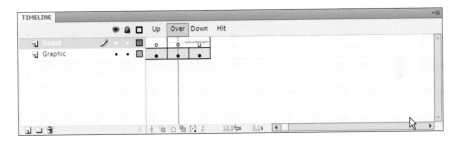

Figure 2-5: Adding a sound to a button's Over state.

8. **Press Ctrl+Enter (Windows) or ⌘+Return (Macintosh).**

   Flash publishes the movie and displays it in another window.

9. **Pause the cursor over the button.**

   The sound plays. Of course there's more to a button than just graphics and sound. In Book VII, Chapter 1, we show you how to create a button and how to create the ActionScript code that makes the button functional.

Using the Flash Sounds Library

Flash CS4 ships with an impressive library of sounds. When you need to find a sound for a button or an animation you need, look no further than the sounds library. To use a sound from the sounds library, follow these steps:

1. **Choose Window⇨Common Libraries⇨Sounds.**

   The sounds library appears (see Figure 2-6).

2. **Select a sound and then click the Play button to preview the sound.**

   You hear the sound unless your speakers are muted.

3. **Drag the sound to the document library.**

   The sound is added to the document library.

4. **Drag the sound to a keyframe.**

   After adding the sound to your project, choose a Sync option and an effect. For more information about synchronizing sounds, see the "Synching sound" section, earlier in this chapter. For more information about sound events, see the Adding Sound Effects section of this chapter.

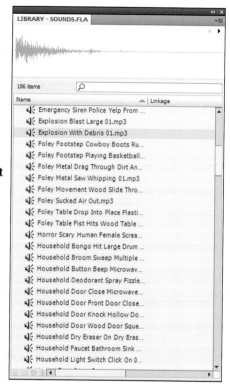

Figure 2-6: A library with sounds? Isn't that an oxymoron?

Use ActionScript to Load an External Sound File

The ActionScript sound classes make it possible for you to load an external sound file into Flash, which enables you to keep the file size of your movie relatively small. In this section, we show you the code needed to load the sound file and to start and stop the movie. The ActionScript is loaded from external ActionScript files. We make the ActionScript files (AS3_Sound.zip) available from this book's companion Web site at www.dummies.com/go/flashallinone.

To load an external sound file using ActionScript, follow these steps:

1. **Choose File⇨New.**

   The New Document dialog box appears.

2. **Accept the default ActionScript 3.0 file type and click OK.**

   Flash creates a new document.

3. **Add two buttons to the document.**

   For the purpose of this example, choose Window⇔Common Libraries⇔Buttons. Choose a Play and Stop button from the Playback Flat group on the Stage.

4. **Select the Play button and then open the Property inspector.**

5. **Name the button instance start.**

   This is the name of the button instance as it will be addressed from the external ActionScript files.

6. **Select the Stop button, and in the Property inspector, name the button halt.**

   It's a rather logical name for a button that stops a sound file.

7. **Save the file.**

   When you save the file, name the file **DoSound**. Leave the document open.

8. **Choose File⇔New and choose ActionScript File from the Type menu.**

   A file named Script-1 appears, and the Actions panel occupies the workspace.

9. **Enter the code from Listing 2-1 in the Actions panel.**

   If you downloaded the ActionScript files, you can copy and paste the code from `SoundPlayer.as` into the Actions panel. Alternatively, you can open the file in Flash.

Listing 2-1: The SoundPlayer ActionScript Code

```
package
{
    import flash.display.Sprite;
    import flash.media.Sound;
    import flash.media.SoundChannel;
    import flash.net.URLRequest;

    public class SoundPlayer extends Sprite
    {
    private var soundCh:SoundChannel;
    private var soundReq:URLRequest;
    private var soundSource:Sound;

    public function SoundPlayer(url:String)
    {
    soundReq=new URLRequest(url);
    soundSource = new Sound();
    soundSource.load(soundReq);
    }
```

(continued)

Listing 2-1: *(continued)*

```
public function playSound():void
{
soundCh=soundSource.play();
}

public function stopSound():void
{
soundCh.stop();
}
}
}
```

10. **Save the file.**

   Name the file **SoundPlayer**. Flash automatically supplies the .as extension.

11. **Choose File⇨New and choose ActionScript File from the Type menu.**

   A file named Script-2 appears, and the Actions panel occupies the workspace.

12. **Enter the code from Listing 2-2 in the Actions panel.**

   This bit of code plays and stops the music file when the appropriate button is clicked. Alternatively, you can cut and paste the code from the DoSound.as file you downloaded.

Listing 2-2:   The DoSound ActionScript Code

```
package
{
    import flash.display.Sprite;
    import flash.events.MouseEvent;

    public class DoSound extends Sprite
    {
    private var soundNow:SoundPlayer;

    public function DoSound()
    {
    start.addEventListener(MouseEvent.CLICK, turnOn)
    halt.addEventListener(MouseEvent.CLICK, turnOff)
    soundNow=new SoundPlayer("mySoundFile.mp3");
    }
    private function turnOn(e:MouseEvent):void
    {
    soundNow.playSound();
    }
    private function turnOff(e:MouseEvent):void
    {
    soundNow.stopSound();
                                                    }
    }
}
```

13. **In the line that starts with** `soundNow=new SoundPlayer`, **select** `mySoundFile.mp3`, **and replace the text with the name of your sound file.**

    Make sure to include the extension in the filename. Also make sure that the file is in the same folder as the ActionScript files and the `DoSound.fla` document.

14. **Save the file.**

    Name the file **DoSound**. Flash automatically supplies the `.as` extension.

15. **Select the DoSound.fla title.**

    If you closed the document, choose File⇨Open, navigate to the file, and then open it.

16. **Press Ctrl+Enter (Windows) or ⌘+Return (Macintosh).**

    Flash publishes the file and opens the movie in a new window.

17. **Click the buttons to start and stop the music.**

Using ActionScript to Load a Soundtrack

Back in the *Jurassic* period of Flash, you created a movie with nothing but a soundtrack and then loaded that soundtrack movie into a target movie clip in your main movie. However, with a bit of ActionScript, you can load a soundtrack into another file. This is an excellent option if you don't own a sound editing application. You can optimize the sound in Flash as outlined in Chapter 3 of this minibook. Whenever you load content from an external file, the main file is as small as possible, which means that it loads quickly. To load a soundtrack from an external source, follow these steps:

1. **Create a new Flash document.**

2. **Open the Property inspector.**

3. **Change the background color to the same color as the document in which the sound file will play.**

4. **Change the W and H values to 1.**

    You're creating a 1-by-1-pixel file that will nestle in a corner of your main Flash movie.

5. **Select the first keyframe and choose File⇨Import⇨Import to Stage.**

    In the Open dialog box, navigate to a sound file and then open it.

6. **In the Property inspector, accept the default Event Synch method, and choose Loop from the Sound Loop menu.**

7. **Select the sound in the document Library, right-click (Windows) or Ctrl-click (Mac) and choose Properties.**

   This opens the Sound Properties dialog box.

8. **Accept the default compression option, or choose a different option from the Compression drop-down menu.**

   To find out everything you ever wanted to know about optimizing a sound in Flash, check out Chapter 3 of this minibook.

9. **Name the document and save it.**

   We prefer using short names, like sndTrk. Remember that you'll end up writing ActionScript to load the file. Why work harder?

10. **Choose File⇨Publish.**

    Flash publishes an HTML file and an SWF file with the name you specify in Step 7.

11. **Create a new Flash document.**

    Alternatively, open another Flash file in which you want to play a background sound.

12. **Select the first keyframe.**

    Typically, you want the sound to load as soon as the file opens in the user's Flash Player.

13. **Choose Window⇨Actions.**

    The Actions panel opens.

14. **Copy the code from Listing 2-3 into the Actions panel.**

15. **Press Ctrl+Enter (Windows) or ⌘+Return (Mac).**

    The soundtrack loads and plays.

Listing 2-3:   Loading an External Movie with a Sound File

```
var sound:Loader;
var url:URLRequest;
   sound=new Loader();
   url=new URLRequest("pixelicious.swf");
   sound.load(url);
   sound.x=0, sound.y=0;
addChild (sound);
```

16. **Press Ctrl+Enter (Windows) or ⌘+Return (Mac).**

    The soundtrack loads and plays. But you need some way to turn off the sound for those who think that silence is golden.

17. **Choose Window⇨Common Libraries⇨Buttons.**

    The Buttons library appears.

18. **Select a button and drag it on stage.**

    For the purpose of this example, choose any button. If you do this technique for your own Flash movies, you can create a spiffy button.

19. **In the Property inspector, name the button instance** btn.

    ActionScript needs to address the button by name.

20. **Select the first frame on the timeline.**

    If you've followed the steps so far, this is where your ActionScript resides.

21. **Add the code in Listing 2-4.**

    This code causes the sound to unload when clicked.

Listing 2-4:   Silencing the Sound

```
btn.addEventListener (MouseEvent.CLICK, removeSound) :
Function removeSound (e:MouseEvent);void
{
     Soujnd.unloadAndStop ();
}
```

22. **Press Ctrl+Enter (Windows) or ⌘+Return (Mac).**

    The sound loads and plays.

23. **Click the button.**

    Ah. Peace and quiet.

Chapter 3: Editing Sound Files

*I*f you don't have sound editing software, you can still do a lot of work in Flash. All you need to do is change some properties in the document library and you can tweak the sound file to sound its best, while also creating a relatively svelte Flash file. The compression method and sampling rate affect the file size of the published SWF file. Tweaking the properties of individual sounds results in files that sound good and are as small as possible. You can also modify effects you apply to sounds, such as the duration of a fade-in or fade-out or panning from one speaker to the next.

Optimizing Sound for Your Project

If you don't have sound editing software, you can accomplish quite a bit in Flash. You can't eliminate background hiss, or slice and dice a sound file to cut out the bits that don't sound good, but you can find the optimal compression method and settings. You can optimize sound globally when you publish a file. (We cover optimizing sound when publishing a document in Book VIII, Chapter 4.)

You can also optimize individual sounds by modifying their properties in the document library. When you modify a sound's properties there, the published sound settings aren't applied. To optimize an individual sound file, follow these steps:

1. **Choose Window➪Library.**

   The document library opens.

2. **Select the sound you want to edit, right-click (Windows) or Control+click (Macintosh), and then choose Properties from the context menu.**

   The Sound Properties dialog box appears (see Figure 3-1).

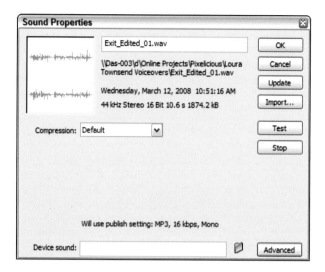

Figure 3-1: Modifying the properties of a sound.

3. **Choose one of the following options from the Compression drop-down menu:**

   - *Default:* Uses the settings specified in the Publish Settings dialog box to compress the sound file on export.

   - *ADPCM:* The option to use when optimizing button and small event sounds.

   - *MP3:* The option to use when optimizing background music.

   - *Raw:* Uses the compression settings from the raw data of the imported files. You can apply compression settings by modifying the sample rate. The sound quality is similar to MP3, but results in a larger file size.

   - *Speech:* Uses settings appropriate for a sound file of a speaker with no background sound.

4. **If the default option is available, accept it to convert stereo to mono.**

   This option decreases the file size because you're not exporting data for two sound channels. Deselect this option if you're creating a Flash movie for a musician's Web site or for another site where stereo sound is important.

5. **Choose settings in the Preprocessing section of the dialog box.**

   The available settings differ depending on the compression setting you choose. The following list offers some guidelines for the compression options that have preprocess setting options:

- *ADPCM:* Choose an option from the Sample Rate drop-down menu. For this format, you can choose a setting from 5 kHz (poor sound quality, smallest file size) to 44 kHz (best sound quality, largest file size). You can also choose an option from the ADPCM Bits drop-down menu. Choose from 2 bits (poor sound quality, smallest file size) to 5 bits (best sound quality, largest file size). These two options determine the data rate of the sound.

- *MP3:* Choose an option from the Bit Rate drop-down menu. You can choose an option from 8 Kbps (poor sound quality, smallest file size) to 160 Kbps (best sound quality, largest file size). You can also choose an option from the Quality menu: Fast, Medium, or Slow. This option determines how long Flash takes to compress the file. Slow takes the longest time to process, but produces the best sound fidelity.

When you initially apply compression settings to an MP3 file, choose the Fast Quality option, as shown in Figure 3-2. It speeds up publishing the file when you're testing your Flash project. When you're satisfied with the file and ready to publish, open the Sound Properties dialog box for the sound and change the Quality setting to Best.

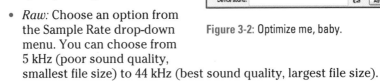

- *Raw:* Choose an option from the Sample Rate drop-down menu. You can choose from 5 kHz (poor sound quality, smallest file size) to 44 kHz (best sound quality, largest file size).

Figure 3-2: Optimize me, baby.

- *Speech:* Choose an option from the Sample Rate drop-down menu. Your options are from 5 kHz (poor sound quality, smallest file size) to 44 kHz (best sound quality, largest file size).

6. **Click Test.**

   Flash applies the compression settings to the sound file and plays it. At this stage, we experiment with different settings. When you're applying compression settings for an individual sound, remember the reason that you're using the file in your project. If it's a simple sound, like a button click, you can apply more compression. If you're creating a site for a public speaker or a musician, applying too much compression results in poor sound quality and doesn't showcase your client's talents. If you're optimizing a long sound file, click Stop when you've heard enough to determine whether the settings are optimal for the file. Figure 3-2 shows a sound file being optimized using the MP3 compression option. Notice the new file size as compared with the original, which is displayed below the Quality setting. This information is in the same spot in the dialog box for the other compression options.

Editing Your Sound Files

When you import a sound file into Flash, you still have the option to edit the file. When you add the sound to the Timeline, you have the option to apply an effect to the sound. You can edit the manner in which the effect is applied or choose the Custom option and then edit the file. If you have sound editing software on your computer, you can make a round trip to the sound editor from Flash.

Editing sound in Flash

When you add sound to a keyframe, you can apply an effect to the sound in the Property inspector, as we outline in Chapter 2 of this minibook. You can also edit the effect that's applied to a sound:

1. **Select the keyframe to which you applied the sound.**

2. **Open the Property inspector.**

   Click Properties to open the Property inspector. If you customized the workspace or are working with a workspace that doesn't display the Property inspector, choose Window⇨Properties.

3. **Click the Edit button that looks like a pencil.**

   The Edit Envelope appears. If you already applied an effect to a sound, it's listed in the Effect field. If the effect changes the volume of the sound as it plays, you see points. Figure 3-3 shows the dialog box with no effect applied. Notice the hollow square at the start of each Timeline. It signifies that the sound plays at full volume in each speaker.

4. **Change the view of the waveform.**

   Click the icon with the magnifying glass and the plus sign to zoom in, or click the icon with the magnifying glass and the minus sign to zoom out.

5. **Change the manner in which the Timeline is displayed.**

   The default option displays the Timeline in seconds. If the sound spans multiple frames and you want to synchronize an edit with a frame, click the Frames icon to display the Timeline as frames. Personally, we found the frames option difficult to use, but try it — you might like it.

6. **Click the Timeline at the point where you want to make a change.**

   This step adds a hollow square to each Timeline.

7. **Drag a point to modify the amplitude (volume) of the sound at that point in its duration.**

   You can edit the left and right speaker Timelines independently. This gives you the option to pan from the left to right speaker or vice versa.

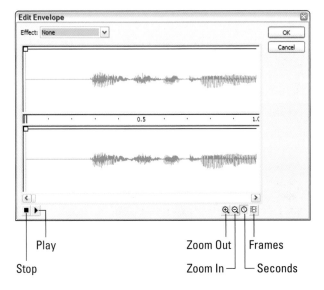

Play

Stop

Zoom Out   Frames

Zoom In   Seconds

Figure 3-3: Editing a sound in Flash.

8. **Add points to the Timeline and modify them as desired.**

If you added a point in error, click it and then drag it off the Timeline. You can add as many points as you need to get the job done.

9. **Click the Play button to preview your handiwork.**

The sound starts playing. You can stop the preview by clicking the Stop button. Figure 3-4 shows a sound that pans between speakers, plays in both speakers, and then fades out evenly from both speakers. Notice that we zoomed out on the waveform to view it in its entirety.

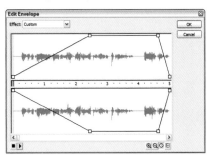

Figure 3-4: A sound that has been edited in Flash.

If you don't have a sound editing application installed on your computer and you like sound, we urge you to experiment with the different effects you can produce by using the Edit Envelope dialog box.

Editing in an external editor

If you have Adobe Soundbooth installed on your computer, you can access the application by selecting a sound file the document library and then choosing Edit with Soundbooth. You can also edit a sound in an external sound editor by following these steps:

1. **Select the sound in the document library.**

2. **Right-click (Windows) or Control+click (Macintosh) and choose Edit With from the context menu.**

   The Select External Editor dialog box appears.

3. **Navigate to the executable (`.exe`) file that launches the external editor you want to use.**

   For example, if you have Adobe Audition installed on your computer, the executable file that launches the application is `Audition.exe`.

4. **After selecting the executable file, click Open.**

   The external sound-editing application launches.

5. **Perform any edits you want, and then save the file.**

   After you save the file and return to the Flash document library, the sound is updated to reflect your changes.

When you edit a sound in an external sound-editing application, you're modifying the original file. Make sure that you have a copy of the original file saved in a different folder.

Book VI
Working with Flash Video

*F*lash works with video on many different levels. You can embed videos directly into a Flash application, progressively download a Flash Video File (FLV) from a Web server, or stream an FLV file from Flash Media Server. The ability to work with video on the Web is a major capability for Flash and anyone developing for the Web.

Book VI shows you how to convert video files from different video formats into both VP6 FLV and H.264 F4V files by using Adobe Media Encoder (included with Flash CS4). You also find out how to play those videos using a video player component or a player you create yourself in a Flash application or with the new Adobe Media Player. We show you how to add cue points and captions to your video for special effects. You even discover how to broadcast a live video and make an audio/video receiver to view the broadcast.

Chapter 1: Playing Video with Flash: The Producer's Chair

In This Chapter

✓ Working with Web video

✓ Embedding video in Flash

✓ Understanding progressive download

✓ Becoming familiar with streaming video

O f all the revolutionary technologies now available with Adobe Flash CS4, the most dramatic is the ability to send video over the Web. Although Web video has been available for a few years, creating Web sites with high-quality display, including high-definition (HD) video, is just now coming to the forefront. You can create videos that use H.264 (MPEG-4, among others) format for spectacular results at a reasonable bandwidth. Using the built-in FLVPlayer component and other tools available in Flash CS4, you can create a Web site that sends video to the viewer just like Flash has delivered animation, text, sound, and graphics. The big difference is that all these elements are combined into a single audio/video file that can be sent smoothly over the Web.

What Is Web Video?

If you've visited YouTube (www.youtube.com), you've seen Web video. In fact, if you've gone to a site such as http://movies.com, you've seen movie trailers done with streaming video. Even some business sites, such as www.sandlight.com, feature streaming video presentations.

If you want to know whether Flash was used to create a Web video, visit YouTube or a favorite site that has movie trailers you can watch online, and right-click a video (Windows) or Option+click it (Mac). If Flash was used to create it, you see About Adobe Flash Player at the bottom of the shortcut menu, as shown in Figure 1-1.

You may have several kinds of experiences with Web video, such as the following:

- Download an entire movie file to your computer and play that movie in a player that recognizes the file type.

  Windows Media Player (which you can also download and use on a Mac) allows you to view files with the extension .wmv, for example. You can also use QuickTime Player (which comes with most Macs and is also available for Windows) to play files with the .mov extension.

- View a podcast in iTunes.

- Click a button to play a movie embedded in a Web page that eventually plays on your computer.

Figure 1-1: Find Flash information on a video's shortcut menu.

If your experience has been primarily with downloaded files, some of which you may have received through e-mail, you're aware that video can be sent over the Internet. But that isn't the kind of video we're talking about in this minibook. Instead, we mean the video that plays as soon as you open the page (or when you click the Play button on the page).

In this chapter, we look at different ways to send video over the Web with Flash CS4.

Embedded Video in Flash: Old School

For as long as we can remember, certain types of video files have been embedded in Flash. Flash treated each frame as a JPEG file and ran through the JPEG files just like frames of a regular movie, with fairly good results. The consequence, however, was that an SWF file with embedded video was huge. Viewers were forced to wait patiently until the giant file loaded, and as often as not, they probably hit the Back button in their browsers and left the file for more patient souls to view.

If you have a short video, however — perhaps a welcome message or a loop of a dumb dog trick — you may be able to include it in a Flash file. This is a quick solution for a specific purpose, however; for the most part, you don't want to embed video in Flash.

Converting a video file for use in Flash

To start, you need a video file. Flash CS4 uses FLV and F4V files — highly compressed file types that take up little space on the server. Chapters 2 and 3 of this minibook provide information about converting different video file types to FLV or F4V.

Figure 1-2 shows a sample AVI file that was recorded on a Webcam, with a background added in Adobe Ultra. The AVI file was shortened and then exported as a small FLV file because only small files in FLV format work for embedded video. (You can download this AVI file from the book's companion Web site at www.dummies.com/go/flashallinone.)

**Book VI
Chapter 1**

**Playing Video
with Flash: The
Producer's Chair**

Figure 1-2: To work as an embedded video, your original video has to be shortened significantly when it's converted to a FLV file.

The AVI file was shortened and then exported as a small FLV file for this demonstration. Only small files and ones set to FLV format work with embedded video.

Embedding the video in a Flash file

To embed the video in a Flash file, follow these steps:

1. **Open a new Flash file.**

2. **Add a graphic background for your movie (see Book I, Chapter 2).**

   Figure 1-3 shows a sample background.

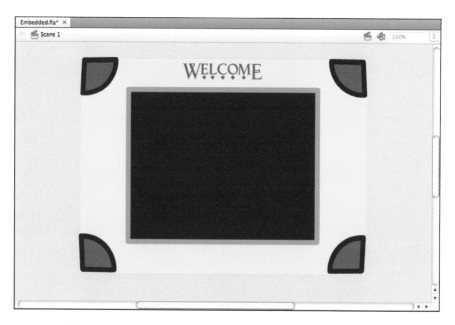

Figure 1-3: A backdrop helps you visualize where the video will appear.

3. **Choose File➪Import➪Import Video (see Figure 1-4).**

    The Import Video dialog box opens, displaying the Select Video page.

4. **Choose the Embed FLV in SWF and Play in Timeline radio button (see Figure 1-5), and then click the Browse button to locate the FLV file to embed.**

    The warning message in the Select Video page tells you that an embedded video is likely to cause audio synchronization issues, so keep audio short or leave it out when you're embedding a video.

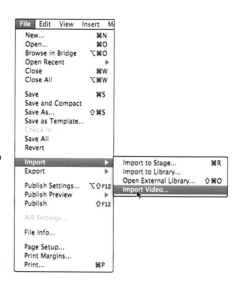

Figure 1-4: Start the video import process.

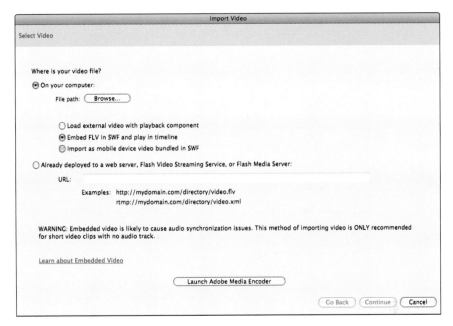

Figure 1-5: Setting the Embed option in the Import Video dialog box.

5. **After you select your video, click the Continue button.**

   The Embedding page opens. By default, the Symbol Type pull-down menu is set to Embedded, and both check boxes — Place Instance on Stage and Expand Timeline If Needed — are selected.

6. **To accept these default settings, click the Continue button.**

   The Finish Video Import page opens (see Figure 1-6).

7. **If the selected video is the one you want, click the Finish button; otherwise, click the Back button (Windows) or the Go Back button (Mac) and load the correct files, as shown in Step 3.**

8. **When you see the video on the Stage, adjust its placement by dragging it or using the Align panel.**

   Figure 1-7 shows an example of what you may see. Notice that the piece of video you see is considerably smaller than the video shown in Figure 1-2, earlier in this chapter.

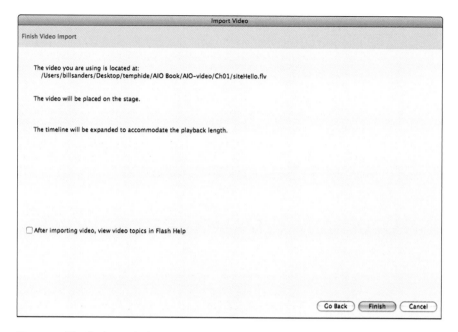

Figure 1-6: The final page before video is embedded.

Figure 1-7: The first frame of the video appears on the Stage.

Essentially, this process cuts the video into separate frames and displays them in a fashion similar to setting a separate JPEG files in each frame. This video can be looped just like any other movie, or it can be stopped and started with ActionScript 3.0.

After you test your Flash application, see how big your SWF file is. In our test of the example embedded video used in this section, the file is 205KB. Considering that the video is only a few seconds long, that file is a large one. Users with slow Internet connections may become impatient as this file loads. Before you decide to use this method for even a small movie, look at the next section for a much smarter alternative.

Progressive Downloading: Almost Streaming from a Web Server

As we note earlier in this chapter, using embedded video is appropriate in only a few situations. In fact, any video more than a few seconds long may be automatically blocked by Flash when you attempt to embed it in Flash CS4.

An alternative method for displaying video on a Web site — *progressive downloading* — is just as easy and generates a much smaller SWF file. In fact, a 10-minute video using progressive download generates the same-size SWF file as a 5-second video, and the size of the video played doesn't affect the size of the player.

Understanding progressive downloading

Progressive downloading uses a Web server, just as a regular HTML or SWF file does. The FLV or F4V file is downloaded in packets, and as the client (browser) begins receiving those packets, the content is displayed in the video player.

Imagine that the FLV file is like a big stack of pancakes. Instead of delivering all the pancakes in one big stack, in progressive downloading, the server delivers the pancakes one at a time. After a few pancakes are delivered, the server begins to display the pancakes until the whole stack is visible. The video appears to show a growing stack of pancakes, but in fact, the pancakes are graphic images shown in sequence to give the illusion of movement.

Progressive downloading is often confused with video streaming or even called HTTP streaming. Progressive downloading is *not* streaming, however. When you use progressive downloading, the video file is actually downloaded to your computer and can be extracted from the browser's temporary cache storage. In actual use, you may not be able to tell the difference, especially in short videos, but the difference is real — as you see in the section "Streaming Video: Leaving the Socket Wide Open," later in this chapter.

Creating a progressive download

Creating a progressive download in Flash CS4 is as easy as pie; so get out your director's chair and get ready to produce your first Web-length feature.

Preparing the folder and files

To start creating your progressive download, follow these steps:

1. **Create a new folder.**

   You use this folder to save the FLA and SWF files for this application.

2. **Locate the F4V file you want to use.**

   For this example, we used the file named `blackBill.f4v`. (It's available for downloading from this book's companion Web site.)

3. **Open a new Flash file and create a background to your taste, leaving an area in the center (approximately 330 by 270 pixels) for the video player.**

   Figure 1-8 shows an example using an art deco theater motif. (The color scheme is a retro one from Kuler.)

4. **Save the file in the same folder as the F4V file.**

   For the example, save the file as **PlayVideo1.fla**.

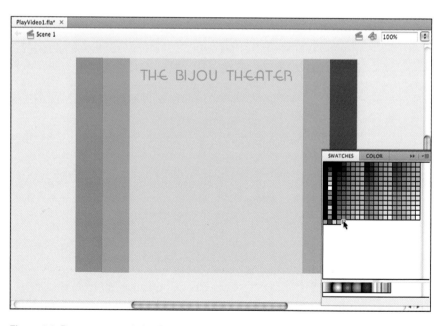

Figure 1-8: Base stage ready for FLVPlayer component.

Importing and customizing your video

Next, you import the video and apply a skin and color scheme to it. Follow these steps:

1. **Choose File⇨Import⇨Import Video.**

   The Import Video dialog box opens, displaying the Select Video page.

2. **Select the Load External Video with Playback Component radio button, and click the Browse button.**

3. **Select the F4V file in the browser window and click Open.**

   Figure 1-9 shows an example. (Notice that the FLA and SWF files are in the same folder.)

4. **Click Continue in the Import Video window.**

   The Skinning page opens.

Figure 1-9: Select the F4V file to play.

5. **From the Skin pull-down menu, choose a skin that has the player controls you want.**

If you select a skin with the word *Under* in its filename, all the controls are below the video. If the word *Under* isn't in the filename, the player controls are superimposed on the bottom portion of the video. (If you prefer to display the entire video, choose an *Under* skin to place the controls below it.)

In some cases, you may not even want any play controls. Select None in the Skin pop-up menu in the Skinning selections in the Import Video Window. In such cases, the video plays once and leaves the last frame displayed on-screen. If you omit the play controls, make sure that you don't allow the video to loop and drive the viewer to distraction!

6. Select a color.

In the example shown in Figure 1-10, the colors from the Swatches panel open when you select a color for the skin. If you have a color scheme that you're using for an entire page, you can select a color from the same color scheme for your video skin so that your video player skin blends in well with your page's color scheme.

7. Click Continue.

The Finish page opens, displaying all the settings you chose.

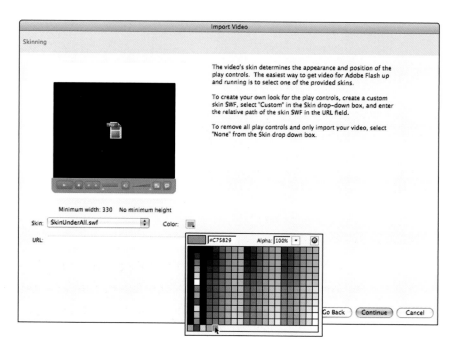

Figure 1-10: Choosing a control skin and color.

8. **Click Finish.**

9. **If you haven't saved your FLA file, do so at the prompt.**

   Remember to save it in the folder with the F4V file.

When you click Finish, you see a big black area where the video is set, because the video is much larger than your default Stage. The selected F4V file in Figure 1-11, for example, is 640 by 480 — way too big. In the following section, you make some adjustments.

Figure 1-11: Video that's too large for the Stage.

Resizing the video

To resize the video, follow these steps:

1. **Open the Properties panel and set the proportion lock icon to lock.**

2. **Change the width to 320 and press Enter (Windows) or Return (Mac).**

   You should see the values in the Properties panel change to 320 by 240 pixels, and your video and page controls should appear on the Stage. Changing the width and height of the video window doesn't affect the length of the video.

3. **Center the video and the play controls, as shown in Figure 1-12.**

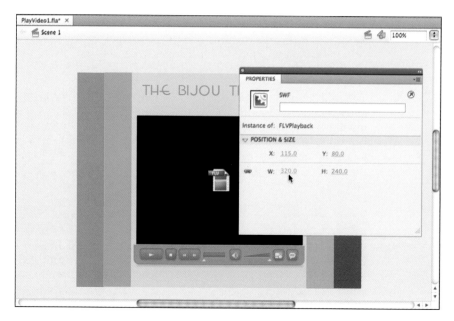

Figure 1-12: Video and play controls after resizing to fit the Stage.

4. **Save everything.**

5. **Press Ctrl+Enter (Windows) or ⌘+Return (Mac) to watch the video.**

   Figure 1-13 shows an example of what you may see.

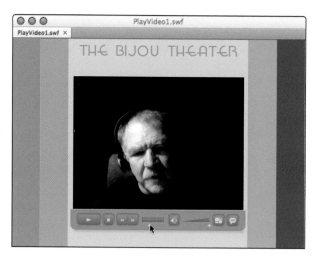

Figure 1-13: A progressive download playing.

Experimenting with the play controls

As a progressive download plays, try using the different play controls. You can pause, rewind, and forward the video to the end, and you can use the scrubber bar to move to different parts of the video.

The first time you run the video, you may have difficulty moving the video ahead because it is still being downloaded. Testing it on your desktop isn't much of a problem, because the video is short and right on your computer. If you place the files on a remote Web server (a host), however, it takes longer for the video to get to your computer. As a result, not all parts of the video are available. Scrubbing ahead may require you to play the whole video once so that all of it is in the cache.

Storing your files

When you finish testing the movie, you see a skin SWF file stored with the FLA file. It's automatically added when you finish importing the video. Depending on the name of the skin you select, you find a different filename describing the skin. (For example, you might find one named `SkinUnderAll.swf`.) If you transfer your application to a Web host, be sure to include the special skin SWF file or else your movie won't work correctly.

Changing videos

After you create an application to play a progressive download, you may want to play a different video. Rather than create a whole new application, you can easily change the FLV or F4V video to be played. The following steps show you how, using the `PlayVideo1.fla` you created in the preceding sections:

1. **Place the new video you want to play in the same folder as the `PlayVideo1.fla` file.**

   For this example, we use the file named `marketing.flv`. This file as well as `PlayVideo.fla` are available for downloading from this book's companion Web site.

2. **Open `PlayVideo1.fla` and click the FLVPlayer component to select it.**

3. **Choose Window⇨Component Inspector to open the Component Inspector panel.**

4. **Click the Parameters tab and locate the source parameter (see Figure 1-14).**

When you're working with the FLVPlayer component, place the Component Inspector panel in the dock to ease the workflow. Think of the Component Inspector as your assistant producer.

5. **Click the magnifying glass icon to the right of the source parameter (refer to Figure 1-15).**

The Content Path dialog box opens.

6. **Type the path to the FLV or F4V file you want to stream, as shown in Figure 1-15, and click OK.**

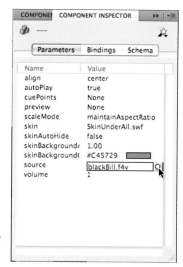

Figure 1-14: The Component Inspector panel showing FLVPlayer parameters.

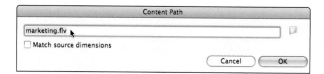

Figure 1-15: Specify the FLV or F4V source file.

If you click the Browse folder icon in the Component Inspector to locate your video file on your system, you assign an absolute address to your video file. When you place your files that play the video on a Web server, the server tries to find that absolute address and fails. The safest approach is to place all the FLV and F4V files you plan to play in the same folder as your SWF file that plays the video, and type the name of the video you want to play in the Component Inspector's source window. You can organize your videos in a separate folder and use a relative address, such as `videos/marketing.flv`, but don't use absolute addressing to your video files that target your computer.

7. **Press Ctrl+Enter (Windows) or ⌘+Return (Mac).**

You see the new video, as shown in Figure 1-16.

Figure 1-16: Playing a different video in the same application.

Changing the appearance of the play controls

When you change a video, you may want to change other features as well, such as how the play controls look. In fact, you can use different play controls without having to change the whole page. Follow these steps:

1. **Open `PlayVideo1.fla` and save it as** PlayVideo2.fla **in the same folder as `PlayVideo1.fla`.**

   This step gives you access to the FLV and F4V files without having to start over.

2. **Click the video icon representing the FLVPlayer component.**

3. **Choose Window⇨Component Inspector to open the Component Inspector panel.**

4. **If it isn't already selected, click the Parameters tab of the Component Inspector (refer to Figure 1-14).**

5. **Click the `skin` parameter.**

   A magnifying glass icon appears in the second column.

6. **Click the magnifying glass icon to open the Select Skin dialog box (see Figure 1-17).**

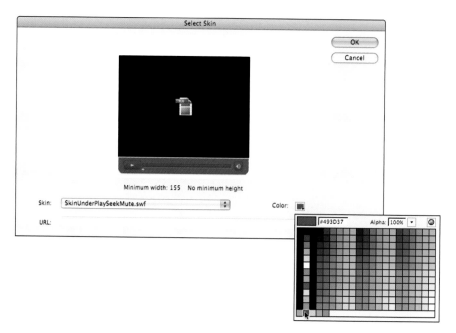

Figure 1-17: The Select Skin dialog box.

7. **Choose an option from the Skin pull-down menu.**

   For this example, we chose `SkinUnderPlaySeekMute.swf`.

8. **Click the Color box to open the color swatches and then choose a color.**

   For this example, we chose dark brown, as shown in Figure 1-18.

   Your color choices come from the color palette used for this design. In this way, you can change the play controls yet stay within the color scheme. (Go nuts, if you want, and make your own color scheme to choose colors from.)

9. **Click OK to close the Select Skin dialog box.**

10. **Test your movie by choosing Control⇨Test from the menu bar (or by pressing Ctrl+Enter [Windows] or ⌘+Return [Mac]).**

    Voilà! The new play controls are different but still fit the overall look, as shown in Figure 1-18.

Figure 1-18: Player with new skin.

Streaming Video: Leaving the Socket Wide Open

The best way to deliver video on the Web is with streaming video. When you use the Web, as soon as the Web page you've requested has arrived, the Web connection between your browser and server is closed. Even with sophisticated animation and pages that appear to be interactive, chances are that you no longer have a Web connection.

Rather than deliver sound and video by opening and closing the connection to the server, you can send streaming data by using *open socket technology*. When you use this technology, after a connection is established, that connection is maintained until the connection is closed by the client or is automatically closed by an event, such as a recorded video coming to an end. (For more on this topic, see Chapter 5 of this minibook.)

The following advantages of streaming technology make it quite popular:

- The stream begins playing almost immediately.

- Recorded video can be scrubbed ahead as soon as the video begins playing.

- Streaming video provides smoother transmission of video and sound.

- Audio (voice, music, sound effects, and so on) can be streamed without video.

- Other types of media, such as text, can be streamed as well.

- Streaming allows for live interaction over the Internet. (Your mother-in-law gets to visit remotely!)

HTTP and RTMP: A tale of two protocols

For the Internet to work, a protocol has to be in place so that a *client* (a computer hooked up to the Internet) can get stuff from a Web *server* (a remote system with lots of stuff on it). The general protocol for this purpose is HTTP (Hypertext Transfer Protocol). A request from the client is sent to the server, creating a connection between the server and client. After everything is delivered to the client computer, the connection is closed. That system makes a lot of sense; the alternative would be keeping all connections open, which would mean that only a few people could use the Internet at the same time.

But what happens when you need a continuous stream of data moving over the Internet, as in a two-way videoconference? If the connection is going to have to be open and closed while the conference is in session, the results are jerky and unintelligible. So Macromedia (now Adobe) came up with RTMP (Real Time Messaging Protocol), which uses the open socket technology mentioned in the preceding section. When the connection between the streaming server and the client is kept open, streaming media over the Internet is much smoother. For this reason, most companies that have media to stream (such as movie studios) use RTMP for streaming instead of HTTP.

A machine that's dedicated to server software is what most people imagine when they think about a server. Actually, servers can be hardware or software — or both.

If you have a Macintosh computer, you have Apache Web Server built in. Likewise, in certain Windows configurations, you can enable Internet Information Services (IIS), which is also a Web server.

In the next section, you see how your computer can be a client, a Web server, and a streaming server at the same time. (Your computer can do more multitasking than a soccer mom.)

Enter Flash Media Server

In Chapter 5, you create an actual streaming-video project by using Flash Media Server. For now, we just provide a brief overview of how the program works. Fortunately, a good deal of what you may already know from reading this book applies to streaming video.

First, look at Figure 1-19, which illustrates the streaming-media process.

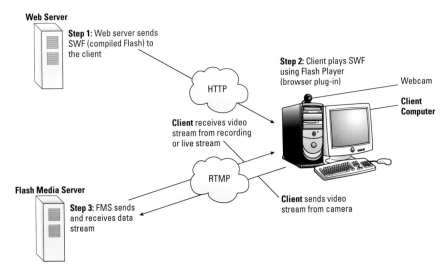

Figure 1-19: HTTP and RTMP data transfer.

The process begins with an SWF file sent from the Web server to the client. The client plays the SWF file on a browser with a Flash Player plug-in. Then the SWF file contacts Flash Media Server and makes a connection that allows streaming.

As you see in the illustration, the client is streaming back and forth between the media server, *not* the Web server. It sends out an audio/video stream from its own camera and microphone, and receives the same back from the media server. All the while, the connection between the media server and the client remains open.

This chapter is an orientation to video and Flash that gets you started and shows different ways to display video with Flash. But as they say in the movies, "You ain't seen nothin' yet!"

Chapter 2: From Camera to Desktop: Getting Video Ready for Prime Time

In This Chapter

✔ **Choosing the right Webcam or digital video camera**

✔ **Finding free video-recording resources**

✔ **Seeing how to use some popular video programs**

*I*f you've worked with just about any kind of graphics on computers, you're aware that images can be saved in JPEG, PNG, or GIF format for use on the Web. The same is true of video files that contain both audio and video (A/V) elements; these files are saved in such formats as WMV, MOV, AIFF, and AVI. As you see in Chapter 1 of this minibook, the formats that Flash video uses for progressive downloads and streaming are FLV and F4V.

In this chapter, you see some fundamental ways to generate different kinds of video files for the Web. Additionally, you see several kinds of cameras and microphones that you can use to make videos.

Whatcha Gonna Do? Video Camera or Webcam

The first question you have to ask yourself is what you plan to do with video on the Web. If your goal is to have video chats or to make fun little videos to share with your friends, all you need is a Webcam. The quality of Webcams varies significantly, but even the least expensive can get the job done for simple video projects.

If you plan to be the next Steven Spielberg, producing everything from movie trailers to your own dramas (or to become a YouTube star), you need a video camera. Video cameras typically have better lenses, more flexibility, and better control options than Webcams. Digital video cameras are relatively inexpensive, but you can get professional-level, high-definition (HD) digital video cameras to get top-quality results. The sky's the limit when it comes to the price of video cameras. (Lucky you!)

If you plan to do a lot of A/V chatting and you want to make videos in locations away from your computer, you're well advised to get both a Webcam *and* a digital video camera. You can use digital video cameras for video chats, but they don't work very well for this purpose because they gobble up a lot of bandwidth.

Choosing a Webcam

Before you go out and buy a Webcam, check your computer; it may have a built-in Webcam already. Many recent laptop and iMac computers do. Check to see whether the top of your screen has a little square window with a small lens inside. Both the Dell laptop and the iMac we use have built-in Webcams, and if we hadn't known where to look, we might have overlooked the cameras. (They've been watching us!)

The decision about which Webcam to buy is based on a few key factors:

- **Resolution:** The camera's *resolution* refers to the size of the screen (in pixels) that the camera can handle. For video chats, 320 x 240 resolution generally is all you need, but you can find Webcams with resolution up to 1600 x 1200 pixels. Also look for the number of *megapixels* that the camera handles (generally, between 1.2 and 2).

    You have to be careful in comparison shopping, because cameras often have two ratings: one for still photos and another for video. The Creative Live! Cam Optia AF, for example, has a rating of 8 megapixels for still images and 2 megapixels for video.

- **Lens:** You need to consider factors including focal length, iris, and lens construction. Price also is a factor: Cheaper lenses generally result in lower quality.

    One of the best lenses we found is the Carl Zeiss Tessar optical system used in the Logitech QuickCam Pro 9000 camera (see Figure 2-1).

- **Light sensitivity:** The more light a camera requires, the less light sensitivity it has. This fact is a two-edged sword. If you have bad lighting in your environment, light sensitivity is important, but often, good light sensitivity results in a lower-quality picture. It's better to improve your lighting than the lighting sensitivity of your camera. (Well, if you live in a bat cave, you may need good light sensitivity.)

- **Autofocus:** This feature automatically keeps the focus on the central figure in the video — generally, you. This important feature is built into the Apple iSight, Logitech QuickCam Pro 9000, and Creative Live! Cam Optia AF cameras, among others.

Figure 2-1: Logitech 9000 Webcam.

Autofocus is very handy, but face-following is not. *Face-following* means that the camera follows you as you move around. The results aren't always what you expect. Sometimes, the camera chooses to follow an unintended object or to *overtrack* (track beyond the point where you stop). On the other hand, zooming and panning features are very handy for framing a shot just the way you want.

✔ **Frames per second (fps):** Generally, you should look for a camera that operates at 15 or 30 fps. Higher resolutions tend to get lower fps. The same camera can have 30 fps at 320 x 240 resolution but only 15 fps at 640 x 480, for example.

✔ **Bandwidth use:** This information is difficult to find, because it generally isn't published. Creative Labs has an excellent reputation for producing Webcams that sip bandwidth, but at the cost of some picture quality.

✔ **Built-in microphone:** This feature can be handy — and also a problem. Depending on how far the camera is from your mouth, you need to consider whether you'd rather have a remote mike.

✔ **Software:** Some cameras come with software that you can use to create videos and special effects.

✔ **Driver compatibility:** You can find yourself in a real nightmare if your camera is incompatible with your computer. You need software drivers that work with your operating system; they may work with Windows XP but not Windows Vista, for example, and may not work with a Macintosh at all. Also check the manufacturer's Web site for the most recent driver updates.

IEEE versus USB

When IEEE 1394 Webcams came out, they were the best ones available. Nowadays, almost all new Webcams use USB instead, so we don't cover IEEE 1394 cameras in this chapter.

If you dig up one of these cameras online, however, and expect it to work because you have an IEEE 1394 port on your computer, be aware that it probably doesn't have software that's compatible with your computer — especially if you have a newer operating system, such as Windows Vista or Mac OS X Leopard.

Choosing a video camera

From the get-go, you should know that a digital video camera is going to use more bandwidth than a Webcam. You're not likely to be using the camera for chat sessions, though, so you shouldn't have to worry about it.

Choosing a digital video camera involves all the same considerations as choosing a Webcam (see the preceding section), as well as the following key factors:

- **Compatibility:** Most older digital video cameras that you can purchase inexpensively at places like eBay are strictly IEEE 1394. Be sure that your computer has an IEEE 1394 port (called a FireWire port on a Macintosh). Newer digital video cameras have both USB 2 and IEEE 1394 connections. Also make sure that the camera has compatible software (see the nearby sidebar "IEEE versus USB" for details).

- **High definition:** Now that Flash can convert your video to H.264 format, you can stream HD video in F4V files. If you need HD for your video projects, you pay more for the camera, but you get high quality.

You can get an inexpensive digital video camera or a professional-level one. The process for getting video files from the camera to your computer is the same for all digital video cameras.

Free Resources for Creating Videos

When you buy almost any new computer these days, you find some kind of video recording program included. Computers that use the Windows operating system (both Windows XP and Windows Vista) have Windows Movie Maker, and Apple Macintosh computers that run Mac OS X include iMovie.

In addition to the free software included with your computer, you can use free software from Adobe to create videos right on your desktop. Adobe

Flash Media Live Encoder 2.5 takes any video source from a Windows computer and converts it to FLV or F4V files; download it at www.adobe.com/ products/flashmediaserver/flashmediaencoder. For playing back FLV and F4V files, you can get Adobe Media Player for both Windows and Macintosh at www.adobe.com/products/mediaplayer.

A final source of free software for creating video files is the software that comes with certain Webcams. Logitech, for example, supplies software for creating, editing, and adding special effects to videos created with its cameras. Likewise, Creative Labs provides software that you can use to create and edit videos.

The following sections discuss a few of these resources in more detail.

Windows Movie Maker

If you have a Windows computer and a digital video camera, get out your director's chair and listen up. Windows Movie Maker works only with a digital video camera, so if you have a built-in or external Webcam but no digital video camera, skip this section.

Windows Movie Maker is a simple-to-use program that captures video directly from your digital video camera or from a storage device in your camera (a digital tape, card, or minidisc) and then stores that video in a WMV file where you specify. To use the program, follow these steps:

1. **Connect your digital video camera to your computer, turn it on, and prepare it to record.**

   Don't forget to remove the lens cap. If you see a dark space where your smiling face should be, check the lens cap first. Also make sure that your camera isn't set for playback.

2. **Launch Windows Movie Maker and click Capture from Video Device.**

   The Video Capture Wizard opens, and you should see the name of your digital video camera (Canon DV Device, Sony DV Device, or a similar name).

3. **Select the icon for your camera and click Next.**

4. **Enter a filename, select a place to save your captured video, and click Next.**

   For this example, we chose to name the file megahit.

   You can accept the default storage folder (My Videos) or browse to another folder where you want to store files for later conversion to FLV or F4V format.

5. **Select Best Quality for Playback on My Computer (Recommended), and click Next.**

The wizard's Capture Video page opens. You should see your face (or whatever the camera is pointing at) in the Preview window, as shown in Figure 2-2.

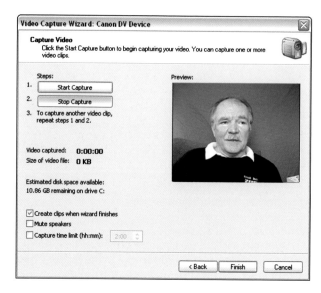

Figure 2-2: Previewing a camera setup in Windows Movie Maker.

6. **Click the Start Capture button; then recite a poem, greet a friend, or say something clever.**

As you record, the Capture Video page provides two vital pieces of information: the amount of space the video is consuming per minute (about 14MB) and the amount of space left on your hard drive to store it. These displays are subtle reminders that videos take lots of memory and can quickly eat up the remaining space on your hard drive.

7. **After no more than a minute, click the Stop Capture button.**

The recording stops.

8. **Click the Finish button.**

A little window displays a progress bar, and then you see a video icon with the name of your movie. To close the wizard and exit Windows Moviemaker, just click the X in the upper-right corner of the screen.

At this point, you've created a video file. You should be able to find it wherever you chose to store it in Step 4. Double-click its icon to play it in Windows Media Player.

In Chapter 3, you see how to use Flash to convert this file to play on the Web.

Adobe Flash Media Live Encoder (Windows)

If you have a Windows computer, you can download Adobe Flash Media Live Encoder and use it with any camera you have connected to your system, including your built-in Webcam. (Get Adobe Flash Media Live Encoder 2.5 or later for the examples in this book.) This program may seem a bit technical when you first open it, but it's easy to use.

Thanks to confusing naming policies, the Adobe Media Encoder CS4 that comes with Flash CS4 is *not* the same thing as (or even similar to) Adobe Flash Media Live Encoder. The former — which is intended solely for converting non-FLV or non-F4V files to FLV or F4V files — is covered in Chapter 3.

Take a quick look at Figure 2-3. Notice that the picture isn't as good as the one shown in Figure 2-2, earlier in this chapter. That's because it was shot on an inexpensive built-in Webcam instead of a digital video camera. Adobe Flash Media Live Encoder does many things (some of which we discuss in detail in Chapter 4), but for now, all you want to do is create a simple video saved in either FLV or F4V format, using either a Webcam or a video camera.

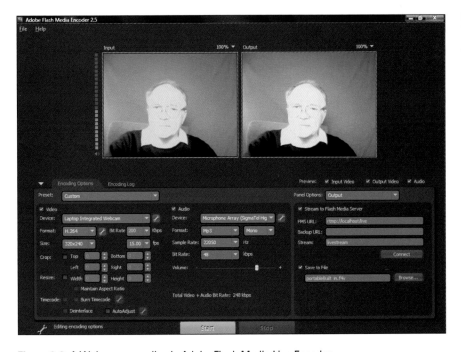

Figure 2-3: A Webcam recording in Adobe Flash Media Live Encoder.

To use Adobe Flash Media Live Encoder for recording, follow these steps:

1. **Connect your camera to your computer, turn it on, and prepare it to record.**

2. **Launch Adobe Flash Media Live Encoder.**

3. **In the lower-left pane of the encoder window, choose your camera from the Device pull-down menu.**

   In Figure 2-3, for example, the selected camera is Laptop Integrated Webcam.

4. **Choose H.264 from the Format pull-down menu.**

5. **Choose 320x240 from the Size pull-down menu.**

6. **In the lower-right pane of the encoder window, select the Save to File check box.**

7. **In the Save to File text box, type a filename.**

   For this example, we named the file `portableBuilt_in.f4v`.

   Whenever you choose the H.264 format, the file extension is `.f4v`; any other format uses the `.flv` extension.

   At this point, you needn't worry about any of the other settings in the encoder window.

8. **Click the green Start button to begin recording.**

9. **When you're finished, click the red Stop button.**

10. **Retrieve the F4V file and play it in Adobe Media Player, as shown in Figure 2-4.**

Figure 2-4: Playing an F4V file in Adobe Media Player.

The best feature of Adobe Flash Media Live Encoder is that it saves your file in a format that Flash can read for progressive download or streaming video. (For details on both progressive download and streaming video, see Chapter 1 and Chapter 5 of this minibook.)

Webcam software

To give you an idea of the software that comes with a Webcam, this section looks at Logitech's QuickCapture. The camera in question, a Logitech Orbit, has a zoom-and-pan feature so that you can center the subject without having to move either the camera or the computer. The files are saved in Windows Media Video format (.wmv), and all you need to do to create them is plug in the camera and click the Record button.

Use the Webcam Settings window to set the pan, tilt, zoom, brightness, contrast, color intensity, and white balance, as shown in Figure 2-5.

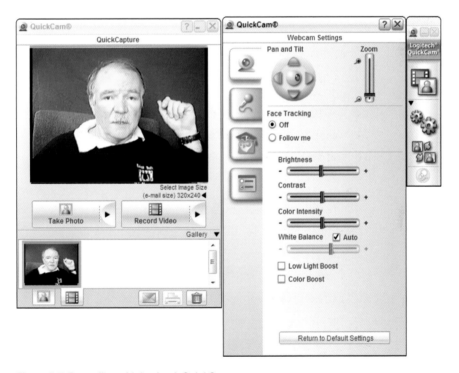

Figure 2-5: Recording with Logitech QuickCapture.

You can also choose Low Light Boost and Color Boost options. A Face Tracking (face-following) option is available as well, but as we note earlier in this chapter, we tend to keep this feature turned off because it causes more problems than it solves. Even on the best Webcams, the feature never seems to work as intended.

Finally, compare the images shown in Figure 2-4 and Figure 2-5. You can see the differences in quality. Both images were taken with a Webcam, but the details and quality of the image shown in Figure 2-5 are much better. These examples give you an idea of the quality range available in Webcams.

You can take advantage of the zoom, pan, and tilt features of the QuickCapture software and at the same time save your files in FLV or F4V format. First, open the software, and set the zoom, pan, and tilt just the way you want. Then close the software, open Adobe Flash Media Live Encoder, and record in the format you want to use.

iMovie (Macintosh)

If you have a recent Macintosh running Mac OS X, you're blessed with an excellent yet simple tool for making all the videos you want: iMovie. You can record using either a Webcam (most likely, a built-in iSight) or a digital video camera. The iSight has excellent quality and autofocus capability, whether it's the built-in version at the top of the screen or the external version connected by a cable.

Recording a video

To record a video in iMovie, follow these steps:

1. **If you're using an external Webcam, connect it to your computer; turn it on; and prepare it for shooting video.**

   If you have a built-in iSight Webcam, the camera is ready to go when you need it; you don't need to connect it.

2. **Launch iMovie (or iMovie HD).**

3. **Choose Create New Project.**

   The Create Project dialog box opens.

4. **Type a filename in the Project text box.**

   For this example, we used `MacMovie`.

5. **From the Where pull-down menu, choose where you want to save the project.**

   For this exercise, we chose Movies to save to the `Movies` folder.

6. **Choose a format from the Video Format pull-down menu.**

   If you're using an iSight camera, choose iSight; if not, choose the format that applies to your camera.

7. Click OK.

The project window opens. Centered below the video window are the play controls; to the left of the play controls, you see a selector switch between a camera icon (Camera mode) and a scissors icon (Edit mode) (see Figure 2-6).

Camera | Edit

Selector switch

Figure 2-6: Recording with iMovie.

Book VI
Chapter 2

Getting Video Ready
for Prime Time

8. Drag the selector switch left, to the camera icon.

At this point, you should see the camera feed from either your external camera or your iSight camera in the video window. A Record button is superimposed on the image at the bottom-center of the video window pointed out in Figure 2-6.

9. Click the Record button to begin recording.

As soon as you click the button, you see a thumbnail image (a clip) in one of the cells to the right of the video window. Here's another chance to make a screen test for YouTube, so get your groove on.

10. **After about 30 seconds, click the Record button again to stop recording.**

    You can record longer, if you like, but even a short recording takes up a lot of hard disk space.

11. **Drag the selector switch to the scissors icon (Edit mode). (See Figure 2-6.)**

    Just to the left of the camera and scissors icons are two other icons: a frame of film (Clip Viewer) and a clock (Timeline Viewer). In Figure 2-6, the clock icon is selected.

12. **Click the film frame icon to open Clip Viewer.**

13. **Drag the movie clip from Step 9 to the area at the bottom of the window that reads `Drag clips here to build your project`, as shown in Figure 2-6.**

    You see the thumbnail of your video in the Clip Viewer, as shown in Figure 2-7, when the move is completed.

Figure 2-7: Playing a recorded movie.

The big guns: Truly powerful video editors

If you want to create some memorable videos using complex editing, special effects, and anything else George Lucas or Steven Spielberg could dream up, you have lots of choices. Three of our favorites are the following:

✔ **Adobe Premiere Pro (Windows and Macintosh):** With Adobe Premiere Pro (www. adobe.com), you can work with most video formats, including HD format. The program offers a wide variety of special effects, titles, transitions, and up to 4000 x 4000 resolution. Premiere Pro integrates easily with three other Adobe products: After Effects, Photoshop, and Soundbooth. The latest version features Ultra 2 chroma keying. Premiere Elements (Windows only) is a scaled-down version, available at a considerable saving.

✔ **Final Cut Pro (Mac OS X):** If you have your heart set on entering a film in the Sundance Film Festival, you may want to take a look

at Final Cut Pro (www.apple.com). Used by many independent filmmakers, this video editor can edit a wide range of video formats, including HD, and has its own special effects, transitions, and other editing essentials. It integrates well with Apple's Soundtrack and LiveType software. To use all its features, be prepared to spend some time learning how to use it. If your budget is limited, try Final Cut Express HD for considerably less money.

✔ **Vegas Pro (Windows):** Sony's Vegas Pro (www.sonycreativesoftware.com/ products/vegasfamily.asp) also has a large following. It's best known for its intuitive interface and ability to handle up to 64-bit channels. Like the other professional editing programs in this list, it can integrate multiple channels of video and audio to create professionally produced and scored digital videos.

---

14. **Click the clock icon to open the Timeline Viewer.**

    You see the video timeline at the bottom of the project window, as shown in Figure 2-7.

15. **Choose File➪Save Project (or press ⌘+S).**

16. **Choose File➪Export.**

    The Export dialog box opens.

17. **Choose Full Quality from the Compress Movie pull-down menu, and click the Share button.**

Testing your video

To test your video file, navigate to the folder where you saved it in Step 5 in the preceding section (the file has a .mov extension), and double-click the file to play it in QuickTime Player. You should get excellent results.

For the test file in Figure 2-6, earlier in this chapter, we used a Canon G2 DV camera, which approaches professional quality. But you can get excellent results from an iSight Webcam too.

Now that you know several ways to capture video as digital files, the next step is modifying those files so that they can be played on the Web — and in such a way that the viewer's experience is the one you want. Chapter 3 in this minibook provides the details.

Chapter 3: Getting Video Files Ready for Flash

In This Chapter

- ✔ Completing preproduction
- ✔ Knowing what can be converted
- ✔ Converting files with Adobe Media Encoder CS4
- ✔ Cropping videos
- ✔ Adjusting file settings
- ✔ Cueing videos

*B*efore you can play a video with Flash CS4, you need to convert all those MOV, WMV, AVI, and other non-Flash-formatted files to FLV or F4V files. The FLV files are standard Flash video files using the VP6 compression format. The new F4V files are based on a standard with a better video quality: H.264. Included with Flash CS4 is Adobe Media Encoder CS4, with which you can easily convert video files to FLV or F4V file format. The encoder also allows you to set different parameters and even crop the video, so you can do a little last-minute editing with it.

In this chapter, we look at the different things you can do before you convert your video file into an FLV or F4V file. We take a look at how the file conversion process works, how to select a video file type, and how to determine which options you have. Films have to be edited, special effects added, and boo-boos removed. You might want to make your video just a little longer or shorter as well. These processes need to be handled before conversion to FLV or F4V files because the main tools for editing such as Adobe Premiere, Adobe After Effects, Apple Final Cut, and even Microsoft Movie Maker cannot edit files converted for running in Flash CS4. So before you get to the point where you cannot edit your FLV or F4V file, you need to do your preconversion work.

Managing Postproduction before Conversion

In show biz, the term *postproduction* refers to everything you do to a video after you have it in the can (*the can* being an old-fashioned reference to those metal cases that hold film). Included in postproduction are simple steps like cutting out those parts of your video that you don't like. You can easily do this kind of simple editing with an application such as Windows Movie Maker or iMovie. More complex editing includes *chroma keying* (electronically cutting out a key color and replacing it with a different background), using a high-end editing program like Adobe Premiere Pro or Final Cut Pro.

Figure 3-1 shows a video in Premiere Pro, with the image on the left featuring a blue chroma screen in the background and the image on the right showing a studio background. The video is the same, but postproduction work changes the image significantly.

Figure 3-1: Complete all preproduction tasks, such as changing a background, before converting a file.

You can't do this kind of editing during or after the conversion process. You must do all your postproduction work before using Adobe Media Encoder to convert the video to a Flash file.

Choosing File Types for Conversion

The number of video file formats seems to grow every day, with new ones being developed or old ones being discovered. We have personally tested the following file types by successfully converting them into FLV or F4V files and running them in a Flash application:

- MPEG-4
- MOV
- AVI
- WMV
- DV

You're likely to find more formats that work and others that don't. The basic test of a file format you can convert is to try dragging a file in that format into Adobe Media Encoder. If the process doesn't work, you see a message such as the one shown in Figure 3-2.

The file /Users/billsanders/Desktop/temphide/AIO Book/AIO-video/Ch02/Web/LogitechOrbit.wmv could not be imported.

OK

Figure 3-2: Video file refused by Adobe Media Encoder.

If you look carefully at the figure, you see that a WMV file is being refused. Although Adobe Media Encoder accepts WMV files, sometimes, an individual file that you try to encode has been corrupted. Being *corrupted* does not mean that the file received a bribe, but that something wrong with it disallows encoding — missing or added code, for example. Also, the Mac version of Adobe Media Encoder doesn't convert WMV files under any circumstances.

Converting Files with Default Options

After your video file is all edited and ready to go, you're ready to convert it. In this section, we show you how to convert files with standard output options; later in this chapter, in the section "Customizing Conversions," we show you how to customize your output.

The companion Web site provides two very big AVI video files (each larger than 100MB): movU.avi and movUF.avi. They are from the same source, but one has been changed so that it has a different background. You can use them to complete the following exercise, if you want.

To convert AVI files to F4V files, follow these steps:

1. **Place the AVI files on the desktop.**

   This step makes them handy for dragging into the converter.

2. **Open Adobe Media Encoder CS4 by double-clicking on the icon.**

   A big gray window opens on-screen.

3. **Drag the two AVI files into the encoder window.**

   You have to wait a few seconds for the files to show up on-screen. When they're ready, you see their names and locations in the Source Name column of the encoder window, as in the example shown in Figure 3-3.

Figure 3-3: Two AVI files loaded in Adobe Media Encoder.

If you have your video files scattered hither and yon on your computer, you can click the Add button in the encoder and browse for the files instead of using the drag-and-drop technique.

4. **From the Preset pull-down menu, choose F4V – Same As Source (Flash 9.2 and Higher).**

   Figure 3-4 shows the selection being made.

Because Flash Player is free, most users update to the latest version. Some users, however, simply keep their old players. How can you tell whether viewers have older players? You receive e-mail complaining that they can't see your movie! (This technique is adopted from the method of locating land mines by stomping on the ground.) If your primary audience is likely to have older versions of Adobe Flash Player, choose one of the formats for older Flash players: FLV – Same As Source

(Flash 7 and Higher), for example, accommodates any player from version 7 to version 10.

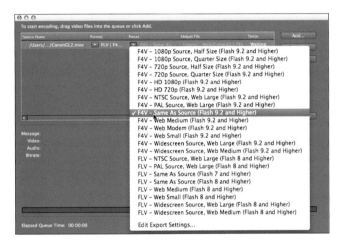

Figure 3-4: Setting the compression type.

5. **Click the Start Queue button and wait while both files are compressed.**

   As the conversion process is taking place, the lower-right corner of the encoder window shows the part of the video that is being compressed.

   When the compression process is complete, a green check appears in the file's Status column.

   In the example shown in Figure 3-5, you see that the first of the two files is finished, but the second one is still in progress.

   Notice what happened to the size of the video file. Right-click the F4V file icon and choose Properties from the shortcut menu (Windows) or Ctrl+click the icon and choose Get Info from the shortcut menu (Mac). You see that the new video is highly compressed. If the original AVI files were 102MB, for example, the F4V files are about 3.8MB. (That would be similar to a 200-pound person going on a diet and weighing only 7.6 pounds when he finished!)

6. **Test the file in Adobe Media Player.**

   You shouldn't see any difference between running it as an F4V file and running it as an AVI file.

Figure 3-6 shows an F4V file playing in Adobe Media Player. This video is ready to be sent over the Internet as a progressive download or streamed.

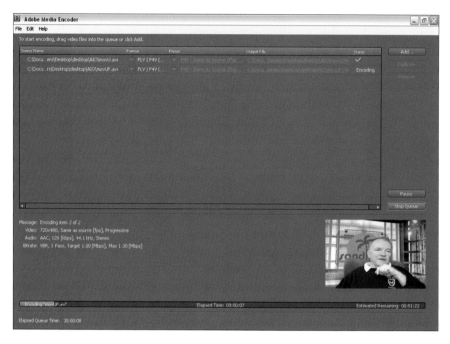

Figure 3-5: File conversion in Adobe Media Encoder.

Figure 3-6: An AVI video playing in F4V format.

Customizing Conversions

When you pull a file into Adobe Media Encoder for conversion, you can make choices from the Format and Preset pull-down menus to customize the process:

- **Format:** The Format pull-down menu provides two choices: FLV | F4V (H.264) and H.264. We don't deal with the H.264 format outside the F4V format, so for the rest of this minibook, you can leave the Format menu set to FLV | F4V (H.264).

- **Preset:** In general, when dealing with FLV/F4V files, you can simply make any choice from the Preset pull-down menu. In this minibook, for the most part, we discuss presets for Flash Player 9.2 or later.

Choosing a compression codec

Each of the three main FLV formats uses one of three codecs. A *codec* (short for *coder–decoder*) is the compression format used to shrink your file. In the section "Converting Files with Default Options," earlier in this chapter, a codec reduces an AVI file to about 4 percent of its original size.

In addition to compressing a file, a good codec optimizes the file's quality — both video and audio.

Flash has had three different codecs since the introduction of streaming video, and you can choose any of them from the Preset pull-down menu in Adobe Media Encoder:

- **FLV (Sorenson Spark):** Used in Flash 7 presets
- **FLV (On2 VP6):** Used in Flash 8 presets
- **F4V (MainConcept H.264 Video):** Used in Flash 9.2 presets

As a rule of thumb, use the newest format because of the increasing quality of audio and video. With larger video formats, you see the greatest difference in quality.

Managing bandwidth

Each preset has several options, and in preparing videos for the Web, you need to consider bandwidth above all else when deciding which option to choose. *Bandwidth* is the amount of stuff you have to port over the Internet to display your video.

Larger formats have more content; smaller ones have less. If your video uses too much bandwidth, you can run into nasty problems because your video can freeze, lose frames, or seemingly become separated from the audio.

The presets are not necessarily set up to optimize bandwidth, so in looking closely at the settings, you need to ask, "How will this affect the amount of bandwidth required and the experience the user has?"

Your original video file is preserved so that you can use it often to try out different settings when you convert it to a FLV or F4V file. You can save bandwidth by using mono audio rather than stereo, lowering the audio quality (lower kHz values), reducing the video window size, and adjusting several other settings discussed later in this chapter. As a rule of thumb, lower quality and smaller size take up less bandwidth.

Trimming Your Video: A Little Nip and Tuck

When you make a video, the ideal is to do as much editing in the camera as possible, which means that you should plan all your shots so that you don't have to do too many cut-and-paste operations in the editing stages. When you're preparing a video for conversion to FLV or F4V format, you should do your editing first, but Adobe Media Encoder allows you to do a little editing in the encoder window.

To trim a bit off the end of a video in the encoder, follow these steps:

1. **Open Adobe Media Encoder by double-clicking its icon.**

2. **Drag a video into the encoder window.**

   We chose `movUF.avi` in the example.

3. **Make a choice from the Preset pull-down menu.**

   We chose F4V – Same As Source (Flash 9.0.r115 and Higher).

4. **Double-click the name in the Preset column.**

   The Export Settings window opens, as shown in Figure 3-7.

   As an alternative to Steps 3 and 4, choose Edit➪Export Settings or choose Export Settings from the Preset pull-down menu.

   In the left panel of the Export Settings window, you see an image from your video. If you drag the playhead left and right, you can see the entire video.

5. **Drag the playhead to the right on the scrubber bar to the spot where you want the video to end, as shown in Figure 3-8.**

6. **Drag the Set Out Point button so that it aligns with the playhead.**

   Figure 3-8 shows the playhead and Set Out Point aligned. At this point, everything is ready for conversion.

Figure 3-7: Editing options in Adobe Media Encoder.

7. **Click the Start Queue button.**

   The file is converted to FLV or F4V format as usual; the only difference is that the converted file will have some of its end cut off.

Figure 3-8: Preparing to crop the duration of a video.

Fine-Tuning Your Settings

If your converted video doesn't look or work as you expected it to, you may be able to make a few changes in Adobe Media Encoder. Suppose that your video is a simple explanation of how to lay tile. You don't need stereo audio set at 96 KHz; a mono audio setting at 48 KHz will do fine, and you won't have as much to port across the Internet. Editing the preset can fix that problem.

Don't depend on Adobe Media Encoder for extensive editing, however. If you don't edit your video before you put it in the encoder, you'll likely regret it.

The following sections show you how to adjust and create presets in various tabs of the Export Settings window. (For details on opening this window, refer to "Trimming Your Video: A Little Nip and Tuck," earlier in this chapter.)

Filters

Back in the old days of moviemaking, technicians rubbed petroleum jelly on camera lenses to blur close-ups of aging beauties. You can create the same kind of effect digitally by using a filter known as a *Gaussian blur.* You can add as much or as little blur to your video as you want; you can also flatten the depth of field to add different moods or focus on certain elements in the frame or to make it look like a foggy night in London.

To add a blur filter to your video, follow these steps:

1. **Click the Output tab in the upper-left corner of the Export Settings window.**

2. **In the right panel of the Export Settings window, click the Filters tab.**

3. **Select the Gaussian Blur box.**

4. **In the Blurriness text box, change the value to something other than the default (0).**

   When you change the Blurriness value, you see its effect in the Output tab, as shown in Figure 3-9.

Figure 3-9: Previewing a Gaussian blur.

5. **From the Blur Dimension pull-down menu, choose the dimension you want to blur: Horizontal, Vertical, or Horizontal and Vertical.**

   As soon as you choose a dimension, you see its effect in the left panel, so try different settings to decide which effect you want.

6. **Click OK to apply your settings.**

7. **Convert the video by clicking on the Start Queue button.**

   The output FLV/F4V file shows the blur.

Format

This setting is easy to change from FLV to F4V and *vice versa*. Follow these steps:

1. **In the Export Settings window, click the Format tab.**

   Even though your video is already set to either FLV or F4V, you again have the choice of FLV or F4V.

2. **Click either FLV or F4V if you want to change your choice.**

Video

When you change the video settings from the default, you can significantly change what the viewer will see. As a rule of thumb, the better the quality of your video, the more bandwidth it will take.

Whenever you work with video editing, be sure to select the Output tab so that you can see a preview of the changes you are making.

In the upper-left corner of the Export Settings window, when the Output tab is selected, you see Deinterlace as the default setting. You should almost always deinterlace your video to reduce moiré patterns that can appear.

Resize Video

The Resize Video check box in the Export Settings window with the Video tab selected allows you to change the size of the video. In Figure 3-10, the size has been changed from 720 x 480 pixels to 320 x 213 pixels.

Generally, making a video file smaller doesn't adversely affect its appearance. If you make the file larger, however, it may look *pixelated*. (Pixels become visible, and the image is blurry and unfocused.)

In the Basic Video Settings section of the Video tab are several pull-down menus, each of which changes some aspect of the video:

Figure 3-10: Changing the size of a video file.

✓ **Frame Rate (frames per second [fps]):** If you want to reduce the amount of bandwidth, choose a lower frame rate. The quality will be lower as well, but if your video has little movement, the change will not be as noticeable as in a video that has a good deal of movement.

✓ **Field Order:** The Field Order option affects two video fields — upper and lower. For a standard-definition format such as DV NTSC, choose Lower; for a high-definition (HD) format, choose Upper. Generally, the default (None – Progressive) setting works well for videos streamed over the Web. For HD video, however, try choosing Upper to see whether it improves output. *Upper* and *lower* refer to odd (upper) and even (lower) fields in a video frame.

✓ **Pixel Aspect Ratio:** If you change the aspect ratio (ratio of width to height), choose Square Pixels. In general, we try to maintain the aspect ratio of the original video, but that isn't always possible or desirable. In Figure 3-10, you see that the original aspect ratio of 4.5:3 in 720 x 480 format is maintained in the reduced format of 320 x 213.

✓ **Profile:** Use the Baseline profile for minimum use of bandwidth — for mobile applications, perhaps, or for users who have limited processing capacity. Use the Main and High profiles when you want to optimize quality for users who have lots of processing power and bandwidth. In Figure 3-10, the High profile has been selected to produce the best quality possible.

✓ **Level:** The Level setting determines the degree of definition. The higher the value, the higher the definition and format. The level set in Figure 3-10 is very high, capable of handling 1280 x 720 resolution at 30 fps. At a lower resolution of 320 x 240, a Level setting of 1.3 would be plenty. As you see in the figure, the level is far greater than required.

After you square away your settings, save them as a preset. Click the disk icon next to the Preset pull-down menu, and provide a name for the settings you used. (In Figure 3-11, the preset name is TwoPass320.) If you decide to improve the settings later, you can overwrite an existing preset with the same name.

Bitrate Settings

Figure 3-11 shows the areas of the Export Settings window where you set bit rates and advanced options. This section covers the Bitrate Settings options; the following section discusses the Advanced Settings options.

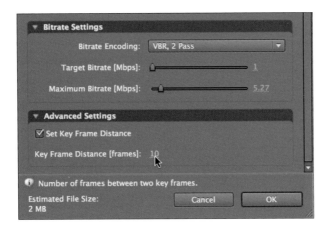

Figure 3-11: Bitrate Settings and Advanced Settings.

The Target Bitrate [Mbps] slider sets the ideal (often, the minimum) amount of bandwidth you want to use. The Maximum Bitrate [Mbps] slider lets users with very-high-speed processors and connections optimize what they can view. The effects of these options are relatively close, but experiment with the sliders to see the range of effects.

A .56 setting doesn't mean 56KB; instead, it means 0.56 of 1MB, or 560KB. Assume that users with dial-up modems are not going to have a very good video experience. Those who have Digital Subscriber Lines (DSL) with low connection rates — less than 1Mbps — will have a good experience if you consider the amount of bandwidth that their connections can handle.

One of the easiest ways to improve the quality of your video and reduce bandwidth is to choose the VBR, 2-Pass option from the Bitrate Encoding pull-down menu. This option sets a two-pass variable bit rate. On the first pass, the program looks for the best settings and then on the second pass, makes those settings. You save, roughly, two-thirds (67 percent) in bandwidth with two-pass compression, which is similar to getting a $100 shirt for only $67 — bandwidth at a discount!

Click OK when you're done with your settings, or go on to make the changes discussed in the following section.

Advanced Settings

When you set the Key Frame Distance options (refer to Figure 3-11), remember that *less is more*. In video, each keyframe is a set image; think of it as a clear snapshot. The frames between the keyframes are filled in by an algorithm, somewhat like tweens. So if you set a low keyframe distance (such as 10; refer to Figure 3-11), the quality is higher but you increase the work required of the processor and the amount of bandwidth. This option is one that you need to tweak and test to your own satisfaction.

Click OK when you're satisfied with your settings.

Audio

Figure 3-12 shows the Audio tab of the Export Settings window.

The Codec pull-down menu allows you to choose one of three flavors of AAC (Advanced Audio Encoding). AAC + Version 1 and AAC + Version 2 allow for more channels and metadata embedded in the sound. For most applications, including music, the default AAC setting is fine.

Of all the settings in this tab, one of the most important — but easiest to overlook — is Output Channels. Mono or Stereo. If your video is simply a talking head, you can halve the amount of audio quality required by selecting the Mono radio button instead of Stereo. For music, however, you most likely want to select Stereo.

Figure 3-12: The Audio tab.

The Frequency setting is important if you find any *latency* — disconnect between the audio and video. (You can see latency in old-time kung-fu movies in which the actors' mouths move at different rates from the sound.) The higher the Frequency setting, the more bandwidth you use, but any latency is reduced. Audio quality doesn't affect latency.

If you have a high-quality recording with your video, you can lower the Audio Quality setting and get good-quality audio at a lower bandwidth. Use the best microphone and sound card you can afford, and set the Audio Quality pull-down menu to a lower setting.

Finally, the Bitrate Settings pull-down menu contains options that are similar to those in the Video tab, except that they're not continuous. You can therefore set them to values only at certain intervals. That is, you can't set them to any value you want, but like frequency, they have certain settings at specified intervals. Yet again, higher settings deliver more quality, but at a higher bandwidth cost.

Others

The Others tab is really an FTP (File Transfer Protocol) tab. (I would have called it the FTP tab, but would Adobe listen to me? Nooooo. . . .) In this tab, you set the FTP address of a nonsecure host folder. Fill in the Server Name, Port, Remote Directory (optional), User Login, and Password boxes, and then Adobe Media Encoder automatically sends the FLV or F4V file to your server. When you have provided the requested information, click the Test button to verify the connection. If the test fails, review your settings and try again until the test indicates a connection. Then when everything is working correctly, click the OK button.

TIP

If you save your settings in a custom preset, every time you convert a file, it's sent to the FTP folder you specify here. Optionally, you can have the encoder send the local file to the trash.

To make sure that the connection works, click the Test button. Figure 3-13 shows a typical setup and verification of a good connection.

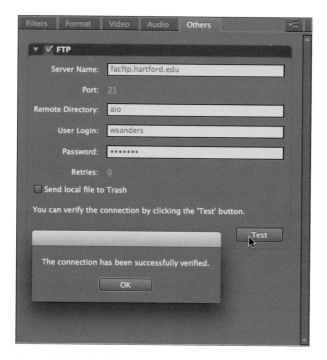

Figure 3-13: Testing FTP settings.

Adding Cue Points

Cue points are like little triggers in a video. You can use them to bring in data and links, but in this section, we show you how to use them to bring up events and labels associated with those events.

Adding cue points to a video allows you to have various things happen at predetermined points. Suppose that you're creating a video about how to lay kitchen tile. As you're explaining how to lay the tile, you want to show viewers different still shots of what the tile looks like at different stages. You can set a cue point so that when you say, "Place the spacers between the tiles," a picture of the tiles pops up with spacers added.

To fill a FLV or F4V file with cue points, follow these steps:

1. **Open Adobe Media Encoder by double-clicking the application icon.**

2. **Drag the video file into the encoder window.**

   You can download the little counting video `cuePoints.mov` from this book's companion Web site at `www.dummies.com/go/` `flashallinone`.

3. **Choose any preset you want to use.**

4. **Double-click the name in the Preset column to open the Export Settings window.**

   The window opens with two panels: one on the left and one on the right. You can expand it into a single left window by clicking the little arrow in the middle of the dividing border. Figure 3-14 shows a single window open.

Book VI
Chapter 3

Getting Video Files
Ready for Flash

Figure 3-14: Adding a cue point.

5. **Drag the playhead to the place in the video where you want to add a cue point, and click the plus (+) icon.**

6. **In the Cue Point Name column, enter a name for the cue point.**

7. **Repeat Steps 5 and 6 to add as many cue points as you want.**

   Figure 3-14 shows a third cue point being added.

8. **After you add all your cue points, return to two-column view by clicking the arrow on the right border; then click OK.**

When you convert the video to FLV or F4V format, you won't see anything different, but your cue points will be hidden inside the video.

In Chapter 4 of this minibook, you see how to unleash the cue points in a Flash application by using ActionScript.

Chapter 4: Getting Fancy with Video

In This Chapter

✔ **Creating your own video player with ActionScript**

✔ **Using embedded cue points**

✔ **Working with metadata**

✔ **Using ActionScript cue points**

✔ **Adding captions to a video**

*N*ow that you can convert different kinds of video files to FLV and F4V files, you're ready to use the different kinds of information embedded in videos. In Chapter 3, you see how to embed cue points into a video during the conversion process. In this chapter, you get the cue points from a NetStream that plays your video; then you get more information that's hidden in the video — the *metadata* — by using the NetStream class. To do all this, you build a simple player with ActionScript 3.0.

You also see how to add cue points to a video that has no embedded cue points, using both the FLVPlayer component and the friendly, incredibly powerful ActionScript 3.0. Then you wrap up the chapter by tweaking some of the controls in the playback process.

Making Your Own Video Player

When you embed cue points in a video, you need to use the NetStream class to get them out. To use NetStream, you need a NetConnection instance, and if you want to see what you're streaming, you need a Video instance as well. That's it!

Understanding the process

Before you start getting those cue points, take a look at what you do to create the simplest video player in the universe:

1. Create a NetConnection instance.

2. Create a NetConnection connection.

   Because this connection uses a progressive download, you more or less plug it into a dead socket; the connection is null. A progressive download doesn't use an open socket server but, rather, uses a regular Web server. As each piece of the file downloads, it's displayed until the entire file is downloaded. (See Book VI, Chapter 5 for streaming video.)

3. Create a NetStream with the NetConnection as a parameter value.

   This procedure — first making a null connection with the NetConnection instance and then passing it as a parameter to NetStream — may seem a little strange. But it's what you do when the video will work with a Web server rather than a streaming server.

4. When you have your NetStream instance, you use its `play()` method to play the video.

5. Finally, you create a Video instance and attach the NetStream playing the video to the Video instance.

Creating a video player

Now you're all set to make your first video player. Follow these steps:

1. **Choose Window⇨File⇨New⇨Flash File (ActionScript 3.0) to open a new Flash file.**

2. **Choose Window⇨Properties (or press Ctrl+F3 [Windows] or ⌘+F3 [Mac] to open the Properties panel, and in the Publish section of the Class window, type EasyPlayer.**

3. **Save the file as** `EasyPlayer.fla` **on the desktop or in a folder of your choice.**

4. **Choose Window⇨File⇨New⇨ActionScript File to open a new ActionScript file, and save it in the same folder as you saved the Flash file.**

   We saved it as `EasyPlayer.as` in the same folder with `EasyPlayer.fla`.

5. **Add the following code to the `EasyPlayer.as` file:**

```
package
{
    import flash.display.Sprite;
    import flash.net.NetConnection;
    import flash.net.NetStream;
    import flash.media.Video;

    public class EasyPlayer extends Sprite
    {
        private var nc:NetConnection;
```

```
        private var ns:NetStream;
        private var vid:Video;

        public function EasyPlayer ():void
        {
            nc=new NetConnection ();
            nc.connect (null);
            ns=new NetStream(nc);
            vid=new Video(320,240);
            ns.play ("myVideo.f4v");
            vid.attachNetStream (ns);
            vid.x=115;
            vid.y=80;
            addChild (vid);
        }
    }
}
```

6. **Save the `EasyPlayer.as` file where you saved the** EasyPlayer.fla **file.**

   In the listing, be sure to substitute the name of your FLV or F4V video in the line ns.play ("myVideo.f4v").

7. **Choose Control⇨Test (or press Ctrl+Enter [Windows] or ⌘+Return [Mac]) to test the application.**

   You should see a 320 x 240 video in the center of the Stage. The Output panel shows an error because the metadata wasn't handled properly, although that shouldn't have affected the video.

Figure 4-1 shows an example of what you should see when you test the video.

Figure 4-1: Playing video.

That process was easy, and it didn't take much code. The best part, though, is that it gives you access to the classes that control the embedded cue points and metadata.

Getting to the Cue Points

Getting cue points out of a NetStream instance looks a little different from most of the event handling you've done. The cue point event is accessed from an Object instance, not directly from NetStream. First you create an object; then you create a NetStream property called `client` to which you assign the object. (This procedure should be clearer when you see the ActionScript.)

The basic code looks like this:

```
checkMeta = new Object();
ns.client=checkMeta;
checkMeta.onCuePoint=cueNow;
```

The reference to `cueNow` is a call to a function that handles the cue-point event — an easy way to deal with `NetStream.client`.

Many developers prefer to write a small client class to handle events. You can write a separate class in the same AS file as the rest of your code or write a separate file. The methods in this class are the event handlers.

Extracting and displaying cue points

In this section, you create an application to extract and display cue points. The application also includes a function that handles metadata (discussed in the section "Managing Metadata," later in this chapter).

To build the application, follow these steps:

1. **Open a new ActionScript 3.0 file, and in the Class text box of the Properties panel, enter** CueOn.

2. **Add a background that suits your taste to act as a "theater" for the video you play.**

   Figure 4-2, later in this section, shows an example.

3. **Save the file as** CueOn.fla **on the desktop or a separate folder.**

4. **Open a new ActionScript file, and save it as** CueOn.as **in the same folder as** `CueOn.fla`.

5. **Enter the following code in the** `CueOn.as` **file:**

```
package
{
    import flash.display.Sprite;
    import flash.net.NetConnection;
    import flash.net.NetStream;
    import flash.media.Video;

    public class CueOn extends Sprite
    {
        private var nc:NetConnection;
        private var ns:NetStream;
        private var vid:Video;
        private var flv:String;
        private var checkMeta:Object;

        public function CueOn ():void
        {
            flv="cuePoints.flv";
            nc = new NetConnection();
            nc.connect (null);
            ns=new NetStream(nc);
            vid=new Video(320,240);
            vid.attachNetStream (ns);
            ns.play (flv);
            addChild (vid);
            vid.x=115, vid.y=92;

            checkMeta = new Object();
            ns.client=checkMeta;
            checkMeta.onMetaData=metaNow;
            checkMeta.onCuePoint=cueNow;
        }

        private function metaNow (mData:Object):void
        {
            trace (mData.duration);
        }

        private function cueNow (cueData:Object):void
        {
            trace (cueData.name);
        }
    }
}
```

In the listing, be sure to substitute the name of your video file in the line `flv="cuePoints.flv"`.

6. **Save CueOn.as again.**

7. **Test the application.**

The example in Figure 4-2 shows both the video and the cue point names. The first number in the Output panel is the length of the video provided by accessing the metadata. (You find out more about metadata in the next section.)

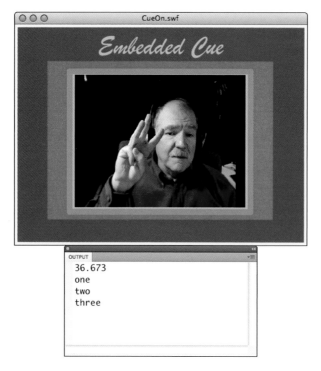

Figure 4-2: Displaying cue points.

Working with cue point properties

Cue points have three properties:

- ✔ name: Whatever name you provide

- ✔ time: The position in the video, returned as a time in the format 00:00:00:00

- ✔ type: Event or navigation

Generally, you can use the cue point name to direct the associated event handler (function) to carry out whatever you want done when a given cue point fires. Often, you find switch statements working out the appropriate set of actions. Alternatively, you can use the names themselves to load a file with the same name plus an extension. You can load text files with cue point names and the .txt extension, for example.

As you see in Book VI, Chapter 3, placing cue points to match the action in the video is simple if you have visual clues. Sometimes, you don't have visual clues — only audio ones. To get your cue point times right, jot down the cue points you want to add by looking at the counter in the player of the original video or by doing the same thing in Adobe Media Player.

Managing Metadata

If you don't place some kind of handler for metadata when you play a video, the Output panel displays an error. Even though your video works fine, it's a good idea to have some kind of handler, even if you don't use the metadata.

What kind of metadata your video contains depends a good deal on the kind of conversion tool you use. Adobe Media Encoder CS4 provides several kinds of metadata. You don't have to use the metadata, but in case you do, you need to know what's in the data and how to get it.

In the preceding section, you see that cue points have only three properties. Metadata, however, has as many or as few as the conversion application's developers decide to add. Because the metadata is stored in an object, you can iterate through the object by using a `for..in` loop and get all the available information about a video.

Book VI Chapter 4

Getting Fancy with Video

In the next example application, everything you see should be familiar from previous examples in this chapter. Rather than output the data with a `trace()` statement, however, this application places the data in a TextArea component that you can see on the Stage. The program allows you to see the metadata in the video file.

To create an application that finds the metadata in your video, follow these steps:

1. **Open a new ActionScript 3.0 file, and in the Class text box of the Properties panel, enter** MetaViewer.

2. **Open the Components and Library panels, and drag an instance of a TextArea component into the Library panel.**

    When the TextArea component is dropped into the Library panel, all the supporting materials also appear in that panel.

3. **Save the file to the desktop or a folder.**

    We saved it as `MetaViewer.fla`.

4. **Open a new ActionScript file, and save it as la in the same location as the Flash (FLA) file.**

    We saved it as `MetaViewer.as` in the same place as `MetaViewer.fla`.

    You can use your own FLV or F4V file with metadata or download from this book's Web site a file named `metaSlave.f4v` and place it in the same folder as `MetaViewer.fla`.

5. **Enter the following code and save the AS file again in the same location as the Flash (FLA) file.**

Use the name `MetaViewer.as` because that's the name of the class and its constructor function.

```
package
{
  import flash.display.Sprite;
  import flash.net.NetConnection;
  import flash.net.NetStream;
  import flash.media.Video;
  import fl.controls.TextArea;

  public class MetaViewer extends Sprite
  {
      private var nc:NetConnection;
      private var ns:NetStream;
      private var vid:Video;
      private var checkMeta:Object;
      private var showMD:TextArea;

      public function MetaViewer():void
      {
          nc=new NetConnection();
          nc.connect (null);
          ns=new NetStream(nc);
          vid=new Video(320,240);
          ns.play ("metaSlave.f4v");
          vid.attachNetStream(ns);
          vid.x=15;
          vid.y=80;
          addChild (vid);

          showMD=new TextArea();
          addChild (showMD);
          showMD.width=180;
          showMD.height=350;
          showMD.x=350;
          showMD.y=10;

          checkMeta = new Object();
          ns.client=checkMeta;
          checkMeta.onMetaData=metaNow;
      }
      private function metaNow (meta:Object):void
      {
          for (var stuff:String in meta)
          {
              if (stuff!="trackinfo"&&stuff!="seekpoints")
              {
              showMD.appendText (stuff + ": = "+meta[stuff]+"\n");
              }
          }
      }
  }
}
```

In the line `ns.play ("metaSlave.f4v")`, be sure to use the filename of your own FLV or F4V file.

6. To test the application, choose Control⇨Test (or press Ctrl+Enter [Windows] or ⌘+Return [Mac]).

When you test this movie, you should see all the metadata except track-info and seekpoints. These properties weren't used, so the output isn't helpful. (All you see are a bunch of Object strings.)

Figure 4-3 shows an example of what your output should look like. Your values will be different, however, and if you used something other than Adobe Media Encoder CS4, you get a different set of metadata properties.

Figure 4-3: Metadata properties.

Book VI
Chapter 4

Getting Fancy
with Video

Depending on what you plan to do with your video, you may find use for the metadata properties. If you decide to make your own scrubber, for example, you need the duration value. Likewise, if you decide that you want to make the video half its original size, you can use the metadata that shows its width and height.

Putting on a Show with ActionScript Cue Points

One aspect of cue points that we haven't discussed much yet are those that you can add by using the FLVPlayer component. Not only can you add cue points after the video has been converted to a FLV or F4V file, but also, you can code in cue points dynamically. Even more important, you can do something more with cue points than just watch them pop up in the Output panel.

In Book VII, Chapter 2, you see how to use the Loader class to load movie clips in the form of SWF files. The movie clips can contain anything from a simple graphic to a full-blown animated feature. Anything that can go into a Flash movie can go into an SWF file, so when you have the capability of loading an

SWF file, you're actually loading a Flash movie. The point is simply to show how to coordinate the actions you see in a video with something else that's going on in the Flash movie.

For this next project, you take a fancy graphic standing cap (a big capital letter) and use the graphic letters to spell out numbers. The video shows each number voiced and shown in hand numbers, and a coordinated SWF file is loaded with the same number shown to the right of the video.

Download a file from the book's Web site named `Count.mov` and convert it into an F4V file. *Do not* add any cue points to the movie. Place the converted video `Count.f4v` in the same folder as `CueThis.fla` that you will create in the project in this section. Optionally, you can download the files `one.swf`, `two.swf`, `three.swf`, `four.swf`, and `five.swf`. The project shows you how to make these files, but you might want to download them to save time.

This next project requires several different files that must be placed into the same folder. Before starting, create a folder named `PlayerCuePoint`. Place into that folder every single file you will create or use from the Web download. Now you're ready to start following these steps:

1. **Open a new Flash File (ActionScript 3.0) and enter the class name in the Class text box in the Properties panel. Save the file.**

   We saved the file as `CueThis.fla`.

2. **Choose File⇨Import⇨Import Video to open the Import Video window.**

   Use the default choices to import a video with the playback component. Select `Count.f4v` as the import file and the SkinUnderPlaySeekMute style for the player controls in color of your choice. Save the file.

3. **Click on the black video block of the player on the Stage and choose Window⇨Properties (or press Ctrl+F3 [Windows] or ⌘+F3 [Mac]) to open the Properties panel. In the Instance Name window, type the name** playBack, **as shown in Figure 4-4.**

   You use that name to address the player component in the program you write later on in this project. Save the file.

4. **Select the FLVPlayer on the Stage and open the Component Inspector panel. Click the cuePoints row and then click on the magnifying glass icon that appears.**

   You now see the Cue Points window open. Add cue points by clicking on the Plus (+) icon. Add a name and a time (in seconds and fractions of seconds), as shown in Figure 4-5, for each cue point. Save the file.

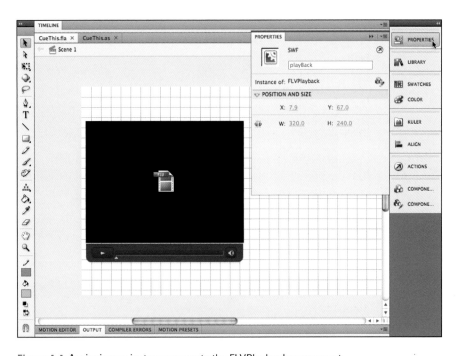

Figure 4-4: Assigning an instance name to the FLVPlayback component.

Book VI
Chapter 4

Getting Fancy
with Video

You can determine what to place in the Time column by watching the video in the Adobe Media Player. Write down the time you want to enter a cue point. After you complete the project, you can go back and change the values in the Time column to more accurately call the cue point events after watching the video. You *cannot* do that with cue points embedded in a video.

5. **(Optional if you didn't download the numbered SWF files) Open a new Flash File (ActionScript 3.0) and set the Stage size to 400 x 400. Save the file as** one.fla.

6. **(Optional if you didn't download the numbered SWF files) Use or create a large standing cap and spell out the word** *One.*

   The work should fill up most of the Stage. Save and test the file. When you test the file, you automatically create a file, one.swf. Repeat Steps 5 and 6 saving the files from one.fla through five.fla. Figure 4-6 shows the fourth file being created. All these SWF files must be saved in the PlayerCuePoint folder. Be sure to save and test all five files so that you have the SWF version of the files.

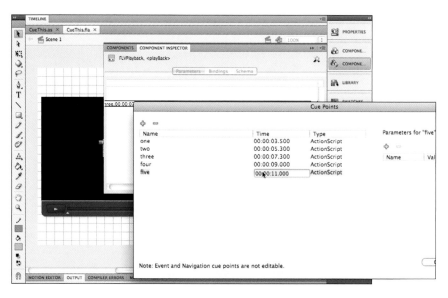

Figure 4-5: Adding ActionScript cue points.

Figure 4-6: Creating number files.

7. **Open a new ActionScript file and save it as** CueMe.as **in the PlayerCuePoint folder. Add the following script and save the file again.**

```
package
{
    import fl.video.MetadataEvent;
    import flash.display.Sprite;
    import flash.display.Loader;
    import flash.net.URLRequest;

    public class CueThis extends Sprite
    {
        private var flv:String = "Count.f4v";
        private var loader:Loader;
        private var url:URLRequest;

        public function CueThis ()
        {
            playBack.source = flv;
            playBack.addEventListener (MetadataEvent.CUE_POINT,onCue);
            loader=new Loader()
        }

        private function onCue (cp:MetadataEvent)
        {
            loader.unload();
            url=new URLRequest(cp.info.name + ".swf")
            loader.load(url);
            addChild(loader);
            loader.x=350;loader.y=3;
        }

    }
}
```

About the only thing new about that program is the line

```
playBack.addEventListener (MetadataEvent.CUE_POINT,onCue);
```

which is an event listener for ActionScript cue points. It's the preferred event handling procedure with ActionScript 3.0 rather than onCuePoint, as is the case with NetStream objects and cue points embedded in the video.

The cue point triggers the onCue() method, which passes the name value of the cue point name property. All that's left to do is invoke the loader. Presto, change-o! Up jumps the SWF file showing the number of the current cue point. Rather than have simple numbers reflect the number spoken and shown in the video, you can have any Flash CS4 movie clip you want appear. Figure 4-7 shows an example of what you may see.

We start with a tag you may know from HTML: the <p> tag. As you may remember, p is for *paragraph,* and everything between the opening <p> and the closing </p> is formatted with the paragraph's formatting attributes. You don't have to worry about formatting for this example, however, because it doesn't use any.

Think of it as you would a PowerPoint presentation — a person talks and illustrates the presentation using graphics and even animation. Using this technique, you can make presentations anywhere in the world over the Web.

Figure 4-7: An SWF file loading in response to a cue point.

Captioning a Video

Adding captions to a video can be both fun and useful. You can make an old-fashioned silent movie and have the captions show what people are saying, or you can add captions for the hearing-impaired to a video that has sound. You can even add foreign-language captions to your video masterpiece. (*¿Porque no?*)

Flash CS4 has a special component, FLVPlaybackCaptioning, that helps you set up captions for a video used with the FLVPlayback component. Before getting started, however, you need to look at a unique timing control.

Using timed text in an XML file

If you have never worked with XML files, rest assured that they're easier than you imagine. Essentially, XML is a tag language like HTML. One of the most interesting applications of these versatile files is that they can be used to provide text on a timer. The plan is to work out the timing for a video and insert text that is displayed in caption format over a video.

For timing, the <p> tag uses the following format:

```
<p begin = "00:00:00" > Message </p>
```

The begin attribute tells when to begin the caption. So if you want the first caption to appear 15 seconds into the video, for example, you write this:

```
<p begin = "00:00:15" > Message </p>
```

As soon as the video reaches 15 seconds, the caption is placed over the video in exactly the same way that you may have seen English translation superimposed on a foreign film. The caption stays in place until the next timed caption is ready to begin. The following tag clears the caption that appears at the 15-second mark and replaces with a different caption at the 18-second mark:

```
<p begin = "00:00:18" > New message </p>
```

The logic is simple. Just because it's an XML file, don't think that it's difficult. It's not.

How do you create XML files? If you can use a text editor such as Notepad (Windows) or TextEdit (Mac), you can create an XML file. Like HTML files, XML files can be saved as plain text with the `.xml` extension to indicate that they are to be treated as XML files. It's that easy.

Download from this book's Web site a file named `rightOn.f4v` for use with this project. All the timing in the XML Timed Text file is based on that video.

Copy the following XML file in your favorite text editor and save it as **mark.xml**. (The captions are from a speech by Mark Antony in William Shakespeare's *Julius Caesar*.)

```
<?xml version="1.0" encoding="UTF-8"?>
 <tt xml:lang="en" xmlns="http://www.w3.org/2006/04/ttaf1">
    <body>
       <div xml:lang="en">
         <p begin="00:00:12.50">For I have neither wit, nor words, nor
            worth,</p>
         <p begin="00:00:16">Action, nor utterance, nor the power of speech,</p>
         <p begin="00:00:18">To stir men's blood: I only speak right on;</p>
         <p begin="00:00:21.30" >I tell you that which you yourselves do
            know;</p>
       </div>
    </body>
 </tt>
```

The first line just establishes the XML file as XML format. The second line is the `<tt>` tag that encompasses the other tags and holds a reference to the Timed Text standard. The rest of the script has the familiar `<body>` and `<div>` tags that you probably know from HTML. The `<div>` tag in this case establishes the language as English ("en"), and the rest is made up of the `<p>` tags with the timing values and caption text.

Launching the captions

After you have the XML file set up, you can create the Flash CS4 application that runs the video in the FLVPlayback component and displays the captions with the FLVPlaybackCaptioning component. Before you get started, place the following files in a folder named CaptionWork:

✔ mark.xml

✔ rightOn.f4v

Use the following steps to create a video with captions to accompany the video:

1. **Open a new Flash File (ActionScript 3.0) and enter** CaptionVid **in the Class text box in the Properties panel.**

    Save the file as **CaptionVid.fla** in the CaptionWork folder.

2. **Drag a FLVPlayback and FLVPlaybackCaptioning component to the Stage, as shown in Figure 4-8.**

    Position the FLVPlayback component in the center below the top and position the FLVPlaybackCaptioning anywhere you want. Because the position of the caption is in the same place over the video, it doesn't matter where you put the component on the Stage. In the example, it's centered beneath the video player.

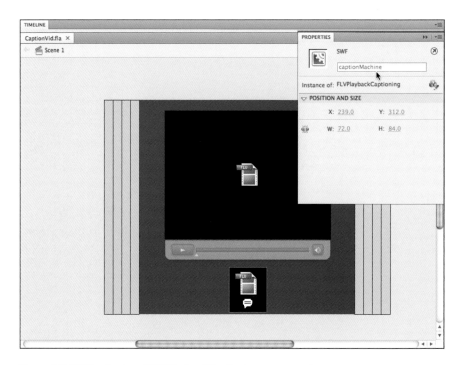

Figure 4-8: FLVPlayback and FLVPlaybackCaptioning components.

3. **Click on the icon on the FLVPlayback component, and in the Properties panel, add the instance name playMachine.**

   Similarly click on the FLVPlaybackCaptioning icon and place the name **captionMachine** in the instance name window in the Properties panel. (Figure 4-8 shows the instance name in the Properties panel for the FLVPlaybackCaptioning component being added.) Save the file.

4. **Open a new ActionScript file and save it as** CaptionVid.as **in the CaptionWork folder. Add the following ActionScript and save the file again.**

Book VI
Chapter 4

Getting Fancy with Video

```
package
{
   import fl.video.CaptionChangeEvent;
   import fl.video.FLVPlayback;
   import fl.video.FLVPlaybackCaptioning;
   import flash.display.Sprite;
   import flash.text.TextField;

   public class CaptionVid extends Sprite {

       private var vidNow:String = "rightOn.f4v";
       private var captionSource:String = "mark.xml";
       private var showCaption:TextField;

       public function CaptionVid() {
           playMachine.source = vidNow;

           captionMachine.flvPlayback = playMachine;
           captionMachine.source = captionSource;
       captionMachine.addEventListener(CaptionChangeEvent.CAPTION_CHANGE,
         getCaption);
       }

       private function getCaption(e:CaptionChangeEvent):void {
           showCaption = e.target.captionTarget;
           playMachine = e.target.flvPlayback;
           //To have the caption below the video
           //remove '//' in following line
           //showCaption.y=300;
       }
   }
}
```

After you save all your files in the CaptionWork folder, test the movie. Figure 4-9 shows a caption appearing at the same time as the spoken version is heard by the viewer.

Figure 4-9: Caption appearing over video.

If you prefer not to have the caption appearing superimposed on the video, you can move it by moving the showCaption object. If you change this line:

```
//showCaption.y=300;
```

to this:

```
showCaption.y=300;
```

the caption appears below the video.

Chapter 5: Live! From Your Desktop!

*F*lash CS4 and the new Adobe tools for video make recording and playing video simple and practical. Even better would be sending live video. Imagine having your own live video broadcasting station! Or what if you could send live audio and video, and also receive it — an A/V chat! Well, using Adobe Flash Media Server 3 and Flash CS4, you can not only stream live video and audio, but also stream data, recorded audio, and recorded A/V files. Hold on to your hat: This operation is going live!

Understanding Streaming versus Broadcasting

When video and audio and other media types are streamed over the Web, they're not really broadcast in the same way that a television station broadcasts TV programs. When you think of a broadcast, the image of a pebble dropped in the water may come to mind: A set of concentric circles sends out waves to receivers.

Also, in a broadcast, it doesn't matter whether the station has one viewer or a million; the amount of power required to send out the broadcast is the same.

With Flash Media Server, however, each connected receiver needs a unique stream. So if 50 people are viewing, Flash Media Server must generate 50 separate streams. Rather than a pebble dropped in water, think of a wagon wheel, with a spoke extending to each receiver.

Moreover, with Flash Media Server, each new connection requires a new stream and added bandwidth. So the number of viewers watching your media streams *does* affect the quality of the experience, because the more viewers you have, the more connections the server has to provide.

Streaming media

What, then, is streaming media? Consider a regular Web page. No matter how interactive a Web page is, after the page reaches your computer, the connection between your computer and the server on which that page resides is cut. Finito! Adios! Kaput! It may not seem that way, especially with a Flash page that contains dancing animation and interaction, but that's the way it is.

To have real streaming — not progressive download, which looks a lot like streaming — you need a server that keeps the connection with your computer open, pushing the data toward you until you decide to cut the link. Flash Media Server (FMS) uses open socket technology (see the following section) to perform that task. A progressive download doesn't use a media server but, rather, a regular Web server. As each piece of the file downloads, it's displayed until the entire file is downloaded. So it's not actual streaming.

Open socket technology

Open socket technology keeps the connection between your computer (the *client*) and the Web server open so that a steady stream of data can flow between server and client.

Using a protocol called Real Time Messaging Protocol (RTMP), Flash Media Server allows you to connect to the server and keep an open connection as the server streams media to you.

Streaming Media with Flash Media Server

Flash Media Server 3 is available in three flavors:

- **Flash Media Interactive Server 3 ($4,500):** Provides the full-range Flash Media Server 3 functionality with an unlimited number of users.

- **Flash Media Streaming Server 3 ($995):** Streams video only to an unlimited number of users.

- **Flash Media Development Server 3 (free):** Has exactly the same functionality as the Flash Media Interactive Server 3 except that it only has ten connections. It's the perfect version of Flash Media Server 3 for learning how to use and develop applications. (Did I mention that it's *free?*)

All the examples in this chapter use Flash Media Development Server 3, which can handle ten consecutive connections. That feature means that you and nine of your friends can connect to the same server at the same time.

Whichever version you use, Flash Media Server is available only for Windows PC and Linux servers. (If you want to install Flash Media Server on a Macintosh, check the following article: `www.flashcomguru.com/index.cfm/2007/7/12/edge-origin`.)

Installing the server

Without further ado, you're ready to download Flash Media Server and get it installed. In this chapter, we assume that you're installing the software on a Windows system. If you have a Linux computer with Red Hat 4 or 5, you can install the software on it as well; for details, check out `www.adobe.com/products/flashmediaserver`.

**Book VI
Chapter 5**

To download and install the software, follow these steps:

1. **Download the application at `www.adobe.com/products/flashmediaserver`.**

2. **Decompress the software.**

   To decompress it, use an unpacking program such as WinZip.

3. **Double-click `FlashMediaServer3.exe`, as shown in Figure 5-1.**

   Note the `Documentation` and `Sample Video` folders. The `Documentation` folder contains several PDF files with detailed documentation on working with the server. You can use the `Sample Video` folder for testing applications, if you want.

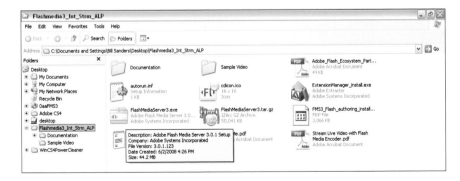

Figure 5-1: Unpacked Flash Media Server 3 files.

4. **Double-click the FMS3 installer you just downloaded to start the installation process.**

   The installer program leads you through a series of steps.

5. **For each step, accept the default settings and click Next.**

6. **When you're asked for a serial number, simply click the Next button.**

   If you decide to purchase the software later, you can add the serial number at that time.

7. **When you arrive at the page requesting an administration name and password (see Figure 5-2), enter any name and password you want; then click Next.**

   Be sure to write down the name and password before you click the Next button.

   You may want to record the username and password in Notepad and store that file along with the other Flash Media Server files.

Figure 5-2: Enter an administration username and password.

8. **In the Configure Flash Media Server ports page, accept or change the default entries, and click Next.**

   The page shows the recommended default ports, as shown in Figure 5-3: 1935 for Flash Media Server and 1111 for the administrative console. If you use those values, viewers connecting to your applications are least likely to run into connection problems. If you know that your system is using Port 1935 for something else, however, use Port 80 or 443 instead.

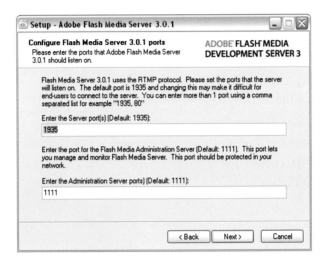

Figure 5-3: Port settings.

Book VI
Chapter 5

Live! From
Your Desktop!

If you do have an application using Port 1935 and can change it to something other than 1935, do so; then use Port 1935 for Flash Media Server.

9. **Check the summary page, which shows the settings you selected, and click Install.**

 If your installation is successful, you see a page that lists three checkbox options: View Readme.htm, Start Adobe Flash Media Server 3, and Start Flash Media Server When the Computer Starts.

10. **Accept the default settings (noted in Step 9), and click the Finish button.**

 If the server is running, it won't seriously affect memory or processor use unless you're actually streaming something.

At this point, your computer is an open-socket server ready to stream media all over the world. (If the lights dim in your neighborhood, don't be alarmed; it's just the powerful server in your machine. Just kidding!)

Connecting to the server

Now that you have Flash Media Server up and running, you need to test the connection. The easiest way is to use Adobe Flash Media Encoder 2.5 or later. Follow these steps:

1. **Open Flash Media Encoder on the same computer where you installed Flash Media Server.**

 Book VI, Chapter 2 introduces this application, which you can download at `www.adobe.com/products/flashmediaserver/flashmedia encoder`.

2. **In the bottom-right pane of the encoder window, check the Stream to Flash Media Server box and clear the Save to File box.**

   You're going to be streaming live video, so there's no point in filling your hard drive with video that you want just to stream out. (If you want to stream and record at the same time, you can do so, but for now, don't save the video to your hard drive.)

3. **In the FMS URL text box, type** rtmp://localhost/live.

4. **Leave the Backup URL text box blank.**

5. **In the Stream text box, type** livestream.

   Your settings should look like the ones shown in Figure 5-4.

6. **Click the Connect button (and hold your breath).**

   If all is working well, the Connect button changes to Disconnect.

   If the connection to the server can't be made, you get an error message (Problem with Primary Server) in a pop-up window. Double-check your spelling of the URL you entered in Step 3, and try again.

Figure 5-4: Stream settings.

The default name for your local Internet host is localhost, but that name isn't necessarily the one configured into your system by whoever configured it (including you). The IP address 127.0.0.1 is universal, however, so try entering **rtmp://127.0.0.1/live** if you can't connect with the localhost URL. (Yes, you can change the IP address as well, but that process is a little trickier.) If you installed Flash Media Server on a remote server, use that server's root URL rather than localhost.

It's easy to forget and enter http:// rather than rtmp://. All your connections to Flash Media Server must use rtmp://, and connections to your Web server must use http://.

At this point, you have a connection to the server. The next step is configuring that connection.

Configuring your connection

After your connection is established, you need to check a few things so that you can stream what you want. You can complete the following steps while you're connected to the server, even though normally, you would have taken care of them before making the connection.

These steps assume that you have Flash Media Encoder up and running and that you've tested your connection successfully.

To configure the connection, follow these steps:

1. **In the Encoding Options tab in the bottom-left pane of the Flash Media Encoder window, set the Preset pull-down menu to Medium Bandwidth (300 Kbps) – H.264.**

2. **Check the Video box.**

3. **Choose the correct camera from the Device pull-down menu directly below the Video check box.**

   (Actually, this menu shows the camera driver, not the camera itself.) After you can see yourself, you know that you selected the correct camera.

4. **Check the Audio box.**

5. **Choose the correct microphone from the Device pull-down menu directly below the Audio check box.**

   You can choose a microphone in the camera or one that's in or connected to your computer.

6. **Check your computer to make sure that the audio feature in your computer is on, has the correct volume settings, and is *not* muted.**

   Audio never works well with a muted mic!

7. **Click the green Start button.**

   You should see the red Stop button and the Encoding Log tab, as shown in Figure 5-5.

   Also, in the Statistics pane in the bottom-right section of the window, you should see continuously updated information about duration and both current and average bit rates for video, audio, and both. In the example shown in Figure 5-5, the current video bit rate is 220 kbps, the current audio bit rate is 47 kbps, and the current total bit rate is 267 kbps.

Making a Live Audio/Video Receiver

Suppose that you have a TV station broadcasting media, but no one has a TV set to receive the signal. Obviously, no one is going to see the broadcast program. That's what you've got now: a transmitting station with no receivers. So you have to make a receiver for the live video being streamed.

Making your own live receiver really isn't too difficult, but you have to use a lot of ActionScript. To help you get a handle on what's required, we start by listing everything that you need; then we show you the actual steps to take.

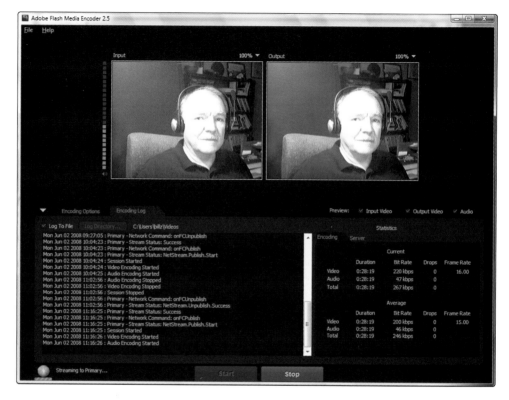

Figure 5-5: Streaming live video.

Making an inventory

Before you build a TV set, you have to make an inventory of the parts required. The same concept applies to making a streaming media receiver.

Following are the parts you need to build (in ActionScript):

- **Connection:** You need some way to connect to Flash Media Server, which requires a NetConnection object.

- **Connection test:** When the connection has been established, it causes a NetStatus event to fire. An event handler tells you when the connection is established.

- **Stream:** After a connection has been established, you need a stream to carry the media being sent. For this task, you need a NetStream object.

- **Video:** So your viewers can see the stream, you need to include a Video object.

- **On/Off controls:** You need controls to allow viewers to start and stop the streamed video. A couple of Button-component instances can do the trick.

✔ **Tuner:** To select the stream they want, viewers need a way to indicate the desired stream. You can give them this capability with a TextInput component.

✔ **Stream data information:** You really don't need to see the information associated with a live streaming video, but to see useful information called *metadata,* include objects that capture any metadata sent to the receiver.

The next several sections take you through creating the different parts of the program. You start with an application named live that is installed automatically when Flash Media Server is installed. Unlike other programs, this one is identified by its folder name. Here's the default location of the program:

```
C:\Program Files\Adobe\Flash Media Server 3\applications\live
```

When you attempt to launch a program by using the `rtmp://` protocol, the program automatically assumes that a reference to live is a reference to the preceding address. When you type this line:

```
"rtmp://localhost/live"
```

the server assumes that you mean the entire path back to the root:

```
. . . /Flash Media Server 3/applications/live
```

Keep that fact in mind when you come to the part of the application where the rtmp reference is defined (see the section "Creating the constructor function," later in this chapter).

Creating the receiver

In this section, you create the actual receiver for streaming media. We've broken the section into several subsections to help you understand what's going on. Essentially, the steps mirror the bullet points in the preceding section.

The complete code listing for the following numbered steps is available for downloading at the book's companion Web site: www.dummies.com/go/flashallinone.

Setting up the application

To begin setting up the application, follow these steps:

1. **Open a new ActionScript file and save it as** H264Live.fla.

2. **In the Class window of the Properties panel, enter H264Live, and save the file again.**

   Optionally, you can add a backdrop to the video, as shown in Figure 5-6.

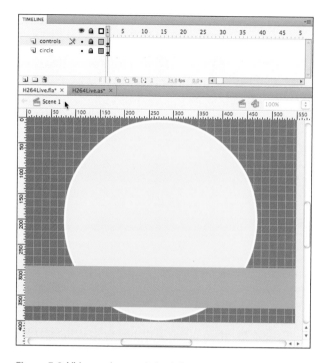

Figure 5-6: Video and controls backdrop.

3. **Drag a Button and TextInput component onto the Stage and then delete both. Save the file.**

   This action places both into the Library panel.

4. **Open another new ActionScript file, and save it as** H264Live.as **in the same folder as** `H264Live.fla`.

5. **Add the following code to the** `H264Live.as` **file to load the necessary classes and components and to declare the class and key variables:**

```
package
{
    import fl.controls.Button;
    import fl.controls.TextInput;
    import flash.display.Sprite;
    import flash.net.NetConnection;
    import flash.net.NetStream;
    import flash.events.NetStatusEvent;
    import flash.events.MouseEvent;
    import flash.events.Event;
    import flash.media.Video;

    public class H264Live extends Sprite
    {
```

```
private var nc:NetConnection;
private var ns:NetStream;
private var rtmpNow:String;
private var msg:Boolean;
private var vid1:Video;
private var playBtn:Button;
private var stopBtn:Button;
private var textInput:TextInput;
private var metaSniffer:Object;
private var serverSniffer:Object;
```

Note that all the imported namespaces and variables are among the elements listed in the section "Making an inventory," earlier in this chapter. The events are related to the different controls and actions generated by the video.

Creating the constructor function

The constructor function helps you construct the core of the application. In this case, you create the NetConnection to Flash Media Server and make the connection by using the RTMP protocol. Notice that the function is referencing localhost as the URL and the application live. Then it uses the `nc.connect()` method to attempt to establish a connection.

6. Add the following code to make the constructor function:

```
public function H264Live ()
{
        nc=new NetConnection ();
        nc.addEventListener (NetStatusEvent.NET_STATUS,checkConnect);

    rtmpNow="rtmp://localhost/live";
    nc.connect (rtmpNow);

    serverSniffer=new Object();
    nc.client=serverSniffer;
    serverSniffer.onBWDone=getDone;

    addMedia ();
    addUI ();

    playBtn.addEventListener (MouseEvent.CLICK,startPlay);
    stopBtn.addEventListener (MouseEvent.CLICK,stopPlay);
    }
```

After implementing the NetConnection in the variable `nc`, an event listener is added to the instance to check on the connection status. Only when the connection is verified can a NetStream be implemented.

The `serverSniffer` is used to respond to a server-side function in the live application through the `nc.client` property. Farther on in the program, you see another sniffer that collects information on the NetStream object.

Adding the worker methods

Whenever you see a private function in a class, you can assume that it is a method belonging to the class. These methods are used within the class to accomplish different chores, but they cannot be accessed outside the class, so they remain encapsulated and safe from unwanted outside influences.

The getDone function simply handles the data returned to the NetConnection. client property. It's really a dummy function — one that handles an event so that it doesn't throw an error (or a tizzy). (A dummy function has nothing to do with the *For Dummies* series, just in case the lawyers are reading this chapter!)

The real workers — the addMedia() and addUI() methods — add the Video object, and create buttons and a text input for the control panel of the live viewer.

7. **Add the following code to create the dummy handler and the worker methods:**

```
private function getDone ():void
    {
        trace("BW eval is done");
    }

private function addMedia ():void
    {
        vid1=new Video(320,240);
        addChild (vid1);
        vid1.x=100;
        vid1.y=50;
    }

private function addUI ():void
    {
      playBtn=new Button ();
        playBtn.label="Play";
        playBtn.x=100;
        playBtn.y=300;
        playBtn.width=60;
        addChild (playBtn);

        stopBtn=new Button ();
        stopBtn.label="Stop Playing";
        stopBtn.width=80;
        stopBtn.x=playBtn.x+180;
        stopBtn.y=playBtn.y;
        addChild (stopBtn);

        textInput=new TextInput ();
        textInput.x=playBtn.x;
        textInput.y=playBtn.y+30;
```

```
        textInput.text="livestream";
        addChild (textInput);
    }
```

Catching the connection and metadata

One of the most important methods in this application is the one that establishes that a connection exists between the client (any computer attempting to connect) and the server. After the connection has been confirmed, the program can create a new NetStream instance. When you're creating a NetStream object, the construction parameter is a connected NetConnection instance. Thus, the statement

```
ns=new NetStream(nc);
```

needs to have a verified NetConnection. As a result, the `checkConnect()` method checks that the NetStatusEvent is `NetConnection.Connect.Success`. If it is, the method goes ahead and creates a NetStream instance, ns.

The other key function in the next segment is a method to read the metadata. First, a new object is created in the `checkConnect()` method to read the metadata in the NetStream. Then the handler, `getMeta()`, uses a `for..in` loop to pull out all the information.

8. **Enter the following code to check the NetConnection, create a NetStream object, and catch the metadata from the NetStream:**

```
private function checkConnect (e:NetStatusEvent):void
{
    msg=(e.info.code=="NetConnection.Connect.Success");

    if (msg)
    {
        ns=new NetStream(nc);
        metaSniffer=new Object ();
        ns.client=metaSniffer;
        metaSniffer.onMetaData=getMeta;
    }
}

private function getMeta (mdata:Object):void
{
    for (var prop:Object in mdata)
    {
        trace (prop+" = "+mdata[prop]);
    }
}
```

Adding the player controls

The last step is adding actions for the buttons. The start button fires and sets in motion a process that begins streaming the live video from Flash Media Encoder. Then it attaches the NetStream instance to the Video object and plays the live stream, getting the name of the stream from the TextInput component.

9. Enter the following code and then save the ActionScript file:

```
private function startPlay (e:Event):void
{
    if (ns)
    {
        playBtn.label="Playing";
        vid1.attachNetStream (ns);
        ns.play (textInput.text);
    }
}

private function stopPlay (e:Event):void
{
    playBtn.label="Play";
    ns.play (false);
    ns.close ();
}
    }
}
```

Testing the player

When you finish and have everything saved, go ahead and test the application with Flash Media Encoder running. You should have the same picture in the H264Live application and in the video in Flash Media Encoder. Figure 5-7 shows that the material you see in the encoder window is the same as the material being streamed. (Compare Figure 5-5 and Figure 5-7.)

Figure 5-7: Streaming video from a live stream.

Seeing yourself on the same computer as the one you're broadcasting on isn't too exciting, but this capability shows that you can view live streams. In the example shown in Figure 5-7, using a local area network (LAN), the audio/video stream was transmitted from a Windows Vista computer and displayed on a Macintosh computer. As long as your computer can run Flash, you can view live streams generated with Flash Media Encoder or another Flash program that streams audio and video.

Furthermore, if you test this program in Flash (press Ctrl+Enter in Windows or ⌘+Return on the Mac), you see the metadata generated by the stream. We saw the following chunk of code in our test of the example in this section:

```
BW eval is done
author =
title =
audiodatarate = 48
avcprofile = 77
videocodecid = 7
audiodevice = Microphone Array (SigmaTel High)
audiocodecid = 2
keywords =
width = 320
videodatarate = 200
copyright =
audiochannels = 1
videodevice = Logitech QuickCam Orbit/Sphere
presetname = Medium Bandwidth (300 Kbps) - H.264
audiosamplerate = 22050
rating =
audioinputvolume = 75
creationdate = Thu Jun 05 08:50:29 2008
framerate = 20
description =
height = 240
avclevel = 21
```

Because you can capture the metadata values, you can use them to make a more flexible receiver. Suppose that the video's width and height are unknown. Using the values in the stream's metadata, you could reconfigure the receiver dynamically to match the video's dimensions.

Creating a Universal Chat Application

In the preceding section, you see that you can receive streamed audio and video on either a Mac or Windows computer. In this section, you create a chat application that streams out *and* in. That way, you can have audio and visual communication with anyone in the world who has an Internet connection, a microphone, and a Webcam.

This application assumes that you have been following along with the examples in this chapter using NetConnection, NetStream, and the other video-related ActionScript.

Sending video and audio

In an audio/visual context, you have two devices that can send something from your computer: a camera and a microphone. Fortunately, Flash has Camera and Microphone classes that you can use to send sound and images over a NetStream. All you need to know is how to connect your camera and microphone to a stream so that when someone plays the stream, they see and hear your media.

Creating the camera object

When you create an instance of a class, you get to use all the methods of that class. The Camera class is no different, but the way to instantiate a camera object is a little different:

```
var myCamera:Camera = Camera.getCamera();
```

When you have your camera object (myCamera), you need to connect it to a stream. To do that, use a NetStream object, which we'll call ns for this example:

```
ns.attachCamera(myCamera);
```

You have one more step to complete before you publish your video:

```
ns.publish("myStream");
```

If you use the camera's default settings, that's all you have to do. With your camera attached to the NetStream, whatever the NetStream instance publishes is going to be what your camera is pointing to.

Changing basic camera settings

Even if you use the default camera settings, you should know how to set three basic options: mode, quality, and keyframe interval.

Mode

The camera has three mode parameters: width, height, and fps (frames per second). You want to match the mode settings with the Video object's width and height:

```
myCamera.setMode(width,height,fps);
```

Generally, fps is 15 or 30, but that value can be more or less, depending on your camera. The following code shows a small format at 15 fps:

```
myCamera.setMode(160,120,15);
```

Smaller formats use less bandwidth but provide smaller images. Likewise, lower `fps` reduces bandwidth, but the video quality is lower.

Quality

The camera quality is set in relationship to the bandwidth you want to allocate. Values range from 1 to 100. A quality setting of 0 assumes that the camera will generate the best quality for a set amount of bandwidth. Likewise, a bandwidth setting of 0 assumes that the program will use enough bandwidth to bring the quality level to the set amount. The following example allocates enough bandwidth for a quality setting of 80:

```
myCamera.setQuality(0,80);
```

Likewise, this setting:

```
myCamera.setQuality(50000/8,0);
```

generates the best picture it can for 500 Kbps.

**Book VI
Chapter 5**

Live! From
Your Desktop!

Although bandwidth is technically measured in bits, Flash sets them in bytes so that by dividing the number of bytes by 8, you end up with bits. When you see the abbreviation *Kbps,* it means kilobytes per second; *kbps* refers to kilobits per second. If you're really smart, you know that a kilobyte consists of 1,024 bits; when measuring bandwidth, however, a kilobyte consists of 1,000 bits. That's because bandwidth does not use real bits and bytes but, rather, a measurement system based on marketing using units that people understand: kilobits per second.

Keyframe interval

The final consideration is the interval between keyframes. The closer together keyframes are, the better the quality is. So when you set the keyframe intervals, closer keyframes (lower values) mean better quality, but at the expense of higher bandwidth. Conversely, the higher the interval, the less bandwidth is used. The following example sets the keyframe interval to a value of 15:

```
myCamera.setKeyFrameInterval(15);
```

Setting the interval between keyframes may be counterintuitive: The *lower* the value, the *higher* the quality.

Making the server-side application

Before you get started with your chat application, you need to set up the server-side application: a single folder named `uchat`. All you have to do is create the folder and place it in the Flash Media Server root. The typical path is

```
C:\Program Files\Adobe\Flash Media Server 3\applications\
```

Place the `uchat` folder in the `applications` folder on your server. The full path is

```
C:\Program Files\Adobe\Flash Media Server 3\
    applications\live\uchat
```

You don't have to place any files in the `uchat` folder. (But you can tell your gullible friends that you created a server-side application!)

Creating the chat application

To build your chat application, follow these steps:

1. **Open a new ActionScript file.**

2. **In the Class window of the Properties panel, type** UniversalChat, **and save the file as** UniversalChat.fla.

3. **Drag a TextInput and a Button component into the Library panel.**

4. **Add a backdrop for the video and controls, as shown in Figure 5-8, and save the file.**

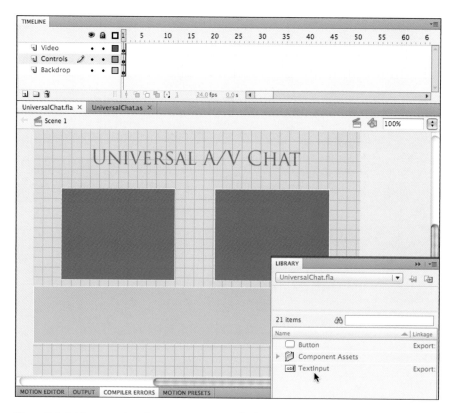

Figure 5-8: Adding user-interface components and a backdrop.

5. **Open a new ActionScript file, and save it as** UniversalChat.as **in the same folder as the** `UniversalChat.fla` **file.**

6. **Add the following program to the** `UniversalChat.as` **file, and save the file again:**

```
package
{
   import flash.display.Sprite;
   import flash.net.NetConnection;
   import flash.net.NetStream;
   import flash.events.MouseEvent;
   import flash.events.NetStatusEvent;
   import flash.media.Camera;
   import flash.media.Microphone;
   import flash.media.Video;
   import fl.controls.Button;
   import fl.controls.TextInput;
   import flash.display.Graphics;
   import flash.display.Shape;

   public class UniversalChat extends Sprite
   {
      private var nc:NetConnection;
      private var nsIn:NetStream;
      private var nsOut:NetStream;
      private var vidLocal:Video;
      private var vidRemote:Video;
      private var startStreamOut:Button;
      private var startStreamIn:Button;
      private var streamIn:TextInput;
      private var streamOut:TextInput;
      private var cam:Camera;
      private var mic:Microphone;
      private var rtmpNow:String;
      private var connectShape:Shape;

      public function UniversalChat()
      {
         nc=new NetConnection ;
         rtmpNow="rtmp://your.server.com/uchat";
         nc.connect(rtmpNow);
         nc.addEventListener(NetStatusEvent.NET_STATUS,checkConnect);
         vidLocal=new Video(160,120);
         vidRemote=new Video(160,120);
         //Camera
         cam=Camera.getCamera();
         cam.setMode(160,120,15);
         cam.setQuality(0,80);
         cam.setKeyFrameInterval(15);
         //Microphone
         mic=Microphone.getMicrophone();
         mic.setUseEchoSuppression(true);
         mic.setSilenceLevel(20,-1);
         mic.rate=11;
         //Video
         vidLocal=new Video(160,120);
         vidLocal.attachCamera(cam);
         vidLocal.x=64,vidLocal.y=111;
         addChild(vidLocal);
         vidRemote=new Video(160,120);
         vidRemote.x=323,vidRemote.y=111;
```

Book VI Chapter 5

Live! From Your Desktop!

```
        addChild(vidRemote);
        //Input text components
        streamOut=new TextInput ;
        streamOut.x=96,streamOut.y=304;
        addChild(streamOut);
        streamIn=new TextInput ;
        streamIn.x=353,streamIn.y=304;
        addChild(streamIn);
        //Button components
        startStreamOut=new Button ;
        startStreamOut.label="Stream Out";
        startStreamOut.x=96,startStreamOut.y=272;
        startStreamOut.addEventListener(MouseEvent.CLICK,goOut);
        addChild(startStreamOut);
        startStreamIn=new Button ;
        startStreamIn.label="Stream In";
        startStreamIn.x=353,startStreamIn.y=272;
        addChild(startStreamIn);
        startStreamIn.addEventListener(MouseEvent.CLICK,comeIn);
        //Red light
        drawLight(0x8A0917);
    }
    private function drawLight(bg:uint):void
    {
        connectShape = new Shape();
        connectShape.graphics.beginFill(bg);
        connectShape.graphics.lineStyle(2, 0xffffff);
        connectShape.graphics.drawCircle(0, 0, 8);
        connectShape.graphics.endFill();
        addChild(connectShape);
        connectShape.x=(550/2),connectShape.y=100;
    }
    private function checkConnect(e:NetStatusEvent)
    {
        if (e.info.code=="NetConnection.Connect.Success")
        {
            nsOut=new NetStream(nc);
            nsIn=new NetStream(nc);
            //Green light
            drawLight(0x595241);
        }
    }
    private function goOut(e:MouseEvent):void
    {
        if (streamOut.text!="")
        {
            nsOut.attachAudio(mic);
            nsOut.attachCamera(cam);
            nsOut.publish(streamOut.text);
        }
        else
        {
            streamOut.text="<add stream name>";
        }
    }
    private function comeIn(e:MouseEvent):void
    {
        if (streamIn.text!="")
        {
```

```
                        nsIn.play(streamIn.text);
                        vidRemote.attachNetStream(nsIn);
                    }
                    else
                    {
                        streamIn.text="<add stream name>";
                    }
                }
            }
        }
```

If you have a dedicated IP address on your computer, you can use its IP for the URL. Otherwise, use the root address where you have Flash Media Server.

Testing the application

Although it may look fairly involved, the program is quite simple. In one window (the left), you see yourself. Add your name for the stream that you want to send out — right below your picture — and click the Stream Out button. In the right window, put the name of the stream that the other person is using, and click the Stream In button.

Figure 5-9 shows a chat in progress. The other person uses the name guest, so he typed guest and clicked Stream Out and then typed bill and clicked Stream In. The application crisscrosses the streams so that the information that one person sends out is the information that the other streams in.

Figure 5-9: Two-way audio/video chat.

None of the controls is shown in the FLA file, but they appear when the application is tested. That's because the controls were added by the code. If the video doesn't correspond with the backdrops, scoot the backdrops around until they do. Alternatively, change the x and y values of the video positions to align with your backdrops.

Chapter 6: Shooting a Video That Looks Good on the Web

Digital video and camcorders are technological marvels. You grab your handy camcorder, point and shoot, and then put your video on the Web. Right? Wrong. If you want to put something that looks like the video from your 5-year-old's birthday party that was captured on your Uncle Frank's and Aunt Mollie's video camera that they forgot to shut off half the time and recorded several minutes of Uncle Frank's wingtips and Aunt Mollie's flip-flops, have at it. We think that you want to post something better on the Web, though. When you create a video for the Web, you must master your camera and think like a director. Web surfers are a savvy lot. When it comes to video, they've seen the good, the bad, and the ugly. If they don't like something, they click the Back button or enter another URL faster than it took to type this sentence. In this chapter, we offer some common sense advice for creating Web-worthy video.

Getting It Right in the Camera

When you shoot digital video and leave the camera to its own devices, you can end up with some gnarly-looking video. Have you ever seen a video that goes a little nuts when another object moves into the scene? The camera is switching focus to the object that just entered the scene. For a second or two, the camera may become confused and let the entire scene go out of focus. Another common issue is when you're panning a subject that's moving through different lighting conditions. If a bright light appears in back of your subject, the camera adjusts its exposure and your subject is backlit, and you then see a silhouette of the subject and no details. That's because you let the camera automatically expose the scene. When you're shooting a video that needs to be pixel perfect, here are several things you should do:

- ✔ **If you're recording a stationary object, such as a speaker in a crowded hall, switch the camera to manual focus and focus on your subject.** This strategy prevents the video from going out of focus when someone in the audience raises her hand and the camera thinks it's time to switch focus.

- ✔ **If you're recording a speaker that will be moving, move far enough away from the speaker to be able to switch to manual focus, focus on infinity, and have the speaker remain in focus.** This strategy keeps the camera focused on the speaker and prevents it from going wonky whenever somebody from the audience stands up to leave.

If you're recording an event, arrive early so that you can get the lay of the land. Ask the event coordinator to turn the house lights to the same level as when the speaker takes the rostrum. Look for any distracting light sources, such as a window behind the speaker. If curtains are in front of the window, draw them so that the backlight isn't an issue.

- ✔ **Don't rely on battery power unless it's absolutely necessary.** Recently, we recorded a speaker at a conference. We arrived early and used one of the conference center's electrical outlets to power our equipment, but the speaker preceding the client we were hired to record rambled on and on. We kept the camera in Standby mode so that we would be ready to record our client when she finally appeared. If we had relied on battery power, we would have had to change batteries in the middle of our client's speech, which would have meant losing several seconds of video — not a good thing.

- ✔ **Compose the scene by using your camera's LCD monitor.** The monitor gives you a better idea of what the scene looks like, and you can pan with your subject. This strategy is also helpful if you're using a tripod. Bending over to compose your scene in the camera viewfinder grows tiring after a while. If you're relying solely on battery power, note that your camera LCD monitor requires extra power.

- ✔ **If you must rely on battery power, carry a spare with you.** When you're recording in cold conditions, battery life is shorter. Keep the spare in your pocket to keep it warm.

- ✔ **Manually set the exposure for the scene.** Most good camcorders have an option to manually set the exposure. Some cameras have a built-in spot meter that enables you to set the exposure for the spot you're recording. If you're panning the camera from shadow to bright light and back again, set the exposure to faithfully record the average brightness of the scene. The brightest areas will be slightly overexposed, and the shadows will be a little dark, but the resulting video looks more natural. If the camera is set to auto-expose the scene, the shadow areas will be brighter than they should and the bright areas of the scene will be darker than they should.

✔ **If your camcorder has the option to manually set the volume, use it.** Cameras with this option have provisions for monitoring the sound input. Even the least expensive camcorders generally have the option for you to monitor the sound through a set of headphones.

✔ **When you record a scene, start recording several seconds before the action takes place.** Having a couple of seconds of *lead-in* time is useful when you're editing the scene. Keep recording for a couple of seconds after the action has stopped; giving yourself some *lead-out* time is also useful when editing. If the resulting video uses other scenes, the lead-in and lead-out periods are useful for providing a transition from one scene to the next.

✔ **If your camera has the provision to accept sound recording from an external microphone, use it.** If you're recording a talking head for a Web site, clip a lavalier microphone to her jacket, plug the mic into your camera, and manually set the sound volume.

✔ **If your camera has a hot shoe that accepts a microphone, don't use it.** A sensitive microphone picks up the mechanical noise of your camcorder's motor. If possible, run a cable from your camcorder to the microphone, and place the microphone as close as possible to the sound source.

✔ **If sound fidelity is important, capture the sound from the event mixing board, if it's available.** You can also use a portable recording device to capture the audio and then synchronize it with the video in your video-editing application.

Book VI
Chapter 6

Shooting a Video
That Looks Good
on the Web

You're a Flash designer, not a videographer. But you have taken the plunge and bought a decent camcorder. Rather than let it sit in the closet and collect dust until your services as a videographer are required, take out the camera occasionally and shoot some video with it. Experiment with the different controls so that you get to know them well. Then whenever a client asks you if you can record the video for the Flash project you're creating, you can smile and answer "Yes" with confidence.

Panning, Zooming, and Other Delights

When you record a moving subject, you have to move the camcorder to keep your subject in the frame. You may also choose to zoom in and out on your subject. If you're not familiar with panning and zooming, the resulting video will be amateurish. The following sections offer some tips for panning and zooming.

To zoom or not to zoom?

I'm sure you watched the vacation video where the camera operator zoomed in and out so much that you got a headache. And he zoomed so fast that you felt slightly sick. When you're recording an event, use the camera zoom feature judiciously. If your subject is a speaker stressing an important point, it may pay to zoom in to add emphasis to it. When you zoom, zoom slowly. If your camera uses a rocker switch to zoom in and out, experiment with the control to know its limits. When you zoom in and out, it also pays to manually focus your camera on your subject if it's stationary.

Panning smoothly and at the right speed

Panning a camcorder is an art. When you pan to follow a subject in motion, you need to pan at the same speed as your subject. If you're recording an event such as an automobile race or a marathon, get to the event early and record the warm-up or practice sessions. You get a feel for the event and know how your subjects move. When you record the event, you can then pan smoothly and capture your subject in motion.

If you're recording video of a building or landscape, you also pan to show the entire scene to your audience. If you pan too slowly, your audience will fall asleep. If you pan too quickly, your audience will click the Stop button and look at something else. When you pan to capture a beautiful scene, remember the *National Geographic* videos you've seen. The camera was level, and the operator panned just fast enough to keep your interest but slowly enough for you to see all the subtle details. When you record video of a beautiful place, you can easily get caught up in the moment. Take a deep breath, relax, and then record your video.

When you pan, plant your feet slightly apart. Cradle the camera with both hands. Your right hand should be positioned so that you can reach the Record button and zoom control easily. Move your elbows close to your chest. This gives you a stable platform. Pivot from your midsection to aim the camera at the point where your subject will enter your field of view. When the subject arrives, press the Record button and pivot to keep the subject within the viewfinder. Make sure that the camera is level at all times; otherwise, it looks like your subject is moving up- or downhill. Follow through after you push the Record button to stop recording. If you don't, your subject will be out of synch during the last second or two of your clip. Remember to record a couple of seconds before and after for a lead-in and lead-out.

Using a tripod

If you're recording a long event, hand-holding the camera wears you out. The resulting video looks like it was shot by an amateur. When you're recording a long event, such as a speech or a conference, a tripod is just what the doctor ordered. When you shoot video with a tripod, the camera is stable at all times. You use the controls to pan the camera with your subject (see Figure 6-1). If you own a tripod, get used to using it with your camcorder. Practice using your camcorder while it's mounted on a tripod. Each tripod is different, but they all have similar controls:

- **A spirit level (bubble level) in the base where the head connects:** Lets you level the legs on any surface

- **A level in the head:** Enables you to level the camera with the ground

- **Retractable spikes in each leg:** Used to plant the tripod when you're using it on surfaces such as dirt or grass

- **A fluid head (on tripods designed for video):** Enables you to pan smoothly

If you don't own a tripod, you can probably rent one from a camera store.

**Book VI
Chapter 6**

**Shooting a Video
That Looks Good
on the Web**

Composing a Scene

Figure 6-1: Use a tripod to keep your video camera stable.

When you create video, you need to capture the attention and imagination of your viewing audience. Therefore you must compose the scene in a manner that creates interesting video while drawing attention to your subject. When you capture video of a person and wonder where the person should be in the frame, the answer "dead center" is dead wrong. Watch your local news and you'll notice that the newscaster is to one side of the frame. This placement not only creates visual interest but also provides room to display text and other objects. We're sure that you've seen a small version of a video playing in another video.

If you capture video of a beautiful landscape, lead the viewer into the scene. Imagine nine squares in your viewfinder divided by two equally spaced horizontal lines and two equally spaced vertical lines. The area where the lines intersect is a point of interest. If you can compose your scene in such a way that your main subject intersects a point of interest, you have a more interesting video as a result. This strategy is known as the *rule of thirds*. We know what you're thinking: Video is motion. However, if you start and end a scene with a subject intersecting a point of interest, you create a more compelling video.

Placing the horizon is also important. If you place the horizon in the middle of your scene, you end up with a boring video. However, if you place the horizon line according to the rule of thirds, you create a more interesting video. If the sky is predominant in the scene, place the horizon line in the lower third of the image. If the main subject of interest is the ocean, for example, place the horizon line on the upper third of the image.

Another factor to consider is your point of view. Do you place the camera above and looking down at your subject, level with your subject, or below and looking up at your subject? If you place the camera below the subject, the subject looks taller than she really is; place the camera above the subject and she appears small and meek.

When you're recording a person, how do you frame him? Do you shoot his whole body from head to toe? Do you shoot his chest and head, or do you zoom in close and crop off the top of his head — also known as an *extreme close-up.* Your choice depends on what your subject is doing.

Lights, Camera, Action!

If you're creating a video for the Web, you have to grab the bull by the horns and be in charge. Whether you're recording a talking head for a Web page or a speaker at a conference, the only way you get decent results is to be in charge. The following sections offer some suggestions for being in charge when you're creating a video production.

Being a director

When you're capturing video of a person or an event, you have a good idea what you want the result to look like. You also have a good idea of what limitations your equipment imposes when recording a video. Therefore, you have to be somewhat of a director. If you're recording a talking head, you have to tell your subject where to look. Many subjects look at the video operator rather than at the camera lens. You may have to pose the subject as well.

If you're a man working with a woman, always ask for permission before touching her.

If you're recording a scripted commercial for the Web, you have to tell your subject the point from which she enters the scene and where she has to stop, for example. You can place a piece of tape on the floor where you want your subject to stop. You can also use hand signals. If you're working with people who haven't been in front of a camera, you have to do a bit of hand-holding and prepare yourself for several takes.

If you're recording a speaker at a conference and the speaker wants you to record the question-and-answer period, tell the speaker to repeat the questions before answering them. This strategy ensures that the viewers of your video hear the question rather than the mumbles of the audience member.

Telling a story

When you capture a video of an event, you should tell a story. Your story should have a beginning, a middle, and an end. If you're creating a video of a speaker at a conference, make sure that you record the introduction (the beginning), the entire speech (the middle), and the audience applause (the end). If you're capturing video of a sporting event, record the athletes preparing to do battle, the actual event, and the awards ceremony.

Conducting an interview

When you conduct an interview and capture the video of it, you play the role of the news reporter. However, you still have to consider the limits of your equipment. Set your camera on a tripod so that you don't have to be a videographer and an interviewer at the same time. Push the Record button, wait a few seconds, and start the interview.

When you interview a person, send him a list of the questions ahead of time. Your subject then has a chance to rehearse his answers. Never surprise your subject unless he is a political person who practices what he preaches — most of the time. When you set up your equipment for the interview, position the sound recording equipment so that you get good audio of your subject. If you're using an on-camera microphone, manually adjust the volume to acquire a clean recording of your subject. Have your subject repeat the question after you ask it and then pause slightly before answering. When you edit the video, you can re-record your audio of the question and cut out the video of your subject repeating the question.

When you're conducting an interview, don't worry about long pauses; you can edit them out. If you're interviewing a subject that may provide short, one-line answers, have some fallback questions that aren't on the list you supplied to your interviewee. Or, you can always ask "How do you mean that? or "Why is that important to you?" or a similar question. Stay on your toes.

Editing DV for the Web

If you already read the other chapters of this minibook, you know that Flash has some powerful tools for encoding video. But Flash has limited tools for editing video. Therefore, you need a video-editing application to convert your raw footage into a finished production. If you don't do a lot of video work, you may hesitate to invest in one of the applications mentioned in Book VI, Chapter 2. The good news is that you don't need to. If you own a PC, you can use Windows Movie Maker to edit your video files. If you own an Apple computer, you can use iMovie to edit your video.

The cutting-room floor

After you capture video, it's time to start editing. This process is the same one that takes place in the revered cutting-room floor in Hollywood production rooms, where you separate the wheat from the chaff. If you're in control of the entire process, be ruthless in your editing. Get rid of the footage where the speaker slurped when she gulped her drink or crashed the microphone on the podium. You should also delete the sections where you forgot to push the Record button when you finished recording a scene and can hear several seconds of your shuffling feet as you moved to the next point of interest.

Video editing applications give you a tool to split video clips and remove unwanted segments. Depending on the sophistication of your application, you may also have tools and menu commands to color-correct video, add contrast, and create special effects, for example. Figure 6-2 shows a video of a speaker being edited in Sony Vegas. Sony Vegas is a non-linear video editing application used by professional and advanced amateur videographers.

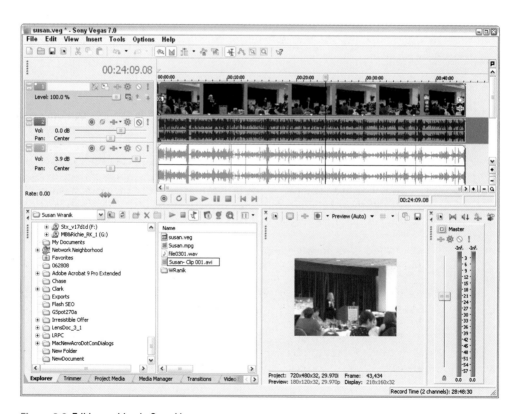

Figure 6-2: Editing a video in Sony Vegas.

Sony also makes a consumer version of the application, which is known as Vegas Movie Studio. For more information on the Vegas family of video editing applications, visit `www.sonycreativesoftware.com/products/vegas family.asp`.

Transitions, transitions

When one scene ends and another begins, what do you use to tell the viewer that something new is happening? You add a transition between scenes. Transitions can cause problems when compressed. The video transition may look squeaky clean on your monitor when you're editing the video. However, when you use Adobe Media Encoder to compress the edited video for the Web and then you choose a low data rate, the transition looks bad. Therefore, whenever you're editing video for the Web, don't use the extravagant video transitions that break the scene into a thousand pieces and reassemble it in the next scene. Use a simple transition that pushes one scene into the next. You're dealing with straight lines rather than pixel magic wherever you see part of one scene and part of the next. The straight line of a transition that pushes a scene in from top to bottom or from left to right renders correctly even when the video is heavily compressed for the Web. When in doubt, the standard straight cut from one scene to another also works well.

Beginning and ending credits

If you create a video for the Web, encode it as an FLV Flash video file, and park it on the Web, your viewers may understand what it's for. Then again, they may not. Here's where beginning and ending credits play a role. You use beginning credits to tell your viewers what the video is about and, if applicable, who the players are. You use ending credits to give credit where credit is due; for example, by listing the name of the videographer, the name of the editor, and the name of the person who made the Flash video. If that's you, list your name next to each role in the ending credits.

Hollywood goes all out when creating starting and ending credits for a movie. You can create some cool beginning and ending credits in most video editing applications. However, when compressed heavily for the Web, the cool credit ends up looking like pixelated junk. When you create beginning and ending credits for a Web video, refrain from using rolling or scrolling credits. Use straight text and display it on-screen for as many seconds as needed, and then create another text credit for the other information you want to display at the beginning or end of your production. Figure 6-3 shows the final frame of a credit for a Web video.

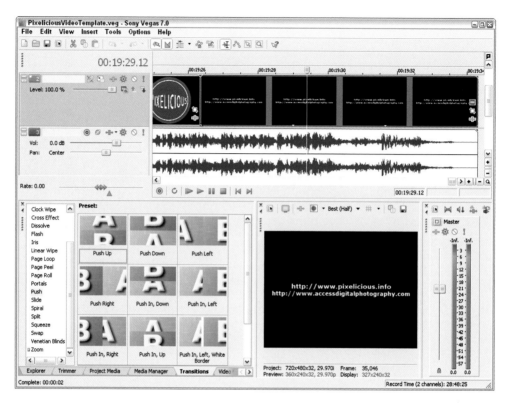

Figure 6-3: Give credit where credit is due.

Rendering for the Web

After you go to all the trouble of recording, capturing, and then editing video, you may think that you have to use some superduper technique for rendering a video for the Web. This belief would be correct if you didn't have Adobe Media Encoder in your hip pocket. Video created for the Web is generally short. Therefore, when you render it from your video editing application, render it using the highest-quality settings available. (When Doug renders a video for his podcast, he renders it as an uncompressed AVI file.) If you compress a file when you render it from your video editing application and then expect it to be squeaky clean when it pops out of Adobe Media Encoder, you're sadly mistaken. As good as the Adobe Media Encoder is, the principle of garbage in, garbage out still applies.

Book VII
Getting Interactive

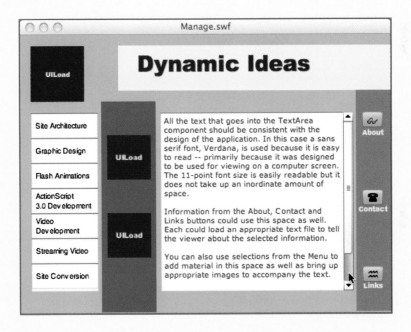

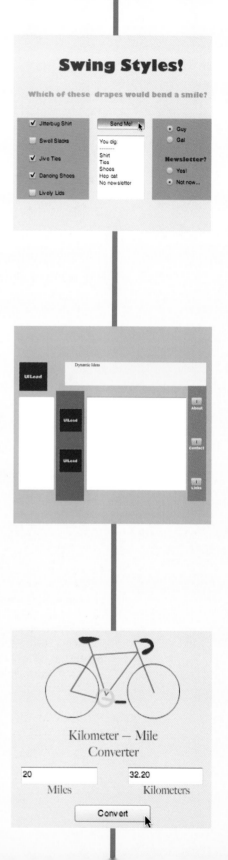

Users interact with Web sites by using the tools the Flash designer and developer make available to them. Starting with buttons, Book VII guides you through the different components that make up a user interface (UI). You find out how to dynamically place information into the components so that the users have the feeling of interacting with a site that wants nothing more than to serve their needs.

Book VII brings together all the UI tools, from buttons to components, and the ActionScript 3.0 to drive them. You discover how to add style to components and make the components do exactly what you want. You find out, as an added attraction, how to use AIR with Flash so that all the interaction that can be done over the Web is possible on the desktop.

Chapter 1: Adding Buttons to a Flash Project

In This Chapter

- ✔ **Creating buttons**
- ✔ **Creating animated buttons**
- ✔ **Using the Button Library**
- ✔ **Bringing buttons to life with ActionScript**

*B*uttons. You click them and something happens. The Web is full of buttons that link to all manner of interesting content. You can create buttons in Flash too. You can create buttons that do interesting things, buttons that do stuff but aren't seen, and buttons that move when you pause the cursor over them. You can create interesting buttons in a flash in Flash. But the buttons don't do a darn thing except display different graphics until you add ActionScript to them. In this chapter, we show you how to create a button, use the button library, and make a button functional with ActionScript.

Creating Buttons

Buttons have timelines, and they also have states. When you create a button, you work with a four-frame timeline — one frame for each state. You can create a simple button with one state or a cool button with four states. When you put a graphic in a state, something different happens in each one, depending on user input. The states are New York, New — just kidding. This list describes what the graphic in each state's frame does:

- ✔ **Up:** What the user sees when the frame on which the button resides is first displayed.
- ✔ **Over:** What a user sees when the cursor pauses over a button.
- ✔ **Down:** What a user sees when clicking the button.

✎ **Hit:** Not seen by the viewer, but it defines the target area for the button. Using a graphic for this state's frame is optional, but is handy when you have a small button or a button with text only.

When you're creating a project with lots of buttons, put them on their own layer. After creating the layer, rename it Buttons so that you can identify it. Remember not to put any other graphics on the layer. When all of your buttons are on a single layer, you can lock the other layers to make editing easier.

Creating a multistate button

A *button* is a symbol that resides in the document library. You create instances of the button as needed on the Stage. When you create a button, you can either create a sedate-looking, functional button or pull out all the stops and create an all-singing, all-dancing button. To create a button symbol, follow these steps:

1. **Choose Insert⇨New Symbol.**

   The Create New Symbol dialog box appears (see Figure 1-1).

2. **Enter a name for the symbol.**

   Choose a name that reflects what the button does.

Figure 1-1: Creating a new button.

3. **Choose Button from the Type drop-down menu and then click OK.**

   Flash enters symbol-editing mode, and a four-frame Timeline with one layer appears (see Figure 1-2).

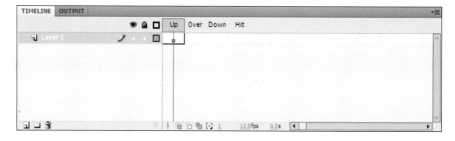

Figure 1-2: A button with four states — ve-e-ery interesting.

4. **Create a graphic for the first state.**

   You can create a graphic (by using the drawing tools), import a graphic, or import an image. There are no rules for your "just right" button. If all you need is a simple button that does something when it's clicked, you can stop here and go to the later section "Making Buttons Functional with ActionScript." But we think that you're cooler than that, so please read on.

5. Click the Over frame.

You need a keyframe when you want something to change.

6. Create a keyframe, or blank keyframe.

Create a keyframe when you want to duplicate the graphic in the first frame, and then modify it. Create a blank keyframe when you want to use a different graphic in the Over frame. Press F6 to create a keyframe, or press F7 to create a blank keyframe. Creating a keyframe copies the graphic from the previous state. Use this option when you want to use the same shape as in the Up frame, but with a different color or some other subtle modification. Create a blank keyframe when you want a different graphic in this keyframe.

7. Modify the existing graphic if you added a keyframe; create or import a new graphic if you added a blank keyframe.

Variety is the spice of life.

8. Click the Down frame.

Yup — you guessed it. This puppy needs a keyframe as well.

9. Create a keyframe or a blank keyframe.

Press F6 to add a keyframe, or press F7 to create a blank keyframe.

10. Modify the graphic in the keyframe; create or import a graphic for the blank keyframe.

11. Click the Hit frame.

This keyframe determines the target area for the button.

12. Press F7 to create a blank keyframe.

13. Create a rectangular shape slightly larger than the largest graphic in any previous keyframe.

This step is especially important if you have a small button or graphics with irregular shapes.

14. Click the Current Scene button or the Back button.

The button is added to the document library.

Creating an invisible button

Invisible buttons can't be seen, but if you add sound to them, they can be heard. An invisible button is useful when you want an area of the document to be a hotspot. Invisible buttons can be used in Flash games or when you want users to click a block of text after reading it to advance to another part of the file. Invisible buttons are easy to make. Here's how to do it:

1. **Choose Insert⇨New Symbol.**

   The New Symbol dialog box appears.

2. **Choose Button from the Type drop-down menu.**

3. **Click OK.**

   Flash enters symbol-editing mode.

4. **Click the Hit frame and then press F7.**

   Flash creates a blank keyframe.

5. **Choose the drawing tool that's best suited for the shape over which you're creating the invisible button.**

   If you're creating an invisible button over a block of text, choose the Rectangle tool. If you're creating an invisible button for an irregular shape, use the Pen tool to create a path and then fill it.

   To create an invisible button for an irregular shape that you want to closely match, create the button as outlined here and add a rectangle or oval to the Hit frame. Press the Back button to leave symbol-editing mode. Drag the button on the Stage and place it over the shape. Right-click (Windows) or Control+click (Mac) and choose Edit in Place from the context menu. Delete the rectangle in the Hit frame, and then use the appropriate tool to create a shape that matches the object over which you placed the invisible button but is slightly larger.

6. **Choose Window⇨Align.**

   The Align panel appears.

7. **Center the shape to the Stage vertically and horizontally.**

8. **(Optional) Click the Over frame and press F6.**

   If you want an alert, such as text to be displayed or a sound to play when a user pauses the cursor over the button, add the keyframe.

9. **Add the text that you want displayed or the sound that you want to play when the user pauses the cursor over the button.**

   Some designers add a sound to alert users that something will happen when this area of the movie is clicked. Other designers add text that tells the viewer what to do.

10. **Click the Current Scene button or the Back button.**

    Flash exits symbol-editing mode, and the invisible button is added to the document library.

11. **Drag the invisible button to a spot on the Stage.**

An invisible button is an opaque blue when you're editing the document (see Figure 1-3). When the document is published or tested, the button is invisible.

Figure 1-3: An invisible button is visible when you edit the document.

Creating an animated button

If you want to create a unique button, add an animation to the button that plays when a user pauses the cursor over the button. You can use a shape tween animation that morphs the original button shape into a different shape or an image sequence animation, which is a good option for a photographer's site. When you use an animation in a button, make sure that it's relatively short. You need only a couple of seconds to pique the viewer's curiosity. To create an animated button, follow these steps:

1. **Create a new movie clip symbol, and then create your animation.**

   If you don't know how to create a movie clip, see Book II, Chapter 4.

2. **Choose Insert⇨New Symbol.**

   The New Symbol dialog box appears.

3. **Choose Button from the Type drop-down menu.**

4. **Enter a name for the button.**

5. **Click the Up state.**

   The graphic you add to this state is what the user sees when the frame on which the button appears is loaded.

6. **Create a graphic for the Up frame.**

   Create a graphic that's the same size as your movie clip.

7. **Choose Window⇨Align.**

   The Align panel appears.

8. **Center the shape to the Stage vertically and horizontally.**

9. **Click the Down frame and press F6.**

   This step creates a keyframe for the Down state frame and copies the graphic from the Up state frame.

10. **Click the Over frame and press F7.**

    This step adds a blank keyframe to the Over state frame.

11. **Drag the movie clip symbol you created in Step 1 on the Stage.**

12. **Choose Window⇨Align.**

    The Align panel appears.

13. **Center the shape to the Stage vertically and horizontally.**

14. **Press Ctrl+Enter (Windows) or ⌘+Return (Mac).**

    Flash publishes the movie and displays it in another window.

15. **Pause the cursor over the button.**

    The movie clip plays.

Creating a navigation menu with buttons

If you're creating a Flash Web site, you need buttons for navigation. If you think that you need to create a separate button for each menu link, you're wrong. You can quickly create a navigation menu in Flash by following these steps:

1. **Decide whether your menu will be vertical or horizontal.**

   The number of buttons needed for navigation and the amount of text you have on each button determine the placement of your menu. If you have lots of buttons and just a bit of text, a vertical placement may be the answer. If you need a menu with just a few buttons, a horizontal menu gives you more room for the rest of your movie.

2. **Divide the available space by the number of buttons needed.**

If you have a horizontal menu, the answer determines the maximum width of each button. If you have a vertical menu, the answer determines the maximum height of each button.

3. **Create a button symbol, as outlined in the earlier section "Creating a multistate button."**

4. **Right-click (Windows) or Control+click (Mac) the first button layer, and then choose Insert Layer from the context menu.**

5. **Create the text for the first button.**

   Figure 1-4 shows a rectangular button for a site home page.

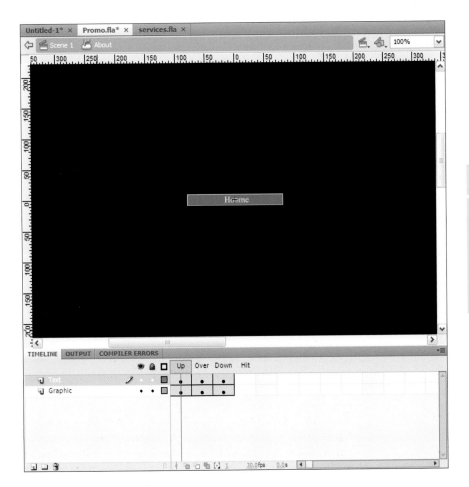

Figure 1-4: Back home again.

6. **Click the Current Scene button or the Back button.**

The button is added to the document library.

7. **Right-click (Windows) or Control+click (Mac) the button you just created and choose Duplicate from the context menu.**

The Duplicate Symbol dialog box appears (see Figure 1-5).

Figure 1-5: Duplicating the button symbol.

8. **Enter a new name for the symbol.**

The menu link name is as good as any.

9. **Click OK.**

The dialog box closes and Flash creates a duplicate symbol.

10. **Repeat Steps 7 through 9 for the other buttons that are needed for the menu.**

11. **Double-click the first duplicated button.**

The button opens in symbol-editing mode.

12. **Change the button text to the name you want.**

13. **Click the Current Scene button or the Back button.**

You exit symbol-editing mode and the button is updated.

14. **In the Timeline panel, right-click (Windows) or Control+click (Mac) the uppermost layer and choose Insert Layer from the context menu.**

15. **Name the new layer** Buttons.

You should create separate layers for the main parts of the site interface.

16. **Drag the buttons from the document library to the Stage.**

We find that it helps to have a guide at the point where you insert the menu buttons.

17. **Align the buttons.**

Choose Window⇨Align to open the Align panel. The alignment depends on how your buttons are positioned. If you have a horizontal menu, you can use one of the distribution options. Figure 1-6 shows a Flash Web site with a navigation menu created by using the methods listed in this section.

Figure 1-6: A flashy navigation menu.

Using the Button Library

If you don't like creating your own buttons, you can use the ones that ship with Flash. The Flash button library contains a wide variety of button presets, all neatly sequestered in groups of similar buttons. To access the button library, follow these steps:

1. **Choose Window⇨Common Libraries⇨Button Library.**

   The button library appears.

2. **Click a title to see all buttons in that group.**

3. **Click a button to preview it.**

   Figure 1-7 shows a button from the Playback group.

4. **Choose Window⇨Library.**

   The document library opens.

5. **Drag buttons from the button library to the document library.**

   You can now drag the buttons from the document library into your project.

Examining the buttons in the button library gives you an idea of the techniques the pros use to create buttons. Select a button that piques your curiosity and drag it into the document library. Double-click the file in the document library to view it in symbol-editing mode. Then you can dissect the button to see how it was built. You can also edit the button to suit your project.

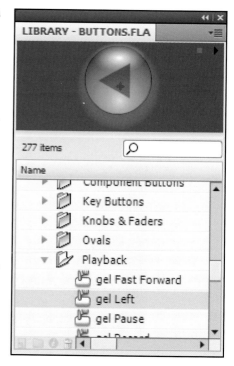

Figure 1-7: A playback button without a cause.

Making Buttons Functional with ActionScript

In previous versions of ActionScript, you could apply actions directly to a button symbol type. However, that isn't the case when you use ActionScript 3.0 to add interactivity to a project. In previous versions of ActionScript, you used event handlers to determine which event triggered the execution of the ActionScript. The onRelease event handler in the earlier versions of ActionScript executed the associated action when the button was clicked with a mouse and then released. In ActionScript 3.0, you use event listeners. ActionScript tells the Flash Player the event to listen for. For example, CLICK is an event that you can tell the Flash Player to listen for.

A *mouse event* is the event that must occur in order to execute the function associated with the mouse event. ActionScript has a class with several mouse events. You can have different things happen when a user interacts with a button. For example, you can have one thing happen when users hover their cursor over the button, and something different when users click the button. You create the function that executes when the mouse event occurs. The events in the following list cover common mouse interaction with a button:

- **CLICK:** Occurs when the user clicks the left mouse button once on the button symbol

- **DOUBLE_CLICK:** Occurs when the user clicks the left mouse button twice on the button symbol

✓ **MOUSE_OVER:** Occurs when the user pauses the cursor over the button symbol

✓ **MOUSE_OUT:** Occurs when the user moves the cursor from the button target area after moving the cursor over the target button area

Creating the ActionScript Code to Make a Button Interactive

If you're a devout coward when it comes to writing any kind of code, there's no need to stress out. The code involved is fairly simple. To show you how easy it is, follow these steps:

1. **Create a new Flash document.**

2. **Click the sixth frame on the Timeline, and then press F6 to create a keyframe.**

3. **Select the Text tool, choose your favorite font, and create a big numeral 6.**

4. **With the keyframe still selected, open the Property inspector.**

5. **In the Label section, enter** big6 **in the Name text field.**

   This bit of text is known as a frame label. You can address a label with ActionScript. Notice that there are no spaces in the frame label.

6. **Click the tenth frame in the Timeline, and then press F7 to create a blank keyframe.**

7. **Select the Text tool, choose your favorite font, and create a big numeral 10.**

8. **With the keyframe still selected, open the Property inspector.**

9. **In the Label section, enter** big10 **in the Name text field.**

10. **Right-click (Windows) or Control+click (Mac) the first layer and choose Insert Layer from the context menu.**

11. **Name the layer** Buttons.

    We know: It's only an exercise. But the sooner you get in the habit of labeling things, the sooner it becomes second nature.

12. **Create two button symbols.**

    If you're pressed for time, open the buttons library and drag two buttons to the Stage. Put the buttons near the top of the document.

13. **Select the first button and open the Property inspector.**

14. **In the Property inspector, enter** btn1 **in the blank text field.**

When you use ActionScript on a button, the button must have an instance name. When you create an instance name, remember to use a logical name with no spaces.

15. **Select the second button, and in the Property inspector, enter** btn2 **in the blank text field.**

    Each button instance must have a unique name.

16. **Right-click (Windows) or Control+click (Mac) the Buttons layer and choose Insert Layer from the context menu.**

17. **Rename the layer** Actions.

    That's right — ActionScript should be on its own layer.

18. **Select the first keyframe on the Actions layer and choose Window⇨Actions.**

    The Actions panel opens.

19. **Add the following code:**

    ```
    stop();
    btn1.addEventListener(MouseEvent.CLICK,bigSix);
    btn2.addEventListener(MouseEvent.CLICK,bigTen);
    ```

    The first line of code stops the movie dead in its tracks on the first frame. The second and third lines of code add the MouseEvent event listener to the buttons. When the buttons are clicked, functions named bigSix and BigTen are executed. Now it's time to create the functions.

20. **Add the following chunk of code to your script:**

    ```
    function bigSix(e:MouseEvent):void
    {
    gotoAndStop("big6");
    }

    function bigTen(e:MouseEvent):void
    {
    gotoAndStop("big10");
    }
    ```

    These lines of code define two functions: bigSix and BigTen. The functions tell the Flash Player to go to, and then stop on, the labeled frames that are specified. At this stage, the Actions panel should resemble the one shown in Figure 1-8.

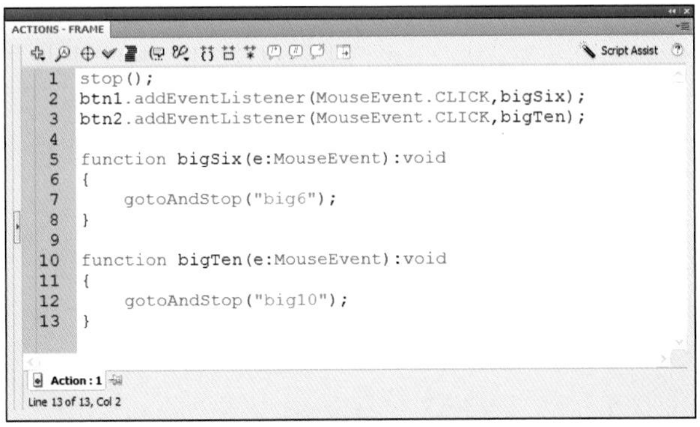

Figure 1-8: Creating ActionScript for buttons.

21. Press Ctrl+Enter (Windows) or ⌘+Return (Mac).

Flash publishes the movie and displays it in a new window.

22. Test the buttons.

When you click the first button, you should see a big numeral 6. When you click the second button, you should see a big numeral 10.

Chapter 2: Using Flash Components

In This Chapter

- ✓ **Understanding components**
- ✓ **Working with the List and Label components**
- ✓ **Using check boxes and radio buttons**
- ✓ **Loading external graphic and SWF files with UILoader**
- ✓ **Creating a Web site**

*M*uch of the time, you work with complex elements in Flash. One set of such elements is the *user interface* (UI). The UI makes the interaction either smooth or awkward, and no designer or developer wants a clumsy or unattractive UI. Whether your UI involves buttons, menus, or something as exotic as dynamic labels, creating these elements from scratch takes time. With Flash's ready-made components, however, most of the work has been done for you. All you have to do is to place the component on the Stage and set the values, and you're good to go.

Some people may think that components take away from the creative aspects of developing with Flash. Actually, components contribute to creativity, because they allow you to do things that you couldn't do otherwise. They even come with their own ActionScript 3 methods and properties, and with very little code, you can make them your own — as you see in this chapter. Topics we cover include how to work with different components, use their methods and properties, use ternary statements to simplify multiple selections, and dynamically change a component's content.

Working with Flash Components

You can use Flash components for a wide variety of tasks. In virtually every application in which you use components, you also use ActionScript 3; for the functionality, you get a lot more bang for your buck. Using a combination of ActionScript 3 and the Component Inspector, you can easily put together relatively sophisticated interfaces.

In working with components, you need to use both the Component and Component Inspector panels. Before you continue, place the Component and Component Inspectors panels in the dock or somewhere else that gives you easy access to them.

Using the List and Label Components

The first two components we examine in this chapter are List and Label. The List component is very handy for creating interactive menus. The Label component can be used for dynamic output — not just for labeling, but also for information display.

In this section, you use these components to make a fruit-calculator application. Each time the user clicks a fruit name in a menu, Flash adds the value of that fruit to a variable that is displayed in a Label component. The simple UI allows the user to add up his purchases and see the results quickly.

Creating a calculator application

To create the application, follow these steps:

1. **Choose New⇨Flash File (ActionScript 3.0) from the menu bar, and save it as `Simple.fla`.**

2. **Choose Window⇨Properties from the menu bar (or press Ctrl+F3 in Windows or ⌘+F3 on the Mac) to open the Properties panel, type Simple in the Class window, and save the file again.**

3. **Choose Window⇨Components (or press Ctrl+F7 in Windows or ⌘+F7 on the Mac) to open the Components panel and drag a List component to the Stage.**

4. **With the List component selected, type Fruit in the Instance Name window of the Properties panel; then press the Tab key and save the file.**

5. **Drag a Label component from the Component panel to the Stage.**

6. **With the Label component selected, type ListTotal in the Instance Name window of the Properties panel; then press the Tab key and save the file.**

7. **Using the Align tool, position the Label component so that it's aligned vertically in the center of the List component.**

8. **Select the Label component, and open the Component Inspector panel.**

   Figure 2-1 shows the window you should see when you open the Component Inspector with the Label component selected.

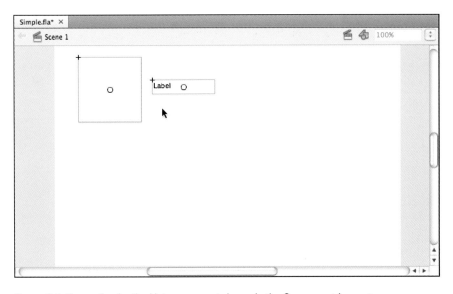

Figure 2-1: Properties for the List component shown in the Component Inspector.

9. **Click the dataProvider row and then click the little magnifying glass that appears.**

The Values window opens (see Figure 2-2). The label is the text of the individual menu item, and the data is a string (even if you use a number) that is associated with the label. In the example shown in Figure 2-2, the data value of Apples is 1.72.

You can easily change numbers that are stored as strings to real numbers. When you use the data, however, you need to know that it's stored in string format and requires conversion to number format if you plan to do any calculations.

10. **Click the plus (+) button at the top of the Values window to add both labels and values; then click OK to return to the Component Inspector panel.**

Using Figure 2-2 as a guide, first type the data value in the Value column; then type the label in the Value column. Make sure that the data values are numbers without any symbols except decimal points (.).

11. **Select the Label component, and enter** Total **in the Value column.**

Before you click any items on the List component, the Label component displays Total. As soon as you start clicking selections in the List component, the values change dynamically and appear in the Label.

12. **Open a new ActionScript file, and save it as `Simple.as` in the same folder as the `Simple.fla` file.**

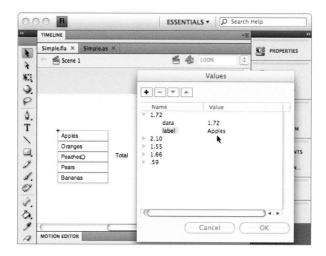

Figure 2-2: Data and label values.

13. **Add the following code to the `Simple.as` file and save the file again.**

```
package
{
    import flash.display.Sprite;
    import fl.controls.List;
    import flash.events.Event;
    public class Simple extends Sprite
    {
        private var total:Number=0;
        private var totalOld:Number=0;
        private var totalStr:String;

        public function Simple()
        {
            Fruit.addEventListener(Event.CHANGE,
        getSelection);
        }

        private function getSelection(e:Event):void
        {
            totalStr=Fruit.selectedItem.data;
            total+=Number(totalStr);
            totalStr=total.toFixed(2);
            ListTotal.text="$"+totalStr;
        }
    }
}
```

The program is a little different from some of the others because it uses the List component (instance name: Fruit) and a CHANGE event. As with a Button component, however, as long as the event is identified, all you need is a function that it fires whenever the event occurs. Rather than use CLICK and the MouseEvent, this program uses CHANGE and the Event event. (Don't worry: You're not seeing double!) So in the parameter of the `getSelection()` function, you see `e:Event` instead of `e:MouseEvent`. The logic is identical, though.

Keeping in mind that the data that you enter in the Component Inspector is *string* data, the variable you store it in is a string as well (`totalStr`). Whatever the user selects is stored in Fruit.selectedItem data. The total variable is a real number, so the string is converted to a number via the Number class. Whatever value is derived is stored is added to the current value of Total to keep a running total. Then the program *reconverts* the number to the `totalStr` string and adds the `toFixed(2)` method so that it has only two decimal points — just like real money!

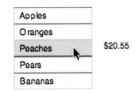

14. **Save the file again.**

15. **Test the application by pressing Ctrl+Enter (Windows) or ⌘+Return (Mac).**

    You see the value of the Label component change to the running total, as Figure 2-3 shows.

Figure 2-3: Interactive element of application built with two components.

Adding a CHANGE choice

When you have an event that uses CHANGE, you can't click the same spot twice and get a different result. Try it with the application you built in the preceding section with the List and Label components. You can pound on the same fruit selection all day, and the value stays the same.

You may reasonably ask, "Why not use the CLICK event?" Well, no such event is available for a selection event. So you have to add another selection that effectively acts as a change with no content. Here's how:

1. **Open `Simple.fla`, select the List component, and open the Component Inspector.**

2. **Select the dataProvider row and then click the magnifying-glass icon to open the Values window.**

3. **Add a data value of 0 and the label *Change*, as shown in Figure 2-4.**

    You still see only five selections on the Stage. The reason is that you can make only five total selections when you use the Component Inspector.

4. **Test the application.**

    By scrolling, you can see the new *Change* selection. So if you alternate between selecting Bananas and *Change*, you see the amount being added to the total.

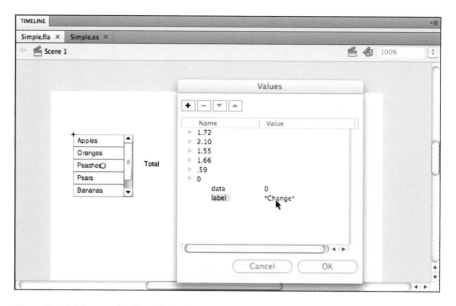

Figure 2-4: Adding a selection with a data value of 0.

That procedure sort of solved the problem, but because the user can't see the *Change* option without scrolling, she may not realize that such an option exists.

Extending visible selections without scrolling

This example shows the limitations of using the Component Inspector. The List component has a property called `rowCount` that determines how many rows are visible. As you see in the preceding sections, no such property is mentioned. In the ActionScript 3 reference document, however, `rowCount` is listed as one of the List class' properties. To change the number of visible rows, follow these steps:

1. **Open the `Simple.as` file that you created in the section "Creating a calculator application," earlier in this chapter.**

2. **Add or change (or both) the following code:**

   ```
   public function Simple()
   {
       Fruit.rowCount=6;
       Fruit.addEventListener(Event.CHANGE, getSelection);
   }
   ```

3. **Test the application again.**

This time, you see all six selections, as shown in Figure 2-5. The List component on the Stage, however, still shows only five, because of the limitations of using the Component Inspector with the List component.

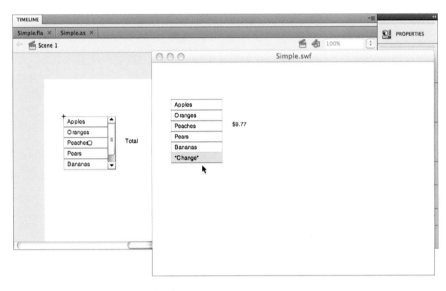

Figure 2-5: Display of added selection.

Book VII
Chapter 2

Using Flash
Components

When you use components, be sure to check what properties they have in addition to those shown in the Component Inspector panel.

The Check Box and Radio Button: Making Life Easier for the User

Some years back, Steve Krug wrote a popular book on human–computer interfaces (HCI): *Don't Make Me Think* (New Riders, 2005). Krug was referring to a simple UI that could be easily and intuitively navigated by the user. The clearest UIs, which you may remember from HTML forms, are the humble check box and radio button. If users have to ponder what you're selling, explaining, or displaying, they're likely to click the Back button in their browsers and never return to your site. Especially when you're asking users to fill out a form or perform some other chore, making things simple (and not making users think) keeps everyone happy.

The best no-brainer UI pair consists of the CheckBox and RadioButton components. (You also find ActionScript classes of the same names.) With check boxes, all the user has to do is to check all the listed items that apply — as many or as few as he wants. What more, the selections can be short or long, but the size of the check box is unchanged.

The only difference between check box and radio buttons is that radio buttons are mutually exclusive. In a group of radio buttons, only one can be selected. If you ask a user to select a dog breed — such as Collie, Poodle, or Bulldog — radio buttons are good to use because a dog can be only a single breed. Breeds are mutually exclusive. If your dog is a collie, it can't also be a poodle. (Where's the Mutt button?)

Reading results

You need a way to determine whether a check box has been checked and whether a radio button has been selected. Then you need a way to pass on the information contained in the selected component. The common property in both components is `selected`. For example, the statement

```
myCheck.selected==true
```

sets up a Boolean value for the selected property. So you could write code like this:

```
if(myCheck.selected==true)
{
    //do something
}
else
{
    //do something else
}
```

That code would work perfectly well with both CheckBox and RadioButton objects. As an alternative, you could use a ternary statement. *Ternary statements* are shorthand versions of `if..then..else` statements. They have the following format:

```
var case1 = cb.selected ? doThis : doThat;
```

This code is the same as writing

```
if (case1==cb.selected)
{
    doThis;
}
else
{
    doThat;
}
```

As you can see, the ternary statement is compact. If you have lots of check boxes and radio buttons, you have much cleaner code if you use ternary statements.

Using ternary statements with lots of components can save time in other ways. After you set up one component with a ternary statement, you can cut and paste the rest, changing only the instance names and values.

Creating a swinging shop

Back in the 1940s, a dance style called swing was popular, along with a style of speech called jive talk. The example in this section creates a swing-oriented online shop to illustrate the use of CheckBox and RadioButton components, along with the ActionScript that gets the job done.

Adding the CheckBox components

To set up the application's check boxes, follow these steps:

1. **Open a new ActionScript file, and save it as** `Swing.fla`.

2. **Open the Properties panel, type** Swing **in the Class window, and save the file again.**

3. **Using the Text tool, add to the top the static text labete** `Swing Styles`. **Below that, add another static text label,** `Which of these drapes would bend a smile?`

4. **Open the Components panel, and drag five CheckBox components to the Stage.**

5. **Place the components in a list on the left side of the Stage.**

6. **Select a component, type a name for it in the Instance Name window of the Properties panel, and press the Tab key, repeating this process until all the components are named.**

   For this example, give the components the following names:
   - jitterbug
   - slacks
   - ties
   - shoes
   - lids

7. **Save the file again.**

   Now you need to add labels for the check boxes.

8. **Select a CheckBox component and type a label for it in the Label row, repeating this process by selecting each one in turn until all the components are labeled.**

   For this example, enter the following labels:

   • Jitterbug Shirt

   • Swell Slacks

   • Jive Ties

   • Dancing Shoes

   • Lively Lids

   Figure 2-6 shows how the check boxes should appear after they're labeled.

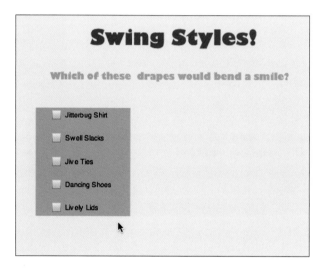

Figure 2-6: Adding CheckBox components to the Stage.

Adding the RadioButton components

Now you're ready to add the radio buttons. Follow these steps:

1. **Using Figure 2-7 as a guide (at the end of this set of steps), drag four RadioButton components from the Components panel to the right side of the Stage.**

2. **Place the components in a list on the right side of the Stage.**

3. **Select a component and type a name for it in the Instance Name window of the Properties panel, selecting each button and repeating this process until all the components are named.**

For this example, give the components the following names:

- guy
- gal
- yes
- no

Now you need to add group names. Radio buttons need both labels *and* group names because only one button in a group can be selected. (See Step 6 in the previous section to see how to open the Components Inspector.)

4. **In the Components Inspector, you see the groupName row and a text box next to it, as shown in Figure 2-7. Enter the group name, and then the label.**

The following list shows what each groupName and label should be:

Group	Label
gender	Guy
gender	Gal
ul	Yes!
ul	Not now. . . .

Figure 2-7 shows where to enter a RadioButton component's group name.

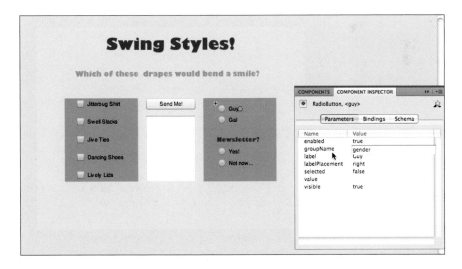

Figure 2-7: Adding a group name to a RadioButton component.

Finishing the application

All you have left to do are add a command button and a text box, enter some ActionScript, and test the application. Follow these steps:

1. **Drag a Button component from the Components panel to the Stage, placing it between the groups of check boxes and radio buttons.**

2. **Select the Button component, and type** send **in the Instance Name window of the Properties panel.**

3. **With the component still selected, type the label** Send Me **in the Component Inspector panel.**

4. **Drag a TextArea component from the Components panel to the Stage, placing it directly below the command button you just created.**

5. **Select the TextArea component, and in the Properties panel, type the instance name** ta **and change the height value to 130.**

6. **Save the** `swing.fla` **file.**

7. **Open a new ActionScript file, and save it as** Swing.as **in the same folder as the** Swing.fla **file.**

8. **Enter the following code:**

```
package
{
    import flash.display.Sprite;
    import flash.events.MouseEvent;

    public class SwingCheck extends Sprite
    {
        private var decision:String="You dig:\n-------
-\n";

        public function SwingCheck()
        {
            sendme.addEventListener(MouseEvent.
CLICK,getAll);
        }

        private function getAll(e:MouseEvent):void
        {
            decision+=(jitterbug.selected==true) ?
"Shirt\n" :"";
            decision+=(slacks.selected==true) ?
"Slacks\n" :"";
            decision+=(ties.selected==true) ? "Ties\n"
:"";
            decision+=(shoes.selected==true) ?
"Shoes\n" :"";
            decision+=(lids.selected==true) ? "Hats\n"
:"";
```

```
            decision+=(guy.selected==true) ? "Hep
cat\n" :"Hep chick\n";
            decision+=(yes.selected==true) ? "Get
newsletter\n" :"No newsletter";
            ta.text=decision;
        }
    }
}
```

9. **Save the** `Swing.as` **file.**

10. **Choose Control⇨Test from the menu bar (or press Ctrl+Enter in Windows or ⌘+Return on the Mac) to test the application.**

    Figure 2-8 shows an example of what you can expect to see.

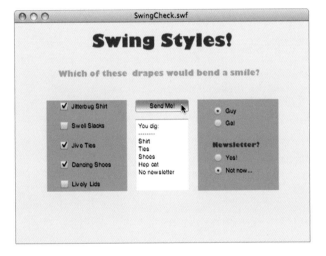

**Book VII
Chapter 2**

**Using Flash
Components**

Figure 2-8: CheckBox and RadioButton data displayed in a TextArea component.

The Button component is incorporated into the application so that the user could make all the selections before processing the information. You could have used a CHANGE event with the check boxes and radio buttons to fire off functions as each selection is made, but you had no reason to do so.

Creating an Interface with Flash Components

To some extent, creating an interface with Flash components is a clear and simple way for users to interact with the application you build. You shouldn't do this with an eye to a static site, however; you have to think, "How will this change?" You must create an interface that has development flexibility but is clear for the user.

In this section, you create a simple interface that you're going to be using in an application later in this chapter. In this interface, the user simply makes a radio-button selection. When she does, the application loads all the necessary materials, and the user sees just the information she needs. What's more, the information arrives just when she needs it and isn't a burden on the overall application.

Setting up the components

To create the simple example interface, you use the following components:

✔ Two UILoader components (discussed in the following section) to load SWF and graphics files when they are requested

✔ One Label component to display a header that shows the user what selection he made

✔ One TextArea component containing data loaded from a text file

✔ Two RadioButton components that let the user make information selections

This architecture makes it simple to change any of the data that's loaded or to add more radio buttons. Figure 2-9 shows the basic layout and the placement and types of components.

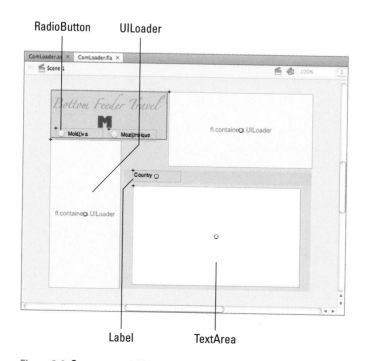

Figure 2-9: Components laid out for flexible interface.

Tracking the elements

With all the components working interactively, you're going to need a system for keeping track of everything. With these components, you'll be keeping track of three key Flash CS4 elements:

- ✓ The component instance names in the Properties panel
- ✓ The data entered directly through the Component Inspector panel
- ✓ Data changed dynamically through ActionScript

Table 2-1 shows the components and their instance names entered in the Properties panel and their initial settings in the Component Inspector.

Table 2-1	**Component Settings**	
Component	*Instance Name (Used as Reference in ActionScript)*	*Initial Component Setting*
RadioButton	mol	Group name=m, label=Moldova
RadioButton	moz	Group name=m, label=Mozambique
Label	country	Selectable=false, label=Country
UILoader (w=150, h=300)	map	Source=mapPH.png scaleContent=true
UILoader (w=300, h=150)	flag	Source=flagPH.png scaleContent=true
TextArea (w=350, h=200)	ta	Editable=false

**Book VII
Chapter 2**

**Using Flash
Components**

When you start building the application, you can use Table 2-1 as a quick reference to help keep everything straight. (Ever hear of a planning stage? This is it!)

Loading As You Go: Why You'll Love the UILoader

The one new component we haven't discussed in this chapter yet is the UILoader. Using the UILoader, you can use the `source` property easily, either directly in the Component Inspector or in ActionScript. Because you can treat the UILoader as a dynamic object, changing the graphic or SWF file stored in the UILoader component is easy. You can't use a text file as the `source`, however.

Graphic versus SWF files

When using the UILoader component, you can choose to resize the SWF or graphic file to fit the size of the UILoader component. If you set the scale-Content property to true, you specify that everything that appears in the UILoader will be resized to fit the dimensions of the component. That practice is great in terms of design considerations, but some graphics become ugly and hard to read when they're resized. So, you have to consider the component size in addition to the graphic size.

Using graphics in the example application

In the example application that you're about to build, you use both national flags and maps of the nations being described as vacation destinations. Our initial experiments showed that the flags could be left as GIF files, and they worked pretty well when they were resized, but the maps were unreadable and blurry.

Vector graphics scale very well, as noted in Book I, Chapter 2, so we took the maps and imported them into Flash. Because the maps were GIF files, Flash treats them as bitmapped graphics.

Converting bitmaps to vector graphics

To convert bitmapped graphics to vector graphics in Flash, all you have to do is the following:

1. **Import a bitmapped graphic to the Stage.**

    In the application we developed, we downloaded maps from the Central Intelligence Agency Web site (www.cia.gov) — a good source of public-domain maps and national flags.

2. **Select the imported graphic and choose Modify⇨Bitmap⇨Trace Bitmap.**

    The Trace Bitmap dialog box opens.

3. **Enter some values in the Color Threshold and Minimum Area text boxes.**

    Figure 2-10 shows settings of 10 and 1, respectively.

4. **Click OK.**

    Flash converts your bitmapped graphic to a vector graphic.

5. **Save the file, which will have the extension .fla.**

6. **Choose Control⇨Test from the menu bar (or press Ctrl+Enter in Windows or ⌘+Return on the Mac) to test the application and to create an SWF file.**

    The SWF file is the one that Flash loads and resizes. Because you now have your graphic in vector format, little distortion occurs when you load it into the UILoader component.

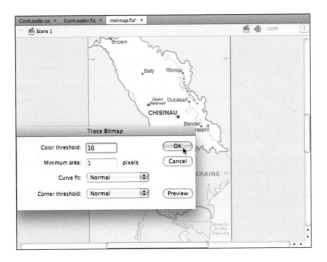

Figure 2-10: Converting a bitmapped graphic to a vector graphic.

When you work with graphics converted from bitmap to vector format, the graphics don't always look as good as you had hoped. Feel free to use the tools in Flash, such as the Text tool, to make everything look better. Remember that the Flash tools create vector graphics as well.

What about loading text and XML files?

We knew you were going to ask that. You can put data from text and XML files in the TextArea component, but you need three classes:

- **URLLoader:** Creates the basic loader object
- **URLRequest:** The request with the actual URL string
- **URLLoaderDataFormat:** Allows you to specify the format of the data being loaded

The process involves instantiating a URLLoader and then using the load method to load the data (a text file) by identifying it in the URLRequest object. The URLLoader `dataFormat` property is assigned a URLLoaderDataFormat set to the constant property TEXT.

As soon as the text file is loaded, an event handler passes the values in the text file to the `text` property of the TextArea component. The process may seem to be a bit convoluted, but as you'll see, it takes just a few lines of code. (Remember, seeming difficult and being difficult are two different things!)

Creating the Bottom Feeder Travel Agency Web Site

Suppose that your client is the Bottom Feeder Travel Agency (BFTA). They make arrangements for their customers to travel to exotic but somewhat damaged locations at cut-rate prices. To reassure clients that these little-known countries they're advertising really exist, they feel obliged to add a map and the country's national flag. Also, they include a lively text description of each country's attractions.

Because their list of countries is so long, they divided it up into alphabetical listings, and you will develop the M countries on their list: Moldova and Mozambique. (I know: You're probably wondering, "What about Mali — the home of the famed Timbuktu?" They're working on it.)

Adding the site's components

Follow these steps to set up the site components:

1. **Open a new ActionScript file, and save it as `ComLoader.fla`.**

2. **Open the Properties panel, type** ComLoader **in the Class window, and save the file again.**

3. **Open the Components panel, and drag the following elements to the Stage:**

   - Two RadioButton components
   - Two UILoader components
   - One Label component
   - One TextArea component

4. **Position the components as shown in Figure 2-9, earlier in this chapter.**

5. **Using Table 2-1 as a guide (refer to the section "Tracking the elements," earlier in this chapter), add the instance name for each component in the Properties panel.**

   Note the different sizes of the UILoader components to name each correctly. The one on the left loads the map with a 150 x 300 image; the one in the top-right corner loads the 300 x 150 image of the flag.

6. **Select the components in turn, and in the Component Inspector, enter the values shown in the Initial Component Setting column of Table 2-1.**

Adding text

Now you're ready to add text to the site. Follow these steps:

1. **Add static text as shown in Figure 2-9. (Feel free to use your own design tastes.)**

2. **Using a text editor (such as Notepad on a Windows computer or TextEdit on the Mac), add the following text files, and save them in the same folder as the `ComLoader.fla` file:**

Mozambique (`moz.txt`)

Mozambique is a beautiful country on the southeast coast of Africa. Although the roads need improvement and fuel prices are high, you'll find savings in other areas. Locally made items show off the country's unique character. Mozambique is quite inexpensive, and you can enjoy its culture and history, and its scuba diving off the coast.

Moldova (`moldova.txt`)

Never heard of Moldova? Don't let that prevent you from visiting this landlocked nation. Part of Romania until the end of World War II, visiting this little country is a bargain. You can easily see the entire country in a couple of days. Enjoy the different local festivals, each showing off a unique flavor of a region or town. Let this country be your starting point for a vacation to all the nearby countries bordering the Black Sea.

Adding maps

In this section, you add maps to the Web site. Follow these steps:

1. **If you decide to place the maps in an SWF file, load the map on the Stage of a new Flash file with the Stage the exact size of the graphic. Center the file horizontally and vertically on the Stage.**

2. **Change the bitmapped graphic into vector graphics using the steps described in "Converting bitmaps to vector graphics," earlier in the chapter.**

   Repeat this process for each graphic you wish to save as an SWF file in the same folder as the other files in the project.

3. **Download the flags from `www.cia.gov` for this application because they're close in size to the UILoader component.**

   If you leave them as GIF files, you find little distortion.

4. **Using a graphics program, create one 150 x 300 placeholder for the flag and one 300 x 150 placeholder, and save them as `flagPH.png` and `mapPH.png`, respectively.**

   Make sure that they're in the same folder as the other files for this project. When users first come to the page, they see the placeholders, but not the map or flag images. You can include a text message to the effect that once a country is selected, the proper flag and map appear. Figure 2-11 shows the kind of message you can leave.

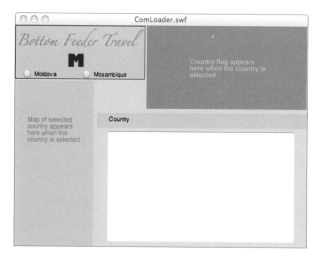

Figure 2-11: The initial page clearly shows areas where information appears.

Finishing the application

To finish the application, follow these steps:

1. **Open a new ActionScript file and save it as** `ComLoader.as` **in the same folder as** `ComLoader.fla`. **Add the following ActionScript 3.0 code:**

```
package
{
    import flash.display.Sprite;
    import flash.events.Event;
    import flash.net.URLLoader;
    import flash.net.URLRequest;
    import flash.net.URLLoaderDataFormat;

    public class ComLoader extends Sprite
    {
        private var loadEm:URLLoader;
        private var txtURL:String;

        public function ComLoader()
        {
            loadEm=new URLLoader();
            loadEm.dataFormat=URLLoaderDataFormat.TEXT;
            loadEm.addEventListener(Event.
COMPLETE,taHandler);
```

```
            mol.addEventListener(Event.CHANGE,
moldova);
            moz.addEventListener(Event.CHANGE,mozam);
      }

      private function moldova(e:Event):void
      {
            txtURL="moldova.txt";
            loadEm.load(new URLRequest(txtURL));
            country.text="Moldova";
            map.source="molmap.swf";
            flag.source="molflag.gif";
      }

      private function mozam(e:Event):void
      {
            txtURL="moz.txt";
            loadEm.load(new URLRequest(txtURL));
            country.text="Mozambique";
            map.source="mozmap.swf";
            flag.source="mozflag.gif";
      }

      private function taHandler(e:Event):void
      {
            ta.text=e.target.data;
      }
   }
}
```

Make sure that you use the same instance names you have for your components in your ActionScript 3.0 code.

2. **Double-check to make sure everything is in the same folder, including the graphics, text, and SWF files. Test it, and if all is in working order, you should see the outcome shown in Figure 2-11.**

When you first load the program, you see the structure of the application, which gives you a visual representation of the use of components on the page. As you can see in Figure 2-12, however, as soon as you make a selection, the structure disappears into the background, and the information is brought to the fore.

Overall, components allow even novice developers to put together very sophisticated applications. More important, you can easily reuse or update the site by changing just the content of the components, leaving the structure intact. Take advantage of the quality of programming behind the components and the ease of using them.

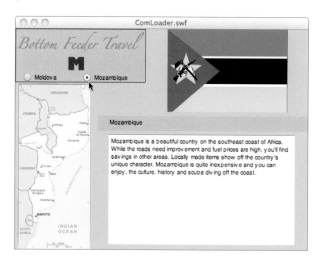

Figure 2-12: The components aid in creating flexible structures and easy updates.

Chapter 3: The Art and Science of Creating a Flash Application

In This Chapter

✓ **Sketching a Flash page**

✓ **Differentiating dynamic and static page elements**

✓ **Setting placeholders to view a page layout**

✓ **Placing and styling page elements with ActionScript**

✓ **Formatting your code**

You can think of a Flash CS4 page in three dimensions. The first two dimensions are the vertical and horizontal planes, where you place objects on your page. The third dimension is the list of possible images, text, videos, and animations that will appear on your site. So when preparing a site, you have to imagine the possible types of media that reside in the different parts of your application and whether they're static or dynamic. This chapter examines the architecture of a Flash application.

You can download the files related to this chapter from www.dummies.com/go/flashallinone.

Apples
Oranges
Peaches
Pears
Bananas

$20.55

Organizing a Flash Page

The first step in creating a Flash page is organizing it. Throughout this book, we discuss organizing everything from symbols to components, and now we're going to let you in on our secret Web-site organization tools: a pen and a piece of paper! Now that you're in on our secret, take a look at a simple piece of Flash CS4 architecture in Figure 3-1.

In this example, you see two of the three dimensions: horizontal and vertical positioning of materials. If the objects and media on the Stage never change, you can think of that space on the page as being two-dimensional. There's nothing wrong with two-dimensional objects, but separating them from the three-dimensional objects on a Flash page is important, because Flash takes a different approach to placing objects on the Stage and the kinds of containers that hold the objects.

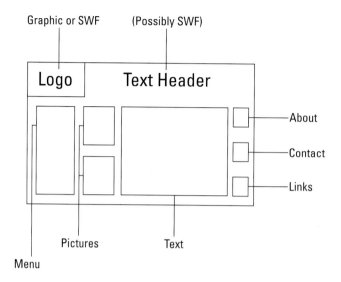

Figure 3-1: Begin with a simple drawing of what you want on a page.

Separating static and dynamic elements

The next step is separating the static materials (two-dimensional) from the dynamic (three-dimensional). *Static* materials don't change, which means that their content doesn't change. (For purposes of this discussion, static materials don't require ActionScript 3 to make changes.) *Dynamic* materials, on the other hand, must have some way of changing.

In looking at your initial sketch of your Web site, think about what won't change. To get you started, Table 3-1 lists some common static and dynamic elements.

Table 3-1	Static and Dynamic Elements
Static	*Dynamic*
Logo	Pictures
Header	About
Menu	Contact
	Links

You can place all static elements by positioning them on the Stage. In looking at these elements in Table 3-1, you can be pretty sure that the logo isn't going to change unless the client is a conglomerate that has several pages each with a different company sporting a unique logo. The header is a little more problematic, because it can be either static or dynamic (a header created with a dynamic text field, for example). Likewise, you may think of a menu as being a fairly stable element, but if the contents of the page change when other materials on the page do, the contents of the menu could change as well.

In Table 3-1, most elements listed are dynamic, and the static elements could be dynamic if the nature of the Web site changed. So you may want to use dynamic containers for all the elements and simply leave the static elements unchanged.

If you spend time creating a design, you probably don't want to reinvent the wheel every time you start a new application that's similar to one you've already made, or to rebuild an entire site to make a few changes.

Build every site with the assumption that it will change. In fact, build every site as though you *want* to make changes. Embrace fluidity even if you create a static site.

Laying out the parts

After you know which elements of your site will be static and which will be dynamic, you need to replace your rough drawing with actual objects. (Chapter 2 in this minibook shows a good cross section of the components you might want to use.) The design is quite simple, keeping the focus on the information design instead of the graphic design. (Good graphic design and information design aren't mutually exclusive, however — quite the opposite.)

Figure 3-2 shows the hand-drawn layout of Figure 3-1 replaced with actual content holders.

**Book VII
Chapter 3**

The Art and Science of Creating a Flash Application

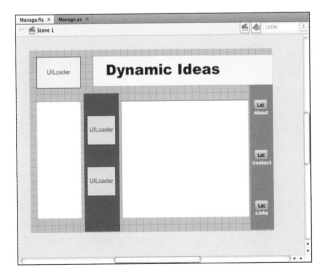

Figure 3-2: Flash page with rough layout of page elements.

UILoader components

Immediately, you see that the UILoader component is used in three places:

- ✔ Logo
- ✔ Picture 1
- ✔ Picture 2

You may wonder why we use a UILoader for the logo; after all, the logo is listed as a static element in Table 3-1, earlier in this chapter. Note that the sketch in Figure 3-1 shows that logo will be either a graphic or an .swf file. The UILoader component can load both graphic files and .swf files, so it provides a dynamic general-use container. Placing a bitmap image, vector graphic, or movie clip in the top-left corner of the Stage is perfectly functional, but when the time comes to make changes or add different content for a new site, you may wish that you had used a more dynamic container.

List component

The menu uses a List component. For this example, we could have used radio buttons, symbol buttons, Button components, or anything else that a user can click to change content, but we chose the List component because a single selection has both *label* and *data* content that can be used with ActionScript. The size of the menu in this example is based on the sketch in Figure 3-1, but if the menu requires only a few selections, we can go back and revise that space.

TextArea component

If the Flash site you're building will have lots of text, the size and position of the TextArea component may be a problem. Instead of having one big TextArea component, as in our example, you may want to use two smaller ones that explain what the pictures mean. Figure 3-3 shows two UILoader placeholders for images and the smaller TextArea components beneath. These small TextArea components act as extended captions.

As you can see, a little rearrangement and the addition of a second TextArea component alter the functionality of the sample page, but the Flash application maintains its basic style and look.

We created the examples in this section from a single sketch. In building a real site, however, we would use many more sketches to experiment with different ideas and looks. In all likelihood, we would have included a sketch with different arrangements and numbers of TextArea components.

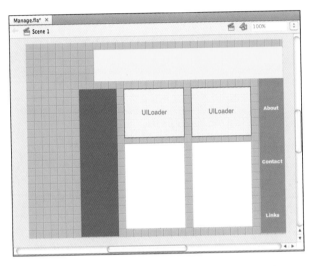

Figure 3-3: Alternative arrangement of picture holders and TextArea.

Header TextField

In our example, the TextField component that serves as the header is a static text field. If we used a dynamic text field instead, would the difference be significant? We don't see how. If we used a dynamic TextField component instead, we could incorporate the same design into other Flash applications that needed a dynamic header.

Button components

On the far right side of Figure 3-2, you see the little Button components that we added to the application. These components are so small that we had no room for labels inside the buttons, so we placed the labels in static TextField components below the buttons. (In a case like this, you may simply want to create new buttons.)

Also, you have to think about where the information from these buttons is going to be placed. The About button could place information in the TextArea component; so could the Contact button. The Links button is a bit more problematic. You could have a separate page appear with the links, or (using HTML text) you could place the links in the TextArea component.

Text labels

The final content holders in the example are the labels that we had to add for the buttons. We could have added other static labels where needed, but because the labels work with either Button components or with buttons created on the Stage or stored in the Library panel, we have other options.

Graphic elements and the grid

The graphic elements are nothing more than a few background rectangles that provide backdrops for the buttons and graphic holders. The 16-pixel squares that make up the grid are the default size in Flash CS4. Virtually every good design book suggests arranging elements on a grid, so if you don't use your grid, you may want to develop the habit of doing so.

Organizing the layout for ActionScript

The most dynamic site imaginable is one in which everything can be placed when you run your application. Using the position information from your rough layout of a page, you can write an ActionScript program that places all the elements you need on the Stage. You can use Flash components for everything other than the TextField class, which you develop wholly from code.

If you have both the Library and Component panels in the dock, you can have only one of these panels open at a time. But if you place a component on the Stage and then delete it, that component stays in the Library panel, so this method is an easy way to get the components you need into the Library.

Finding the coordinates

In Figure 3-2, all the components are laid out in the positions shown in the sketch in Figure 3-1 and resized to fit the area required. By selecting each component in your design and examining the values in the Properties panel, you can construct a table that contains all the coordinates information you need. Table 3-2 shows the instance names, x and y coordinates, and width and height of the components. Your own application will differ, but you need to make a record of similar information for the components in your layout.

Table 3-2	**Element Coordinates**				
Element	*Instance Name*	*X*	*Y*	*W*	*H*
UILoader	logo	16	16	80	80
List	menu	16	112	100	256
UILoader	pix1	130	144	64	64
UILoader	pix2	130	256	64	64
TextField	header	172	16	262	49
TextArea	ta	208	112	286	256
Button	b1	508	112	30	22
Button	b2	508	224	30	22
Button	b3	508	334	30	22

At this point, you should remove everything from the Stage except the underlying design and static text labels for the buttons.

Figure 3-4 shows what the application example looks like when all the elements that ActionScript 3 will generate are removed.

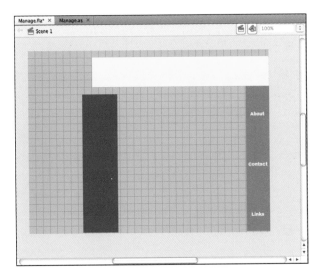

Figure 3-4: Base page.

Book VII
Chapter 3

The Art and Science of Creating a Flash Application

Placing the objects on the Stage

The next step is placing the dynamic elements of your page on the Stage. Follow these steps:

1. **Open a new ActionScript file and save it as `Manage.fla`.**

2. **Place the background elements of your application on the Stage.**

   For this example, use the elements shown in Figure 3-4, earlier in this chapter.

3. **Choose Window⇨Extensions⇨Kuler from the menu bar to open the Kuler panel.**

   For this example, type **Bordeaux** in the search window (the one with the little magnifying glass) of Kuler. After `Bordeaux` is found, select it and click the right-pointing arrow and choose Add to Swatches Panel. The following colors (using their hexadecimal values) appear in the Swatches panel:

   - *F7F2B2:* Header backdrop, button label
   - *ADCF4F:* Background
   - *84815B:* Button backdrop
   - *4A1A2C:* Header text
   - *8E3557:* Image backdrop

   Feel free to use a different Kuler palette or to design your own.

4. **Save the file.**

5. **Open the Properties panel, type** Manage **as the class name, and save the file again.**

   Dynamically created UILoader components have no visible parts when they're loaded to the Stage without any content, so you have to provide some.

6. **Using your favorite graphics program, create a UILoader placeholder.**

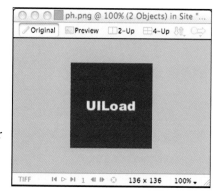

Figure 3-5: Placeholder for UILoad components.

   For this example, create a square, 136 x 136 pixels, colored burgundy (0x4A1A2C). Add the text label "UILoad", colored cream (0xF7F2B2). Then save the placeholder as ph.png in the same folder as the Manage.fla file. Figure 3-5 shows what the example looks like.

   If you don't have a graphics program handy, you can always use Flash CS4. For this example, a 136 x 136 square with the features specified in Step 6 will do the trick. Name it ph.swf. Later, when you write the ActionScript, use "ph.swf" instead of "ph.png" where you see source="ph.png".

7. **Open a new ActionScript file, and save it as Manage.as in the same folder as Manage.fla.**

8. **Using your coordinates table as a guide, enter ActionScript code to populate the Stage with dynamic containers.**

   For this example, use the coordinates in Table 3-2 to enter the following code:

```
package
{
    import flash.display.Sprite;
    import flash.text.TextField;
    import flash.text.TextFieldAutoSize;
    import flash.text.TextFormat;
    import flash.text.TextFieldType;
    import fl.containers.UILoader;
    import fl.controls.Button;
    import fl.controls.TextArea;
    import fl.controls.List;

    public class Manage extends Sprite
    {
        private var logo:UILoader;
        private var menu:List;
```

```
private var pix1:UILoader;
private var pix2:UILoader;
private var header:TextField;
private var ta:TextArea;
private var about:Button;
private var contact:Button;
private var links:Button;
private var textStyle:TextFormat;

public function Manage()
{
    logo=new UILoader();
    logo.scaleContent=true;
    logo.autoLoad=true;
    logo.source="ph.png";
    logo.x=16, logo.y=16;
    logo.width=80, logo.height=80;
    addChild(logo);

    menu=new List();
    menu.x=16, menu.y=112;
    menu.width=100, menu.height=256;
    addChild(menu);

    pix1=new UILoader();
    pix1.x=130, pix1.y=144;
    pix1.width=64, pix1.height=64;
    pix1.scaleContent=true;
    pix1.autoLoad=true;
    pix1.source="ph.png";
    addChild(pix1);

    pix2=new UILoader();
    pix2.x=130, pix2.y=256;
    pix2.width=64, pix2.height=64;
    pix2.scaleContent=true;
    pix2.autoLoad=true;
    pix2.source="ph.png";
    addChild(pix2);

    //TextFormat goes here

    header=new TextField ;
    header.type=TextFieldType.DYNAMIC;
    header.x=172, header.y=16;
    header.width=262,header.height=49;
    header.autoSize=TextFieldAutoSize.LEFT;
    header.selectable=false;
    header.textColor=0x4A1A2C;
    header.text="Dynamic Ideas";
    addChild(header);

    ta=new TextArea();
    ta.x=208, ta.y=112;
```

Book VII
Chapter 3

The Art and Science
of Creating a Flash
Application

```
                    ta.width=286, ta.height=256;
                    addChild(ta);

                    //Buttons
                    about=new Button();
                    about.x=508, about.y=112;
                    about.width=30, about.height=22;
                    about.label="|";
                    addChild(about);

                    contact=new Button();
                    contact.x=508, contact.y=224;
                    contact.width=30, contact.height=22;
                    contact.label="|";
                    addChild(contact);

                    links=new Button();
                    links.x=508, links.y=334;
                    links.width=30, links.height=22;
                    links.label="|";
                    addChild(links);

                }
                //handler functions go here
            }
        }
```

9. **Save the file.**

10. **Test the application.**

At this point, the example looks like Figure 3-6.

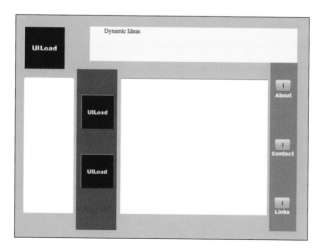

Figure 3-6: Dynamically created elements on the Stage.

In looking at Figure 3-6, you see immediately that the header text is the wrong size and not necessarily in the font you want. (It certainly is different from the example shown in Figure 3-2.) Nevertheless, what you see is very close to the initial sketch. You can remedy the problems by adding a section of code that takes care of styling issues.

Styling Code

In the preceding section, you may have noticed that a comment in the code reserved some space for styling. You may think of style as being a static feature of any page, but like content in a Flash page, style can also be dynamic. In this particular case, we're not suggesting making a dynamic change to a page's style, but pointing out that style is in fact a dynamic element because it can be changed after the page is launched.

In this section, you see how to set the style of the elements on the page.

Formatting the TextField class with the TextFormat class

To format text in a TextField object, you must adopt a TextFormat object. The TextFormat class has the following properties (among others) that you need to format text just the way you want it:

**Book VII
Chapter 3**

**The Art and Science
of Creating a Flash
Application**

- bold
- color
- font
- italic
- size

To work its magic, the TextFormat instance is assigned to a TextField instance, using this statement:

```
MyTextField.defaultTextFormat=MyTextFormat;
```

So all that's necessary is to add the styles you want to the TextFormat instance and then assign the whole thing to the TextField instance. (Those among you who are sharp of eye will notice a little overlap with one of the properties. We'd never dream of insulting your intelligence by pointing out which property that is, though.)

In the application example, you haven't specified a font. Some fonts, such as Arial Black are big and bold to begin with, so you may not have to specify that the font is bold — as you'd expect for header text. You have to add to the script in the Manage.as file to get the style you want for the header.

By great good fortune, you've declared a variable, `textStyle:TextFormat`, that you can use. The necessary class import of TextFormat has been taken care of as well. So all you need to do is to find the commented line

```
//TextFormat goes here
```

and add the following code just below it:

```
textStyle=new TextFormat();
textStyle.font="Arial Black";
textStyle.size=32;
textStyle.color=0x4A1A2C;
```

Next, right after the line

```
header=new TextField();
```

add this line:

```
header.defaultTextFormat=textStyle;
```

You're good to go. Test the application again, and you should see what you do in Figure 3-7.

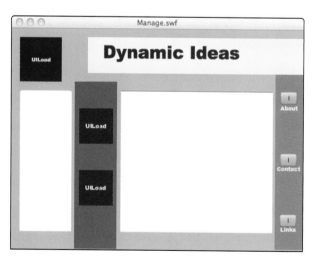

Figure 3-7: Styling a TextField instance with a TextFormat instance.

Applying dynamic text style to UI components

Reformatting the text in a TextField is easy. All you have to do is whip up a TextFormat you like and apply it to the TextField instance. Can you do the same with UI components? Fortunately, the answer is yes. (You knew that. We can't surprise you no matter what!)

If you look at the ActionScript 3.0 Reference that jumps up when you click the Help icon in an ActionScript file, you can find the UIComponent class — the parent class for all the UI components discussed in this chapter. For most classes, you find properties and methods, as well as events that can be used with the class. For the UIComponent class, you find four types of styles:

- disabledTextFormat
- focusRectPadding
- focusRectSkin
- textFormat

Of these four styles, all you need is the textFormat style. With it, you can apply styles from a TextFormat class. So you can not only style the text in your UI components but also use the TextFormat class to do so. (In other words, you don't have to find out about a whole separate class to style the text in UI components.)

The little things always get people in trouble. The class TextFormat uses an uppercase *T,* and the style textFormat uses a lowercase *t.* This difference is little, but it may jump up and get you when you least expect it.

Following is the general format for adding a text format to a UI component:

```
var uiFormat:TextFormat = new TextFormat();
uiFormat.property="value"
uiComponent.setStyle("textFormat", uiFormat);
```

The property can be any of the TextFormat class properties, such as `font`, `color`, and `size`.

This example shows you how to set the text style for a Label component. Follow these steps:

1. **Open a new ActionScript file, and save it as `LabelStyle.fla`.**

2. **Type** LabelStyle **in the Class box of the Properties panel, and save the file again.**

3. **Open a new ActionScript file, and save it as `LabelStyle.as`.**

4. **Enter the following code:**

```
package
{
  import fl.controls.Label;
  import flash.display.Sprite;
  import flash.text.TextFormat;
```

```
public class LabelStyle extends Sprite
{
    private var labFormat:TextFormat;
    private var formLabel:Label;

    public function LabelStyle()
    {
        labFormat=new TextFormat();
        labFormat.font="Comic Sans MS";
        //labFormat.font="Blackoak Std";
        labFormat.size=24;
        labFormat.bold=true;
        labFormat.color=0xcc0000;

        formLabel=new Label();
        formLabel.x=100,formLabel.y=100;
        formLabel.height=36;
        formLabel.width=150;
        formLabel.text="Styled Label";
        formLabel.setStyle("textFormat",labFormat);
        addChild(formLabel);
    }
}
}
```

5. Save the file.

6. Test the application.

When you do, you should see the output shown in Figure 3-8.

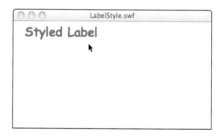

Figure 3-8: Label UI component with styled text.

In looking at the ActionScript, notice that the size of the font is set to 24 points (`labFormat.size=24`) and that the height of the Label component is set to 36 (`formLabel.height=36`). The reason for those settings is that font designs determine the actual size. If you used a small font like Times New Roman, you would have been able to set the Label height to 24, and everything would have fit fine. Comic Sans MS, however, is designed for use as a display font. Display fonts tend to be larger in both height and width; they're typically used in headers, because their size attracts the user's attention. A typical body-text font like Times New Roman, though, will fit, based on matching the font size to the Label text container.

Likewise, fonts take up different amounts of horizontal space. If your system has a large font such as Blackoak Std, change the lines to use the larger font, as follows:

```
//labFormat.font="Comic Sans MS";
labFormat.font="Blackoak Std";
```

Test the application again. This time, you see the image shown in Figure 3-9.

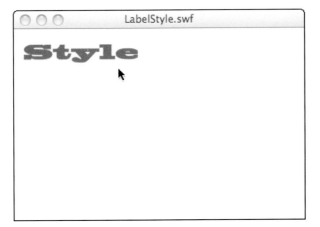

Figure 3-9: Label UI component with styled text.

Because Blackoak Std is a wider font than Comic Sans MS, you would have to change the width of the Label component to see all the label text. The heights of the two fonts are close to the same, however. When you use different fonts with UI components, you have to make adjustments based on the font family in use *and* the selected font size.

Styling the Button components

In the fast world of the Internet, you often see icons on buttons to show the user at a glance what those buttons are for. In this section, you see how to add graphic characters to buttons by using the Wingdings font, which features graphic symbols instead of just alphanumeric characters. (*Note:* The Wingdings font is a common graphics font. If you don't have it in your system, use another with symbols of your own choosing.)

The plan is to place the following symbols from the Wingdings font on the buttons in the application example:

Button	*Symbol*	*Code*
About	👓	[$]
Contact	☎	[(]
Links	≈	[h]

The About button has a pair of reading glasses next to it; Contact, a telephone; and Links, a couple of wavy lines. In the code, you use the character to the right in brackets.

Make changes to the button-code section where you see the line

```
//Buttons
```

Replace the existing code with the following in that section of the `Manage.as` file:

```
//Buttons
btnFormat=new TextFormat();
btnFormat.font="Wingdings";
btnFormat.size=16;

about=new Button();
about.label="$";
about.setStyle("textFormat", btnFormat);
about.x=508, about.y=112;
about.width=30, about.height=22;
addChild(about);

contact=new Button();
contact.label="(";
contact.setStyle("textFormat", btnFormat);
contact.x=508, contact.y=224;
contact.width=30, contact.height=22;
addChild(contact);

links=new Button();
links.label="h";
links.setStyle("textFormat", btnFormat);
links.x=508, links.y=334;
links.width=30, links.height=22;
addChild(links);
```

Save the file, and test your application. Figure 3-10 shows what the buttons in the sample application should look like.

Adding selections to the List component

Next, you need to turn to the blank menu and see what you can do about adding content. For the application example, use the following list of services:

- Site Architecture
- Graphic Design
- Flash Animations
- ActionScript 3.0 Development
- Video Development
- Streaming Video
- Site Conversion

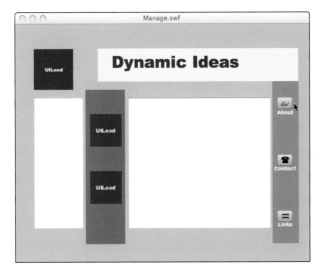

Figure 3-10: Buttons with styled text.

To add content to a List component, you need a DataProvider object. Next, you add the menu selections to the DataProvider. Finally, you assign the DataProvider to the List.dataProvider and all the data to the List object.

You create and add data to a DataProvider instance by using the following format:

```
var appData:DataProvider=new DataProvider();
appData.addItem({label:"Row Name", data: 22});
```

The first element is the label that appears in the List as a row name; the second value, data, is a numeric or string value. In this example, the List component would display "Row Name" and the data value 22.

Next, to assign the data in the data provider to a List component, you use the following format:

```
appList.dataProvider=appData;
```

List.dataProvider is a List property, so a simple assignment is all you need.

In the application example, the List has the instance name menu, so all you have to do is add the items to the data provider and then assign the data provider to menu. First, though, you need to import the DataProvider, so add the following line to the list of import statements:

```
import fl.data.DataProvider;
```

Where you have all the private variables lined up, attach the following to the bottom of the list:

```
private var menuData:DataProvider;
```

Now you're ready to change the menu ActionScript in the Manage.as file:

```
//Menu data and menu
var asd:String="ActionScript \n3.0 Development";
menuData=new DataProvider();
menuData.addItem({label:"Site Architecture"});
menuData.addItem({label:"Graphic Design"});
menuData.addItem({label:"Flash Animations"});
menuData.addItem({label: asd});
menuData.addItem({label:"Video \nDevelopment"});
menuData.addItem({label:"Streaming Video"});
menuData.addItem({label:"Site Conversion"});

menu=new List();
menu.rowHeight=36
menu.rowCount=7;
menu.labelField="label";
menu.dataProvider=menuData;
menu.x=16,menu.y=112;
menu.width=100,menu.height=256;
addChild(menu);
```

Save the changes you made, and test the application. This time, you see menu selections for the List component, as shown in Figure 3-11.

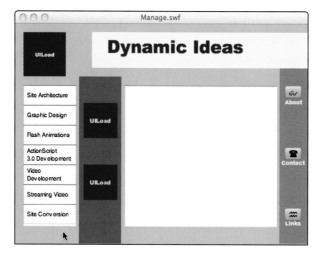

Figure 3-11: Menu choices added dynamically.

As you see in Figure 3-11, two menu selections take up two lines: ActionScript 3.0 Development and Video Development. By establishing a row height of 36, you have plenty of room to have text on two lines in a single row. Rather than make the List component wider, all you need to do is use the \n character to inject a line break.

Adding text to the TextArea component

Your last task in the application example is to get some text to the TextArea component and add the style you want. In Chapter 2 of this minibook, you see how to pull data out of a text file and display it in a TextArea component. You do that again in this section and at the same time add some style.

At this stage, you've made so many changes that we decided to provide the entire code for the Manage.as file. In this way, you can see how everything works together without having to flip back and forth too much. Just follow these steps:

1. **Replace the current `Manage.as` code with the following code:**

    ```
    package
    {
        import flash.display.Sprite;
        import flash.text.TextField;
        import flash.text.TextFieldAutoSize;
        import flash.text.TextFormat;
        import flash.text.TextFieldType;
        import fl.containers.UILoader;
        import fl.controls.Button;
        import fl.controls.TextArea;
        import fl.controls.List;
        import fl.data.DataProvider;
        import flash.net.URLLoader;
        import flash.net.URLRequest;
        import flash.net.URLLoaderDataFormat;
        import flash.events.Event;

        public class Manage extends Sprite
        {
            private var logo:UILoader;
            private var menu:List;
            private var pix1:UILoader;
            private var pix2:UILoader;
            private var header:TextField;
            private var ta:TextArea;
            private var about:Button;
            private var contact:Button;
            private var links:Button;
            private var headerText:String;
            private var asd:String;
            private var textStyle:TextFormat;
            private var btnFormat:TextFormat;
            private var taFormat:TextFormat;
            private var menuData:DataProvider;
            private var taLoader:URLLoader;
            private var textURL:String;
    ```

```
public function Manage()
{
    //Holder for logo
    logo=new UILoader();
    logo.scaleContent=true;
    logo.autoLoad=true;
    logo.source="ph.swf";
    logo.x=16,logo.y=16;
    logo.width=80,logo.height=80;
    addChild(logo);

    //Menu data provider
    asd="ActionScript \n3.0 Development";
    menuData=new DataProvider();
    menuData.addItem({label:"Site Architecture"});
    menuData.addItem({label:"Graphic Design"});
    menuData.addItem({label:"Flash Animations"});
    menuData.addItem({label:asd});
    menuData.addItem({label:"Video \nDevelopment"});
    menuData.addItem({label:"Streaming Video"});
    menuData.addItem({label:"Site Conversion"});

    //Create menu
    menu=new List();
    menu.rowHeight=36;
    menu.rowCount=7;
    menu.labelField="label";
    menu.dataProvider=menuData;
    menu.x=16,menu.y=112;
    menu.width=100,menu.height=256;
    addChild(menu);

    //Create two image containers
    pix1=new UILoader();
    pix1.x=130,pix1.y=144;
    pix1.width=64,pix1.height=64;
    pix1.scaleContent=true;
    pix1.autoLoad=true;
    pix1.source="ph.png";
    addChild(pix1);

    pix2=new UILoader();
    pix2.x=130,pix2.y=256;
    pix2.width=64,pix2.height=64;
    pix2.scaleContent=true;
    pix2.autoLoad=true;
    pix2.source="ph.png";
    addChild(pix2);

    //TextFormat goes here
    textStyle=new TextFormat();
    textStyle.font="Arial Black";
    textStyle.size=32;
    textStyle.color=0x4A1A2C;

    //Create header
    headerText="Dynamic Ideas";
    header=new TextField();
    header.defaultTextFormat=textStyle;
    header.type=TextFieldType.DYNAMIC;
    header.x=172,header.y=16;
    header.width=262,header.height=49;
```

```
            header.autoSize=TextFieldAutoSize.LEFT;
            header.selectable=false;
            header.textColor=0x4A1A2C;
            header.text=headerText;
            addChild(header);

            //Format style for TextArea content
            taFormat=new TextFormat();
            taFormat.font="Verdana";
            taFormat.size=11;
            taFormat.bold=false;
            taFormat.color=0x4A1A2C;

            //Create TextArea component
            ta=new TextArea();
            ta.editable=false;
            ta.x=208,ta.y=112;
            ta.width=286,ta.height=256;
            addChild(ta);

            //Create loader for TextArea
            taLoader=new URLLoader();
            taLoader.dataFormat=URLLoaderDataFormat.TEXT;
            taLoader.addEventListener(Event.COMPLETE,taText);
            textURL="text.txt";
            taLoader.load(new URLRequest(textURL));
            ta.setStyle("textFormat", taFormat);

            //Format for buttons
            btnFormat=new TextFormat();
            btnFormat.font="Wingdings";
            btnFormat.size=16;

            //About, Contact and Links buttons
            about=new Button();
            about.label="$";
            about.setStyle("textFormat", btnFormat);
            about.x=508,about.y=112;
            about.width=30,about.height=22;
            addChild(about);

            contact=new Button();
            contact.label="(";
            contact.setStyle("textFormat", btnFormat);
            contact.x=508,contact.y=224;
            contact.width=30,contact.height=22;
            addChild(contact);

            links=new Button();
            links.label="h";
            links.setStyle("textFormat", btnFormat);
            links.x=508,links.y=334;
            links.width=30,links.height=22;
            addChild(links);
        }
        //handler functions go here
        private function taText(e:Event):void
        {
            ta.text=e.target.data;
        }
    }
}
```

2. **Create a text file using Notepad (or TextEdit on the Mac), and enter the following text:**

   All the text that goes into the TextArea component should be consistent with the design of the application. In this case, a sans serif font, Verdana, is used because it is easy to read — primarily because it was designed to be used for viewing on a computer screen. The 11-point font size is easily readable but doesn't take up an inordinate amount of space.

   Information from the About, Contact, and Links buttons could use this space as well. Each could load an appropriate text file to tell the viewer about the selected information.

   You can also use selections from the Menu to add material in this space as well as bring up appropriate images to accompany the text. Because the image holders are adjacent to this text, the association is better enforced.

3. **Save the file as `text.txt`.**

4. **Place the `text.txt` file in the same folder as the `Manage.fla` file.**

   Figure 3-12 shows what you see.

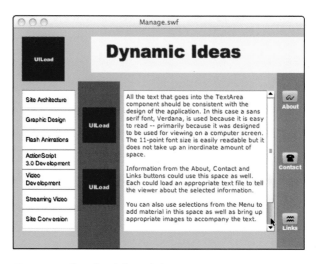

Figure 3-12: Completed dynamic layout.

ActionScript provides a great deal of flexibility for developing dynamic Flash applications. For some people, this approach may appear to be a great deal more work than a static layout should require. Remember, however, that other than the few things placed on the Stage, the entire application is dynamic. Now you can develop virtually everything on a page by using code and change it while the application is running.

Chapter 4: Up in the AIR

In This Chapter

⮑ **Understanding AIR applications**

⮑ **Working with AIR files**

⮑ **Converting Flash to AIR**

⮑ **Writing AIR-only ActionScript applications**

*B*esides using Flash on the Internet, you can use Flash as a desktop application, just as you would your word processor or favorite game. While Adobe AIR was introduced in Flash CS3, using it in Flash CS4 is even simpler and more robust. The idea behind AIR is that if you have developed a skill set for an Internet application such as Flash, you can leverage that skill to make applications that run directly from the desktop without having to have Flash open and running.

The AIR on Your Desktop

Flash CS4 lets you create AIR applications, just as you would create any other Flash application to run on a Web hosting service. What's more, ActionScript 3 classes that are available for exclusive use with AIR allow you to do things on your desktop that may be difficult or impossible to do on the Internet. So you're getting bonus classes by creating AIR applications.

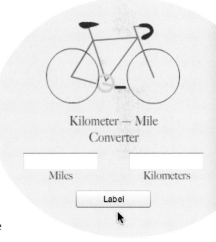

You'll be surprised by how easily you can develop AIR applications. If you want, you can even convert existing Flash applications to AIR versions, as you see later in this chapter.

If you don't already have AIR, download it from www.adobe.com. It's a free application, and you can use it with Adobe Dreamweaver and applications other than Flash CS4.

Making a Simple AIR Application

To get up and running with AIR, in this section you create a simple application that uses standard Flash and ActionScript. The application, which converts miles to kilometers and kilometers to miles, is a conversion program for bicyclists who compete in both American and European cycling events. It helps users get an intuitive feel for the length of the cycling course by converting it to the units of measurement with which they feel most comfortable, and it's simple to use: If the user enters values in the miles box, any values in the kilometer box are cleared, and vice versa.

Creating the Flash file

In this first set of steps, you create a Flash file. Because certain subtle differences exist, we go into a little more detail than usual to keep you on track. Follow these steps:

1. **Open a new AIR file, as shown in Figure 4-1.**

2. **Save the file as `KlickConvert.fla`.**

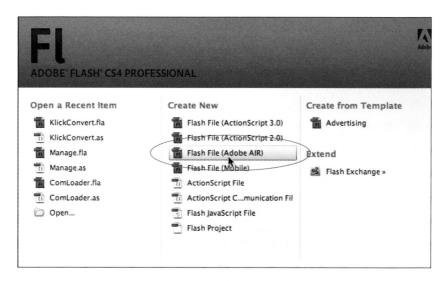

Figure 4-1: Opening a new AIR file.

3. **Open the Properties panel, type** KlickConvert **in the Class window, and save the file again.**

4. **Set the background color to E5DFC2 (tan), and put the following colors in the Swatches panel for easy access:**

   - F0D513 (yellow)

   - D40022 (red)

   - 61261E (brown)

   - E5DFC2 (tan)

   Check out Book II, Chapter 2 for details on using hexadecimal values for colors.

5. **Use the Oval, Paint, and Line tools to draw an abstract bicycle, using the colors in the Swatches panel.**

   Figure 4-2 shows a simple bicycle drawing.

6. **Select the image and convert it to a symbol by choosing Modify⇨Convert to Symbol from the menu bar (or press F8) to open the Convert to Symbol dialog box.**

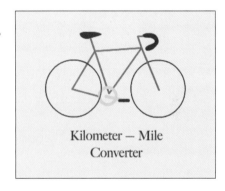

Figure 4-2: Graphic image in symbol format.

Book VII
Chapter 4

Up in the AIR

7. **Place the image in the top center of the Stage (refer to Figure 4-2). Below it, add the static text** Kilometer – Mile Converter **and save the file.**

8. **Drag two TextInput components and one Button component to the Stage.**

9. **Place one TextInput component on the left side of the Stage and give it the instance name** miles **in the Properties panel; place the other TextInput component on the right side of the Stage and give it the instance name** klicks.

10. **Add the static text** Miles **below the left TextInput component and the static text** Kilometers **below the right TextInput component.**

    At this point, your application should look like the one shown in Figure 4-2.

11. **Center the Button component on the Stage below the two TextInput components, and give it the instance name** convert **in the Properties panel (see Figure 4-3).**

12. **Save the file.**

Figure 4-3: A completed application.

Creating the ActionScript file

Now you're ready to create the ActionScript. Follow these steps:

1. **Open a new ActionScript file, and save it as** KlickConvert.as **in the same folder as the** KlickConvert.fla **file.**

2. **Add the following code:**

```
package
{
    import flash.display.Sprite;
    import flash.events.MouseEvent;
    import flash.events.FocusEvent;

    public class KlickConvert extends Sprite
    {
        private var distance:Number;

        public function KlickConvert()
        {
            convert.label="Convert";
            klicks.addEventListener(FocusEvent.FOCUS_IN,clearMiles);
```

```
        miles.addEventListener(FocusEvent.FOCUS_IN,clearKlicks);
        convert.addEventListener(MouseEvent.CLICK, doConvert);
    }

    private function clearMiles(e:FocusEvent):void
    {
        miles.text="";
    }

    private function clearKlicks(e:FocusEvent):void
    {
        klicks.text="";
    }

    private function doConvert(e:MouseEvent):void
    {
        if (klicks.text=="")
        {
            distance=Number(miles.text)*1.61;
            klicks.text=distance.toFixed(2);
        }
        else
        {
            distance=Number(klicks.text)/1.61;
            miles.text=distance.toFixed(2);
        }
    }
}
}
```

3. **Save the `KlickConvert.as` file.**

4. **Test the application as you would any other Flash file.**

    As soon as you enter a number in one of the TextInput boxes, the application clears the text in the other box. The algorithm is set up to multiply or divide by 1.6, depending on which TextInput component is selected. Figure 4-4 shows what you can expect to see.

Notice that the Output panel shows the following:

```
[SWF] KlickConvert.swf - 41873 bytes after decompression
```

This message is characteristic of an AIR application. When the test is complete, the Output panel adds the following:

```
Test Movie terminated.
```

That message, too, is characteristic of an AIR application. When you see those messages, you know you're on the right track.

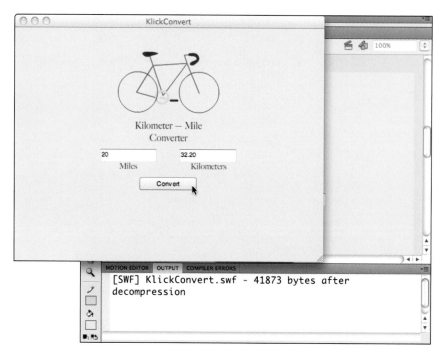

Figure 4-4: Converting miles to kilometers.

Publishing the AIR file

Unlike publishing a regular Flash file, publishing a Flash file as an AIR file is a bit more involved. In this section, you publish as an AIR file the Flash file you created in the preceding sections. Follow these steps.

1. **Select the KlickConvert.fla file and choose File⇨AIR Settings.**

   The AIR – Application & Installer Settings dialog box appears.

2. **Fill out the dialog box as shown in Figure 4-5.**

   The first four windows are filled out for you. Adding a description and copyright are optional. Likewise, the Destination and Included files are filled out.

3. **Click the Publish AIR File button.**

   The Digital Signature dialog box appears, as shown in Figure 4-6.

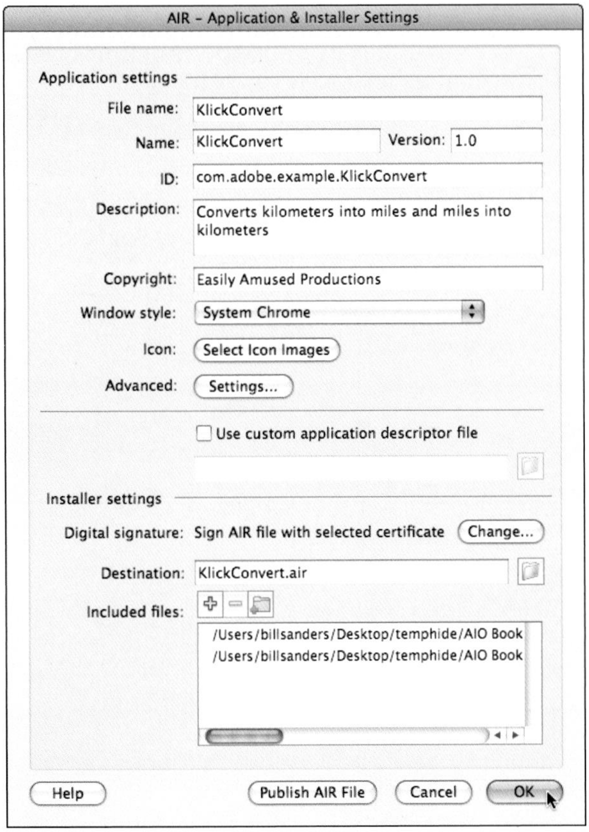

Figure 4-5: The AIR – Application & Installer Settings dialog box.

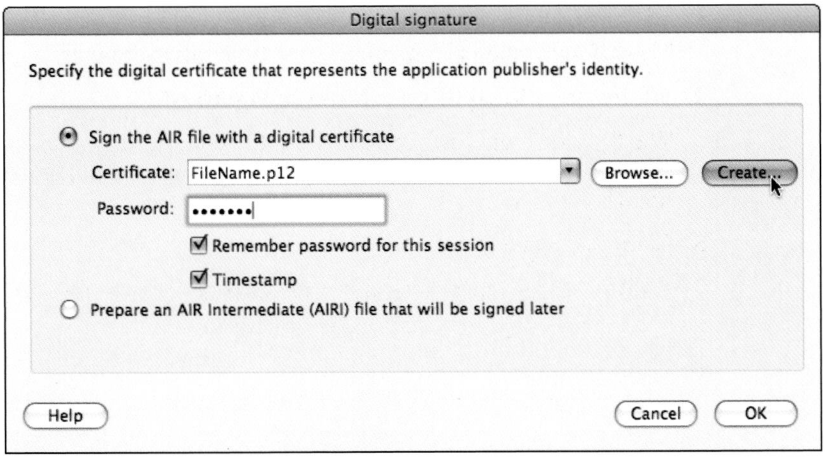

Figure 4-6: Setting up a digital signature.

4. **Click the Create button to the right of the Certificate box.**

   (After you create other digital certificates, you can browse for them or choose them from the pull-down Certificate menu in this dialog box.)

   The Create Self-Signed Digital Certificate dialog box opens (see Figure 4-7).

Figure 4-7: Creating a digital certificate.

5. **When you fill out the dialog box, fill out all windows. Click OK when you're finished.**

   You can use any name your want for the publisher name, organizational unit, and organization name. Then select a country from the pop-up menu and add and confirm a password. Leave the type as 1024-RSA, and save it as a name of your selection. As soon as you click OK, the digital certificate is complete.

6. **After you click OK for the digital certificate, click OK for both dialog boxes — Create Self-Signed Digital Certificate and AIR – Application & Installer Settings.**

   Your AIR application is now created.

Installing and testing the application

To install the AIR file on your computer to run as a standard application, follow these steps:

1. **Open the location where you saved your AIR file.**

   Figure 4-8 shows the group of files that are created when you create an AIR file. Notice that the group contains an `.xml` and an `.air` file in addition to the files you usually see in a Flash application. The `.xml` file holds the information you entered for your digital signature.

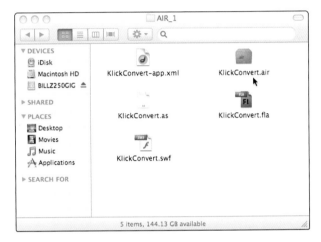

Figure 4-8: Group of files created in the AIR application.

**Book VII
Chapter 4**

Up in the AIR

2. **Double-click the `KlickConvert.air` file.**

   The Application Install dialog box appears (see Figure 4-9).

   You're the publisher, so you shouldn't have to concern yourself with the Publisher Identity warning. With unrestricted System Access, however, you may want to be careful. Later, if you believe that the application opened the door to Internet gremlins, repeat this install procedure to uninstall any installed AIR program.

3. **Click the Install button.**

   The Installation Preferences page of the Application Install dialog box opens.

4. **From the pull-down menu, choose the location where you want to install the application, and check or clear the check box to specify whether you want to start the application after installation (see Figure 4-10).**

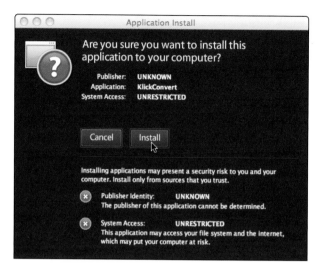

Figure 4-9: Start page of the Application Install dialog box.

Figure 4-10: Choosing the installation directory.

5. **Click Continue.**

   At this point, you should see the application icon (or its name in a list) in the directory you specified, as shown in Figure 4-11. The icon has the AIR logo and the `.app` extension.

6. **Double-click the icon to launch your application.**

Figure 4-11: Your AIR application in the directory.

Given the power and extent of both Flash and ActionScript, your capacity to create professional applications is similar to that provided by languages such as C++ and Java.

Converting Standard Flash Applications to AIR

In addition to creating an AIR application from scratch, you can take one of your old Flash applications and convert it to AIR. This ability opens your entire library of applications for use on the desktop.

We refer to an example application from the book. However, you can use the same process for any Flash application you already created. Chapter 2 of this minibook is an application named `Simple.fla` (which is available for downloading from `www.dummies.com/go/flashallinone`). It includes List and Label components. As each item is selected in the List, it is totaled in the Label — a calculator that totals how much fruit you've purchased. A separate `Simple.as` file contains the code. Make copies of the FLA and the ActionScript files you convert. The following steps show you all you need to do to convert these files so that they can be installed on your computer and run as AIR applications (you don't have to change any of the ActionScript 3.0):

Book VII Chapter 4

Up in the AIR

1. **Open a new Flash (Adobe AIR) file and save it.**

   The example we used was saved as `SimpleAIR.fla` in the Convert2AIR folder. In the Properties panel, we typed `Simple` for the class name. You use the same ActionScript 3.0 file (we used `Simple.as`) with no changes. We saved the file `SimpleAIR.fla` again. Be sure to leave it open, though.

2. **Open the FLA file. Make sure that all layers are unlocked. Press Ctrl+A (⌘+A on the Mac) to select all the objects.**

   We opened the `Simple.fla` file.

3. **Select the tab or window with the FLA file you're using and press Shift+Ctrl+V (⌘+V on the Mac) to paste everything from the original FLA file to the new AIR file. Save the file.**

   We copied the stage of `Simple.fla` and pasted it into the `SimpleAIR.fla` file.

4. **Choose File⇨AIR Settings from the File menu and follow Steps 1 through 6 from the previous section.**

After you're finished, you can run the application on your desktop. It looks and acts no different from the Flash CS4 version when you test it. Also note that you will have both a new `.xml` and `.air` file. (We had `SimpleAIR-app.xml` and `SimpleAIR.air` in the `Convert2AIR` folder.) You will find that most applications can be converted to AIR by using the same method.

Made for AIR: Using ActionScript Exclusively for AIR

When ActionScript 3 was released, several classes were created exclusively for AIR applications. Many actions that are common in desktop applications wouldn't work the same way if they were used with Internet applications, so rather than limiting AIR applications to what would make sense for Web applications, Adobe created a special subset for AIR.

In this section, you find out how to use some of the AIR classes created exclusively (members *only*) for AIR. Using these special AIR classes, you can do things that you cannot do with applications in Flash created for the Web. The few AIR classes we examine provide you with far more capability than using non-AIR Flash.

Open the ActionScript 3.0 Language and Component Reference site by opening an ActionScript file and clicking on the question mark icon (?) at the top of the window. When the ActionScript 3.0 Language and Component Reference site is open make sure that frames are enabled. Then find and open the File class. Figure 4-12 shows what you see.

The little red icons next to several of the classes indicate that they are AIR-only classes. File, FileListEvent, FileMode, and FileStream, for example, can be used with Flash AIR applications but not with non-AIR Flash projects. They simply don't work on the Web.

To see how to work with AIR ActionScript, in the following section you create a simple application that allows you to read the directories on your computer. To make it more interesting, all the directories are displayed in a List component. This application illustrates that filename information can be placed in a selectable container, which has implications for more sophisticated file work on your system.

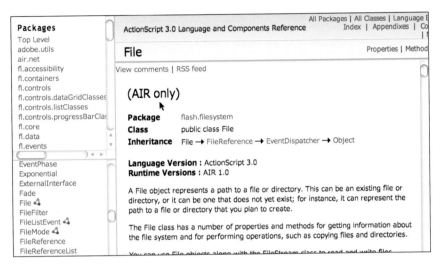

Figure 4-12: Some ActionScript is for AIR applications only.

Making a Desktop AIR Browser

**Book VII
Chapter 4**

Up in the AIR

The main practical purpose of this application is placing file names in a List component for future development. But you also can use the application to look at different parts of your computer without disrupting your desktop or losing your place in an open folder that you're using. To get started, you look into the AIR-only File class.

Using the File class

For this particular use of the File class, you create a File instance, just as you would with any other class, but you're going to do something a little different.

The File class has three directory properties:

✓ documentsDirectory

✓ desktopDirectory

✓ userDirectory

When you declare a File instance, you can do it just as you would any other instance. For this application, you use the name `folder` for the File instance name, declared as follows:

```
private var folder:File;
```

When the variable is instantiated, however, you include the property:

```
folder=File.documentsDirectory;
```

Two differences are important to notice:

⮑ **The new statement wasn't included.** Typically, you expect to see

```
folder= new File();
```

The new statement is unused in the instantiation.

⮑ **The type of directory — a property of the File class — is included in the instantiation.**

Including the name of the directory property isn't a general feature of all AIR classes; it's unique to File when you're creating a specific kind of directory. FileStream, for example, is another AIR class, and you declare it by using the new statement:

```
private var fStream:FileStream;
fStream = new FileStream();
```

So although you can instantiate File instances without using new and include a class property in the process, doing so isn't typical of all AIR classes.

Creating the AIR application

You should treat this application like any other AIR or Flash project. Using special AIR-only ActionScript changes nothing, other than the fact that you must use an AIR file.

Setting up the AIR file

To set up the AIR file for the application, follow these steps:

1. **Open a new AIR file and save it as `BrowsePod.fla`.**

2. **Add the following colors to the Swatches panel:**
   - 91003A (red)
   - 0B4C9F (blue)
   - C8A67A (tan)

3. **Open the Properties panel and enter BrowsePod as the class name.**

4. **Choose Window⇨Properties (Ctrl+F3, ⌘+F3 on the Mac) from the menu bar to open the Properties panel. Add the tan from the Swatches panel for the Stage color in the Properties panel and save the file.**

5. **Add a layer to the timeline, and name the top layer** Components **and the bottom layer** Background.

   Book I, Chapter 2 describes how to work with layers.

6. **Lock the Components layer.**

7. **Click the Background layer; and draw a blue rectangle with the dimensions w=550, h=32; and position it at x=0, y=59.**

8. **Lock the Background layer.**

9. **Drag a Button component to the Stage, centering it on the blue rectangle, and give it the instance name** browse **in the Properties panel.**

10. **Drag a List component to the Stage, centering it below the blue rectangle; set the dimensions to w=200, h=240; and give it the instance name** list **in the Properties panel.**

11. **Save the file.**

12. **Centered above the button, add** Desktop Browser **in static 24-point red text. Then save the file again.**

    Figure 4-13 shows how the Stage should appear.

**Book VII
Chapter 4**

Up in the AIR

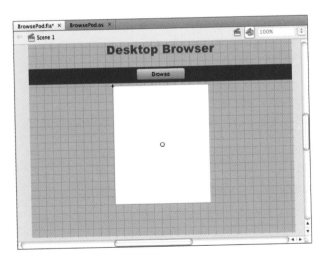

Figure 4-13: Component and color-scheme layout.

Entering the ActionScript

Now you add the ActionScript. Follow these steps:

1. **Open a new ActionScript file, and save it as `BrowsePod.as` in the same folder as the `BrowsePod.fla` file.**

2. **Enter the following code:**

```
package
{
    import flash.display.Sprite;
    import flash.filesystem.File;
    import flash.events.Event;
    import flash.events.MouseEvent;
    import flash.text.TextFormat;

    public class BrowsePod extends Sprite
    {
        private var folder:File;
        private var files:Array;
        private var browseFormat:TextFormat;

        public function BrowsePod()
        {
            folder=File.documentsDirectory;
            //folder=File.desktopDirectory;
            //folder=File.userDirectory;

            browse.addEventListener(MouseEvent.CLICK, showDir);

            browseFormat=new TextFormat();
            browseFormat.color=0x91003A;
            browse.setStyle("textFormat",browseFormat);
        }

        private function showDir(e:MouseEvent):void
        {
            try
            {
                folder.browseForDirectory("Select Folder");
                folder.addEventListener(Event.SELECT, folderSelected);
            }
            catch (error:Error)
            {
                trace("Arrrrg!:", error.message);
            }
        }

        private function folderSelected(e:Event):void
        {
            list.removeAll();
            folder=e.target as File;
            files=folder.getDirectoryListing();
            for (var fli:uint = 0; fli < files.length; fli++)
            {
                list.addItem({ label:files[fli].name});
            }
        }
    }
}
```

Completing the application

To finish the application, follow these steps:

1. **Select the `BrowsePod.fla` tab (or window) and choose File➪AIR Settings.**

    The AIR – Application & Installer Settings dialog box opens.

2. **Fill out the dialog box as described in Steps 2 through 6 in the section "Publishing the AIR file" (earlier in the chapter) and in Figures 4-4 through 4-14.**

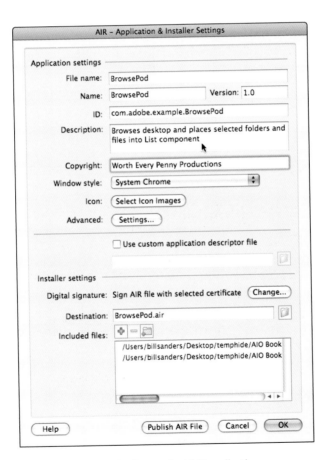

Figure 4-14: Settings for BrowsePod AIR application.

3. **Click the Publish AIR File button.**

    This time, you see that a certificate has been provided for you (assuming that you're using the same computer and Flash application).

4. **Enter a password and click OK.**

   You should find `BrowsePod.air` in your application folder.

5. **Double-click the BrowsePod.air icon to install the application on your computer.**

   A warning page appears.

6. **Click OK.**

   You see the Application Install dialog box, shown in Figure 4-15.

   This figure is slightly different from the image shown in Figure 4-10, earlier in this chapter, because Figure 4-11 was taken on a Macintosh and Figure 4-15 was taken on a Windows Vista PC. The Windows version gives you the additional option of adding a shortcut icon to the desktop. (The default installation location also is different for the two platforms.)

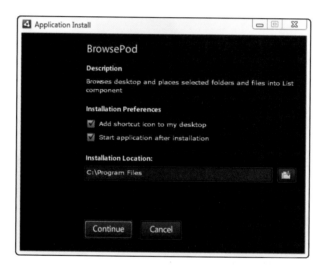

Figure 4-15: The Application Install dialog box on a Windows Vista PC.

7. **Click Continue.**

   The AIR file is created and the dialog box closes.

8. **Click the BrowsePod AIR icon.**

9. **Test the application.**

   Figure 4-16 shows a typical page in Windows Vista.

Figure 4-16: Browsing directories with the AIR application.

Modifying the AIR application

One of the options you have with the File class is the kind of directory that your BrowsePod application works with. You can change the following lines to use different kinds of initial directories:

```
folder=File.documentsDirectory;
//folder=File.desktopDirectory;
//folder=File.userDirectory;
```

Comment out the top line (that's geek for "add two slashes in front of the line — //"), and uncomment the second line (remove the slashes) to see the difference in the starting points.

You can also test the third line to see where it begins the directory search. If you decide that you like one type of directory better than another, you can republish your AIR application. Or you can modify the program to offer different options for the type of directory in use.

Book VIII
Finalizing a Flash Project

```
 1   //Buttons
 2   btn1.addEventListener(Mou
 3   btn2.addEventListener(Mou
 4   btn3.addEventListener(Mou
 5   btn4.addEventListener(Mou
 6
 7   //Button Functions
 8   function full(e:MouseEver
 9   {
10       glass1.gotoAndStop(3(
11   }
12
13   function half(e:MouseEver
14   {
15       glass2.gotoAndStop(15
16   }
```

*A*ll things must pass — even your most revered Flash project. When the time comes and you say it's "Soup!" (ready to be served to the world), it's time to publish your project. But if you publish a project without doing some testing and debugging, you'll probably have to deal with one or more of Murphy's laws.

In Book VIII, we show you what you need to know to test and debug a project. In addition, we show you how to optimize your project and determine how much bandwidth your creation uses when it's downloading to visitors' browsers. And, if you bust the bandwidth bank, we show you how to create a preloader. Last but not least, we show you how to publish your project.

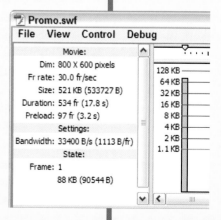

Promo.swf

File   View   Control   Debug

Movie:	
Dim:	800 X 600 pixels
Fr rate:	30.0 fr/sec
Size:	521 KB (533727 B)
Duration:	534 fr (17.8 s)
Preload:	97 fr (3.2 s)
Settings:	
Bandwidth:	33400 B/s (1113 B/fr)
State:	
Frame:	1
	88 KB (90544 B)

128 KB
64 KB
32 KB
16 KB
8 KB
4 KB
2 KB
1.1 KB

Chapter 1: Testing and Debugging a Flash Project

In This Chapter

✔ Testing a movie

✔ Previewing a movie

✔ Debugging a movie

*A*fter you slave and toil to create a compelling Flash movie, you have to make sure that it works as expected. Otherwise, you'll end up with copious amounts of egg on your face. And, if you created the Flash project for a client, after the client wipes the egg off his face, you'll get a nasty phone call — hopefully, not from that person's lawyer. So, no matter how large or small your project, you need to test and retest your project to make sure that it performs as planned.

Testing a Movie

When you're creating a Flash project, you should test the project after you make a major change. When you test often, you can detect a mistake or an inconsistency right after you create a new animation or create a new ActionScript rather than after you do a couple of hundred other things to the document and have no idea how to track down the rotten smell in the state of Denmark.

You can perform quite a few tests in Flash authoring mode. This option is handy when you don't want to wait for Flash to publish the document as an SWF file and play it in another window. You can test a movie in authoring mode by choosing one of these methods:

✔ **Drag the playhead** to scrub the Timeline. This option comes in handy when you want to check a few frames of animation or preview the manner in which a sound is synchronized to the Timeline.

✔ **Choose Control⇨Play or press Enter or Return** to play the movie in movie editing mode. This action plays the Timeline in its entirety, unless you use ActionScript to stop the movie on one or more keyframes.

✔ **Choose Control⇨Rewind** to rewind the movie to the first frame after playing the movie.

✔ **Choose Control⇨Go To End** to navigate to the last frame in the movie.

✔ **Choose Control⇨Enable Simple Frame Actions** to preview simple frame actions, such as stop and goto in Flash authoring mode.

✔ **Choose Control⇨Enable Simple Buttons** to test the functionality of simple buttons when testing a movie in Flash authoring mode.

✔ **Choose Control⇨Enable Live Preview** to preview component animation and 9-slice scaling when working in Flash authoring mode.

✔ **Choose Control⇨Mute Sounds** to mute Timeline and button sounds when testing a movie in Flash authoring mode.

Testing a Movie in Another Window

Sometimes it's important to see the entire movie, such as when you make radical changes to your ActionScript or extensively modify an animation or swap several symbols. When you need to preview the entire movie, follow these steps:

1. **Choose Control⇨Test Movie.**

   Flash displays a dialog box telling you that it's exporting the Flash movie. After a few seconds, the movie appears in another window (see Figure 1-1). The movie plays in its entirety and loops continuously.

2. **Choose Control⇨Rewind.**

   Flash rewinds the movie to the first frame and stops playing it.

3. **Choose Control⇨Play.**

   Flash plays the movie. While the movie plays, make sure that the animations are smooth and that any ActionScript executes flawlessly. Test each button to make sure it does what it's supposed to do.

4. **Choose View⇨Show Redraw Regions.**

   Flash displays a red rectangle around all areas that are redrawn, such as animations.

Figure 1-1: Testing a movie.

Previewing a Movie

Testing a movie is all well and good, but there comes a point when you want to see what viewers will see on the Web. You can preview your movie in the Flash Player or in a browser. To preview a Flash movie as your viewers will see it, choose File➪Publish Preview➪Default. This action publishes the movie using the default Publish settings and displays it in the default device. You can choose a different option from the Publish Preview menu. The available options are those you select in the Publish Settings dialog box. For example, if you choose to publish the document as a Flash SWF movie, a JPEG image, and a Flash projector, those options appear on the menu.

Debugging a Movie

If you have gobs of ActionScript in a document, or even just a paragraph or three, you can make sure that your code is performing flawlessly when you debug a movie. The debugging interface differs depending on whether you're debugging a document with ActionScript 2.0 or ActionScript 3.0. The available options are identical.

When you debug a movie, you can add breakpoints to your ActionScript. A *breakpoint* tells the debugger to stop the movie at this point in your script. When you stop a movie at a breakpoint, you can examine various elements to make sure that they're performing as you expect. For example, if your ActionScript causes an object to move, you can add a breakpoint at a point in your script where the object is supposed to be at a known coordinate. When the movie halts, you can examine the variable data for the object, such as the X and Y position, in the Variables pane of the debugger.

Setting breakpoints

The first step in debugging a project is setting breakpoints. You can set breakpoints at any point in your script. You can set as many breakpoints as you need to make sure that your script executes as envisioned. You should set your breakpoints at the beginning of a function, so that whenever you debug the movie, you can step through the function, one line at a time. To set breakpoints, follow these steps:

1. **Choose Window⇨Actions.**

   The Actions panel appears.

2. **Click the blank space to the left of the line number of the code where you want a breakpoint to appear.**

   Alternatively, you can select a line of code, right-click (Windows) or Control+click (Macintosh) and choose Toggle Breakpoint from the context menu. Using either method causes Flash to add a red dot to the left of the line number.

   If no line numbers are visible in the Actions panel, you can add a breakpoint by clicking the blank space to the left of the line of code you want.

3. **Continue adding breakpoints as needed.**

   Figure 1-2 shows a script with several breakpoints.

Using the debugger

After you add breakpoints to your ActionScript, you're ready to debug your movie. When you debug your movie, you can check your code and make sure that your animations play as you envisioned. To debug your movie, follow these steps:

1. **Choose Window⇨Actions.**

   The Actions panel opens.

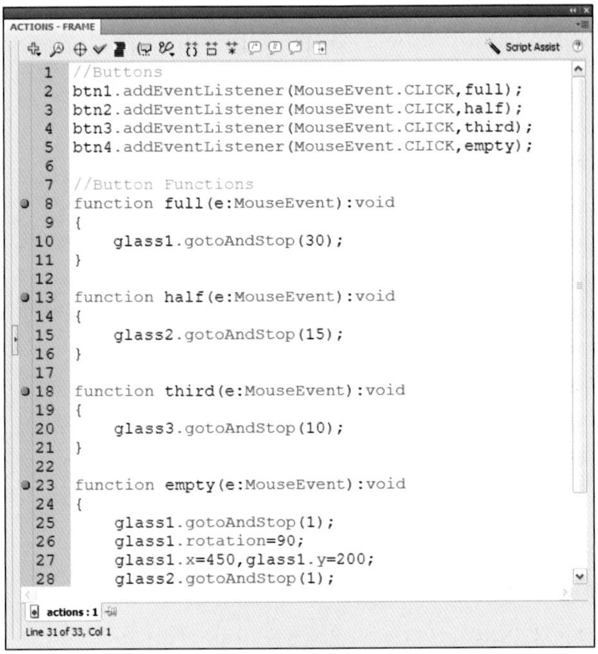

Figure 1-2: Don't confuse breakpoints with breakdances.

2. **Set breakpoints as needed.**

   If you fast-forwarded to this section and don't know how to set breakpoints or, for that matter, don't know what they are, read the previous section.

3. **Choose Debug⇨Debug Movie.**

   The Flash workspace is reconfigured to show the debug options (see Figure 1-3). The debugging workspace is divided into five panels:

   • *The Debug console:* Has the controls you use to debug the movie.

   • *The Variables panel:* Displays values for parameters, such as the size of an object and its current position.

   • *The panel to the right of the Debug console:* Displays symbols and scenes.

   • *Your script:* Lies directly beneath the list of symbols and scenes lists the breakpoints.

   • *The Output panel:* Displays information about the tasks being performed by the Debugger.

Continue

Exit Debugger

Step Over

Step In

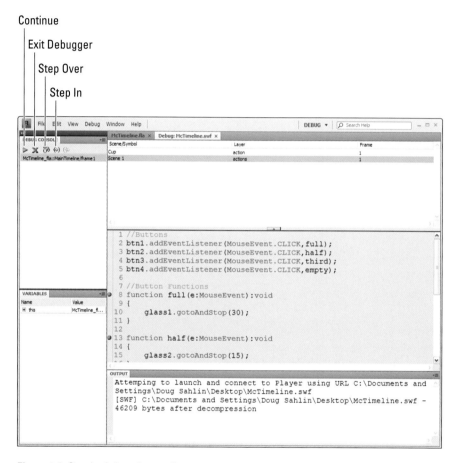

Figure 1-3: So what's bugging you?

4. Click the Continue button in the Debug console.

The Flash Player plays the movie.

5. If buttons are in your movie, click them.

If you have a breakpoint at the function associated with the button, the Debugger halts the movie (see Figure 1-4).

6. In the Variables panel, click a plus sign to view the parameters for the object at this point in the movie.

The current values for each applicable parameter are displayed in the Variables panel (see Figure 1-5).

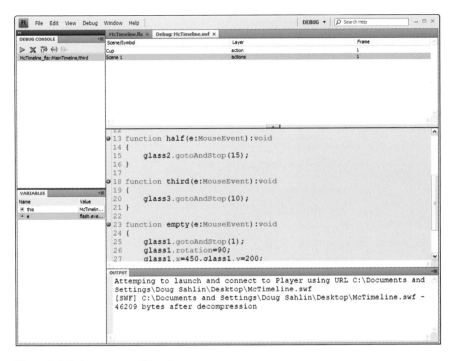

Figure 1-4: Debugger says "Stop."

7. Continue debugging the movie.

At this point, you can either click the Step Over button to step over the next step in the function or click the Step In button to advance to the next step in the function. Alternatively, you can click the Continue button to continue playing the movie.

If you find errors in your script, note the line or lines on which the errors appear. If you find errors in your script, you have to correct them in Flash authoring mode and debug the movie again to make sure that it plays properly.

8. Click the End Debug Session button, which looks like a red X.

The default Flash workspace appears and you can edit your movie. Run the Debugger as many times as needed until your movie is perfect.

9. After running an error-free debugging session, choose Debug — Remove All Breakpoints.

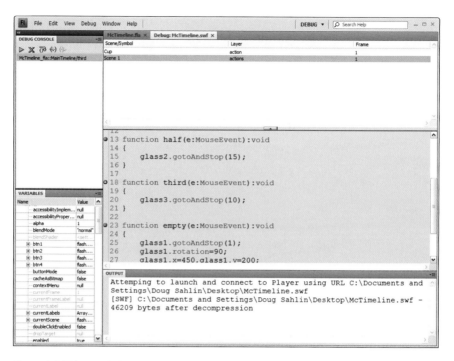

Figure 1-5: This panel shows the winds of change.

This step removes all breakpoints you added to your script. You can also remove individual breakpoints in the Debugger by right-clicking (Windows) or Ctrl+clicking (Macintosh) a line of code with a breakpoint and then choosing Toggle Breakpoint from the context menu. You can also remove all breakpoints by choosing the Remove All Breakpoints command from the context menu. Removing a breakpoint is useful when you've identified that the code associated with the breakpoint is performing perfectly. The same context menu is available in the Actions panel in Flash authoring mode.

Chapter 2: Fine-Tuning and Optimizing Your Flash Project

In This Chapter

✔ Analyzing your movie

✔ Optimizing your project

*A*fter you create your Flash masterpiece, you want to make sure that it's squeaky-clean and that everything works as planned. You have a lot of tools at your disposal to check out every facet of your Flash project. You use the Movie Explorer to quickly navigate to and find items in your Flash movie. You can configure the Movie Explorer to display everything in your movie or limit the display to individual categories, like ActionScript, movie clips, and buttons. Before you do any serious heavy lifting before publishing the file, you should make the file as lean and mean as possible — otherwise known as *optimizing* your movie.

Using the Movie Explorer

The Movie Explorer shows all elements in your Flash movie in outline form. You choose which items are displayed in the Movie Explorer. When you need to, you can cut straight to the chase and find the element in your project. To analyze your movie with the Movie Explorer, follow these steps:

1. **Choose Window⇨Explorer.**

   The Flash Movie Explorer appears (see Figure 2-1).

2. **To search for a specific item, enter its name in the Find text box.**

   You can search for an item name, a font name, a string of ActionScript code, or a frame number. After you enter the search query, the Movie Explorer refreshes to show all instances that match your query.

3. **Filter your results by clicking the icons that correspond to the items you want to view.**

   You can limit the view to a single item such as text, several items, or all items.

4. Click an item to select it.

The path to the item is displayed at the bottom of the Movie Explorer.

5. Click the Customize Which Items to Show icon.

The Movie Explorer Settings dialog box appears (see Figure 2-2).

6. Select the items you want to show.

You can also display context for movie elements and symbol definitions.

7. Right-click (Windows) or Ctrl+click (Macintosh) and choose an option from the context menu (see Figure 2-3).

The available menu commands differ depending on the item you select. You can use commands from this menu to navigate to the item in your movie, show the object in the document Library, or edit the item, for example.

8. If you prefer working from a menu, click the Movie Explorer Panel Options icon.

This step reveals a menu with the same options as the context menu. You have the following commands at your disposal:

- *Go To Location:* Moves the focus in the document to the frame, layer, or scene you select in the Movie Explorer.

- *Go To Symbol Definition:* Shows the symbol definition in the document library. This option is available only if you select Symbol Definitions from the Movie Explorer Settings dialog box.

Show ActionScript

Show Text

Show Frames and Layers

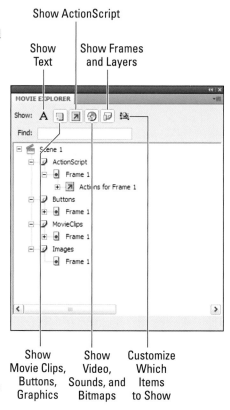

Show Movie Clips, Buttons, Graphics

Show Video, Sounds, and Bitmaps

Customize Which Items to Show

Figure 2-1: The Flash Movie Explorer.

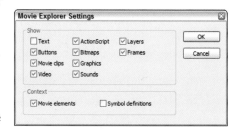

Figure 2-2: Customize Movie Explorer settings.

- *Select Symbol Instances:* Shows the instances of a symbol you select in the Movie Explorer. This option is available only if you select Movie Elements from the Movie Explorer Settings dialog box.

- *Show in Library:* Highlights the selected symbol in the document library.

- *Rename:* Highlights the text for the item you select. Enter new text to change the name.

- *Edit in Place:* Enables you to edit the selected symbol instance on the Stage.

- *Edit in New Window:* Opens the selected object in a new window in which you can edit the object.

- *Show Movie Elements:* Changes the Movie Explorer display and shows all elements in the document organized by scene.

- *Show Symbol Definitions:* Displays symbol definitions at the bottom of the Movie Explorer. Click the plus sign to the left of a symbol to show all layers and elements used to create the symbol.

```
Go to Location
Go to Symbol Definition
Select Symbol Instances
Show in Library

Rename
Edit in Place
Edit in New Window

✔ Show Movie Elements
✔ Show Symbol Definitions
  Show All Scenes

Copy All Text to Clipboard
Cut
Copy
Paste
Clear

Expand Branch
Collapse Branch
Collapse Others

Print...
```

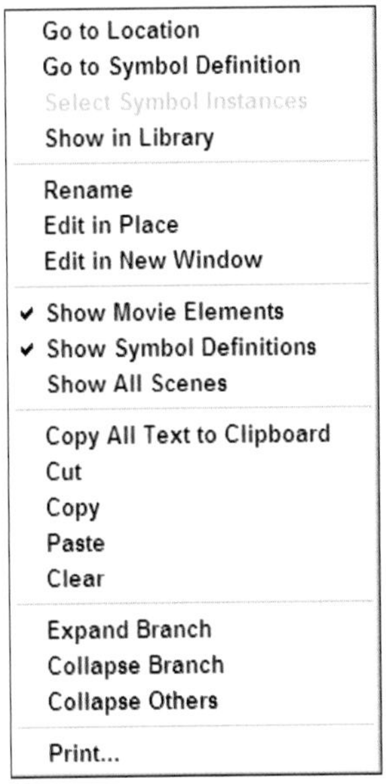

Figure 2-3: Using the Movie Explorer context menu.

- *Copy All Text to Clipboard:* Copies all text in the Movie Explorer to the Clipboard.

- *Expand Branch:* Expands the tree at the selected element.

- *Collapse Branch:* Collapses the tree at the selected element.

- *Collapse Others:* Collapse all branches other than those associated with the selected element.

- *Print:* Creates a hard copy of the list displayed in the Movie Explorer.

Book VIII
Chapter 2

Fine-Tuning and Optimizing Your Flash Project

Optimizing a Flash Movie

Whenever possible, your goal as a Flash designer is most likely to create a thing of beauty that's interactive and that downloads quickly. In this regard, you need to optimize your project before you publish it. You also need to think about the final output during all phases of your project. When you optimize a document, the published movie downloads quicker and isn't processor intensive. This section shows you a few techniques you can use to make sure that you publish a lean, mean Flash movie.

Your first step is to get rid of the dead weight. Eliminate unused objects by following these steps:

1. **Choose Window⇨Library.**

   The document library appears.

2. **From the Library Options menu, choose Select Unused Items.**

   Flash selects the unused items. Before you delete them, make sure that they're not items you can use in another project. If they are, create a new document, pin the library of the movie you're optimizing, and drag the unused but useful symbols into the new document.

3. **Press Delete to remove the unused items.**

   Even if you remove just a few unused items, the document is still smaller when published.

Here are some other actions you can take to optimize a document:

- **Use symbol instances whenever possible.** When you use a symbol instance, the Flash Player re-creates the instance using information from the document library.

- **Avoid animating images whenever possible.**

- **Use the Alpha color effect judiciously.** This effect uses computer memory and may slow down playback on older, less powerful computers.

- **Use gradients sparingly.** When you use gradients, the file size of the published movie increases.

- **Limit the number of font faces you use.** Embedding fonts increases the file size of the published documents.

- **Whenever possible use device fonts.** When the Flash Player encounters a device font, it gets the information from the viewer's computer.

- **Whenever you create a complex shape, choose Modify⇨Shape⇨ Optimize.** This command enables you to simplify an object by reducing the number of points required to define the object.

- **Avoid embedding movies in a document.** Whenever possible, load external movies into the document.

- **Optimize individual objects in the document library.** This strategy enables you to apply more compression to a sound or an image than the global settings in the Publish Settings dialog box. This option is useful when you have either small images you're using for buttons or sounds you're using for buttons. As a rule, you can apply more compression to these objects because they're not as important to the overall look and feel of the published movie.

Chapter 3: Dealing with Bandwidth

In This Chapter

✓ **Measuring the bandwidth of your movie**

✓ **Creating a preloader**

Done right, a Flash movie is a svelte thing of beauty that loads faster than a speeding locomotive or jet plane. But sometimes you have to add some squeaky-clean video while your client's target audience accesses the Internet with a tin can and a tight string. In other words, your file may run the risk of breaking the bandwidth of some of the computers belonging to your client's intended audience. At other times, you have to create a Flash movie for an audience with dialup connections and tailor your movie to the connection. How do you perform these feats of magic? And, if you do break the bandwidth of your intended audience, is a "band aid" available to fix it? The answer to both questions is yes. In this chapter, we show you how to know whether your Flash project will break the bandwidth of your intended audience and what to do if it does.

Using the Bandwidth Profiler

The handy Bandwidth Profiler tells you how fat or skinny your Flash file is. When you access the Bandwidth Profiler, you see how much information is contained on each frame, and which frames may be a potential bottleneck at a given download speed. You can view the Bandwidth Profiler as either a frame-by-frame graph or a streaming graph. When you view the Bandwidth Profiler and simulate a download, the movie starts playing when enough frames have been downloaded. If a frame contains enough data to stop the movie from playing, the movie pauses until enough data has downloaded to continue playing the movie. Whenever this happens, you know that you have the problem of movie interruptus. To analyze your movie with the Bandwidth Profiler, follow these steps:

1. **Choose Control⇨Test Movie.**

   Flash publishes the document as an SWF file and displays it in another window. Alternatively, you can press Ctrl+Enter (Windows) or ⌘+Return (Macintosh).

2. **Choose View⇨Bandwidth Profiler.**

   The Bandwidth Profiler appears — see Figure 3-1, which shows the Bandwidth Profiler as a frame-by-frame graph. The left window shows information about your movie. For the purpose of this demonstration, we use a rather large promo that Doug created for his photography business. Because the promo was distributed on CD discs, the file downloaded a lot faster than it would on most types of Internet connections. The Bandwidth Profiler also shows how many frames must preload before the movie plays. The profiler also shows the selected frame and the amount of data that's on the frame.

3. **Choose View⇨Download Settings and choose a connection speed from the menu.**

   You can choose a speed from the ridiculously slow to the outrageously fast. If your customer is displaying the published SWF file on a *muy rapido* intranet server, you can create settings to match the speed of your client's intranet:

   a. *Choose Customize to open the Custom Download Settings dialog box.*

   b. *Enter the speed in one of the Bit Rate text fields of a user setting.*

   You also see a red line appear across the graph. When a frame is higher than the red line, Flash Player stops until the frame loads in its entirety. If you have several frames packed with a lot of data at the start of a movie, the file takes longer to load. If the frames with a lot of data are at the end of the movie and your intended audience connects at a fairly fast speed, the movie may play without stopping. The only way to know for sure is to simulate a download.

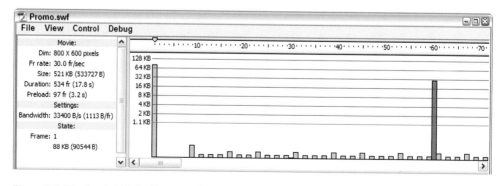

Figure 3-1: The Bandwidth Profiler at work.

4. Choose Simulate Download.

The movie begins playing as soon as enough frames have downloaded. A green bar appears across the top of the profiler, indicating the total number of frames that have loaded (see Figure 3-2). The playhead shows which frame of the movie is playing. If the playhead catches up with the green progress bar, the movie stops playing until enough frames have loaded for it to continue playing. If the playhead stops in the simulated download, your movie is a candidate for a preloader. Alternatively, you have to change some compression settings on sound files, video clips, and bitmaps that are in the movie. You can change individual settings by choosing the item in the document library and then modifying the properties. The topic of sounds is covered in Book V, Chapter 3.

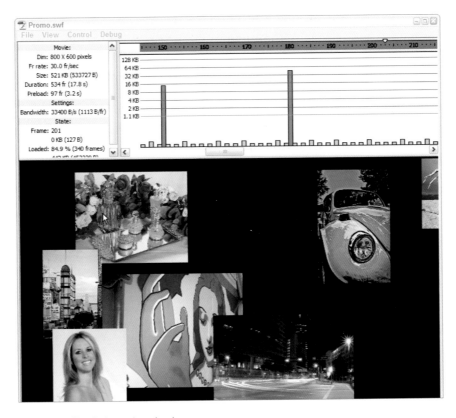

Figure 3-2: Simulating a download.

5. **Choose View⇨Streaming Graph.**

This step changes the display to Streaming Graph mode. Frame content is displayed as alternating light and dark bands. The first frame of a symbol contains its content and information and is therefore larger than subsequent frames. The Bandwidth Profiler in Streaming Graph mode is shown in Figure 3-3.

Figure 3-3: The Bandwidth Profiler in Streaming Graph mode.

Creating a Preloader

To create a preloader, follow these steps:

1. **Create a new document.**

For the document type, choose ActionScript 3.0. Name the document **myPreloader** and save it.

2. **Choose Insert⇨New Symbol.**

   The New Symbol dialog box appears.

3. **Name the symbol** bwRX **and choose Movie Clip from the Type menu.**

   So we had a little fun with the name — bandwidth RX. You can give the movie clip any name you want. The name becomes critical when you name the movie clip instance.

4. **Using the Primitive Rectangle tool, create a rectangle that's 1 pixel wide by 50 pixels long.**

   You can change the dimensions of the rectangle in the Property inspector. Use any color that suits your fancy. This document will be your generic preloader for any movie with bandwidth issues. You can change the color of the rectangle to suit the movie for which you're creating the preloader by editing the symbol.

5. **Click the Stroke color swatch to open the Swatches panel, and then click the No Color icon.**

   You'll change the dimensions of the rectangle and use a motion tween to animate it. Strokes do wonky things during motion tween animations.

6. **In the Property inspector, change the X value to –100 and the Y value to –25.**

   This step positions the rectangle off-center horizontally and centered vertically. You see the method to our madness in a few steps.

7. **Select the rectangle and press F8 to convert it to a symbol.**

   The Convert to Symbol dialog box appears.

8. **Name the symbol** preloadBar, **choose Graphic from the Type menu, and then click the center left registration point.**

   You'll animate this symbol by using a classic motion tween.

9. **Click OK.**

   The symbol is added to the document library.

10. **Click frame 100 and then press F6.**

    The blank frame is converted to a keyframe.

11. **Right-click (Windows) or Ctrl+click (Mac) one of the in-between frames and then choose Classic Tween.**

    That's right — this is one time that you use the old tried-and-true motion tween to get the job done.

12. **Select the symbol in the 100th frame, click the chain icon in the Property inspector, and then change the W value to** 200.

    Click the chain icon, which enables you to resize the width without changing the height.

13. **Click the current scene or Back button.**

    The movie clip is added to the document library.

14. **Drag an instance of the bwRX movie clip on Stage.**

15. **In the Property inspector, change the X value to** 225 **and the Y value to** 200.

    This step places the movie clip in the center of the Stage when the animation is completed.

16. **In the Property inspector, enter** bwRX_mc **in the text field.**

    You use this name in the ActionScript to make the preloader bar move while the specified movie loads.

ActionScript makes the preloader spring to life. In addition to moving the preloaderBar symbol, it loads the file. The bwRX movie clip animation is 100 frames in duration. When 10 percent of the movie has loaded, the animation is on Frame 10; when 50 percent has loaded, the animation is on Frame 50; and so on. When the movie is completely downloaded, the preloader animation disappears and the movie plays.

Adding ActionScript to the preloader

To add the ActionScript to the preloader, follow these steps:

1. **Right-click (Windows) or Ctrl+click (Mac) the layer on which your Movie Clip symbol resides, and from the context menu, choose Insert Layer.**

   A new layer is added to the Timeline.

2. **Double-click the current layer name and enter** actions.

   This is only a one-frame preloader, but it still pays to develop good habits. Naming layers is a good habit to form.

3. **Click the keyframe on the actions layer, right-click (Windows) or Ctrl+click (Mac), and choose Actions from the context menu.**

   The Actions panel appears.

4. **Enter the ActionScript code shown in Listing 3-1.**

   You can download a text file of the script (385395_bk08ch03_preloader. txt) from this book's companion Web site at www.dummies.com/go/ flashallinone. Download the file preloader.txt from this chapter's folder.

Listing 3-1: The Preloader ActionScript Code

```
var fileToLoad:String = "myFile.swf"; var req:URLRequest = new
    URLRequest(fileToLoad);
var loader:Loader = new Loader();

    loader.contentLoaderInfo.addEventListener(ProgressEvent.PROGRESS,
        fileLoading);
    loader.contentLoaderInfo.addEventListener(Event.COMPLETE, fileLoaded);
    loader.load(req);


function fileLoading(event:ProgressEvent):void
{
    var percent:Number = event.bytesLoaded/event.bytesTotal;
    var roundedPercent:uint = Math.ceil(percent * 100);
    bwRX_mc.gotoAndStop(roundedPercent);
                                                                }


bwRX_mc.stop();


function fileLoaded(event:Event):void
{
    removeChild(bwRX_mc);
    addChild(loader);
}
```

5. **Replace the text `myFile.swf` in the first line of code with the file-name of the file you want the preloader to load.**

   Make sure that the file you're loading is in the same folder as the pre-loader. You can also use this preloader to load any file type that can be loaded into a Flash movie.

6. **Press Ctrl+Enter (Windows) or ⌘+Return (Mac).**

   Flash publishes the movie and plays it in another window. The file loads so quickly that you don't even see the preloader.

7. **Choose View⇨Download Settings and then select a connection speed from the menu.**

   Choose the speed at which your intended audience connects to the Internet.

8. **Choose View⇨Simulate Download.**

   When the movie plays, the bwRX animation plays. The preloaderBar symbol moves to show how much of the movie has been loaded. When the animation stops, the movie you specified in Step 5 plays.

The code in Listing 3-1 has all the components to run the animation and load the movie. The first three lines of code declare variables:

- ✏ **First line:** Identifies the file to load
- ✏ **Second line:** Creates an instance of the URLrequest object
- ✏ **Third line:** Creates an instance of the Loader object

The next lines of code add event listeners and instructions for the loader. Notice the function names at the end of the event listener statements.

The `fileLoading` function creates a variable named percent, which is the result of the number of bytes in the file divided by the number of bytes loaded. This returns a number between zero and one. The next line of code creates a round number between 0 and 100. The final line of code tells the instance of the bwRX symbol (bwR_mc) to go to and stop at the value roundedPercent, which is a number between 1 and 100, the exact number of frames in the motion tween animation. The next line of code tells the instance of the movie clip to stop playing when the file is fully loaded. The `fileLoaded` function loads the file, which then begins playing without interruption, thanks to Freddy the Preloader.

Displaying the percentage of a file that's been loaded

The progress bar gives you an indication of how quickly the associated file is loading, but you can show visitors the actual percentage that has been loaded by following these steps:

1. **Choose Insert⇨New Symbol.**

   The New Symbol dialog box appears.

2. **Choose Movie Clip from the Type drop-down menu, and name the movie clip `dispText`.**

3. **Click OK.**

   Welcome to Symbol Editing mode.

4. **Select the Text tool.**

5. **In the Property inspector, choose Dynamic Text from the Type drop-down menu.**

   Dynamic text can be updated by ActionScript. In this case, the text box will display the percentage of the file that has loaded and will update until 100 is reached, at which point the movie associated with the pre-loader is fully loaded and plays.

6. **Enter `progress_Display_txt` in the blank text field at the top of the Property inspector.**

   This is the instance name for the text box that will be addressed by ActionScript.

7. **Choose an option from the Family drop-down menu and then specify the font size.**

   These options determine what the progress text looks like. We suggest you choose _sans, _sans serif, or _typewriter. If you choose a different family, you run the risk of choosing a font that is not on the user's computer. We're talking about a preloader here; there's no need to choose an artsy-fartsy font.

8. **Click the current scene or Back button.**

   The movie clip is added to the document library.

9. **Drag an instance of the dispText movie clip on the Stage and position it above the progress bar movie clip.**

   If you want to get real persnickety, use the Align panel to align the movie clip horizontally to the center of the stage.

10. **In the Property inspector, name the instance of the dispText movie clip `progress_Text_mc`.**

    If you guessed that you're going to address the movie clip with ActionScript, you would be voyant, Claire.

11. **Click the first frame.**

    This is where all of your ActionScript for the preloader resides.

12. **Add the following code to the fileLoading function:**

    ```
    progress_Text_mc.progress_Display_txt.text=(roundedPercent + ' %');
    ```

    Your fileLoading function code should resemble Listing 3-2.

Listing 3-2: The Revised fileLoading Function

```
function fileLoading(event:ProgressEvent):void
{
        var percent:Number = event.bytesLoaded/event.bytesTotal;
        var roundedPercent:uint = Math.ceil(percent * 100);
        bwRX_mc.gotoAndStop(roundedPercent);
    progress_Text_mc.progress_Display_txt.text=(roundedPercent + ' %');
}
```

13. **Press Ctrl+Enter (Windows) or ⌘+Return (Mac).**

    Flash publishes the movie and plays it in another window. At this stage, you may see 100% before the movie starts playing.

14. **Choose View⇨Simulate Download.**

    Flash simulates downloading the file. If you've followed the steps correctly, you'll see a number followed by the percent sign, which signifies the percentage of the movie that has downloaded.

Chapter 4: Publishing Your Flash Project

After you spend lots of hours creating a cool Flash file, tweaking the ActionScript to add every ounce of interactivity that the law allows and then testing the file, you're ready to publish the file in a format supported by Flash. Before you can publish the file, you have to choose one or more formats and then specify the publish settings for each format. When you specify publish settings, you also specify the quality of the sound and image files in your Flash document. The publish settings determine the file size and other factors, such as the version of Flash Player with which the file is compatible. That's what this chapter is all about — publishing your Flash file to share with a few friends or the world!

. cG quality:

☐ Enable JPEG de

Audio stream: MP3, 16 kbps, Mor

Audio event: MP3, 16 kbps, Mor

☐ Override sound

☐ Export device s

Publishing a Flash File

The default publish settings yield a Flash SWF file and an HTML document. The HTML document contains the code needed to embed the SWF file within the document. In addition, the code detects the version of Flash Player used by the viewer. The HTML code also contains JavaScript that enables the movie to play instantly in any browser without triggering an ActiveX warning.

SWF Settings

☑ Compress movi

☑ Include hidden

☑ Include XMP me

☐ Export SWʳ

You can publish your file in other formats, such as JPEG, GIF, or PNG, with an HTML document to display the published file on the Web. Another option is publishing the file as a Flash Projector. A *projector* is an executable file that can be played whether or not the Flash Player is installed on the user's computer. In the following sections, we show you the steps needed to publish a file in supported formats.

Specifying publish settings

The file format you choose determines the available settings you have. In this section, we cover publish settings for Flash SWF files, the associated HTML document, and image files. The default publish settings yield a Flash SWF file and an HTML file. The settings you use match the settings you specify when you create a new document. For example, if you create a new document for a mobile device, your publish settings must match the settings you specified in Device Central. To start the publishing process, follow these steps:

1. **Choose File⊅Publish Settings.**

   The Publish Settings dialog box appears (see Figure 4-1).

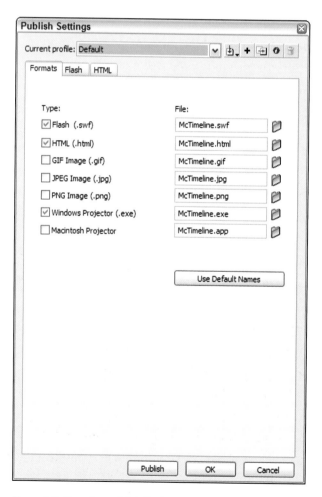

Figure 4-1: Choosing publish file formats.

Publishing a Flash projector

When you create a Flash application, you can publish it as a Windows projector or a Macintosh projector. Projector files are stand-alone applications that can be used on the desktop or from a CD disc. A Windows projector file is a stand-alone executable with an .exe (executable) file extension. A Flash projector file is a stand-alone application with an .app (application) file extension. You specify publish settings for a projector file on the Flash tab of the Publish Settings dialog box.

2. **Select the file formats in which you want to publish the document.**

   The default settings are for a Flash SWF file and an HTML document.

3. **Click a tab to specify settings for that format.**

   Each tab is covered in detail in upcoming sections.

4. **Click Publish.**

   Flash publishes the file in the formats you specified in Step 2.

   You can publish a document with the current settings by either choosing File⇨Publish or pressing Shift+F12.

5. **After the files are published, click OK.**

   The Publish Settings dialog box closes.

Specifying SWF settings

From the Flash tab of the Publish Settings dialog box, you specify the version of Flash Player with which the published file is compatible, the global settings for image and sound quality, SWF settings, and more. To specify SWF settings, follow these steps:

1. **Choose File⇨Publish Settings.**

   The Publish Settings dialog box appears.

2. **Choose Flash as one of the file formats.**

3. **Click the Flash tab.**

   The Flash settings appear (see Figure 4-2).

4. **Choose an option from the Player drop-down menu.**

   This version of Flash Player is the one with which the published file is compatible. If your document uses ActionScript 3.0, you're limited to Flash Player 9 and Flash Player 10. If you're using features such as inverse kinematics animation that are exclusive to Flash CS4, your only option is Flash Player 10.

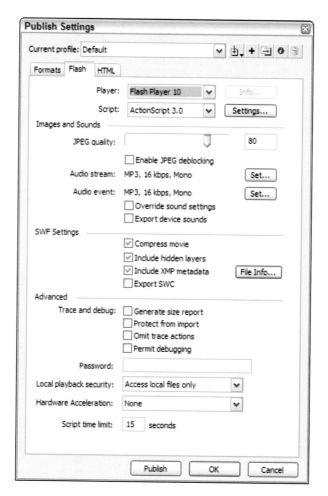

Figure 4-2: Choosing Flash publish settings.

5. Choose an option from the Script drop-down menu.

Choose the version of ActionScript that's the same as the one with which you created the document.

6. Click Settings.

This step opens a dialog box that enables you to specify advanced ActionScript settings, such as the Document class or the frame on which to export classes. Unless you have a computer science degree from MIT (or the equivalent), don't mess with the advanced settings. Just hustle your behind to Book IV, and don't you dare send an e-mail to us and ask about advanced AS 3.0 settings until the ink on your MIT diploma is dry.

7. **Drag the slider to set the JPEG quality.**

   This step determines how much compression is applied to images. The default value of 80 gives good results in most instances. Choose a lower setting for a smaller file size at the expense of image quality.

8. **Select the Enable JPEG Deblocking option if you specify a low-quality setting globally or have specified high compression when changing an image's properties in the document library.**

   This option smoothes images with high compression to prevent them from looking pixelated (or blocky, if you will).

9. **Accept the default Audio Stream settings or click Set to open the Sound Settings dialog box (see Figure 4-3).**

   From within the Sound Settings dialog box, you can specify global compression settings. For more information on sound settings, see Book V, Chapter 3.

Figure 4-3: Specifying global sound settings.

10. **Accept the default Audio Event settings or click Set to open the Sound Settings dialog box (refer to Figure 4-3).**

    This dialog box enables you to specify global settings for event sounds.

11. **(Optional) Click Override Sound Settings.**

    This option overrides any sound settings you apply by changing a sound's properties in the document library.

12. **(Optional) Click Export Device Sounds.**

    Use this option when you're creating Flash files for handheld units, like mobile phones.

13. **In the SWF Settings section, you have the following options:**

    - *Compress Movie:* Compresses the movie, which results in a smaller file size and faster download; selected by default.

    - *Include Hidden Layers:* Exports hidden layers with the published movie.

    - *Include XMP Metadata:* Includes metadata with the file.

    - *Include SWC file:* Exports an SWC file with the document. SWC files are used with remote debugging sessions.

14. **In the SWF Settings section, click File Info.**

This step opens the dialog box shown in Figure 4-4. From within the dialog box, you can add a description of the file, contact information, and International Press Telecommunications Council (IPTC) information, for example. This information is stored as metadata with the file.

Figure 4-4: Adding metadata to a Flash file.

15. **In the Advanced section, choose from the following Trace and Debug options:**

- *Generate Size Report:* Generates a report in the Output panel that shows the amount of data in the published file.

- *Protect from Import:* Prevents people from importing the resulting SWF file into Flash and using some of your graphics or converting the file into an FLA document. When you choose this option, the Password text field becomes available. Enter a password, and users are prompted for a password when attempting to import the file into Flash.

- *Omit Trace Actions:* Eliminates any trace actions you may have added to your ActionScript to test and debug the file.

- *Permit Debugging:* Makes it possible for you to remotely debug the file.

16. **Choose an option from the Local Playback Security drop-down menu.**

    You can restrict access to files on the local computer or on the network.

17. **Choose an option from the Hardware Acceleration drop-down menu.**

    The default option is None. Alternatively, you can choose Level 1 Direct, which uses DirectX for hardware acceleration, or Level 2 – GPU, which uses a graphics processing unit attached to the user's video card for hardware acceleration.

18. **Accept the default script time limit of 15 seconds, or enter a different value.**

    This option limits the amount of time a script plays. Most scripts should execute in a fraction of a second. When a script continues to execute in an effort to resolve an error, the host computer CPU slows to a crawl and a crash may incur.

19. **Click OK. Or click Publish to publish the document.**

If you modify Flash and HTML settings and will use the settings frequently, click the plus sign (+) next to the Current Profile drop-down menu, to open the Create New Profile dialog box. Enter a name for the profile and click OK. This action adds the new profile to the Current Profile drop-down menu for future use.

Specifying HTML settings

The default publishing option includes an HTML file with the Flash document. You can choose a template and modify settings on the HTML tab of the Publish Settings dialog box. To specify HTML settings, follow these steps:

1. **Choose File⇨Publish Settings.**

    The Publish Settings dialog box appears.

2. **Choose HTML as one of the file formats.**

3. **Click the HTML tab.**

    The HTML settings appear (see Figure 4-5).

4. **Choose an option from the Template drop-down menu.**

    We'd put you to sleep if we listed every detail about each template. You can get a down-and-dirty description of what a template is used for by clicking Info after selecting a template.

5. **(Optional) Choose the Detect Flash Version option.**

    Choose this option, and Flash adds code to the HTML page that searches the user's computer for the optimum Flash Player version that's needed to play the SWF file as designed.

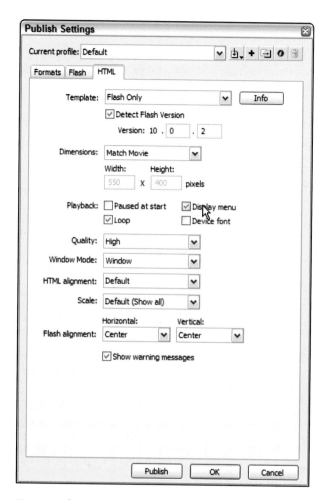

Figure 4-5: Specifying HTML settings.

6. **Choose one of the following options from the Dimensions drop-down menu:**

   • *Match Movie:* Embeds the width and height dimensions of the movie in the HTML file.

   • *Pixels:* Opens the Width and Height text fields with the current pixel dimensions of the movie. You can manually change these values. However, Flash doesn't change the other dimension. Unless you do the math and change the value of the other dimension to preserve the original document aspect ratio, the published file will be distorted.

It's also not advisable to increase the dimensions of a file that has bitmap images because they will be distorted.

- *Percent:* Enables you to specify the percentage of the browser that's filled with the Flash movie. You can manually change these values. However, Flash doesn't change the other dimension. Unless you do the math, the resulting file will be distorted.

7. **In the Playback section, you have the following options:**

   - *Paused at Start:* The movie is paused on the first frame until the user clicks a button or selects a command from the context menu.

   - *Loop:* The default option plays the file and loops it continuously.

   - *Display Menu:* The user has the option of using a context menu when viewing the movie. Users access the context menu by right-clicking (Windows) or Ctrl+clicking (Mac). Then they can choose how the file is played in their version of the Flash Player.

   - *Device Font (Windows only):* When Flash Player encounters a font not installed on the user's computer, it substitutes a smooth-edged system font from the user's computer.

8. **Choose one of the following options from the Quality drop-down menu:**

   - *Low:* Yields a low-quality movie in which playback speed is more important than the quality of the graphics. Anti-aliasing isn't used with this option.

   - *Auto Low:* Favors playback speed over quality when the movie begins playing. However, if Flash Player senses that the quality can be improved without sacrificing playback speed, it increases the quality as the movie plays. When the movie starts playing, anti-aliasing is disabled until Flash Player decides that it can be used without reducing playback speed.

   - *Auto-High:* Starts out playing the movie with high-quality graphics and anti-aliasing. If the frame rate starts to drop, Flash Player lowers quality and, if necessary, disables anti-aliasing.

   - *Medium:* Uses some anti-aliasing, but doesn't smooth bitmap images.

   - *High:* Always uses anti-aliasing; the default option. High-quality graphics are favored over playback speed. Bitmap images are smoothed if the SWF file contains no animation, but aren't smoothed if the file contains animation.

   - *Best:* Provides the highest-quality display. All output is anti-aliased and bitmaps are smoothed.

9. **Select one of the following options from the Window Mode drop-down menu:**

   - *Window:* Renders the background of the Flash movie opaque and uses the background color of the HTML document; the default option. If you have HTML or JavaScript code for items like pop-up menus, they don't render above or below the window provided for the Flash movie.

   - *Opaque Windowless:* Causes the background of the Flash movie to be opaque. Anything in the HTML document below the Flash content isn't visible. HTML content will be visible above the Flash movie.

   - *Transparent Windowless:* Causes the background of the Flash movie to be transparent. HTML content is rendered above or below the Flash movie.

10. **Choose one of the following options from the HTML Alignment drop-down menu:**

    - *Default:* Places the content in the default browser position, which doesn't necessarily center the content in the browser.

    - *Left, Right, Top, or Bottom:* Positions the Flash content in the corresponding position in the browser.

11. **Choose one of the following options from the Scale drop-down menu:**

    - *Default (Show All):* Displays the entire Flash content in the specified window while preserving the aspect ratio.

    - *No Border:* Resizes the Flash content in the specified window without a border. The content is distorted if the aspect ratio of the window doesn't match that of the Flash content.

    - *Exact Fit:* Resizes the Flash content to fit the specified window. Distortion may occur if the aspect ratio of the window isn't the same as the Flash content.

    - *No Scale:* Preserves the original size of the Flash content when the window is resized.

12. **Choose an option from the Flash Alignment drop-down menus to determine how the content is placed in the application window.**

13. **Check the default Show Warning Messages option to display a warning message if tag settings are in conflict.**

14. **Click OK to apply the settings to the current document.**

Publishing Flash documents in other formats

In addition to publishing a Flash document as a SWF file, you can publish the file as an image. You can publish the document in either the GIF or JPEG file format.

To publish your file as a GIF image, follow these steps:

1. **Choose File⇨Publish Settings.**

   The Publish Settings dialog box appears.

2. **Choose GIF as one of the file formats.**

3. **Click the GIF tab.**

   The GIF publish settings are displayed (see Figure 4-6).

Figure 4-6: Specifying GIF publish settings.

4. **In the Dimensions section, accept the default Match Movie option.**

   If you deselect this option, you can manually enter values for the size you want. Note that Flash doesn't recalculate values to resize the resulting file proportionately.

5. **Choose an option in the Playback section.**

   You can publish the option as a static image or an animated GIF. If you choose the latter option, you can create an animation that loops endlessly or specify the number of times the animation repeats.

6. **In the Options sections, choose one of the following options:**

   - *Optimize Colors:* Removes from the GIF color palette any colors not used in the document. This option reduces the file size.

   - *Interlace:* Causes the image to be displayed in stages when it loads into the viewer's browser. The first stage gives the viewer an idea of what the image looks like. Each stage adds more information until the image is displayed at full fidelity.

   - *Smooth:* Produces a higher-quality image by applying anti-aliasing.

   - *Dither Solids:* Applies dithering to approximate colors in the image that aren't in the GIF color table.

   - *Remove Gradients:* Doesn't display gradients in the published image. The gradient is displayed as a solid color using the first color in the gradient. Gradients may cause banding to appear when the GIF format attempts to display them. If you use this option, choose the first color of your gradient carefully.

7. **Choose one of the following options to determine how transparency is handled:**

   - *Opaque:* Renders the background a solid color.

   - *Transparent:* Renders the background transparent.

   - *Alpha:* Renders the background as partially transparent. When you select this option, the Threshold text field appears. The default value of 128 renders the background with 50 percent transparency. Lower values make the background more transparent, and higher values make the background more opaque.

8. **Choose one of the following options from the Dither drop-down menu:**

   - *None:* Doesn't apply dithering. When a color is encountered that isn't on the color palette, it's replaced with the closest approximation that's in the palette. This option creates images with smaller file sizes, but the colors don't match the original document perfectly.

- *Ordered:* Applies dithering with the smallest increase in file size.

- *Diffusion:* Applies higher-quality dithering and produces the greatest color fidelity with the original document. This results in a larger file size and is available only when you select the Web 216 color palette.

9. **Choose one of the following options from the Palette Type drop-down menu:**

- *Web 216:* Renders the image using the colors from the Web 216 color palette, which is the default color palette for the Swatches panel.

- *Adaptive:* Analyzes the colors you used in the document and creates a color palette to faithfully render the image.

- *Web Snap Adaptive:* Analyzes the colors you used in the document and creates a palette using the colors from the Web 216 palette.

- *Custom:* Enables you to assign to the document a color palette you created. When you choose this option, the Palette field becomes active. Click the Folder icon to navigate to the color palette. Flash supports ACT color palettes.

10. **If you choose the Adaptive or Web Snap Adaptive color palette, the Max Colors field becomes available. Enter a value for the maximum number of colors that will be used to render the image.**

The maximum number of colors for a GIF image is 255. Entering a lower value results in a smaller file size with poorer image quality.

11. **Click OK.**

The Publish Settings dialog box closes. The GIF settings are applied to the image that's generated when you publish the document. Alternatively, click Publish to publish the document.

To publish your file as a JPEG image, follow these steps:

1. **Choose File⇨Publish Settings.**

The Publish Settings dialog box appears.

2. **Choose JPEG as one of the file formats.**

3. **Click the JPEG tab.**

The JPEG settings appear (see Figure 4-7).

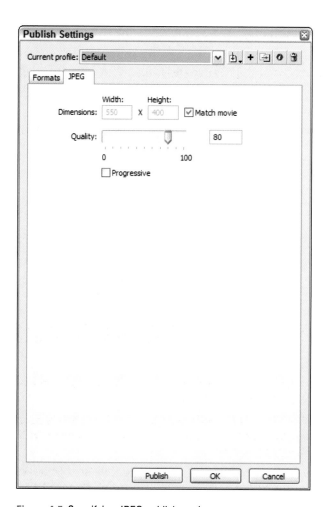

Figure 4-7: Specifying JPEG publish settings.

4. In the Dimensions section, accept the default Match Movie option.

If you deselect this option, you can manually enter values for the size you want. Flash doesn't recalculate values to resize the resulting file proportionately.

5. Drag the Quality slider to specify image quality.

The default setting of 80 gives you good image quality. Specifying a lower setting results in a smaller file size with poorer image quality. A setting of 100 produces the best image quality.

6. **(Optional) Choose the Progressive option.**

    This step produces a JPEG file that loads into the user's browser in stages. Each stage is progressively better. The full image quality is revealed after the final pass.

7. **Click OK.**

    The Publish Settings dialog box closes. The JPEG settings are applied to the image that's generated when you publish the document. Alternatively, click Publish to publish the document.

Integrating Flash Movies with HTML Documents

When you choose Flash and HTML for your publishing options and choose Default, the SWF file appears in the left corner of your browser. You can easily change this by editing the HTML document in an HTML editor such as Dreamweaver or a word processing application such as Notepad. You use a <div> tag with the alignment option set to the center to display the Flash file in the center of the Web browser. The exact location of the code you need to modify differs depending on the HTML option you choose in the Publish Settings dialog box. To center the Flash SWF file in the Web browser, follow these steps:

1. **Open the HTML document in an HTML editor or a word processing application such as Notepad.**

    Don't use Word to edit the document. When Word opens an HTML document, the application has a tendency to mess with the code — not always in a good way.

    Less is more. Open the application in the most basic word processing application on your computer. If you edit the file in an HTML editor, switch to the mode that lets you edit the code.

2. **Add the following bit of code before the spot where the Flash SWF file appears:** <div align="center">.

    If you're using the HTML template that includes JavaScript to run ActiveX content, place the tag before the line of code that reads

    ```
    <script language="JavaScript" type="text/
        javascript"> AC_FL_RunContent (
    ```

3. **Add the following bit of code at the end of the code to embed the Flash file:** </div>.

    If you're using the HTML template that includes JavaScript to run ActiveX content, place the tag after the line of code that reads </noscript>. Listing 4-1 shows the HTML code with the added tags to center the Flash file in the Web browser.

Listing 4-1: Centering the SWF File in the Browser

```
<div align="center">
      <!--url's used in the movie-->
      <!--text used in the movie-->
      <!-- saved from url=(0013)about:internet -->
      <script language="JavaScript" type="text/javascript">
      AC_FL_RunContent(
      'codebase','http://download.macromedia.com/pub/shockwave/cabs/flash/
          swflash.cab#version=10,0,0,0',
      'width', '550',
      'height', '400',
      'src', 'McTimeline',
      'quality', 'best',
      'pluginspage', 'http://www.adobe.com/go/getflashplayer',
      'align', 'middle',
      'play', 'true',
      'loop', 'true',
      'scale', 'showall',
      'wmode', 'window',
      'devicefont', 'false',
      'id', 'McTimeline',
      'bgcolor', '#f7f2b2',
      'name', 'McTimeline',
      'menu', 'true',
      'allowFullScreen', 'false',
      'allowScriptAccess','sameDomain',
      'movie', 'McTimeline',
      'salign', ''
      ); //end AC code
</script>
  <noscript>
    <object classid="clsid:d27cdb6e-ae6d-11cf-96b8-444553540000"
        codebase="http://download.macromedia.com/pub/shockwave/cabs/flash/
        swflash.cab#version=10,0,0,0" width="550" height="400" id=
        "McTimeline" align="middle">
      <param name="allowScriptAccess" value="sameDomain" />
      <param name="allowFullScreen" value="false" />
      <param name="movie" value="McTimeline.swf" />
      <param name="quality" value="best" />
      <param name="bgcolor" value="#f7f2b2" />
      <embed src="McTimeline.swf" quality="best" bgcolor="#f7f2b2"
          width="550" height="400" name="McTimeline" align="middle"
          wmode="window" allowScriptAccess="sameDomain"
          allowFullScreen="false" type="application/x-shockwave-flash"
          pluginspage="http://www.adobe.com/go/getflashplayer" />
  </object>
  </noscript>
</div>
```

Index

Numbers and Symbols

A

N

Q

R

U

Notes

Notes

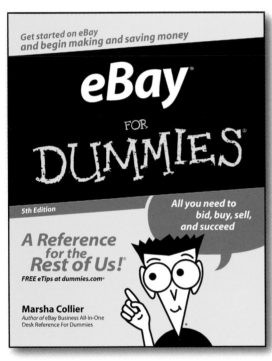
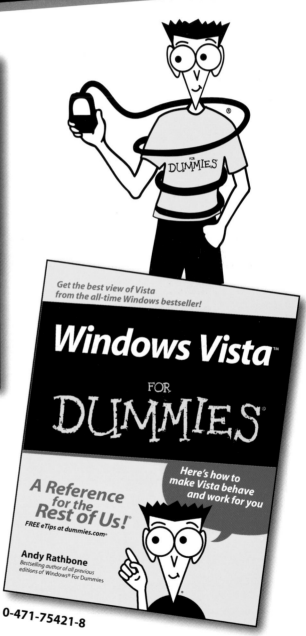

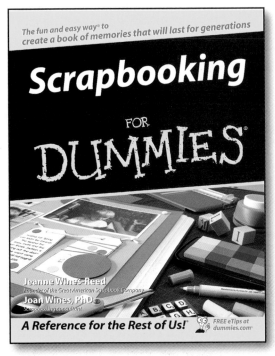
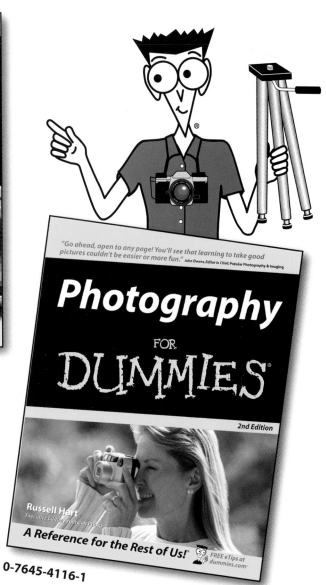